CARBON NEUTRALITY IN THE GULF

With its in-depth investigation of the opportunities and obstacles facing the region, this book offers data-driven assessments and policy recommendations to guide the process of energy transition in the Gulf Cooperation Council (GCC) region. It provides a comprehensive analysis of the current state of carbon reduction initiatives in the GCC and the sustainable development practices that are driving progress. The chapters are divided into four parts: circular economy and pathway frameworks; infrastructure; policy and data transparency; and behavioural and human factors. The book includes case studies to offer unique insights into the policy frameworks, technological innovations, and behavioural changes needed to transition to cleaner, knowledge-based economies. It unpacks the interplay between the ambitions of the GCC countries regarding climate change and sustainable development and the challenges they face in trying to achieve these. It is an indispensable resource for researchers and policymakers in environmental policy, climate change, and the Gulf States.

DR WAEL A. SAMAD holds the position of Associate Professor of Mechanical Engineering and serves as the Chair of the Department of Mechanical and Industrial Engineering at the Rochester Institute of Technology, Dubai Campus. Throughout his research endeavours, Samad has delved into areas such as experimental solid mechanics, smart cities, and material characterisation of 3D-printed artefacts. His commitment to research is demonstrated by the extensive array of over fifty publications he has authored, encompassing peer-reviewed journal articles, book chapters, and conference proceedings. Among his contributions is a coedited volume with Elie Azar, titled *Smart Cities in the Gulf: Current State, Opportunities, and Challenges* (2019). Since setting foot in the UAE almost ten years ago, Samad has been proactive in forging collaborations with prominent local industries. Notably, his work with Emirates Global Aluminium has played a pivotal role in projects that aim to extend the lifespan of ingot molds, promoting more sustainable aluminium production in the Emirates.

DR AHMED BADRAN is Associate Professor of Public Policy and Head of the Department of International Affairs, College of Arts and Sciences at Qatar University. Badran has also worked as Postdoctoral Research Fellow at the Aston Centre for Critical Infrastructure and Services, Aston Business School, Aston University, Birmingham, UK. Badran's research interests extend to cover different areas of regulatory governance and the politics of regulation in liberalised public utilities. This includes telecoms, water, and energy sectors, particularly in transition and developing economies. At present, Badran is leading an international research team working on modeling and assessing the transition towards a low-carbon economy in the GCC. This National Priorities Research Program project is funded by the Qatar National Research Fund.

DR ELIE AZAR is Canada Research Chair and Associate Professor of Civil and Environmental Engineering at Carleton University in Ottawa, Canada. His main research focus is on sustainable buildings and communities through the modelling and analysis of complex building systems and human behaviour. Azar has authored more than 100 scientific articles, in addition to three books on sustainability, smart cities, and artificial intelligence in the Gulf. He is the recipient of various prestigious awards, including the Government of Dubai Emirates Energy Award for his contributions to the field of energy modeling, and was named one of the World's Top 2% Scientists in 2022. Before joining Carleton University, Azar was a faculty member at Masdar Institute and Khalifa University in the UAE.

CARBON NEUTRALITY IN THE GULF

Between Well-intentioned Pledges and the Harsh Reality

Edited by

WAEL A. SAMAD
Rochester Institute of Technology – Dubai

AHMED BADRAN
Qatar University

ELIE AZAR
Carleton University

CAMBRIDGE
UNIVERSITY PRESS

CAMBRIDGE
UNIVERSITY PRESS

Shaftesbury Road, Cambridge CB2 8EA, United Kingdom

One Liberty Plaza, 20th Floor, New York, NY 10006, USA

477 Williamstown Road, Port Melbourne, VIC 3207, Australia

314–321, 3rd Floor, Plot 3, Splendor Forum, Jasola District Centre, New Delhi – 110025, India

103 Penang Road, #05–06/07, Visioncrest Commercial, Singapore 238467

Cambridge University Press is part of Cambridge University Press & Assessment,
a department of the University of Cambridge.

We share the University's mission to contribute to society through the pursuit of
education, learning and research at the highest international levels of excellence.

www.cambridge.org
Information on this title: www.cambridge.org/9781009471558

DOI: 10.1017/9781009471527

When citing this work, please include a reference to the DOI 10.1017/9781009471527

First published 2025

A catalogue record for this publication is available from the British Library

Library of Congress Cataloging-in-Publication Data
Names: Samad, Wael A., author. | Badran, Ahmed, author. | Azar, Elie, author.
Title: Carbon neutrality in the gulf : between well-intentioned pledges and the harsh reality /
edited by Wael A. Samad, Rochester Institute of Technology – Dubai, Ahmed Badran, Qatar University,
Elie Azar, Carleton University.
Description: Cambridge, United Kingdom ; New York, NY : Cambridge University Press, [2025] |
Includes bibliographical references and index.
Identifiers: LCCN 2024021478 | ISBN 9781009471558 (hardback) | ISBN 9781009471527 (ebook)
Subjects: LCSH: Gulf Cooperation Council. | Sustainable development – Persian Gulf States. |
Environmental policy – Persian Gulf States. | Sustainability – Persian Gulf States. |
Climatic changes – Persian Gulf States.
Classification: LCC HC415.3.Z9 E573 2025 | DDC 338.9536/07–dc23/eng/20240607
LC record available at https://lccn.loc.gov/2024021478

ISBN 978-1-009-47155-8 Hardback

Contents

List of Contributors — *page* vii
Acknowledgments — x
List of Abbreviations — xi

Part I Introduction

1 Carbon Neutrality in the GCC: An Overview — 3
WAEL A. SAMAD, AHMED BADRAN, AND ELIE AZAR

Part II Circular Carbon Economy and Pathway Frameworks

2 Circular Cities: One of the Pathways to Carbon Neutrality — 11
OKAN GERAY AND GAMZE HAKLI GERAY

3 The GCC and the Circular Carbon Economy: Progress and Potential — 30
MARI LUOMI, FATIH YILMAZ, AND THAMIR AL SHEHRI

4 Net Zero Saudi Arabia: How Green Can the Oil Kingdom Get? — 57
JIM KRANE

Part III Infrastructure

5 Energy Efficiency and Carbon Neutrality Potentials for the Building Sector in the GCC Region — 85
MONCEF KRARTI

6 Electrifying Public Transport Networks in Dubai: Environmental Benefits, Urban Improvements, and Social Challenges — 117
GIOVANNA POTESTÀ AND MARIO TARTAGLIA

7 Net Zero Emissions in the GCC Region: Challenges and Opportunities for Green Hydrogen Applications 134
AHMED BADRAN

Part IV Policy and Data Transparency

8 GCC Carbon Neutrality and Net Zero Policy Tracker: Framing, Methodology, and Findings 153
ANDREAS RECHKEMMER, LOGAN COCHRANE, AND NOUREDDINE RADOUAI

9 Data Policies and Governance for Greenhouse Gases Reports and Initiatives 176
HESHAM M. AL-AMMAL

10 Key Issues for Long-Term Climate Policy Design in GCC Countries with a Focus on Qatar 201
FREDERIC BABONNEAU, AHMED BADRAN, MAROUA BENLAHRECH, ALAIN HAURIE, MAXIME SCHENCKERY, AND MARC VIELLE

Part V Behavioural Aspects and Human Factors

11 Energy Transition in Oil-Rich Countries: The Role of Resource Nationalism 225
SUSAN KURDLI AND RENATO LIMA-DE-OLIVEIRA

12 Toward Smart Buildings and Communities in the Gulf States: Analysis of Human and Social Dimensions in the Transition to Carbon-Neutral Cities Using Artificial Intelligence 245
AMMAR ABULIBDEH, ESMAT ZAIDAN, AND MOHSEN JAFARI

13 EU–GCC Cooperation Opportunities on Behavioural Energy Efficiency 282
KONSTANTINOS KOASIDIS, NIKOLAOS VOURGIDIS, VANGELIS MARINAKIS, FILIPPOS SEREPAS, AND HARIS DOUKAS

Part VI Conclusion

14 Outlook of Net Zero GCC States 309
WAEL A. SAMAD, AHMED BADRAN, AND ELIE AZAR

Index 315

Contributors

Ammar Abulibdeh, PhD, Associate Professor of Geography and Urban Planning, Qatar University, Qatar.

Thamir Al Shehri, PhD, Senior Research Lead, King Abdullah Petroleum Studies and Research Center, KSA.

Hesham M. Al-Ammal, PhD, Professor of Computer Science, University of Bahrain, Bahrain.

Elie Azar, PhD, Canada Research Chair and Associate Professor of Civil and Environmental Engineering, Carleton University, Canada.

Frederic Babonneau, PhD, Professor of Operation Management, Supply Chain, and Information Systems, KEDGE Business School, France.

Ahmed Badran, PhD, Associate Professor of Public Policy, Qatar University, Qatar.

Maroua Benlahrech, Senior Researcher Assistant, Qatar University, Qatar.

Logan Cochrane, PhD, Associate Professor of Public Policy, Hamad Bin Khalifa University, Qatar.

Renato Lima-de-Oliveira, PhD, Assistant Professor of Business and Society, Asia School of Business, Malaysia.

Haris Doukas, PhD, Associate Professor of Electrical and Computer Engineering, National Technical University of Athens, Greece.

Okan Geray, PhD, Strategic Planning Advisor, Dubai Digital Authority, UAE.

Gamze Hakli Geray, Visiting Faculty in Business, Middlesex University – Dubai, UAE.

Alain Haurie, PhD, Professor Emeritus of Operations Research, University of Geneva, Switzerland.

Mohsen Jafari, PhD, Professor and Department Chair of Industrial and Systems Engineering, Rutgers University, USA.

Konstantinos Koasidis, PhD Candidate, National Technical University of Athens, Greece.

Jim Krane, PhD, Wallace S. Wilson Fellow for Energy Studies, Rice University, USA.

Moncef Krarti, PhD, Professor and Director, Building Energy Smart Technologies Center University of Colorado Boulder, USA.

Susan Kurdli, PhD Candidate, Nanyang Technological University, Singapore.

Mari Luomi, PhD, Research Fellow, King Abdullah Petroleum Studies and Research Center, KSA.

Vangelis Marinakis, PhD, Assistant Professor at the School of Electrical and Computer Engineering, National Technical University of Athens, Greece.

Giovanna Potestà, PhD, Visiting Professor of Architecture, Rochester Institute of Technology – Dubai, UAE.

Noureddine Radouai, Graduate Student of Public Policy, Hamad Bin Khalifa University, Qatar.

Andreas Rechkemmer, PhD, Professor of Public Policy, Hamad Bin Khalifa University, Qatar.

Wael A. Samad, PhD, Associate Professor of Mechanical Engineering, Rochester Institute of Technology – Dubai, UAE.

Maxime Schenckery, PhD, Director of the Energy Economics and Management Centre, French Institute of Petroleum, France.

Filippos Serepas, Software Developer, Holistic PC, Greece.

Mario Tartaglia, Associate Professor, University of Florence. Italy.

Marc Vielle, PhD, Scientist at the Laboratory of Environmental and Urban Economics, Federal Institute of Technology Lausanne, Switzerland.

Nikolaos Vourgidis, PhD Candidate, National Technical University of Athens, Greece.

Fatih Yilmaz, PhD, Research Fellow, King Abdullah Petroleum Studies and Research Center, KSA.

Esmat Zaidan, PhD, Associate Professor, College of Public Policy, Hamad Bin Khalifa University, Doha, Qatar.

Acknowledgments

This volume owes its existence to the dynamic gathering of scholars and practitioners at the "Carbon Neutrality in the GCC: Between Good-Intentioned Pledges and the Harsh Reality" workshop, hosted on July 14–16, 2022 at the University of Cambridge in the United Kingdom. We, the editors, extend our heartfelt gratitude to all the participants who actively contributed to this three-day event. Their academic papers and lively discussions have profoundly influenced the content of this edited volume, helping us collectively to explore key themes, confront challenges, and propose innovative solutions related to promoting NetZero in the six GCC member states.

We would also like to express our deep appreciation to the organisers of the 2022 Gulf Research Meeting, held under the auspices of the Gulf Research Centre Cambridge. We extend our thanks to the following individuals for their unwavering commitment and support:

Dr. Abdulaziz Sager, Chairman and Founder of the Gulf Research Council (GRC), Jeddah
Dr. Christian Kokh, Director of the GRC Foundation Geneva
Layla Ali, Researcher at the GRC
Dr. Oskar Ziemelis, Director of Cooperation at the GRC
Sanya Kapasi, Administration Manager at the GRC

We sincerely appreciate your tireless efforts, which have been instrumental in the success of this endeavour.

Abbreviations

AC	Air Conditioning
BAS	Baseline Scenario
BAU	Business as Usual
BEEC	Building Energy Efficiency Code
CC	Cooling Capacity
EE	Energy Efficiency
EEI	Energy Efficiency Indices
EER	Electrical Efficiency Ratio
EU	European Union
GCC	Gulf Cooperation Council
GDP	Gross Domestic Product
GSAS	Global Building Assessment System
HVAC	Heating, Ventilating, and Air Conditioning
IEA	International Energy Agency
KSA	Kingdom of Saudi Arabia
LCC	Life Cycle Cost
LCOE	Levelized Cost of Energy
LED	Lighting Emitting Diode
LEED	Leadership in Energy and Environmental Design
MEPS	Minimum Energy Performance Standard
NZEB	Net Zero Energy Building
PRS	Pearl Rating System
PV	Photovoltaic
RISE	Regulatory Indicators for Sustainable Energy
SASO	Saudi Arabia Standards Organization
TFEC	Total Final Energy Consumption

TPES	Total Primary Energy Supply
TOE	Ton of Oil Equivalent
UAE	United Arab Emirates
US	United States
USD	US Dollar

Part I

Introduction

1

Carbon Neutrality in the GCC

An Overview

WAEL A. SAMAD, AHMED BADRAN, AND ELIE AZAR

1.1 Background

Since the discovery of oil in the Gulf Cooperation Council (GCC) region in the 1930s, energy policies and strategies have been centred around exploiting fossil fuels to supply local energy demands and export this important and lucrative resource to the world (Ulrichsen, 2015). However, challenges posed by climate change issues, along with the restrictions imposed by international accords, such as the Paris Agreement in 2015, necessitate a fundamental reconsideration and revisions of current energy and development strategies in this region (UN, 2015).

The global push towards a more sustainable future has recently taken a new and promising direction. Countries and major companies worldwide are receiving pledges to achieve 'Carbon Neutrality' by 2050, the Paris Agreement's long-term strategy, or even earlier. Carbon Neutrality is defined as a state of net zero carbon-dioxide (CO_2) emissions, which can be reached by balancing the emissions of CO_2 with its removal and/or by reducing or eliminating the need for it in society (Masson-Delmotte et al., 2018). While the main and direct benefits of a carbon-neutral future are the anticipated reductions in greenhouse gas emissions, indirect benefits and payoffs are numerous, including improved air quality, reduced healthcare costs, job creation, and improvements in the overall quality of life, among others (US EPA, 2022).

In line with global trends, the Gulf countries announced several ambitious pledges to achieve carbon neutrality by 2050 or earlier. Most of the climate pledge announcements were made just before the 26th UN Climate Change Conference (COP26), which took place in Glasgow, Scotland, on 31 October–13 November 2021. The degree of commitment to carbon neutrality varied from country to country. For instance, Saudi Arabia, the United Arab Emirates (UAE), and Bahrain all committed to achieving net zero emissions by 2060, 2050, and 2060, respectively, while Kuwait, Oman, and Qatar only committed to a certain percentage reduction in emissions by different dates (Kramer et al., 2022). Parallel to the pledges, the Gulf countries have taken steps towards carbon neutrality. The UAE has launched the world's largest single-site solar energy project, while Saudi Arabia has announced plans to develop 200 gigawatts of solar energy by 2030. Qatar has also launched several initiatives to promote renewable energy and reduce carbon emissions.

While the mentioned pledges and initiatives are commendable, they face significant challenges in the harsh geographical and socioeconomic reality of the Gulf region. First, the hot and arid climate puts tremendous stress on critical resources, such as energy, water, and food, in addition to presenting unique challenges for renewable energy sources like solar and wind power. Furthermore, the region's rapid development and population growth have resulted in increased energy consumption, making it challenging to reduce emissions without impacting economic growth and development – GCC economies heavily rely on the oil and gas industry. Another challenge facing the Gulf countries is the lack of public awareness of and engagement in the issue of climate change. Many people in the region view climate change as a distant problem that does not affect them directly, and as a result, there is a lack of urgency and political will to address the issue.

1.2 Problem Statement and Objectives

Despite the heightened level of GCC interest, commitments, and investments in carbon neutrality, surprisingly there are no serious efforts to date to pull together scholarship on the adoption challenges for a successful carbon neutrality transition, the implications for the economy and society, and the infrastructure and regulatory requirements that need to be in place. Related efforts have typically been segregated and remain limited in comparison to other growing economies, such as China (CICC Global Institute, 2022). However, the rewards of carbon neutrality are significant, both in terms of mitigating the impacts of climate change and promoting sustainable development and economic growth. Important barriers are expected to hinder the full transition towards carbon neutrality in the GCC. These include – but are not limited to – technology readiness, economic barriers, availability of locally generated knowledge, energy-intensive lifestyles, and rigid institutional and policy structures (Bayoumi et al., 2022; Zaidan et al., 2019).

This edited volume aims to provide the first systematic assessment and understanding of the current trends, challenges, and opportunities for the GCC region to achieve carbon neutrality. Through a compilation and synthesis of scholarly essays and case studies, it offers unique insights into the policy frameworks, technological innovations, and behavioural changes needed to transition from oil-based to cleaner, knowledge-based economies. The book is intended for policy-makers, scholars, researchers, and students interested in the transition to a sustainable, low-carbon future and offers valuable insights for anyone interested in the global energy transition. Its scope is well along the lines of the United Nations (UN's) Sustainable Development Goals (SDGs); in particular the 11th pillar on 'Sustainable Cities and Communities'.

The core chapters of the book come as a result of the compilation of some of the insightful papers, presentations, and discussions by participants at the 12th Gulf Research Meeting, which was organised by the Gulf Research Center and held at the University of Cambridge in July 2022. Participating authors included a diverse mix of experts from various disciplines and sectors such as policy-makers, engineers, political and social scientists, architects, educators, and researchers.

1.3 Book Structure

Following this Part I introduction (Chapter 1), the chapters of the book are divided into a further five parts, each one focusing on a theme of a particular aspect of the transition to carbon neutrality.

Part II, 'Circular Carbon Economy and Pathway Frameworks', provides a roadmap for GCC countries to transition from oil-based to cleaner, knowledge-based economies. Chapter 2, 'Circular Cities: One of the Pathways to Carbon Neutrality', by Okan Geray and Gamze Hakli Geray, discusses the concept of circular cities and its social, economic, and environmental implications for urban contexts in the GCC. Chapter 3, 'The GCC and the Circular Carbon Economy: Progress and Potential', by Mari Luomi, Fatih Yilmaz, and Thamir Al Shehri, compares the GCC countries' progress towards Circular Carbon Economies (CCEs) and their potential to achieve carbon neutrality by mid century. Finally, Chapter 4, 'Net Zero Saudi Arabia: How Green Can the Oil Kingdom Get?', by Jim Krane, examines the implications of Saudi Arabia's goal to achieve net zero emissions by 2060 and the challenges of transitioning from a fossil fuel-driven economy to a net zero carbon future.

Part III, 'Infrastructure', discusses the infrastructure required to achieve net zero emissions. Chapter 5, 'Energy Efficiency and Carbon Neutrality Potentials for the Building Sector in the GCC Region', by Moncef Krarti, presents an overview of the current trends in energy demands in the building sector for the GCC region and countries with an emphasis on historical trends in the energy efficiency performance of buildings. Chapter 6, 'Electrifying Public Transport Networks in Dubai: Environmental Benefits, Urban Improvements, and Social Challenges', by Giovanna Potestà and Mario Tartaglia, examines the potential benefits and social challenges of Dubai's plan to electrify its public transport network. Finally,

Chapter 7, 'Net Zero Emissions in the GCC Region: Challenges and Opportunities for Green Hydrogen Applications', by Ahmed Badran, examines the potential benefits of green hydrogen technology for GCC countries in reducing carbon emissions and greenhouse gases and the challenges that may hinder its adoption in the region.

Part IV, 'Policy and Data Transparency', explores the regulatory and reporting frameworks needed to measure progress towards carbon neutrality. Chapter 8, 'GCC Carbon Neutrality and Net Zero Policy Tracker: Framing, Methodology, and Findings', by Andreas Rechkemmer, Logan Cochrane, and Noureddine Radouai, presents a policy tracker for climate policies of GCC states aimed at achieving mitigation goals of the Paris Agreement and carbon neutrality targets. Chapter 9, 'Data Policies and Governance for Greenhouse Gases Reports and Initiatives', by Hesham M. Al-Ammal, examines the lessons learned from the Kingdom of Bahrain's national initiative for reporting on the its state of carbon and greenhouse gases. Finally, Chapter 10, 'Key Issues for Long-Term Climate Policy Design in GCC Countries with a Focus on Qatar', by Frederic Babonneau, Ahmed Badran, Maroua Benlahrech, Alain Haurie, Maxime Schenckery, and Marc Vielle, tackles the challenges and options of designing an efficient long-term global climate policy for GCC countries.

Part V, 'Behavioural Aspects and Human Factors', examines how the GCC's transition to carbon neutrality will be influenced by behavioural and human factors. Chapter 11, 'Energy Transition in Oil-Rich Countries: The Role of Resource Nationalism', by Susan Kurdli and Renato Lima-de-Oliveira, explores how domestic political factors related to oil and gas resource nationalism influence energy transition capabilities. Chapter 12, 'Toward Smart Buildings and Communities in the Gulf States: Analysis of Human and Social Dimensions in the Transition to Carbon-Neutral Cities Using Artificial Intelligence', by Ammar Abulibdeh, Esmat Zaidan, and Mohsen Jafari, investigates the interaction of people with their built environments to better understand drivers of occupants' indoor comfort and related energy behaviours. Finally, Chapter 13, 'EU–GCC Cooperation Opportunities on Behavioural Energy Efficiency', by Konstantinos Koasidis, Nikolaos Vourgidis, Vangelis Marinakis, Filippos Serepas, and Haris Doukas, aims to facilitate a knowledge transfer between the European Union (EU) and the GCC to enhance the ability of the two regions to trigger end-user behavioural changes and help them achieve their energy efficiency targets.

The book concludes with Part VI, Chapter 14, 'Outlook of Net Zero GCC States', by Wael A. Samad, Ahmed Badran, and Elie Azar. This chapter synthesises the key findings and lessons learned from the various chapters, reflecting on the policy measures, technological innovation, and behavioural change enablers needed for a successful carbon neutrality transition in the GCC region.

References

Bayoumi, M., Luomi, M., Fuller, G., and AlSarihi, A. (2022). *Arab SDG Index and Dashboard Report. Mohammed bin Rashid School of Government (Dubai, UAE), Anwar Gargash Diplomatic Academy (Abu Dhabi, UAE), and UN Sustainable Development Solutions Network.* Report. New York: MBRSG, AGDA, and SDSN.

China International Capital Corporation Global Institute (CICC Global Institute) (2022). *Guidebook to Carbon Neutrality in China.* Singapore: Springer Nature.

Kramer, N., Croker, A., and Ajoodha, R. (2022). *Is Net-Zero a Reality in the Middle East?* London: Norton Rose Fulbright, England.

Masson-Delmotte, V., Zhai, P., Pörtner, H. O., Roberts, D., Skea, J., Shukla, P. R., and Waterfield, T. (2018). *Global Warming of 1.5 C.* Intergovernmental Panel on Climate Change (IPCC), Geneva: IPCC.

Ulrichsen, K. C. (2015). *The Political Economy of Arab Gulf States.* Houston, TX: Rice University's Baker Institute for Public Policy.

United Nations (2015). Adoption of the Paris Agreement, 21st Conference of the Parties, Paris, France. Paris: United Nations.

United States Environmental Protection Agency (US EPA) (2022). *Greenhouse Gas Emissions.* US EPA. Washington, DC. Retrieved from: www.epa.gov/ghgemissions/sources-greenhouse-gas-emissions (accessed 15 January 2023).

Zaidan, E., Al-Saidi, M., and Hammad, S. H. (2019). Sustainable development in the Arab world – is the Gulf Cooperation Council (GCC) region fit for the challenge? *Development in Practice*, 29(5), pp. 670–681.

Part II

Circular Carbon Economy and Pathway Frameworks

2

Circular Cities

One of the Pathways to Carbon Neutrality

OKAN GERAY AND GAMZE HAKLI GERAY

2.1 Introduction

Cities globally take up approximately 3% of the earth's land area, yet they command disproportionate amounts of energy consumption, economic activity, and greenhouse gas (GHG) emissions. In this context, cities in general, including Gulf Cooperation Council (GCC) cities, pose a significant opportunity for fighting climate change. Carbon neutrality is a state of net zero carbon-dioxide emissions and can be achieved by balancing carbon-dioxide emissions with its removal, reduction, or elimination. Cities play an important role in attaining carbon neutrality. More specifically, they accommodate half of the global population (predicted to reach 70% by 2050) and generate 60% of global gross domestic product (GDP), produce more than 70% of human-induced GHG emissions, and account for 60–80% of energy consumption (UN SDG11). Hence, most of our social, economic, and environmental challenges are predominantly manifested in urban environments. This also makes cities a natural target for achieving carbon neutrality given their importance and overall impact globally.

Achieving carbon neutrality by the mid twenty-first century has been deemed crucial in order to constrain global warming to 1.5°C, a limit the Intergovernmental Panel for Climate Change suggests is safe. This target is part of the Paris Agreement signed by 193 parties in the French capital on 12 December 2015, reflecting their commitment to mitigate climate change. Three GCC countries have already pledged their timeline commitments as well. On the other hand, there are still significant challenges remaining for signatories, including GCC countries, to define their detailed road maps and executions.

Net zero pledges from governments and businesses are vital to mitigating climate-related risks. Commitments have been made to significantly reduce GHG emissions. Governments, financial organisations, international bodies, energy companies, and businesses are engaging in environmental, social, and governance strategies. A circular economy and cities' full readiness to leverage transition drivers such as climate financing, implementation of circularity initiatives, use of technology, and so on are needed to achieve a resilient net zero world.

Before the United Nations Climate Change Conference, COP26, was held in Glasgow, UK, in late 2021, three GCC countries released their net zero pledges. The United Arab Emirates (UAE) was the first Gulf country to make a net zero commitment, setting the target for 2050, ensued by Saudi Arabia and Bahrain, pledging to be net zero by 2060 (ECIU, 2022).

COP27 at Sharm el-Sheikh, Egypt, reaffirmed the commitment to limit global temperature rise to 1.5°C above pre-industrial levels. The 2023 United Nations (UN) Climate Change Conference referred to as COP28 was held from 30 November to 12 December 2023 in Dubai, UAE.

This chapter aims to introduce a unified high-level methodology inclusive of four steps coupling the concept of circular cities with carbon emissions. Cities can apply the methodology iteratively over time as they progress and refine their implementations. Circularity is associated with carbon emissions and the proposed methodology prioritises circularity actions toward reducing them.

2.2 From Linear to Circular Economy

Various definitions have been introduced in the past for 'circular economy'. A circular economy is restorative and regenerative by design, and aims to keep products, components, and materials at their highest utility and value at all times, while reducing waste streams (ITU-T, 2018). It has been indicated that 'circular economy' refers to the production and consumption of goods through closed-loop material flows that internalise environmental externalities linked to virgin resource extraction and the generation of waste (Sauvé et al., 2016).

Circular economy is deemed as an approach that transforms the function of resources in the economy (Preston, 2012). Waste becomes a valuable input to another process – and products have the potential to be repaired, reused, or upgraded, as opposed to being discarded. It can be regarded as an alternative to linear economy whereby resources are kept in use as long as possible to extract the maximum value from them, followed by recovery and reuse of products and materials (Mitchell, 2015). Therefore, the circular economy is a restorative and regenerative industrial system in which the 'end-of-life' concept is replaced by restoration (Ellen, 2013a; Ellen, 2013b; Ellen 2015a). It preserves the value of products, materials, and resources in the economy for as long as possible, while minimising the generation of waste (European Commission, 2015). The proliferation of circular economy definitions and characterisations also led to arguments against clarity on the definition of circular economy (Yuan et al., 2008; Lieder and Rashid, 2015) and it was indicated that this clarity is yet to emerge (Blomsma and Brennan, 2017). However, pragmatic and beneficial aspects of the circular economy have enabled its implementation at local, national, and supranational levels (C40, 2018; EUKN, 2015; EC, 2015).

This novel circularity concept has profound implications on urban contexts in terms of social, economic, and environmental aspects. The industrial economy throughout most of its history has adopted a linear model of production and consumption. Goods manufactured from raw materials are sold to consumers, who then use them for a certain amount of time and then discard or dispose of them as waste. This linear model of production and consumption is material- and energy-intensive and has been widely used in providing affordable goods, services, and resources to consumers and material welfare to a large extent. However, this linear model relies on the principle of economies of scale to produce large amounts of goods at minimal cost. It is unsustainable in the long run as it consumes resources on an ongoing basis but is also inherently limited by the earth's resources. The concept of a circular economy has emerged as an alternative to the linear model of production and consumption for economic activities. The alternative to the linear method is to increase the utilisation of our consumed goods (e.g. assets and products), extend their lifetimes, and feed them back into the city economy and society for further usage through various means. These form the basis of the circular method. It aims to decouple resource use from economic growth, which in turn contributes to sustainable development (UNEP, 2011; McKinsey & Company, 2015; EC, 2015; OECD, 2016; Ghisellini et al., 2014; Geissdoerfer et al., 2017). The challenge is that our existing systems and supply chains are not yet completely geared up for it as the linear method has been de facto the predominant one.

2.3 Circular Cities

Implementation of a circular economy can be undertaken at different levels such as the micro- (products, companies, and consumers), the meso- (industrial symbiosis), and the macro-level (cities, regions, and nations). In this chapter, an approach described in *A Guide to Circular Cities*, published by the United for Smart Sustainable Cities (U4SSC, 2020) initiative is adapted. The initiative brings together seventeen UN agencies with the International Telecommunication Union (ITU), the United Nations Economic Commission for Europe, and UN-Habitat serving as the secretariat. Subsequently ITU Study Group 5 (Environment, climate change, and circular economy) turned *A Guide to Circular Cities* into a global standard, namely ITU-T L.1620 (08/2022), to be adopted by UN member states (Recommendation ITU-T L.1620, 2022). This approach entails defining a broad set of city assets and products (CAPs) comprising three main categories, namely, city infrastructure, city resources, and city goods and services. Each category is further composed of several subcategories forming a hierarchical structure with potentially multiple levels (U4SSC, 2020).

Circular actions are specific actions that can be applied to CAPs, which increase their utilisation, extend their lifetimes, or feed them back for further usage. Six specific actions have been identified for circularity, which are sharing, recycling, refurbishing, reusing, replacing, and digitising (U4SSC, 2020). Circular actions applied to CAPs create a staggering potential for circularity due to the vast number of combinations of CAPs and circular actions. Some examples of circularity are:

Commercial buildings as part of city infrastructure can be shared.

- Fossil fuel-based energy as a city resource can be replaced with renewable energy.
- Waste as a city resource can be recycled.
- Commercial assets can be refurbished extending their lifetime.
- Household appliances can be shared.
- Buildings can be disassembled, and their modular parts can be reused in other buildings or commercial products.
- Physically available books and videos can be digitised.

These examples are non-exhaustive and in fact reflect a negligible portion of the actual potential available for circularity in cities. GCC countries are also capturing or planning to capture circularity potential at national or city levels. Saudi Arabia launched the circular carbon economy (CCE) as a framework during its presidency of the Group of Twenty (G20) in 2020 (Al Shehri et al., 2022). CCE leverages a circular economy with an emphasis on energy and carbon dioxide (or more generally GHG emissions). Different conceptualisations of CCE (Williams, 2020; G20, 2020) have utilised different circularity actions such as recycling, reusing, and so on to cope with carbon dioxide or GHG emissions. Wakud, the biofuel plant in Oman, converts waste products into biodiesel fuel to reduce GHG emissions. Qatar's Minister of Municipality and Environment indicated in 2022 that a comprehensive strategy to deal with all types of waste produced was formulated and the development of an integrated national programme for solid waste was underway. The application of the circular economy's potential for sustainable resource management in Kuwait was highlighted (Gulseven and Mostert, 2017).

The UAE Cabinet approved the UAE Circular Economy Policy, which is a ten-year policy for identifying priorities in terms of circular economy and green infrastructure and sustainable transportation, sustainable manufacturing, sustainable food production, and consumption have been selected as priority sectors. The UAE also approved twenty-two policies to accelerate the transition to a circular economy. The UAE Government announced 2023 as the 'Year of Sustainability' under the theme 'Today for Tomorrow', which will include several initiatives, environmental activities, and various events. Dubai Net Zero Energy Buildings Framework aims to reduce the energy consumption of buildings in Dubai and to promote the use of renewable energy sources. The UAE Energy Strategy 2050 aims to achieve an energy mix that combines renewable and clean energy sources to balance economic and environmental goals. The strategy consists of five main pillars: infrastructure, legislation, funding, building capacities and skills, and having an environment-friendly energy mix. The infrastructure pillar includes initiatives such as the Mohammed bin Rashid Al Maktoum Solar Park, the largest single-site solar energy project in the world. The strategy plans to increase the use of solar energy, promote energy efficiency, and encourage the adoption of electric vehicles. The Mohammed bin Rashid Al Maktoum Solar Park supports the Dubai Clean Energy Strategy 2050 and the Dubai Net Zero Emissions Strategy 2050. The hydroelectric power station in Hatta will generate electricity by making use of the water stored in Hatta Dam with a storage capacity of 1,500 MWh.

In May 2023, Dubai's Roads and Transport Authority (RTA) announced its 'Zero-Emissions Public Transportation in Dubai 2050', strategy which aims to reduce carbon emissions in public transportation, buildings, facilities, and waste management. This initiative is in line with the Paris Climate Agreement and the United Nations Sustainable Development Goals adopted in 2015. It is also consistent with the UAE Net Zero 2050 Strategic Initiative, the UAE's Green Agenda – 2030, the National Climate Change Plan of the UAE 2050, and the UAE Energy Strategy 2050.

The Abu Dhabi Industrial Strategy (2022) aims to strengthen the emirate's position as the region's most competitive industrial hub. The Abu Dhabi Industrial Strategy also includes plans for a smart circular economy to enhance sustainability in line with the UAE Net Zero by 2050 and the National Climate Change Strategy. The circular economy programme will drive industry-wide sustainability by enabling responsible industrial production and consumption. Masdar City is a planned sustainable city located in the Emirate of Abu Dhabi designed to be a hub for clean technology and renewable energy. The city features green buildings, sustainable transportation options, and also waste management systems.

These are just a few examples of circular cities and net zero carbon initiatives from the UAE. Such non-exhaustive examples suggest that there are several initiatives launched to promote circularity in GCC countries.

2.4 Circularity Potential and Carbon Neutrality

Nationally determined contributions (NDCs) constitute an integral part of the Paris Agreement and the achievement of the long-term goals and targets established therein. NDCs represent various pledges, legal and regulatory actions, and other efforts undertaken by countries to reduce national emissions and adapt to the impacts of climate change.

The key findings of the synthesis report on NDCs published by the United Nations Framework Convention on Climate Change (UNFCCC, 2021) in 2021 indicate that

26% of the communicated NDCs included the promotion of circular economy as a mitigation option for GHG emissions (UNFCCC, 2021). Energy supply-related NDCs are the highest category with a focus on energy generation, transmission, and storage accounting for 89% of signatory parties' NDCs. More specifically, the transition to renewable energy and energy efficiency has been at the forefront.

The framework created at the Stockholm Conference in 1972 still leads the way in how countries negotiate their climate deals. In 1992, countries joined an international treaty, the United Nations Framework Convention on Climate Change, as a framework for international cooperation to combat climate change by limiting average global temperature increases. The climate change negotiation meetings have grown significantly through the years aiming to accelerate climate actions and investment needed for a sustainable carbon-neutral future.

The Article 6 'rulebook' negotiations of the Paris Agreement were finally completed in Glasgow COP26. The COP27 climate summit in Sharm el-Sheikh, Egypt, concluded with a decision to help vulnerable countries deal with their losses and damages from the impacts of climate change. In 2023, the UAE hosted COP28 in Dubai to create a platform for the solutions to accelerate the global energy transition. These energy-related efforts are indeed important and in line with the circularity concept. Energy-related emissions are estimated to account for 55% of total emissions globally whereas the remaining 45% are due to products consumed (Ellen, 2021) and land use. Consequently, there is a big potential for circularity to reduce these remaining emissions by adopting a circular model in the way we produce and consume globally, hence the establishment of Sustainable Development Goal number 12, 'Responsible Consumption and Production' in 2015. Industry-level circular actions can significantly reduce or eliminate GHG emissions (Ellen, 2015b, 2021; UK, 2021). Circular actions can be tailored to challenges faced in GHG emissions in a specific industry (Ellen, 2021). Therefore, circularity is a significant pathway to carbon neutrality.

2.5 A High-Level Methodology for Circular Cities towards Carbon Neutrality

Cities are a main producer of carbon emissions and circularity plays a key role in achieving carbon neutrality. Therefore, this chapter suggests a high-level pragmatic methodology adapted from an approach described in the U4SSC publication *A Guide to Circular Cities* for implementing circularity in cities to reduce or eliminate carbon emissions. It considers the fact that each city has its particular context and differs in terms of its social, economic, and environmental aspects and its aspirations for achieving carbon neutrality. The methodology has four high-level steps for a given city:

1. Assess current carbon emissions and circularity.
2. Identify target circularity actions.
3. Accelerate circularity actions.
4. Implement circularity actions.

The methodology can be applied in a cyclical manner iteratively as cities progress and revise their implementations over time. The proposed methodology couples circularity with carbon emissions and aims to prioritise circularity actions towards the achievement of carbon emissions reduction. Each step of the methodology will be described in the following subsections.

2.6 Assess Current Carbon Emissions and Circularity

The first step in the methodology entails identifying the current landscape of the city in terms of circularity and carbon dioxide emissions. Hence, it is important to identify city's:

- Carbon-dioxide inventory (total emissions), its progression over time, and breakdown by sector if available.
- Carbon-dioxide emissions reduction targets at the local and national levels if available.
- Carbon-dioxide emissions reduction action plans (e.g. national strategies and plans, NDCs, city strategies, and plans).
- Circularity targets at the local and national levels.
- Circularity action plans (e.g. national strategies and plans, NDCs, city strategies, and plans). Note, Table 2.1 can be used to analyse and categorise existing circularity action plans.
- Estimates of carbon-dioxide emissions reduction due to circularity actions if available; otherwise predictions can be made where possible.

Table 2.1 *Circularity potential for cities.*

	Circular action items					
City assets and products	CAI 1	CAI 2	CAI 3	CAI 4	....	CAI N
CAP1						
CAP2						
CAP3						
CAP4						
...						
CAP N						

This step allows a simple baselining exercise for the city in terms of carbon-dioxide emissions, circularity, and the linkage between the two.

2.7 Identify Target Circularity Actions

The second step consists of identifying the circularity action plans to reduce or eliminate carbon-dioxide emissions. During this step, the city collectively can innovate circularity action plans based on the innovation potential discussed in Section 2.4. The city during this step can generate a large number of circularity action ideas. These ideas can reflect the city's own context and stakeholder priorities. Table 2.1 illustrates the innovation potential available to cities for implementing circularity in their urban contexts.

The purpose of this table (proposed methodology adapted from U4SSC *A Guide to Circular Cities*) is to present a template showing the immense potential where circular action items can be mapped against CAPs. Novel business models focused on reuse, repair, recycling, digitising, and sharing may offer circularity-based innovative opportunities.

City assets and products span various stakeholders such as individuals, private companies, public sector organisations, city municipal administrations, NGOs, and so on. Hence, broad participation during the circularity innovation stage might help generate a vast number of circularity action ideas at the city level. However, it would be important to evaluate and possibly shortlist circular action ideas due to resource constraints (e.g. budget, capabilities). A simple prioritisation scheme is suggested in this chapter and cities can further tailor it to their own needs, priorities, and contexts. The prioritisation scheme has two main criteria: contribution to carbon-dioxide emissions reduction and feasibility. Contribution to carbon-dioxide emissions can include projected (estimated) percentage reduction in the overall carbon-dioxide emissions. It can either be:

- estimated quantitatively as a number or
- assessed qualitatively at a high level with varying levels of degree (e.g. low, medium, or high reduction potential).

On the other hand, the feasibility of the circularity action ideas may include the following sub-criteria, among others:

- Cost of implementation.
- Complexity.
- Capabilities required.
- Predicted time to achieve targeted carbon-dioxide emissions reduction.
- Extent of cultural change required.

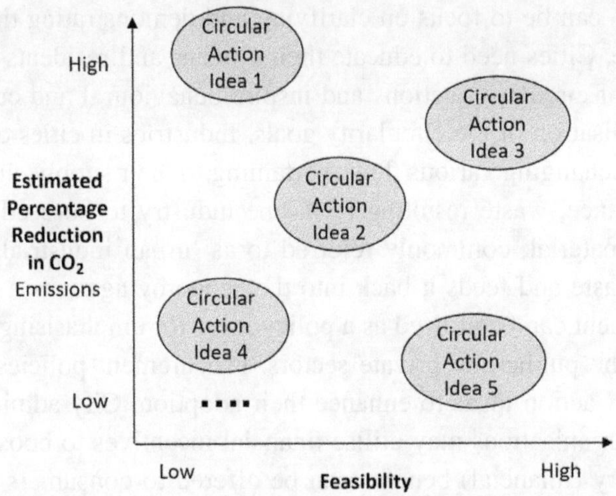

Figure 2.1 Prioritisation tool for circular action ideas.

The sub-criteria can be tailored based on city needs and requirements by adding new or deleting and modifying existing ones. This simple prioritisation scheme allows cities to evaluate and shortlist their circularity action ideas. Figure 2.1 illustrates the simple prioritisation scheme proposed in this chapter to help cities in their decision-making progress.

It would be logical to give priority to highly feasible action items, which highly contribute to the carbon-dioxide emissions reduction. Assessing the remaining circularity action ideas can follow them. The low-feasible and low-contributing circularity action ideas may be eliminated unless there is a strong need to include them in the overall city action plans.

2.8 Accelerate Circularity Actions

The third step involves identifying and utilising various auxiliary means to accelerate the implementation of circularity action plans to reduce or eliminate carbon-dioxide emissions. Climate change is a pressing issue for all cities including GCC ones. Augmenting circularity action plans with miscellaneous means helps in their smoother, faster, and better execution and potentially reduces risks. Further on are some of these non-exhaustive means that cities can consider during the implementation of their circular action ideas. Existing smart city or circular economy strategies and plans at national and local levels may help in accelerating circular action items. Newly formulated circular action ideas can be piggybacked onto these existing strategies and plans to further boost and accelerate them.

Cities can benefit from public and stakeholder engagement and awareness before and during the implementation of circularity action ideas. One of the imminent tasks can be to focus on clarifying and demonstrating their impacts on climate change. Cities need to educate their citizens and residents about the concrete benefits of circularity actions and inspire behavioural and cultural changes toward the realisation of the circularity goals. Industries in cities can engage and cooperate in exchanging various flows pertaining to their supply chains. This may allow, for instance, waste resulting from one industry to be used by another as an input raw material, commonly referred to as 'urban industrial symbiosis'. It circumvents waste and feeds it back into the economy again as a circular action item. Procurement can be utilised as a policy lever for emphasising and enforcing circularity in the public and private sectors. Procurement policies can prioritise various circular action ideas to enhance their adoption. City administrations and public sector organisations may utilise financial incentives to boost circularity in a city. Monetary (financial) benefits can be offered to consumers and producers of circular CAPs. Financial incentives include, but are not limited to, green bonds and other green financing mechanisms, tax incentives, preferred loan rates, impact investment alternatives, VAT deductions, and so on.

Cities can flourish an innovation ecosystem to help boost circularity in cities. Circularity is a system, rather than a single initiative or action item. In this context, entrepreneurs can be encouraged and supported via incentives to establish start-ups related to circulatory challenges in the cities. Accelerators and incubators can be created to advance circularity by helping start-ups and small and medium enterprises (SMEs). Both public and private sector organisations may collaborate and form partnerships to support and accelerate the circular actions. Partners may combine their forces to align and unify their circular goals and share the risks and rewards of implementations. Specific research and development (R&D) programmes can be developed to address the particular challenges for cities in implementing circular action ideas. Certain circularity action ideas may require further research before embarking upon implementation. R&D programmes can help bridge this knowledge gap and smooth implementation.

Additionally, capacity-building programmes can create substantial benefits in instilling and promoting the concept of circularity in cities. These programmes include academic ones and executive training programmes, for example university degrees, short- or long-term certificate and diploma programmes, vocational and professional training and coaching programmes, and corporate training programmes to teach circularity at individual, organisational and societal levels. Encouraging the creation, sharing, and dissemination of green and circularity-related knowledge, research, and skills both inside and outside academia (e.g. virtual conferences, think tanks, dedicated not-for-profit organisations) would help to develop talented human capital for implementing circularity in the cities and communities. Laws and regulations about circularity may be used as an enabler to boost circular action ideas. Certifications are designated credentials that can provide a competitive advantage for certified organisations undertaking circular action ideas. Certification can provide independent verification of a certain level of expertise in a particular area of circularity. Certifications depend on verifiable and well-defined standards to measure performance on circularity and allow organisations to demonstrate their skills, knowledge, and competence towards the achievement of circular goals and targets.

Cities can leverage existing certifications or introduce new ones to incentivise circular action ideas. Circularity certificates can also act as indicators of compliance related to pre-defined circularity standards or well-defined criteria identified by the city and are usually issued by an accredited third party after an independent audit process. Communities can be established to boost circularity at different levels. Corporate social responsibility programmes and platforms can be established to exemplify the reuse, repair, and other actions of circularity and to facilitate the exchange of circular practices to attain collective sustainability goals and mitigate climate change. For instance, the Circular Community Foundation (CCF) stimulates communities around the world to create value in their neighbourhood by co-designing interventions that are aimed at closing resource loops at the local level. Table 2.2 exhibits instances of cities utilising various auxiliary means in their circularity actions (C40, 2018; Williams, 2022). These examples illustrate the adoption of various auxiliary means by cities in helping to accelerate and enhance their circular action ideas.

Cities need to identify which of the aforementioned auxiliary means would be relevant and positively impact their circularity action plans. Cities can then augment their action plans with the relevant means to accelerate their implementation. For example, a lack of skills and capabilities in certain areas may trigger training programmes or long-term R&D programmes and investments. Governments can utilise procurement as a lever to boost circular action plans in the public sector. Financial incentives and innovation ecosystems may accelerate start-ups and private sector investment in requisite fields. These non-exhaustive examples elucidate the acceleration potential of circularity action ideas and their implementation plans in a dynamic landscape. Cities should tailor these generic means to their own needs to capture specific requirements in their urban contexts. Many cities around the world are implementing circular strategies with net zero principles to achieve more sustainable and resilient urban systems. For instance, Helsinki has implemented a range of circular initiatives, including a circular economy roadmap that sets out a vision for a circular Helsinki by 2050, a circular economy platform that connects circular businesses, and a circular procurement programme. Ljubljana has been named as the European Green Capital in 2016, partly due to its ambitious circular economy initiatives. The city has implemented a range of

Table 2.2 *Cities' circular auxiliary means – this table is a non-exhaustive compendium of selected city cases across the globe.*

	Cities	Amsterdam	Paris	Stockholm	London	Cape Town	Glasgow	Kristiansand	Quezon	Seoul	Basel	Toronto	Dubai
Auxiliary means													
		Handling waste/ strategic and city–regional approach to circular resources of construction and organic waste	Local circular food-waste mechanism via recycling	Circular thinking for development decisions	Circularity in major new and existing neighbourhood projects–eco districts	Industrial symbiosis initiative	Business innovation	Competition for green businesses, citizens, and business collaboration	Regulations about the use of plastic bags	Social innovation encouraging new circular business opportunities	Low energy city / Gold award	Circular procurement	Green building certificate
Public stakeholder engagement		X	X	X	X		X				X	X	
Capacity-building programmes		X	X	X	X	X	X	X	X	X		X	
Urban industrial symbiosis		X	X			X	X						
Circular procurement		X	X	X	X			X				X	X
Financial incentives									X		X		
Public–private partnership		X				X		X		X			

Innovation ecosystem		X		X	X			X					
Research and development (R&D)			X				X			X			
Laws and regulations		X	X	X	X			X	X	X			X
Certifications													X
Circular communities		X	X	X	X								X

circular projects, including a zero-waste programme that aims to reduce waste and increase recycling, a circular procurement programme that encourages the use of circular products and services, and a green business network that connects sustainable businesses. The Western Cape Industrial Symbiosis Program (WISP) in South Africa provides businesses a resource-sharing environment connecting organisations with materials, energy, water, assets, logistics, and expertise. The success of WISP has inspired other industrial symbiosis programmes in other South African provinces. Copenhagen's vision is to become the world's first carbon neutral capital by 2025. The plan targets 70% of municipal waste to be recycled by 2024, equating to 59,000 tonnes of CO_2 reduction. The city aims to become a leader in the circular economy through further targets, such as tripling the amount of goods reused by municipalities. The city of Sydney aims to co-create industry guidelines for circular office refurbishments. The city's target is to reduce GHG emissions by 70% by 2030 (from 2006 levels) (C40, 2018).

2.9 Implement Circularity Actions

Last but not least, the fourth step entails the actual implementation of circularity action ideas as prioritised and planned in the preceding steps. The auxiliary means identified in the third step can be used to accelerate the implementation of cities' circular actions. The fourth step is a crucial one since carbon-dioxide emissions reduction will be attained at this step. Therefore, success depends on the appropriate execution of this step for cities. This step may require complex coordination and facilitation as well as execution of requisite tasks and activities in the circularity action plans. After implementation, cities can go back to the first step of the proposed methodology and can iteratively apply it for further reduction of carbon dioxide (or GHG) emissions.

Cities can measure and assess their progress concerning implementation and achievement of results, that is carbon-dioxide emissions reduction. They can also assess the effectiveness of auxiliary means they have adopted during their circularity actions implementation. They can fine-tune and revise their circular action ideas and the selected auxiliary means. Ineffective circular action ideas and auxiliary means can be eliminated, or revised, and new ones can be added for enhancement.

2.10 Potential Benefits of the Proposed Methodology

The proposed methodology holds significant potential for addressing the urgent deadline of the United Nations Sustainable Development Goals (SDGs). The methodology's primary objective is to create a comprehensive, systematic, and integrated framework that enables cities to define, implement, expedite, and evaluate circularity initiatives at the local level. This is particularly crucial as globally circularity efforts are fragmented and decentralised. Circular initiatives and Sustainable Development Goals (SDGs) are intimately related. The proposed methodology can help cities implement various SDGs, especially SDGs 7 and 11. Net zero initiatives supported by circularity allow for the harmonisation of economic progress with social equity and environmental protection – ultimately driving forward the agenda for global sustainability. Cities are complex ecosystems with intricate flows of energy, water, materials, and waste.

When initiatives are isolated and uncoordinated, it becomes challenging to optimise the use of resources and minimise environmental impact. By adopting a holistic model, cities can align their efforts and coordinate actions across sectors such as energy, transportation, waste management, and urban planning. Policy-makers, cities, businesses, and individuals can identify synergies and trade-offs among different sectors to achieve the most efficient and cost-effective solutions for decarbonising their economy. Additionally, a holistic strategy allows for a clearer understanding of potential unintended consequences or rebound effects that might arise from isolated actions. Therefore, circularity initiatives must encompass an integrated and coherent framework with well-defined pragmatic steps along with circularity actions that incorporate all relevant sectors to ensure long-lasting and sustainable results in mitigating climate crisis and preserving the planet for future generations. By considering the entire resource lifecycle and adopting an integrated approach, cities can effectively manage resources, enhance resilience, and reduce their ecological footprint. Moreover, a holistic model fosters innovation and creativity by encouraging cross-sector collaboration and knowledge-sharing and creates a fertile ground for generating new ideas and solutions.

Cities can learn from each other's experiences, leverage expertise, and find synergies that lead to innovative approaches. For example, collaboration between urban planners, architects, and renewable energy experts can result in the design of energy-efficient and sustainable buildings that utilise renewable energy sources. This interdisciplinary collaboration can drive technological advancements, policy innovations, and business models that accelerate the transition towards net zero. In conclusion, a holistic methodology for circular cities is crucial in overcoming the limitations of isolated and uncoordinated initiatives.

2.11 Potential Future Research

There is no 'one-size-fits all' approach in terms of circular action ideas for implementing the proposed methodology in all cities. Each city has also a different starting point and will progress at a different pace towards the circularity and carbon neutrality goals and objectives. But there is also an enormous potential for circularity with a very broad scope in cities for implementation.

Further research may be beneficial in quantifying carbon-dioxide emissions reduction for a broad set of circular action items, or for selected or prioritised circular action items for a given city. Future research can focus on the economic viability of circular cities and how they can contribute to achieving carbon neutrality by adopting circular approaches compared to traditional linear approaches. Another area can be identifying key critical indicators for measuring the success of circular cities in achieving carbon neutrality.

Assessing the impact of circular approaches on innovative jobs and evaluating the impact of circular models on employment is another important area for research. The evaluation of policy interventions such as subsidies, tax incentives, and regulations in promoting circular approaches is a potential area for researchers. The Circularity Gap Report 2023 explains that the global economy is currently only 7.2% circular. The global economy increasingly relies on non-circular materials and poses a serious threat to the sustainability of the planet (The Circularity Gap Report, 2023). Cities around the world need to take immediate action to address the pressing challenges of climate crisis and resource depletion. Adopting circular economy principles can be a powerful tool for achieving carbon neutrality while also promoting sustainable development. Cities are urged to embrace circularity, benefit from best practices, and implement net zero strategies to reduce their carbon footprint and enhance their resilience to combat the negative impact of the climate crisis.

This also involves investing in renewable energy and circular infrastructure, promoting innovative circular business models, and engaging and educating citizens and stakeholders in the transition to a circular economy. Following are some observations that can be drawn given the challenge cities and nations face in implementing circularity for reducing or eliminating carbon dioxide emissions:

- Cities may consider city products and assets categories and subcategories individually and identify appropriate circular action ideas.
- Cities may consider taking an industry-based approach for private sector products and assets in determining their circular actions.
- Cities can create cross-industry circular synergies by creating supply-chain loops among industries to innovate circular action ideas, commonly referred to as 'urban industrial symbiosis'.
- It might be challenging to predict the carbon-dioxide emissions reduction potential for certain circularity actions.
- Cities would benefit from sharing circularity best practice action ideas in reducing carbon-dioxide emissions and also in terms of which auxiliary means to boost their circularity action ideas more effectively and efficiently.

- Cities can utilise circularity and carbon neutrality as an economic opportunity and build a rich innovation ecosystem around it while concomitantly creating wealth around it.
- Cities can leverage the collective city capital existing in a broad range of city stakeholders by effectively engaging them and ensuring their participation in formulating circular city action ideas with a focused perspective on reducing carbon-dioxide emissions.

The implementation of the methodology is hindered by various challenges, particularly the scarcity of prediction tools and reliable emissions data specific to individual circular actions. These practical barriers make it difficult to accurately gauge the effectiveness of each measure within an actual urban setting. Moreover, the limited availability of data and evidence further exacerbates the challenge as it may hamper the ability to assess the real-world impact of these actions.

2.12 Conclusion

This chapter has introduced circularity as one of the alternative pathways to achieving carbon neutrality. It has adopted a high-level, unified and coherent four-step methodology to utilise circularity for carbon neutrality. The proposed methodology is deliberately designed to flexibly accommodate the particular needs of cities. It also relies on dependable and accurate predictions of carbon-dioxide reduction potential for circular action items. The proposed methodology furthermore provides a non-exhaustive set of auxiliary means and policy instruments to accelerate the implementation of circular action items.

References

Al Shehri, T., Braun, J., Howarth, N., Lanza, A., and Luomi, M. (2022). Saudi Arabia's climate change policy and the circular carbon economy approach. *Clim. Policy* 23 (2), pp. 151–167.

Blomsma, F., and Brennan, G. (2017). The emergence of the circular economy: a new framing around prolonging resource productivity. *J. Ind. Ecol.* 21 (3), pp. 603–614.

C40 (2018). Municipality-Led Circular Economy Case Studies; In Partnership with the Climate-KIC Circular Cities Project.

Circular Community Foundation Website. Available online: https://circularcommunity.org/ (accessed 21 June 2022).

Ellen MacArthur Foundation (2013a). Towards the Circular Economy: Economic and Business Rationale for an Accelerated Transition. Cowes, UK. Available online: https://tinyurl.com/hzfrxvb (accessed 21 June 2022).

Ellen MacArthur Foundation (2013b). Towards the Circular Economy: Opportunities for the Consumer Goods Sector. Cowes, UK. Available online: https://tinyurl.com/ztnrg24 (accessed 21 June 2022).

Ellen MacArthur Foundation (2015a). Potential for Denmark as a Circular Economy A Case Study From: Delivering the Circular Economy – A Toolkit for Policy Makers. Cowes, UK. Available online: https://archive.ellenmacarthurfoundation.org/assets/downloads/government/20151113_DenmarkCaseStudy.pdf (accessed 21 June 2022).

Ellen MacArthur Foundation (2015b). Towards a Circular Economy: Business Rationale for an Accelerated Transition. Cowes, UK. Available online: https://tinyurl.com/zt8fhxw (accessed 21 June 2022).

Ellen MacArthur Foundation (2021). Completing the Picture: How the Circular Economy Tackles Climate Change. Cowes, UK.

Energy & Climate Intelligence Unit (ECIU) Website. Available online: https://eciu.net/netzerotracker (accessed 21 June 2022).

European Commission (EC) (2015). Communication from the Commission to The Parliament, The Council, The European Economic and Social Committee of the Regions. Closing the Loop – An EU Action Plan for the Circular Economy (COM/2015/0614 Final). Available online: www.eea.europa.eu/policy-documents/com-2015-0614-final (accessed 21 June 2022).

European Urban Knowledge Network (EUKN) (2015). *The Circular City. Lessons from Europe*. Factsheet for Policy Lab Netherlands. The Hague: EUKN.

G20 (Group of Twenty) Saudi Arabia (2020). *G20 Climate Stewardship Working Group. Managing Emission in the Context of the Circular Carbon Economy Platform*. Presidency Report. September. Saudi Arabia.

Geissdoerfer, M., Savaget, P., Bocken, N. M. P., and Hultink, E. J. (2017). The circular economy: a new sustainability paradigm? *J. Clean. Prod.* 143, pp. 757–768.

Ghisellini, P., Cialani, C., and Ulgiati, S. (2014). A review on circular economy: the expected transition to a balanced interplay of environmental and economic systems. *J. Clean. Prod.* 114, pp. 11–32.

Gulseven, O., and Mostert, J. (2017). Application of circular economy for sustainable resource management in Kuwait. *Int. J. Soc. Ecol. Sustain. Dev.* 8 (3), Article 6, 13.

International Telecommunication Union (ITU-T) L.1620 Telecommunication Standardization Sector of ITU (08/2022). Recommendation ITU-T L.1620.

International Telecommunication Union Telecommunication Standardization Sector (ITU-T) (2018). Recommendation L.1020 Circular Economy: Guide for Operators and Suppliers on Approaches to Migrate towards Circular ICT Goods and Networks.

Lieder, M., and Rashid, A. (2015). Towards circular economy implementation: a comprehensive review in the context of manufacturing industry. *J. Clean. Prod.* 115, pp. 36–51.

McKinsey & Company (2015). *Europe's Circular Economy Opportunity*. Available online: www.mckinsey.com/business-functions/sustainability/our-insights/europes-circular-economy-opportunity (accessed 21 June 2022).

Mitchell, P. (2015). *Employment and the Circular Economy – Job Creation through Resource Efficiency in London*. Report produced by WRAP for the London Sustainable Development Commission, the London Waste and Recycling Board, and the Greater London Authority.

Organisation of Economic Co-operation and Development (OECD) (2016). *Forum 2016 Issues: International Collaboration*. Available online: www.oecd.org/forum/issues/forum-2016-issues-international-collaboration.htm (accessed 21 June 2022).

Preston, F. (2012). *A Global Redesign? Shaping the Circular Economy*, Briefing Paper, London: Chatham House.

Sauvé, S., Bernard, S., and Sloan, P. (2016). Environmental sciences, sustainable development and circular economy: alternative concepts for trans-disciplinary research. *Environ. Dev.* 17, pp. 48–56.

The Circularity Gap Report (2023). *An Initiative of Circle Economy*. Available online: www.circle-economy.com (accessed 5 April 2023).

UK Government (2021). *Net Zero Strategy: Build Back Greener*. London: Department for Energy Security and Net Zero, UK Government.

United for Smart Sustainable Cities (U4SSC) (2020). *A Guide to Circular Cities*.

United Nations Environment Programme (UNEP) (2011). Fischer-Kowalski, M., Swilling, M., von Weizsäcker, E. U., Ren, Y., Moriguchi, Y., Crane, W., Krausmann, F., Eisenmenger, N., Giljum, S., Hennicke, P., Romero Lankao, P., and Siriban Manalang, A., *Decoupling Natural Resource Use and Environmental Impacts from Economic Growth. A Report of the Working Group on Decoupling to the International Resource Panel*. Nairobi: UNEP.

United Nations Framework Convention on Climate Change (UNFCCC) (2021). *Nationally Determined Contributions under the Paris Agreement*. Revised Synthesis Report by the Secretariat. Bonn: UNFCCC.

United Nations Sustainable Development Goals (UN SDG11) Website. Available online: www.un.org/sustainabledevelopment/cities (accessed 21 June 2022).

Williams, E. (2020). *CCE Guide: Overview. A Guide to the Circular Carbon Economy (CCE)*. Riyadh: KAPSARC.

Williams, J. (2022). Circular cities: planning for circular development in European cities. *Eur. Plan. Stud.* 31 (1), pp. 14–35.

Yuan, Z., Bi, J., and Moriguichi, Y. (2008). The circular economy: a new development strategy in China. *J. Ind. Ecol.* 10 (1–2), pp. 4–8.

3

The GCC and the Circular Carbon Economy

Progress and Potential

MARI LUOMI, FATIH YILMAZ, AND THAMIR AL SHEHRI

3.1 Introduction

After joining the 2015 Paris Agreement, all six Gulf Cooperation Council (GCC) countries have updated their medium-term greenhouse gas (GHG) emission targets by submitting revised nationally determined contributions (NDCs) under the Paris Agreement. In addition to these medium-term targets, all GCC countries except Qatar have also, at the time of writing, announced net zero emission targets. Work is now ongoing to develop more detailed roadmaps and implementation plans, some elements of which are already laid out in the updated NDCs. As the region embarks on this ambitious journey, its energy stakeholders will need to make key choices about the technologies they wish to support and invest in. In parallel, they will need to foster the right kind of enabling conditions that will facilitate the transitions to carbon neutrality. These include more detailed policies and regulatory frameworks, strengthened financial and logistical infrastructures, robust innovation support, and attractive business environments, among others.

The circular carbon economy (CCE) is a concept developed jointly by Saudi and international researchers and energy sector actors and endorsed by G20 leaders in 2020. Its ultimate goal is full carbon circularity or, in other words, carbon neutrality or net zero carbon dioxide (CO_2) emissions. The concept aims to provide a holistic, technology-agnostic, and cost-effective framework for assessing climate change mitigation options and pathways at a global, national or organisational level. The CCE builds on the three 'Rs' of the circular economy concept – reduce, recycle, and reuse – but adds a fourth 'R' for removal, and focuses on energy and emissions flows instead of materials and products. The CCE approach embraces all mitigation technologies (e.g. renewable energy and carbon capture, utilisation and storage (CCUS)) and activities (e.g. energy efficiency, fuel switching, and natural carbon sinks). In simple terms, the CCE draws attention to the need to focus on preventing CO_2 emissions and other GHGs from reaching the atmosphere, instead

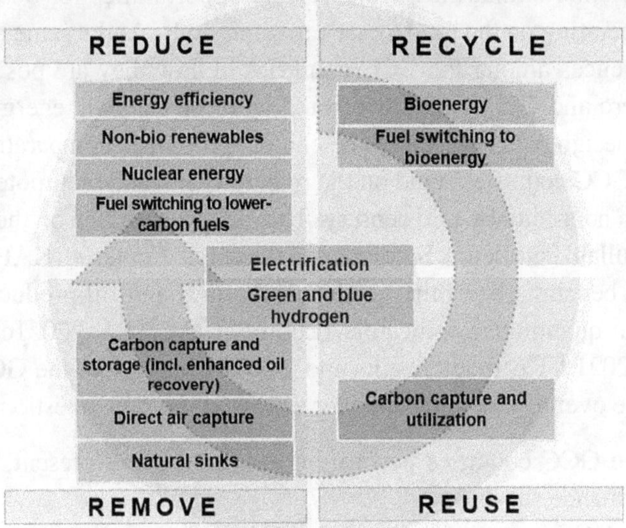

Figure 3.1 The circular carbon economy.

of focusing on specifying a list of technologies (McDonough, 2016; Williams, 2019; Luomi et al., 2021a). An illustration of the CCE concept is provided in Figure 3.1.

Using the CCE concept can help raise the level of mitigation ambition globally because it broadens the scope of available technology options. First, the framework can help any country assess a wider variety of mitigation options side by side, conduct cost comparisons, assess different technologies' potential, and identify where support needs to be scaled up to reach this potential. Second, the CCE's technology-agnostic approach can help with achieving buy-in from many industries, sectors, and countries that have large hydrocarbon endowments and/or limited cost-effective options to decarbonise without using fossil fuels. Despite their significant potential to contribute to emission reductions, for example, through large-scale CCUS deployment, these actors are often seen mainly as incumbents in the current energy transition discussion discourse, which has created barriers to their engagement. While the CCE concept is sometimes seen as putting exclusive emphasis on CCUS-related applications, it considers these technologies as a part of a broader mix of mitigation solutions that each country will apply according to its strengths and priorities. The end goal of the CCE is an economy in which carbon emissions are either avoided in the first place, removed permanently, or circulated through it while generating value, ultimately resulting in net zero emissions.

This chapter starts from the premise that although each country will have its own, unique pathway to net zero and CCEs, the GCC countries share a number of structural and other similarities, which create opportunities for both sharing lessons and cooperating on the road to net zero emissions. At the same time, there are marked differences among the GCC countries in how they are positioned on the road to net zero and CCEs, and understanding these can help energy and climate stakeholders design better policies. The chapter presents a comparative evaluation of where the GCC countries stand on the road to CCEs and their potential to move toward carbon neutrality by mid century. The analysis is based on the 2021 edition of King Abdullah Petroleum Studies and Research Center's (KAPSARC) CCE Index, which benchmarked thirty major economies and oil-producing countries on forty-seven quantitative indicators (Luomi et al., 2021b, 2021c). After summarising the 2021 CCE Index results and a brief overview of the GCC countries' standing in the overall Index, the chapter zooms in on three questions:

- How are the GCC countries performing on the CCE at present, based on the CCE performance sub-index?
- How are the GCC countries positioned to transition toward CCEs going forward, based on the CCE enablers sub-index?
- How are the GCC countries' oil and gas sectors and related industries performing, and how are they positioned to make progress on CCEs, based on the CCE Oil Producers' Lens indicators?

The results of the analysis indicated that as a group, the GCC countries outperform their non-OECD peers and neighbours in the Middle East and Africa region while ranking slightly below the high income and global average. They should undertake further efforts to increase emissions circularity if they wish to maintain their competitiveness amidst the global transition to net zero in many performance and enablers areas of the CCE transition. Among the key technologies and activities covered under the CCE performance sub-index, GCC countries indicate strong performance especially in preserving their natural sink capacity, improving energy efficiency, and implementing fuel switching, along with the penetration of emerging technologies, such as CCUS and hydrogen. Renewable energy and nuclear power continue to be underutilised technologies with large potential amidst ambitious projects in the pipeline.

Out of the five enabling dimensions considered in the CCE Index, most gaps are observed in the three dimensions across the countries in the region: policies and regulation; technology, knowledge, and innovation; and finance and investment. In particular, the current CCE investment levels as well as the size of sustainable flows tend to be low in the region despite the enormous potential. There remains significant potential in the regional countries to improve their penetration of the relevant technologies, transition investment, and sustainable finance with the implementation of more ambitious policies and incentives.

The following section provides a high-level discussion of the total CCE Index scores across the GCC and other included countries. Section 3.3 focuses on the performance gaps across the GCC countries in terms of utilising key technologies such as renewable energy, CCUS, and clean hydrogen. Similarly, Section 3.4 identifies cross-country enabling gaps. Section 3.5 brings oil producers' perspectives. Section 3.6 analyses the strengths, weaknesses, and gaps in the GCC countries' internationally communicated climate plans and Section 3.7 concludes.

3.2 2021 CCE Index: A High-level Overview of the Scores

The CCE Index provides a composite score for comparing countries' standings vis-à-vis CCEs on two sub-indices: current performance and future potential. The total index score is consequently comprised of two parts with equal weights: the CCE performance score measures the diversity and depth of countries' engagement with eight different CCE activities, each of which receives an equal weight in the performance sub-index score calculation: energy efficiency, renewable energy, electrification, nuclear energy, fuel switching, natural sinks, CCUS, and green hydrogen. It consists of eight quantitative indicators, derived from harmonised, reputable datasets. The CCE enablers score gauges how well countries are positioned to make progress toward CCEs going forward. The enablers score consists of five parts, or dimensions, of equal weight: policies and regulation; technology, knowledge, and innovation; finance and investment; business environment and energy infrastructure; and socioeconomic context. The enablers sub-index has a total of twenty-nine different indicators, classified under these five areas. The CCE enablers score is computed by first calculating the average scores of each of the dimensions and then calculating the average score of these dimensions. Data for all indicators is derived from reputable, harmonised datasets, and indicator values are scaled to a score of 0–100, which is in most cases based on the top and bottom performing countries' values.[1]

Given the aim of this chapter, to identify both similarities and differences between the GCC countries, the analysis below examines the GCC countries both as a group, comparing them to other peer country groups, and each GCC country individually, comparing them to the GCC countries' average and each other. Since the 2021 edition of the CCE Index only includes the G20 member countries and top-20 global oil-producing countries (a total of 30 countries), Bahrain is not

[1] The CCE Index framework, indicator descriptions, and the score aggregation logic are available in the Appendix. The full CCE Index methodology, results, underlying data, and various other resources are available online: http://cceindex.kapsarc.org/. The CCE Index will be updated annually, and the 2022 edition included a significantly expanded list of countries.

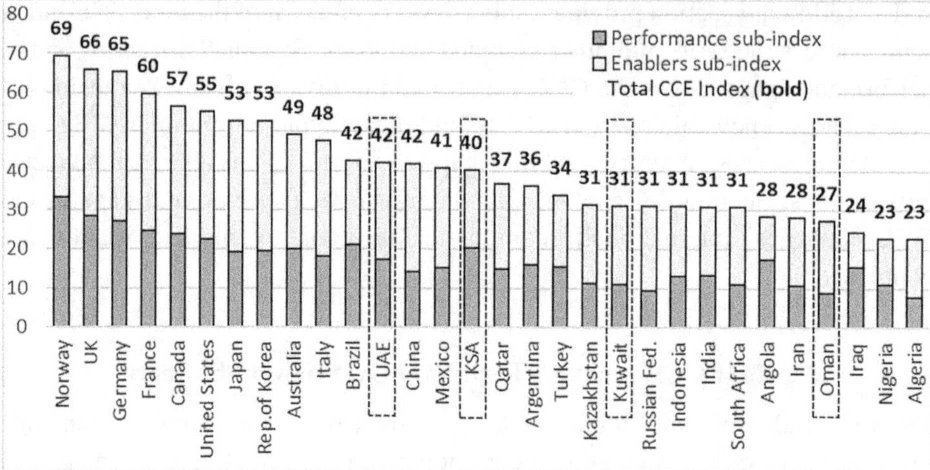

Figure 3.2 The GCC countries in the 2021 CCE Index – performance and enablers sub-indices.

included in the index. Throughout the chapter, therefore, 'GCC average' always refers to the average score of the five other GCC member countries.

Figure 3.2, adopted from (Luomi et al., 2021b) shows the 2021 CCE Index total scores, with a breakdown of the relative contributions of the performance and enablers sub-indices. Among the '30 countries' (as they shall henceforth be referred to) included in this edition, the ranks of the GCC countries range from twelfth to twenty-seventh, with the United Arab Emirates (UAE) ranking the highest and Oman the lowest.

As a group, the GCC countries, with an average total CCE Index score of 35, rank below the average score of the 30 countries included in the index (41), as well as the average scores of the 15 high-income countries (50) and 19 major oil producers (39). As a group, on average they score higher than the 18 non-OECD countries and the 11 Middle Eastern and African countries included in the index. Similarly, on both the CCE performance and enablers sub-indices, the GCC countries as a group score lower than the 30-country, high-income, and oil producers' averages and higher than the non-OECD and Middle East and Africa averages (see Figure 3.3, Panel A).

Individually, as displayed in Figure 3.3, Panel B, the UAE (42), Saudi Arabia (KSA, 40), and Qatar (37) have total CCE Index scores above the GCC group average (35), and Kuwait (31) and Oman (27) score below this average. The five countries' CCE performance and CCE enablers scores show a similar pattern, with two exceptions: Saudi Arabia has a higher performance score (41) than the UAE (35), while its enablers score (40) ranks just below the GCC average (42).

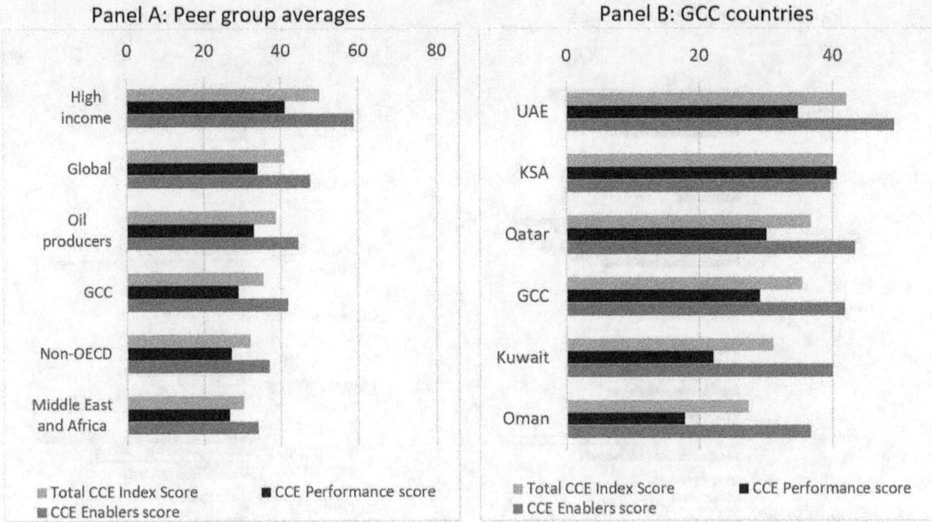

Figure 3.3 The GCC countries in the 2021 CCE Index – group and individual comparisons.
Note: The 'high-income' country group includes 15 countries; 'global' includes the 30 countries included in the 2021 CCE Index; 'oil producers' includes the top 19 oil producers; 'GCC' includes the 5 GCC countries included in the 2021 CCE Index; 'non-OECD' includes 18 countries, and 'Middle East and Africa' includes 11 countries. The order of the GCC countries in Figure 3.7, Panel B and in subsequent figures is based on their ranking in the total 2021 CCE Index.

Measured by the variation between the five GCC countries' scores, as expected, the GCC is a more homogeneous group than the broader 30-country group. Among the 30 countries, there is a 46-point difference in the total CCE Index scores between the top and bottom performers, whereas this difference reduces to 15 points between the GCC countries. At the same time, as shown by the high-level overview of the CCE Index total and sub-index scores above, there are major differences among the five GCC countries. The following sections unpack these differences – and similarities – by deconstructing the two sub-indices.

3.3 CCE Performance: The Diversity and Depth of Current Activities

The CCE performance sub-index measures how countries are engaging with eight CCE activities and technologies, which cover the major climate change mitigation options presently available worldwide. The indicators draw from harmonised international datasets and are designed to serve as representative proxies for each activity. Energy efficiency, for example, is measured by the energy intensity of an economy, and renewable energy by the share of renewables in the energy mix.

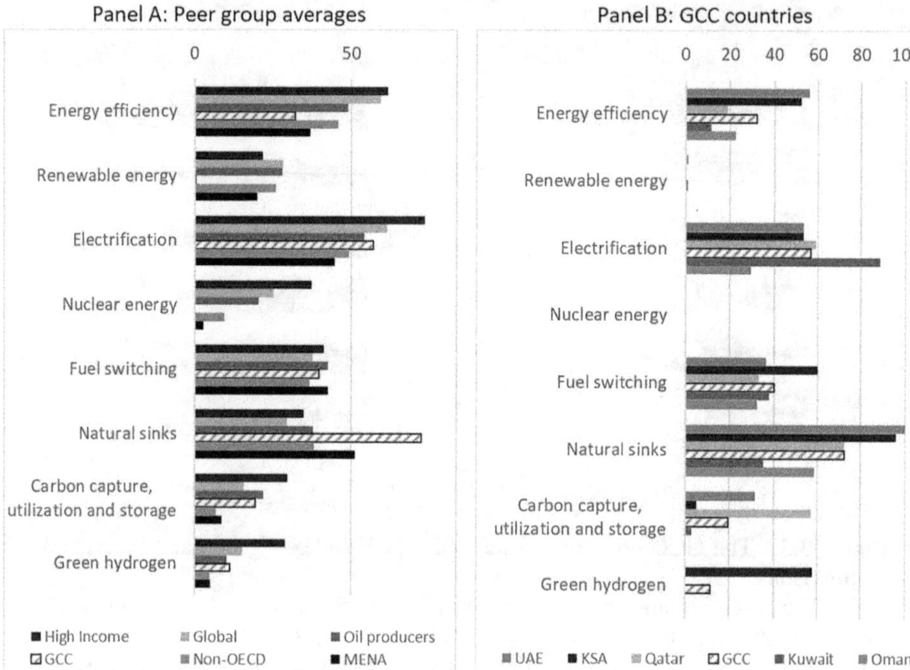

Figure 3.4 The GCC countries' CCE performance scores compared (excluding Bahrain).

Because the CCE Index gives each CCE activity an equal weight, countries that engage in a broader variety of activities score better.[2]

Figure 3.4 shows how the GCC countries, as a group and individually, are faring on each of the eight CCE activities. In the figure, Panel A illustrates how the GCC countries score on average compare to the 30 countries' average and four peer groups. The GCC as a group scores higher than all others in only one area, natural sinks. This indicator, taken from Yale University's Environmental Performance Index, measures how well countries are preserving their *existing* ecosystems, primarily forests. Countries are therefore rewarded for what they preserve, irrespective of the size of these natural carbon sinks.

There are two areas where the GCC countries, as a group, perform significantly worse than other groups measured: renewable energy and nuclear energy (see Figure 3.4, Panel A). All countries score either zero or close to zero on both activities. While not all countries can be expected to deploy nuclear energy,[3] renewable energy resources are abundant in the GCC region and technologies

[2] All CCE activities receive an equal weight because finding consensus around a system for different weights.
[3] Data for nuclear energy is for 2019 and therefore does not account for the UAE's Barakah nuclear power plant, which has been connected to the grid since 2021.

are also cost-effective there. The GCC countries' hydrocarbon endowments are the obvious explanation for the low levels of other energy sources in the mix. However, as will be discussed further on, significant scaling-up is expected in the coming years in some GCC countries, based on their current renewable energy targets.

In the other areas, the GCC averages do not stand out in the group comparisons, but there are high variations among the individual GCC countries (see Figure 3.4, Panel B). Fuel-switching measures the total share of coal and oil – the most carbon-intense fossil fuels – in the total electricity mix. It considers a country's starting point (the share of these sources in 2014) and how rapidly it has moved away from them over the past five years (2014–2019). Here, Saudi Arabia ranks significantly higher than its GCC peers, owing to a 21%-point drop in the share of oil in its electricity mix (from 62% in 2014 to 41% in 2019).

There is a wide variation in the GCC countries' electrification scores (Figure 3.4, Panel B). This indicator measures the share of electricity in the country's total energy mix. Among other things, it can be used to indicate how well countries are positioned to electrify their economies (in the CCE Index it is also used as a control for the share of commercial renewables). However, high shares of electricity in the energy mix can also be a sign of other things, such as an absence of heat-intensive industries or inefficiencies on the demand side. In the case of Kuwait, high per capita electricity demand (16.3 megawatt hours [MWh] per capita in 2019) indicates a more inefficient use of energy than in other GCC countries. Oman's electricity per capita consumption, in contrast, was only 7.0 MWh in 2019 (IEA, 2021).

Given the presently low levels of deployment, the CCUS and green hydrogen[4] indicators also factor in projects that are in the pipeline (e.g. in planning or development, and financed or under construction). On these indicators, two countries – Oman and Qatar – had no registered projects as of September 2021. Capacity data for both indicators is divided by the country's gross domestic product (GDP) to consider its economy size. On green hydrogen, Saudi Arabia's Neom project, which in the BloombergNEF's (BNEF's) database features a 2-gigawatt capacity, grants the country a high score. On CCUS, Qatar achieves a high score from an enhanced oil recovery (EOR) project and methanol production facility, with a total capacity of 2.28 million tonnes of carbon dioxide ($MtCO_2$) per year. The UAE similarly gets a high score from two EOR projects and a urea production facility with a total capacity of 3.25 $MtCO_2$/year.

[4] The 2021 edition of the CCE Index only measures green hydrogen projects because the authors were unable to locate sufficiently comprehensive datasets for blue hydrogen projects. At the same time, blue hydrogen is also indirectly covered through the CCUS indicator.

3.4 CCE Enablers: Potential to Transition to Net Zero and CCEs

The 2021 CCE Index results indicate larger gaps among countries in three of the five areas of the enablers sub-index, which can unlock countries' potential to accelerate CCE transitions. These are policies and regulations; technology, knowledge, and innovation; and finance and investment (see Figure 3.1). The GCC region's average in these areas is lower than that of the high-income, 30-country, and oil-producers' groups (Figure 3.1, Panel A). Compared to the non-OECD and Middle East and Africa group averages, the GCC group average is either slightly higher or equivalent. For instance, the GCC group's average finance and investment score is 21, while that number is 48 for the high-income group, 35 for the 30 countries, and 30 for the oil producers. The average scores for the non-OECD and the Middle East and Africa are 20 and 16, respectively.

As displayed in Figure 3.5, Panel B, the GCC countries appear to score similarly on the business environment energy security and socioeconomic context dimensions. While there are minor differences among them in terms of their scores on socioeconomic context, their scores for the business environment and energy infrastructure dimension are strikingly similar.

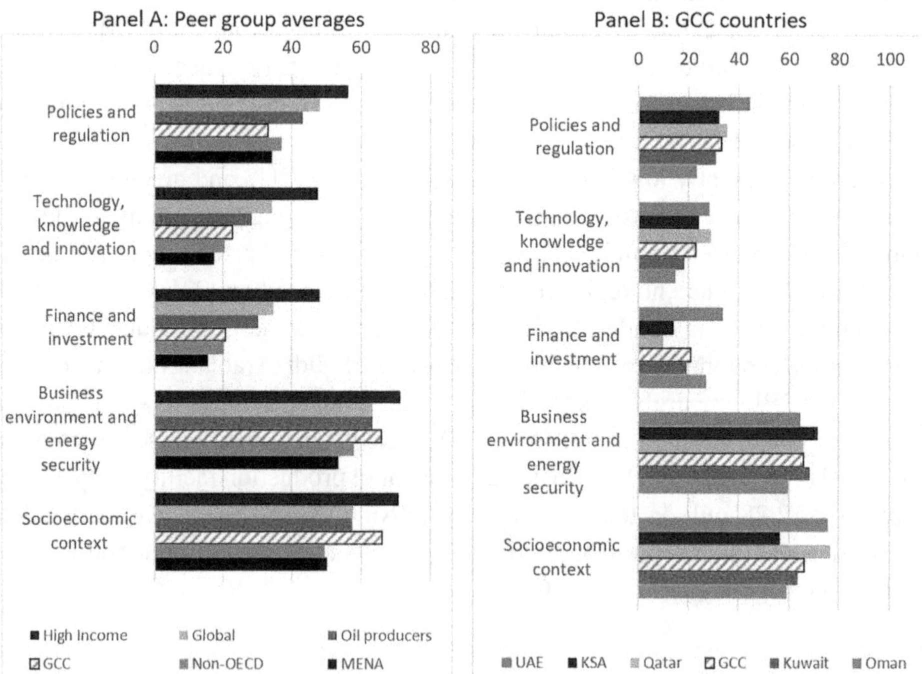

Figure 3.5 The GCC countries' CCE enablers scores compared (excluding Bahrain).

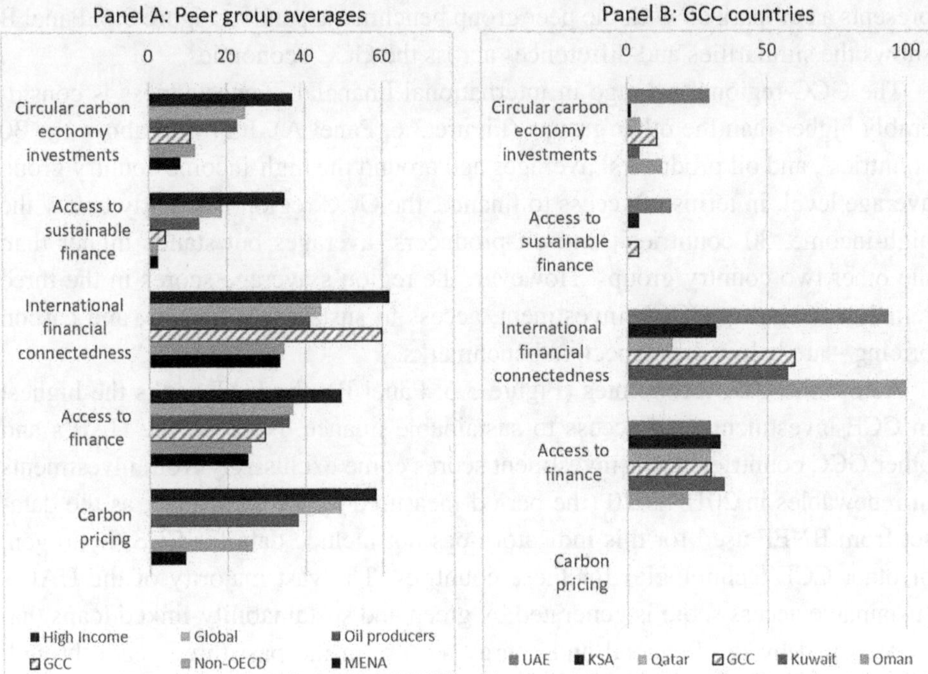

Figure 3.6 The GCC countries' CCE enablers scores compared: finance and investment.

Significant gaps exist in the other three enabling dimensions across the GCC countries (Figure 3.5, Panel B). More specifically, the UAE ranks the highest in the region in the policies and regulation dimension; Saudi Arabia, Qatar, and Kuwait lie around the GCC average; and Oman scores below the group average. The technology, knowledge and innovation dimensions have a similar distribution, but the group average and country-level scores here are lower than in the policy and regulation dimension.

The largest gaps across the GCC countries exist in the finance and investment dimension (Figure 3.6, Panel B). The UAE leads this dimension, while Oman records the second-highest score. Kuwait's performance is around the GCC average, while Saudi Arabia and Qatar are below the average. Considering the large differences across the countries, the finance and investment dimension deserves a closer look, which is provided in Figure 3.6. The figure presents the key metrics covered under this dimension, which measure CCE investments (in renewable energy, hydrogen, carbon capture and storage, energy storage, and electrified heat and transportation); access to sustainable finance (sustainable debt); international financial connectedness (foreign direct investment, net inflows, and outflows); access to conventional finance (access to credit, size of stock, and bond markets); and carbon pricing (emissions trading scheme or carbon tax). Figure 3.6, Panel A presents a comparison with the peer group benchmarks, and in Figure 3.6, Panel B shows the similarities and differences across the GCC economies.

The GCC regional average in international financial connectedness is considerably higher than the other groups (Figure 3.6, Panel A). It is well above the 30 countries', and oil producers' averages and around the high-income country group average level. In terms of access to finance, the GCC region is slightly below the high-income, 30 countries', and oil producers' averages but stands higher than the other two country groups. However, the region's average scores in the three remaining metrics – CCE investment, access to sustainable finance, and carbon pricing – are below the respective benchmarks.

Across the GCC economies (Figure 3.6, Panel B), the UAE ranks the highest in CCE investments and access to sustainable finance. Notably, the UAE's and other GCC countries' CCE investment scores come exclusively from investments in renewables in 2018–2020 (the period measured by the indicator), as the dataset from BNEF used for this indicator does not include data for CCS, hydrogen, or other CCE technologies for these countries. The vast majority of the UAE's sustainable access score is generated by green and sustainability-linked loans that were issued by the financial and energy sectors in the past three years through September 2021 (the period measured by the indicator), but some green-bond issuance has also taken place in the country over this period.

The other GCC economies also scaled up their CCE investments during this period; Oman stood around the GCC average and others remained below. Similarly, they also leveraged some sustainable finance in the period between 2019 and 2021, although the general flows were quite low compared to the peer-group benchmarks. Here, Saudi Arabia recorded around the GCC average, while others stood significantly below. Finally, none of the GCC economies currently engages in subnational or national-level carbon-pricing activities, which gives them a zero score on this indicator.

3.5 Oil Producers' Lens: Gauging Industry's CCE Performance and Potential

The CCE Index contains an additional set of indicators aimed at enabling further comparisons among major global oil producing countries, which face both challenges and opportunities unique to only this group that stem from the size of their hydrocarbon industries. The 2021 CCE Index included 19 top global oil producers (henceforth referred to as the '19'). The 2021 Oil Producers' Lens score was calculated by adding five indicators to the performance sub-index and five indicators to the enablers sub-index. The score aggregation logic is shown in the Appendix. The 2021 ranking for the Oil Producers' Lens is shown in Figure 3.7, Panel A. There

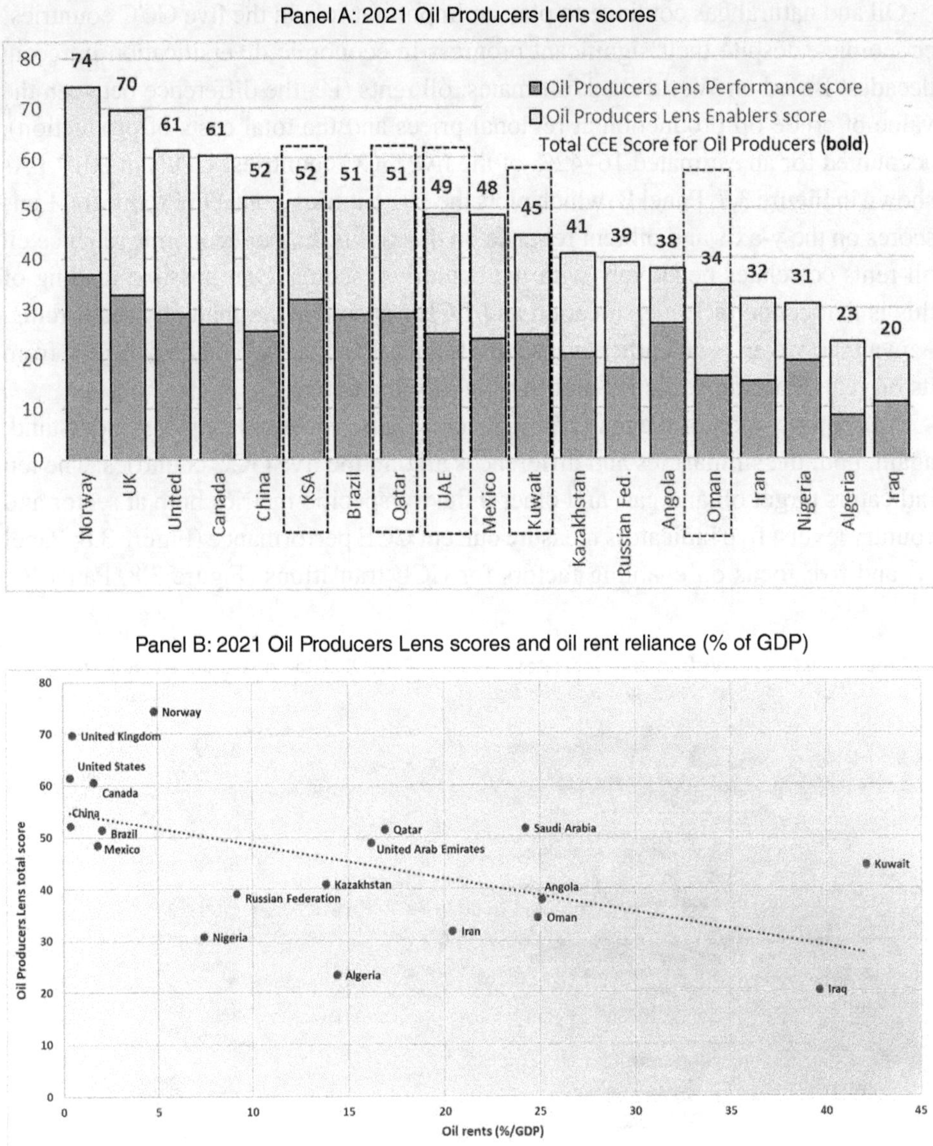

Figure 3.7 The GCC countries in the 2021 Oil Producers' Lens ranking and oil rent levels.

are some changes in rank compared to those of the same 19 countries in the 2021 total CCE Index. For the GCC countries, the major changes are Saudi Arabia's higher ranking – it ranks sixth on the Oil Producers' Lens, compared to ninth among the 19 oil producers included in the total CCE Index score – and the UAE's lower ranking – ninth compared to sixth in the total CCE Index. Data presented in Figure 3.7 is adopted from (Luomi et al., 2021b; World Bank, 2021b).

Oil and natural gas continue to play an important role in the five GCC countries' economies, despite their significant progress in economic diversification in recent decades. Based on World Bank estimates, oil rents (i.e. the difference between the value of crude oil production at regional prices and the total costs of production), accounted for an estimated 16–42% of the five GCC countries' GDPs in 2019.[5] As shown in Figure 3.7, Panel B, which plots the 19 countries' total Oil Producers' Lens scores on the y-axis and oil rent reliance on the x-axis, higher economic reliance on oil rents correlates negatively with the countries' scores. One possible reading of this is that economic diversification and CCE transitions are mutually reinforcing. Kuwait, however, is an outlier as it scores higher than what would be expected from its oil rent dependence, as is Saudi Arabia to some extent.

A decomposition of the ten Oil Producers' Lens indicators helps us understand, again, both the similarities and differences among the five GCC countries. The ten indicators target oil and gas, and other industry-specific metrics both at sector and country levels: five indicators measure current CCE performance (Figure 3.8, Panel A) and five focus on enabling factors for CCE transitions (Figure 3.8, Panel B).

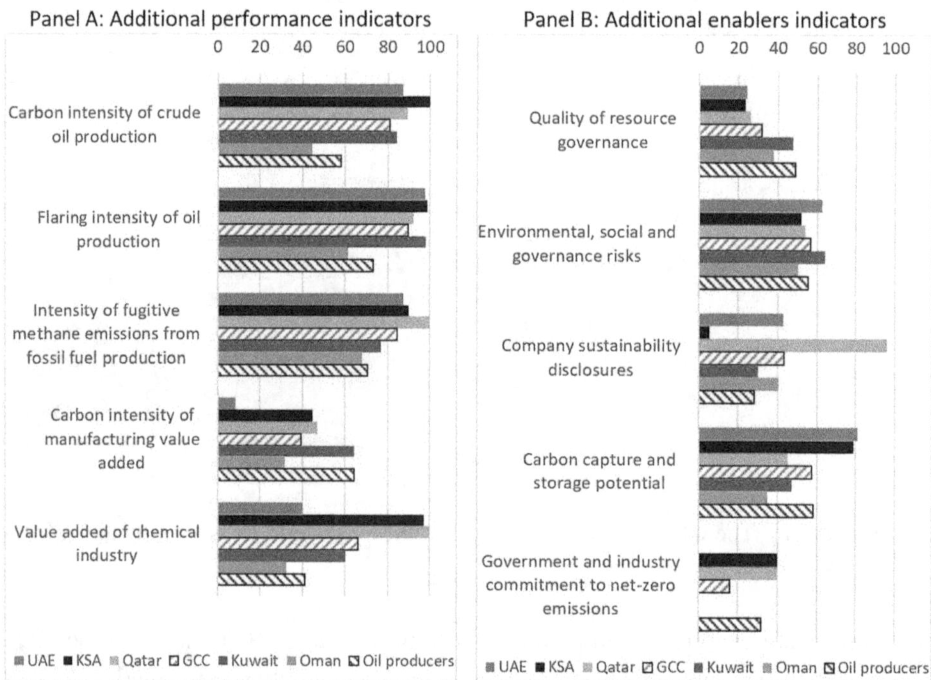

Figure 3.8 The GCC countries (excluding Bahrain) compared to other major oil producers on key CCE metrics.

[5] Natural gas rents are not included. These are a significant source of external revenue for Qatar and Oman.

Focusing first on the performance indicators (Figure 3.8, Panel A), overall, with the exception of the carbon intensity of manufacturing value added, the GCC as a group ranks higher than the 19-country group on average on all indicators. Individually, however, there is important variation in the scores.

As the world moves toward net zero and many countries continue or start pricing emissions, a lower carbon intensity of production will become an asset for oil producers. At present, four GCC countries have among the world's least carbon-intensive crude oil production processes. Saudi Arabia scores 100 on this indicator, which covers a country's production, transportation and refining of crude oil. Oman stands out with a score of only 44. Flaring and venting remain significant sources of emissions from the oil industry, even while reductions would often deliver cost savings. In 2020, flaring alone was estimated to have generated 377 $MtCO_2$ worldwide, roughly equal to the combined annual emissions of the UAE and Oman (World Bank, 2021a; WRI et al., 2021). Again, the GCC countries, apart from Oman, score high in reducing the amount of gas flared per barrel of oil produced. They also perform well compared to their peers in avoiding fugitive methane emissions from their oil and gas industries, with Qatar scoring the highest and Oman the lowest.

As oil-producing countries diversify their economies both vertically (within the oil and gas sector) and horizontally (beyond the oil and gas sector), the carbon intensity of their manufacturing sectors becomes increasingly important.[6] On the indicator measuring the carbon intensity of their manufacturing value added ($kgCO_2$/USD), all but Kuwait performs well below the 19-country average. The UAE has the second lowest score among the 19 countries (9), only higher than that of Iraq (0). A further analysis to understand the structure of the country's manufacturing industry compared to its peers would be required to identify possible causes. The chemicals industry is an important area of vertical diversification for Gulf oil producers and has the potential to make a significant economic contribution to CCEs in the region. Qatar and Saudi Arabia receive top scores on chemical industry value added as a share of GDP, while Oman and the UAE rank below the 19-country average. It should be kept in mind, however, that more diversified economies may have higher contributions from other economic sectors, which might explain the UAE's lower score in particular.

Figure 3.8, Panel B shows the GCC countries' scores on the five oil producer-specific enablers indicators. A general challenge in measuring this area is that environmental, social and governance (ESG) and broader long-term sustainability-related issues have emerged relatively recently on the global industry's agenda. As a result, there is a general dearth of harmonised datasets that would help measure oil industry preparedness for CCE transitions. The first two indicators, quality of resource

[6] Carbon intensity of manufacturing value added measures the carbon intensity of the energy mix used in the manufacturing sector, the structure of the sector, the energy efficiency of production technologies, and the economic value of the various outputs.

governance and ESG risks draw from existing indices and focus on the country level. On the former, Kuwait stands out for its higher score (48), which is on par with the 19-country average, while the other four score below this average. On the latter, all five receive scores around the broader group's average. Company sustainability disclosures are used as a proxy of how mainstreamed sustainability and ESG reporting is among oil-producing countries' energy-related industries. It measures the number of reports published by multinational and large energy, energy utility, and chemical companies over the past decade divided by the country's GDP. On this metric, Qatar has a high score (96) with a total of 58 reports registered in the Global Reporting Initiative's database. Saudi Arabia has 21 reports in the database but, due to its larger economy size, scores the lowest (6).

CCS will be a key technology for global oil producers to continue exploiting their hydrocarbon resources as the world transitions to net zero (IEA, 2021). On CCS potential, which is measured using an existing indicator from the Global CCS Institute's CCS Readiness Index that tracks the development of countries' storage resources, the UAE (81) and Saudi Arabia (79) score well above the 19-group average, while the other three receive lower than average scores. The final enablers indicator measures the level of government and industry commitment to net zero emissions. Data for the 2021 CCE Index was retrieved at the end of September 2021, which means the scores do not capture the net zero announcements made by the UAE, Saudi Arabia, and Saudi Aramco (as well as Bahrain) in October 2021. If these were factored in, the UAE would score 40, on par with Qatar, and Saudi Arabia would score 80.

3.6 The GCC Countries' Climate Targets and the CCE

While net zero targets establish a clear, absolute long-term goal (net zero equals full carbon circularity in which the balance of emissions and removals of CO_2 emissions is zero), they alone tell little about how individual countries and industries plan to reach that goal. Countries' Paris Agreement NDCs generally provide some of this detail for the medium term (currently through 2030 or 2035). The GCC countries submitted their new or updated NDCs to the UN Framework Convention on Climate Change (UNFCCC) between December 2020 and November 2021. Key CCE-related elements featured in these documents are presented in Table 3.1. The table seeks to demonstrate how using the CCE as a framework for analysing countries' emissions plans and targets not only enables comparisons across countries but also allows for an examination of strengths and weaknesses. It also helps to identify possible gaps in countries' internationally communicated climate plans compared to their domestic plans and ongoing developments. The table can also be used to compare GCC countries' 2021 CCE performance scores with their medium- and long-term plans and targets, to gauge where activities could be expected to be scaled up in the near term.

First, Table 3.1 identifies where GCC NDCs contain quantitative (dark grey) versus qualitative (light grey) targets. It shows that most quantitative targets fall under the 'reduce' pillar of the CCE, namely renewable energy and energy efficiency. Most GCC countries mention natural sinks in their climate plans, even if their potential may not be as large as that of many other world regions. CCS is also mentioned in most NDCs, but concrete plans or targets still appear to be missing. Hydrogen, in turn, is only mentioned in the UAE's and Saudi Arabia's NDCs, while Oman has also signalled high ambition in this area and recently announced the establishment of a national hydrogen alliance (PDO, 2021).

However, some of the quantitative targets mentioned in the NDCs, both for CCE activities and for emissions, do not include baseline information. Baselines are quantitative points of comparison for targets that are expressed concerning business-as-usual or other quantitative milestones. A baseline allows for set targets to be quantified by providing a clear point of comparison. In some cases, governments have this information, but for various reasons choose not to disclose it. This means, however, that researchers, for example, cannot conduct policy-relevant scenarios and other quantitative analyses in support of effective policy-making. Domestically, baseline information can also help improve policy outcomes by providing all stakeholders with a clear sense of direction. Also, the Paris Agreement calls for transparency in disclosing key assumptions related to targets that countries communicate, as this, among other things, helps quantify the aggregate impact of countries' efforts.

Second, as noted above, the major gap in GCC countries' current CCE performance, measured by the CCE Index, is in the area of renewables (along with nuclear energy, which not all countries can be expected to pursue). Based on the GCC countries' current NDCs, Saudi Arabia, which has set a 50% by 2030 renewable electricity target, and the UAE, which has a 50% clean electricity capacity by 2050 target, can be expected to see significant scaling up of these technologies in the immediate and medium term.

In two CCE activities, namely CCUS and green hydrogen, three GCC countries – Saudi Arabia, Qatar and the UAE – score significantly higher on the CCE Index than their peers. These countries also seem to have somewhat more defined plans in these areas, based on what they have communicated in their NDCs. Given the recent rise in global interest in clean hydrogen, the GCC countries' next NDC updates, which are due by 2025 at the latest, can be expected to contain further details. This is particularly the case for Oman, which has been ramping up its engagement in this area but does not yet refer to hydrogen in its 2021 NDC. CCUS, in turn, will be a critical area for all GCC countries, should they wish to pursue net zero emissions and CCEs, which is why more detailed plans, by the countries' national oil companies in particular, should also be forthcoming.

Table 3.1 *Activities, technologies, and targets listed in GCC countries' latest NDCs from 2021 onwards, mapped onto the CCE framework.*

	Bahrain	Kuwait	Oman	Qatar	Saudi Arabia	UAE
Energy efficiency	6% EE (energy consumption reduction) target for 2025 (no baseline*)	Energy and water efficiency measures; energy subsidy reforms (only past mentioned)	Improving gas-fired power plants' efficiency by 11% during 2021–2025; other energy and water efficiency measures; subsidy reforms	Energy and water efficiency measures	Energy and water efficiency measures	Reduction of final energy demand by 40% by 2050 (no baseline*); energy and water efficiency measures; energy price reforms (only past mentioned)
Renewable energy	Solar, wind and biogas; 10% peak capacity target for 2035	Increasing renewable energy generation by 2030	20% of electricity from renewables (solar and wind) by 2027 (and 35–39% by 2040)	(800 MWh solar plant operational soon)	50% of electricity from renewables by 2030; (plans for solar, wind, geothermal, waste to energy, green hydrogen)	Installed clean power (mainly solar and nuclear) capacity of 14 GW by 2030; renewables and nuclear energy accounting for 50% of installed power-generation capacity by 2050
Electrification			Electrification of equipment in the oil and gas industry	Transition to electric vehicles; electrification of port operations	(Electrification mentioned as part of the CCE framework)	2% share of electric and hybrid cars in the Emirate of Dubai's road fleet by 2030

Nuclear energy						Installed clean power (mainly solar and nuclear) capacity of 14 GW by 2030; renewables and nuclear energy accounting for 50% of installed power-generation capacity by 2050
Fuel switching		Increasing the share of liquefied natural gas to 70% in energy generation by 2022	Decarbonisation of the power sector		50% electricity from natural gas by 2030	(International cooperation in cleaner hydrocarbons welcomed)
Natural sinks	National project for afforestation; mangrove transplantation project	Mangrove cultivation (reductions increasing by 50 kilo tonnes of CO_2 per year)		Growing mangroves and planting indigenous trees	Increasing sinks through tree planting, green belts, rehabilitating land, and planting mangroves (blue carbon)	20% of marine blue carbon habitats within protected areas by 2025; planting 30 million mangrove seedlings by 2030
Carbon capture, utilisation, and storage (CCUS)	Support to carbon capture and utilisation, direct air capture (DAC), other mitigation technologies for hard-to-abate sectors	CCS project(s) resulting in an annual reduction of 216 kilotons of CO_2 in 2022		CCS included for new LNG facilities and concepts	Plans to transform industrial cities of Jubail and Yanbu into global hubs for CCUS; enhanced oil recovery; (DAC also mentioned)	Plans to expand CCS capacity; CCS as part of national oil company's GHG emissions intensity reduction target of 25% by 2030 (no baseline*)

Table 3.1 (*cont.*)

	Bahrain	Kuwait	Oman	Qatar	Saudi Arabia	UAE
Clean hydrogen				(International cooperation in hydrogen fuels and technologies mentioned as important)	650 tonnes /day of green hydrogen by electrolysis and 1.2 million tonnes / year of green ammonia produced by 2025; plans for blue hydrogen and National Hydrogen Strategy under development; (clean hydrogen deployment and collaboration mentioned as crucial)	(Pilot electrolysis facility mentioned; international cooperation in hydrogen welcomed)
GHG emissions targets for 2030/2035		7.4% reduction in GHG emissions by 2035 relative to a business-as-usual (BAU) trajectory	7% reduction in GHG emissions by 2030 compared with a BAU trajectory	25% reduction in GHG emissions by 2030 compared with business as usual (no baseline*)	278 million tonnes CO_2e reduction in GHG emissions by 2030 (no baseline*)	23.5% reduction in GHG emissions by 2030, relative to BAU emissions
CO_2/GHG emissions targets for 2050/2060	Net zero CO_2 emissions by 2060	(Low-emissions development strategy for 2050 planned)			Net zero CO_2 emissions by 2060	Net zero CO_2 emissions by 2050

Key

(light shading)	Activities/technologies mentioned. *The absence of an emissions/other baseline means the absolute target cannot be quantified.
(dark shading)	Quantitative target associated with an activity/technology.

Note: The table is not exhaustive, based on the GCC countries' latest NDC documents as of 3 January 2022. Mid century targets are in many cases not enshrined in the NDCs but have been included in the table as additional information.

3.7 Conclusion

The analysis above has shown that, although as a group, the GCC countries outperform their neighbours in the Middle East and Africa region and their non-OECD peers in most areas measured by the CCE Index, they should undertake further efforts if they wish to improve their position, or retain competitiveness, in the global transition to net zero.

Apart from identifying areas where there is scope for further work in individual countries, the analysis in this chapter also highlighted areas where some GCC countries are leading the way. Individually, among the GCC countries, there are several bright spots: in the area of current CCE performance, Saudi Arabia has made significant progress in switching from oil to natural gas in the power sector and has a significant green hydrogen production capacity in the pipeline. The UAE, in turn, has a sizable CCUS project capacity and pipeline. However, the GCC as a whole is still lagging in renewable energy deployment.

In terms of CCE transition enablers, the GCC countries on average fare very well compared to their peer groups in providing attractive business environments and energy infrastructure stability and security. Their lowest group score is in the area of finance and investment, which is where the largest differences among the five countries also exist. Oman and the UAE have managed to leverage the highest foreign direct investment flows (in proportion to their economy size), and the UAE also scores better than its neighbours in CCE investments and sustainable finance. Even so, all GCC countries still have significant work ahead in scaling up CCE transition finance and investments, including through exploring different carbon pricing instruments.

On many oil-producer-specific metrics, some GCC countries perform significantly better than their peers. Saudi Arabia, the UAE, and Qatar perform well in terms of present-day oil industry emissions metrics; major Qatari companies have well-established sustainability reporting practices; and the UAE and Saudi Arabia have well-developed CCS resources. If the recent net zero targets are factored in, the same three countries – Saudi Arabia, the UAE and Qatar – also score well compared to other oil producers on long-term policy ambition.

There is also significant scope for emissions reductions or avoidance with a minimal or negative cost in the areas of energy efficiency and fuel-switching across the GCC. Setting new or higher quantified targets in these areas could help send policy signals to markets and further raise the level of ambition in the GCC countries' NDCs.

Finally, in most CCE activities, there is significant, still unexploited potential for cooperation among the GCC countries in leveraging their similarities and complementarities. An example of the former would be collaborative efforts on major CCUS initiatives and hydrogen exports. There are also major complementarities that a strengthened market around the GCC interconnection grid could bring that could help scale up renewable and other forms of clean energy and increase the rate of electrification across the region.

Appendix

Supplementary Data Showing (a) 2021 CCE Index Indicator Framework, (b) Indicator List, and (c) Aggregation Logic

Table A.a *2021 CCE Index indicator framework.*

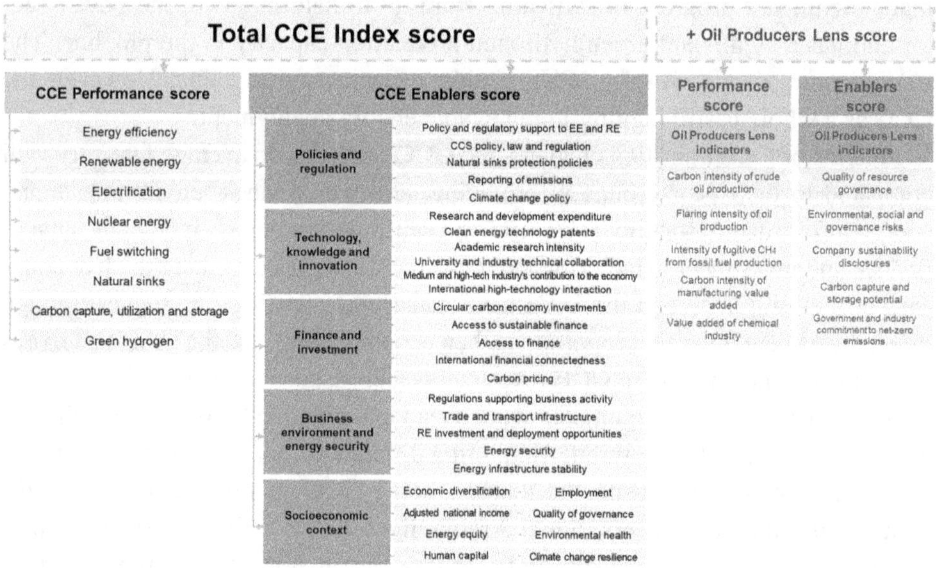

Table A.b *Indicator list.*

Sub-index	Sub-dimension	Indicator name	Indicator description
Performance	(n/a)	Energy efficiency	Energy intensity of the GDP at purchasing power parities
		Renewable energy	Share of renewables in primary consumption
		Electrification	Share of electricity in total final energy consumption
		Nuclear energy	Share of nuclear electricity in primary consumption
		Fuel switching	Change in the share of oil, coal and lignite and derived gas in electricity production over a five-year period, and overall share of oil, coal, lignite, and derived gas in electricity production at the start of the period
		Natural sinks	Ecosystem services, including carbon sequestration and storage, biodiversity habitat, nutrient cycling, and coastal protection (from the Environmental Performance Index)
		Carbon capture, utilisation and storage	Total capture capacity of CCUS projects (operational, in construction, advanced development, and early development)
		Green hydrogen	Total capacity of green hydrogen projects (commissioned, financed/under construction, and announced/planning begun)
Oil Producers' Lens	Performance	Carbon intensity of crude oil production	Volume-weighted average carbon intensity of crude oil production, transportation, and refining by source country (Source Country Upstream and Refining Combined CI)
		Flaring intensity of oil production	Gas flared per barrel of oil produced
		Intensity of fugitive methane emissions from fossil fuel production	Fugitive methane emissions from fossil fuel industry/ total fossil fuel production
		Carbon intensity of manufacturing value added	CO_2 emissions per unit of manufacturing value added
		Value added of chemical industry	Value added of chemical industry as a share of the GDP

Table A.b (*cont.*)

Sub-index	Sub-dimension	Indicator name	Indicator description
Enablers	Policies and regulation	Policy and regulatory support to energy efficiency and renewable energy	Regulatory Indicators for Sustainable Energy (RISE) indicators for energy efficiency and renewable energy
		Carbon capture and storage policy, law, and regulation	CCS Legal and Regulatory Indicator and CCS Policy Indicator (from the CCS Readiness Index)
		Natural sinks protection policies	Average proportion of terrestrial, freshwater, and marine key biodiversity areas covered by
		Reporting of emissions	Fulfilment of reporting obligations under the UNFCCC
		Climate change policy	Climate Policy score (from the Climate Change Performance Index)
	Technology, knowledge and	Research and development expenditure	Research and development expenditure
		Clean energy technology patents	WIPO patent applications/capita (fuel cells, geothermal, solar and wind energy), sum of 5 latest
		Academic research intensity	Nature Index, 'share'
		University and industry technical collaboration	University/industry research collaboration
		Medium and high-tech industry's contribution to the economy	Medium and high-tech industry value added (of total manufacturing value added)
		International high-tech interaction	High-tech trade (export and import total trade after excluding re-imports/exports,
	Finance and investment	Circular carbon economy investments	Investments in renewable energy, hydrogen, CCS, energy storage, electrified heat, and electrified transport, sum of 3 latest years
		Access to sustainable finance	Sustainable (green, social and sustainability-linked) debt (bonds and loans) issued per country of domicile, 5 latest years)
		Access to finance	Average % of GDP: (1) domestic credit to private sector; (2) stock market capitalisation, and (3) corporate bond issuance volume

		International financial connectedness	Average %GDP of: (1) foreign direct investment net inflows by foreigners; and (2) foreign direct net outflows by residents
		Carbon pricing	Emissions trading scheme or carbon tax implemented (national level 1, subnational level 0.75); scheduled (0.5); or under consideration (0.25)
	Business environment and energy security	Regulations supporting business activity	Ease of Doing Business score
		Trade and transport infrastructure	Logistics Performance Index
		Renewable energy investment and deployment	Renewable Energy Country Attractiveness Index
		Energy security	Share of fuel imports of total imports of goods and services (current USD)
		Energy infrastructure stability	Average of System average interruption duration index (SAIDI) and System average interruption frequency index (SAIFI)
	Socioeconomic	Economic diversification	Economic Complexity Index
		Adjusted national income	Adjusted net national income per capita
		Energy equity	Energy Equity score (from the Energy Trilemma Index)
		Human capital	Human Capital Index
		Employment	Employment to population ratio, 15+, total (modeled ILO estimate)
		Quality of governance	Worldwide Governance Indicators aggregate score
		Environmental health	Mortality rate attributed to household and ambient air pollution, age-standardised
		Climate change resilience	Global Climate Risk Index

Table A.b (*cont.*)

Sub-index	Sub-dimension	Indicator name	Indicator description
Oil Producers' Lens	Enablers	Quality of resource governance	Value Realisation and Revenue Management Scores for oil and gas (from the Resource Governance Index)
		Environmental, social and governance risks	ESG Index
		Company sustainability disclosures	Number of sustainability disclosure reports by multinational and large energy, energy utility, and chemicals companies (ten latest years)
		Carbon capture and storage potential	CCS Storage Indicator (from the CCS Readiness Index)
		Government and industry commitment to net zero emissions	National net zero target in law, policy, or under discussion, and participation in major industry net zero partnerships

Table A.c *Aggregation logic.*

Index level	Sub-index level	Sub-dimension/indictor level					No.
CCE Index	Performance score (50%)	Performance indicators (6.25% each)					8
	Enablers score (50%)	Enablers sub-dimensions					29
		Policies and regulation (10%)	Tech., knowledge and innovation (10%)	Finance and investment (10%)	Business environment and energy sector (10%)	Socioeconomic context (10%)	
Oil Producers' Lens	Oil Producers' Lens performance score (50%)	Performance indicators (3.13% each)					8
		Oil Producers' Lens performance indicators (5% each)					5
	Oil Producers' Lens enablers score (50%)	Enablers sub-dimensions					29
		(8.33%)	(8.33%)	(8.33%)	(8.33%)	(8.33%)	
		Oil Producers' Lens enablers indicators (1.67% each)					5

References

International Energy Agency (IEA) (2021). *Data and Statistics*. Available online: www.iea.org/data-and-statistics/data-browser?country=WORLD&fuel=Energy%20consumption&indicator=ElecConsPerCapita (accessed 9 January 2022).

Luomi, M., Fatih, Y., and Alshehri, T. (2021a). How the Circular Carbon Economy Index Can Serve Policymaking: Case Study of Saudi Arabia. *KAPSARC Commentary*. October 2021. Available online: www.kapsarc.org/rewsearch/publications/how-the-circular-carbon-economy-index-can-serve-policymaking-case-study-of-saudi-arabia/ (accessed 9 January 2022).

Luomi, M., Fatih, Y., and Alshehri, T. (2021b). The Circular Carbon Economy Index 2021 – Results. *KAPSARC Discussion Paper*. No. ks-2021-dp021. Available online: www.kapsarc.org/research/publications/the-circular-carbon-economy-index-2021-results/ (accessed 9 January 2022).

Luomi, M., Fatih, Y., and Alshehri, T. (2021c). The Circular Carbon Economy Index 2021 – Methodology. *KAPSARC Methodology Paper*, No. ks--2021-mp02. Riyadh: KAPSARC. Available online: www.kapsarc.org/research/publications/the-circular-carbon-economy-index-2021-methodology/ (accessed 9 January 2022).

McDonough, W. (2016). Carbon is not the enemy. *Nature*, 539 (17 November): pp. 349–351. Doi: https://doi.org/10.1038/539349a.

Petroleum Development Oman (PDO) (2021). *Oman's Hydrogen Alliance to Drive National Hydrogen Economy*. 12 August. Available online: https://pdo.co.om/en/news/press-releases/Pages/Oman%E2%80%99s%20Hydrogen%20Alliance%20to%20Drive%20National%20Hydrogen%20Economy.aspx.

Williams, E. (2019). Achieving Climate Goals by Closing the Loop in a Circular Carbon Economy. *KAPSARC Instant Insight*, 9 November. Riyadh: KAPSARC. Available online: www.kapsarc.org/research/publications/achieving-climategoals-by-closing-the-loop-in-a-circular-carboneconomy/.

World Bank (2021a). *Global Gas Flaring Data: Global Gas Flaring Reduction Partnership*. Available online: www.worldbank.org/en/programs/gasflaringreduction/global-flaring-data (accessed 5 January 2022).

World Bank (2021b). *Oil Rents (% of GDP)*. Available online: https://data.worldbank.org/indicator/NY.GDP.PETR.RT.ZS (accessed 9 January 2022).

World Resources Institute (WRI) et al. (2021). *Global Historical Emissions*. Available online: www.climatewatchdata.org/ghg-emissions?end_year=2018&regions=ARE%2COMN&start_year=1990 (accessed 5 January 2022).

4

Net Zero Saudi Arabia

How Green Can the Oil Kingdom Get?

JIM KRANE*

4.1 Introduction

In October 2021, Saudi Arabia told the world it would eliminate or offset its greenhouse gas emissions by 2060, adopting the same "net zero" target date as governments in China, Russia, Kazakhstan, and Nigeria. A year earlier, the kingdom's national oil company, or NOC, Saudi Aramco, announced it would decarbonize its own operations even earlier, by 2050 (Saudi Aramco, 2021).

The gargantuan task of decarbonizing Saudi Arabia is evident in a few simple statistics. A country that ranked 41st in the world by population and 20th by economic activity consumed more oil in 2021 than any country outside the United States, China and India (BP, 2022). On a per capita basis, Saudi Arabia emits more CO_2 than the United States – 17 metric tons a year versus 14 in the US – on average incomes are just 75 percent as large. A serious program to decarbonize Saudi Arabia would impose a sweeping restructuring of a fossil fuel-driven society and economy in less than four decades. Transformational changes would alter energy consumption, power generation and storage, transportation, and industrial operations.

At the time of writing in 2023, the Saudi government had only hinted at its decarbonization path, with government statements and reports mentioning initiatives, favored technologies and investment targets. This chapter extrapolates from those hints to lay out a plausible path toward decarbonizing Saudi Arabia's energy and emissions systems. This work also examines potential secondary effects on the kingdom, as well as its competitive advantages and disadvantages.

* For their helpful comments on this chapter, the author would like to thank David Reiner at the University of Cambridge Energy Policy Research Group, the World Bank's Jon Strand, Renato Lima-de-Oliveira of the Asia School of Business, Andreas Rechkemmer and Logan Cochrane of Hamad bin Khalifa University, and the Baker Institute's Michael Maher. An earlier version of this chapter was presented at the 2022 Gulf Research Meeting at the University of Cambridge and released as a working paper by the Baker Institute and the University of Cambridge's Energy Policy Research Group.

Briefly stated, a net zero program might see demand-side reforms revoking fuel and utility subsidies, driving efficiency gains and technology switching, some of which would be legally mandated. The Saudi transport sector might shift toward electric vehicles, swapping petroleum fuels whose export underpins the economy for a network of charging stations.

On the supply side, the transformation would push oil products from being combusted in the kingdom's electricity generation sector, replacing liquid fuels with natural gas with carbon capture capability, along with solar and wind plants connected to electricity storage. In the medium term, as generation and transmission capacity are expanded to address transport and industrial needs, a Saudi nuclear power sector is likely to emerge.

Desalination plants, refineries, petrochemical plants and other emitters in the kingdom's industrial zones would see their emissions captured, compressed, and piped to underground storage, perhaps in depleting oilfields or in vast aquifers below the western half of the Arabian Peninsula. In the long term, carbon capture would facilitate replacing natural gas with low-emission fuels based on hydrogen, including ammonia and methanol.

The reward for the successful implementation of Saudi Arabia's Net Zero 2060 ambition could be significant. A kingdom struggling to retain geostrategic importance as the world's central banker of oil would leverage domestic decarbonization to establish credibility in the global climate arena, revitalizing the kingdom's influence and allowing Saudi policymakers to shape the energy transition in ways that could retain a greater long-term role for hydrocarbons. Saudi Aramco's 2021 sustainability report suggests such an ambition. "Developing low-carbon products and solutions helps to *sustain and diversify demand for oil and gas* through competitive technologies," the report states (Saudi Aramco, 2022, p. 5, emphasis added).

Net zero success might also be economically counterproductive. A vigorous decarbonization push by Saudi Arabia could inspire other petrostates to more seriously pursue reductions of their own. Any decline in oil combustion outside the kingdom would reduce oil prices and rent flows to the kingdom, all else constant. Therefore, a Saudi role that motivates global momentum toward climate action might be viewed negatively inside domestic policymaking circles.

For this reason and others, it remains possible that the Saudi leadership will not earnestly pursue its commitment to full decarbonization. The credibility of past Saudi environmental policy declarations has been lacking, which suggests a level of comfort with disregarding official targets. For instance, the Saudi government did not pursue a 2012 announcement to build 23.9 gigawatts (GW) of renewables by 2020, nor a 2018 memorandum of intent to build 150–200 GW of renewables by 2030; while a 2011 plan to build sixteen nuclear power reactors within twenty years was also shelved (World Nuclear Association, 2022). As of mid 2022, Saudi Arabia reported a renewables installation of just 700 megawatts (MW) (Carpenter, 2022).

Decarbonization commitments of other regional governments have had mixed effects on energy policy. The United Arab Emirates' (UAE) net zero goal appears to have driven Dubai's utility to convert the just-built Hassyan coal-fired power plant to run on natural gas (Rahman, 2022). But Turkey's decarbonization commitment does not seem to be constraining policy. Ankara's ongoing expansion of its coal-fired power generation was unaffected by President Erdogan's declaration of intent to reach net zero by 2053 (Pitel & Kıraç, 2022).

Therefore, any demonstrated lack of determination by Riyadh in pursuit of its decarbonization goals might also signal to other oil-exporting governments that climate commitments need not be adhered to in the near term. Only by observing interim progress can the sincerity of the Saudi net zero commitment be determined. An early milestone comes in 2030, the date by which the kingdom has pledged to reach its Paris Agreement goal of a reduction of 278 million tonnes of CO_2 per year (below a 2019 baseline of 580 million tonnes) (Government of Saudi Arabia, 2021). Some USD187 billion has been earmarked toward 2030 climate targets including GHG reduction (Financial Times, 2021; MEES, 2021).

The objective of this chapter is to describe a potential pathway toward the Saudi net zero goal while accounting for the kingdom's conflict of interest in embracing a project that would undermine its economic model. Section 5.2 describes these conflicts in detail. The chapter then turns to examine the Saudi emissions profile in Section 5.3 and in Section 5.4 lays out the policy and investment steps toward a net zero status that leverages the kingdom's advantages. Section 5.5 discusses governance attributes and shortcomings; Section 5.6 assesses the geopolitical fallout from an energy transition; and the discussion in Section 5.6 ties together the various outcomes of each section to suggest the advantages of a Saudi adoption of climate action strategy.

4.2 Inherent Contradictions

The specter of the world's premier petrostate making a serious bid at carbon neutrality is not without its contradictions. Saudi Arabia's net zero pursuit comes alongside plans to ramp up production and export of oil, the source of more than a third of the world's fuel-based emissions.[1] Saudi Aramco in 2020 announced capital investment aimed at boosting production capacity from 12 to 13 million

[1] IEA data show global fossil fuel emissions in 2018 were distributed as follows: coal 44.1%; oil 34.4%; natural gas 21.5%.

barrels per day by 2027 (Kennedy, 2021; Walt, 2022). Leadership messaging on the energy transition has been at odds with carbon neutrality. Regular statements underscore the view that fossil fuels must remain a key part of the future energy mix and oppose a global transition away from the technologies that combust these fuels.

Saudi Arabia's updated Paris Climate Pledge, or nationally determined contributions (NDCs), more than doubles its emissions reduction target to 278 million tonnes of CO_2 equivalent through massive installations of renewable power and hydrogen production connected to carbon capture and sequestration. But the document also exemplifies the policy dichotomy, declaring that cutting Saudi emissions by 2030 is contingent upon "a robust contribution from hydrocarbon export revenues to the national economy" (Government of Saudi Arabia, 2021, p. 3). And, as mentioned above, Aramco states that it seeks to leverage transition technologies to "sustain and diversify demand for oil and gas" (Saudi Aramco, 2022).

Clearly, the kingdom's planners are counting on oil and oil-based products remaining important exports for decades. This is borne out by forecasts depicting a long and slow energy transition, and by scenarios showing low-cost oil producers in the Middle East expanding their share of the global market.[2] Even scenarios modelling a rapid transition retain demand for oil as a petrochemical feedstock and fuel for heavy and specialized transport. Saudi Arabia's Paris NDC makes no suggestions for abating or mitigating combustion emissions from the kingdom's oil exports.

Further contradictions are evident in contrasting attitudes toward an energy transition *inside* versus *outside* the kingdom. There are numerous tangible benefits from a major shift to renewables inside the kingdom. Replacing carbon-based power and transportation with cheaper clean electricity allows for increased hydrocarbon exports and revenues since domestic oil and gas consumption is heavily subsidized and exports are priced on global benchmarks. Indeed, several utility-scale renewables installations were under construction, as will be discussed. Reducing subsidies and imposing other market-based economic reforms remains attractive regardless of decarbonization goals.

Outside the kingdom, however, a transition from combustible fuels to clean electricity – coupled with efficiency mandates and bans on internal combustion engine vehicles – threatens to undermine Saudi Aramco's oil income. If no replacement is found for oil's contribution to the Saudi government budget, usually between 80 and 90 percent of the total, the kingdom's patronage-based governance model will be undermined.

[2] The IEA forecasts that the Middle East will increase its share of the global oil market in 2030 in two of three scenarios, and by 2050 in one scenario (the "stated policies" scenario; see IEA, 2022, pp. 336–341).

In 2022, however, that was not the case. The Russian invasion of Ukraine and a stronger-than-expected pandemic recovery provided Saudi Aramco with record profits of more than USD161 billion, including nearly USD1 billion per day in the spring (Abu Omar, 2022; Saudi Aramco, 2023). Longer term, however, changes in vehicle propulsion promised by automakers and nearly three dozen national governments look likely to shave down oil demand (although one 2019 estimate suggests a worldwide ban on ICE engines in light vehicles would only cut oil demand by around 15 million b/d) (Fulton et al., 2019).

Within Saudi Aramco a similar internal–external conflict is apparent. As shown in Figure 4.1, Saudi Aramco is the largest single commercial entity producing carbon-based fuel in the world. Combustion of Aramco's oil and gas accounted for roughly 5 percent of global emissions in 2018 and about 4 percent of total historic atmospheric accumulations since Saudi oil production began in 1938 (Climate Accountability Institute, 2020).

It is clear that the success of global climate action hinges on halting or abating GHG emissions from the combustion of oil and gas marketed by Saudi Aramco. However, abatement plans of Saudi Aramco ignore the so-called Scope 3 emissions

Entity	$MtCO_2e$	% of global
1. Saudi Aramco, Saudi Arabia	1,931	4.84%
2. Gazprom, Russia	1,527	3.83%
3. National Iranian Oil Co.	1,266	3.17%
4. Coal India, India	1,214	3.05%
5. PetroChina / China Natl Petroleum	883	2.22%
6. Rosneft, Russian Federation	846	2.12%
7. Abu Dhabi, United Arab Emirates	692	1.74%
8. ExxonMobil, USA	580	1.45%
9. Iraq National Oil Co., Iraq	566	1.42%
10. Royal Dutch Shell, The Netherlands	550	1.38%
11. BP, UK	549	1.38%
12. Kuwait Petroleum, Kuwait	444	1.11%
13. Chevron, USA	443	1.11%
14. Total SA, France	404	1.01%
15. Peabody Energy, USA	398	1.00%
16. Sonatrach, Algeria	398	1.00%
17. Petrobras, Brazil	385	0.97%
18. Pemex, Mexico	380	0.95%
19. Glencore, Switzerland	355	0.89%
20. Lukoil, Russian Federation	341	0.86%
Top Twenty	14,152	35.49%
Global (2018)	39,878	100.00%

Figure 4.1 Top 20 global sources of fossil fuels and implied GHGs emitted during combustion in 2018.
Source: Carbon Majors Database 2020, available online: https://climateaccountability.org/carbonmajors_dataset2020.html.

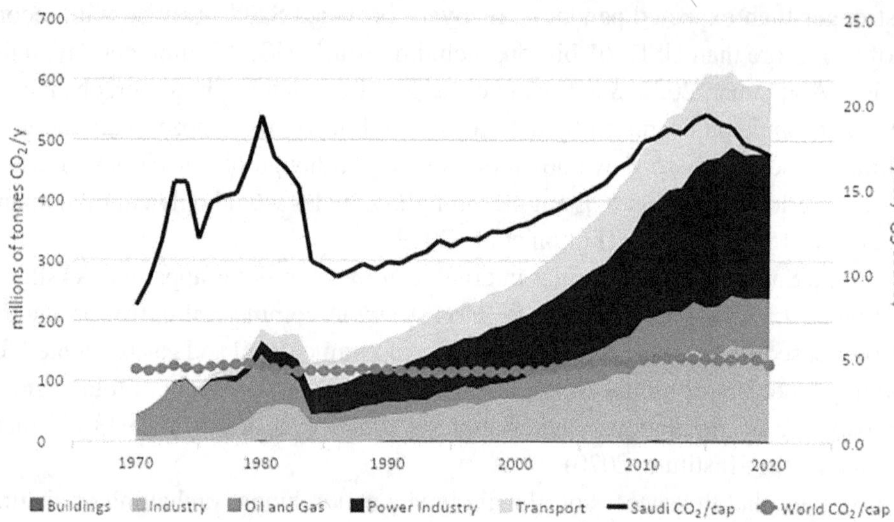

Figure 4.2 Saudi CO_2 emissions by sector since 1970.

from combustion of Aramco products. Scope 3 emissions refer to the indirect greenhouse gas emissions that are not directly produced by a company, but are associated with the company's activities. The national oil company's decarbonization plans focus on much smaller Scope 1 and 2 emissions from Aramco's "wholly owned and operated assets."[3]

Despite being a small portion of Aramco's emissions portfolio, Figure 4.2 shows emissions from oil and gas production account for roughly 14 percent of GHG emissions within Saudi Arabia. Aramco has agreed to eliminate or offset those emissions by 2050. Such a commitment is aimed not at constraining the NOC's business model but at enhancing the competitiveness of Aramco's oil exports. Carbon has emerged as a new arena for competition among global oil producers, particularly as global oil production plateaus and begins to decline. "When it comes to oil and gas, the future now clearly belongs to the lowest cost, least-carbon intensive producers," CEO Amin Nasser has stated, "We intend to be one of those producers" (Saudi Aramco, 2022).

Rent windfalls in 2022 provided capital for NOCs like Aramco to invest in reducing their emissions and providing clean energy for the domestic market. Serious commitments, however, did not appear forthcoming. NOCs with large resource bases had invested less in diversification and transition technologies than

[3] Aramco's sustainability report addresses Scope 3 emissions briefly, saying that: "To date, we have not reported Scope 3 emissions from our supply chain or from customers' use of our products" (Saudi Aramco, 2022, p. 39).

shareholder-owned counterparts. Research from Wood Mackenzie shows that, as of early 2022, Aramco had not announced any capital commitment to decarbonization or transitioning to clean energy (Wood Mackenzie, 2022). (In 2021, Aramco's USD315 million in "sustainability" research amounted to a third of its R&D budget but just 1 percent of its USD32 billion capital spending (Saudi Aramco, 2022)) The lack of decarbonization investment extended beyond Aramco to NOCs in Qatar, UAE, Iran, Algeria, Russia, and Mexico. None of the world's major state-owned oil firms had dedicated more than 5 percent of investment capital toward decarbonization or renewables. By contrast, shareholder-owned IOCs had allocated an average of 15 percent and European IOCs 20 percent (Wood Mackenzie, 2022). Some IOCs have introduced net zero plans that go well beyond Aramco's to include Scope 3 emissions.[4]

4.3 Current GHG Emissions Accounting

The task of decarbonizing Saudi Arabia should not be underestimated. At nearly 600 million tonnes, Saudi Arabia's domestic CO_2 emissions in 2020 ranked ninth in the world, just behind South Korea and ahead of Canada. At 17 tonnes per capita, Saudi emissions were nearly quadruple the world average. As shown in Figure 4.2, (EDGAR, 2022), power generation accounted for 40 percent of the kingdom's emissions, with another 40 percent from industry (including refining and petrochemicals) and the oil and gas sector. Transport added a further 19 percent, with the building sector contributing just 1 percent (EDGAR – Emissions Database for Global Atmospheric Research, 2022).

4.4 Steps to Net Zero in Saudi Arabia

For most countries, the disruption involved in replacing fossil fuels with renewables and low- or zero-carbon substitutes is expected to be costly, particularly in the initial decades, before allowing for a potential return to profitability in later decades (Martin and Zhou, 2022). Exposure to economic damage from the energy transition is even greater in hydrocarbon exporters and carbon-intensive economies like Saudi Arabia.

However, the carbon intensity of the Saudi economy also presents policymakers with several inexpensive opportunities to reduce emissions while improving economic competitiveness. Chief among these is a reduction in oil use. In 2021, the kingdom consumed an average of 3.6 million barrels per day of oil and gas liquids

[4] As of June 2022, oil companies with net zero plans including Scope 3 (combustion) emissions include Shell PLC, TotalEnergies SE, Equinor ASA, Occidental Petroleum Corp., Eni SpA, Suncor Energy Inc., Williams Cos. Inc., and Neste Oyj. For a full list of oil firms and their climate pledges, see Holland (2022).

(BP, 2022). Almost a third of that was burned to produce electricity, roughly 430,000 b/d of crude oil and 600,000 b/d of refined products, on average (Mees, 2022d). In most of the world, oil combustion in power generation was displaced decades ago by cleaner and cheaper substitutes. Expunging oil from the domestic power sector is attractive for reasons of competitive cost and efficiency, as well as the environment.

How might a plan to reach net zero in the kingdom start? The following sections propose one potential pathway that begins with subsidy reform and efficiency improvements, then shifts toward decarbonizing power and transport. Follow-on steps target emissions from industry and the oil and gas sector.

4.4.1 Eliminate Subsidies to Improve Efficiency

Under the net zero plan, subsidized energy prices inside the kingdom, serving to encourage fossil fuel consumption and emissions, will come under intense pressure for reform. The net zero goal aligns with the already strong aspiration for rationalized prices and energy efficiency.

Major increases in administered prices were imposed in 2016 and 2018, which succeeded in dampening demand for transport fuels and electricity. Figure 4.3, adopted from (BP, 2022) shows that Saudi demand for oil appears to have peaked

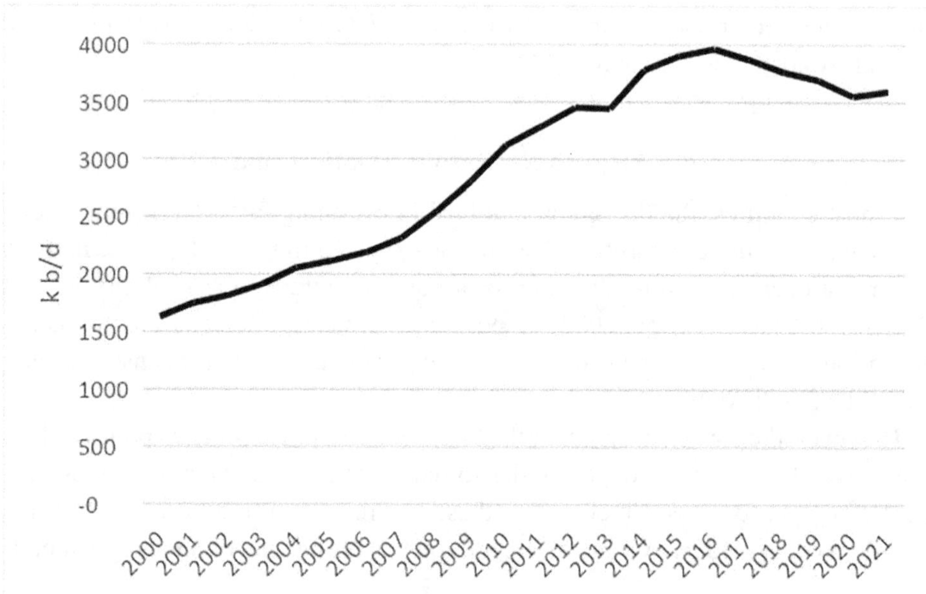

Figure 4.3 Domestic demand for oil and natural gas liquids has slipped since the subsidy reforms of 2016 and 2018.

in 2016 and dropped by almost 10 percent, or 367,000 b/d, through the end of 2021 (BP, 2022).

The Fiscal Balance Program of 2018, part of the Vision 2030 effort, was supposed to mandate "progressive increases of prices to market levels for electricity, fuel, and water for households and businesses" by 2020 (Kingdom of Saudi Arabia, 2018). By 2023, however, the promised reforms had still not taken place and most energy prices remained at levels set in 2018, far below global averages. Saudi gasoline was cheaper in March 2023 than all but seventeen other countries, averaging 62 US cents/litre (USD2.35/US gallon). Diesel in the kingdom, at 20 cents/litre (76 cents/gal) was cheaper than everywhere except Libya, Venezuela, and Iran. Residential electricity prices, averaging less than 5 US cents/KWh, were less than a third of the US average and just 10 percent of Britain's (GlobalPetrolPrices.com, 2023). Figure 4.4 depicts Saudi prices on a global scale.

Further increases would align Saudi energy prices closer to world prices, encouraging efficiency and technology switching. Higher prices would also reduce the financial penalty on Saudi Aramco for providing energy to the domestic market. Weakening domestic demand would allow surplus oil to be exported at market prices or used as feedstock for higher value-added products like petrochemicals and fertilizers. While subsidy reforms have long been a priority among Saudi technocrats (Krane, 2019), public opposition has slowed implementation (Nereim, 2021), even with cash compensation under the Citizens Account Program.

The Saudi net zero goal provides a rationale for further price increases, which could give policymakers political cover for reforms of distortionary subsidies valued at more than 5 percent of GDP. Figure 4.5 shows that Saudi energy subsidies are substantially larger as a portion of GDP than those of the neighboring monarchies. The IMF and World Bank have urged continued subsidy retractions, with the World Bank stating in 2022 that the energy efficiency improvements flowing from subsidy reforms are "the single most important element of moving to net zero emissions" (World Bank, 2022, p. 25).

Aligning Saudi electricity prices with those of other emerging economies in the G20 – Argentina, Brazil, China, India, Indonesia, Mexico, Russia, South Africa, and Turkey – would reduce 2030 demand by 11 percent, according to research from the King Abdullah Petroleum Studies and Research Center. Aligning prices with the full G20 average would bring demand down by nearly 20 percent. Imposing energy efficiency measures in buildings and energy-consuming technology would compound the savings, potentially reducing 2030 power demand by nearly a third (Soummane & Ghersi, 2022). Such reforms would ease the route to carbon neutrality in three other ways; first, by reducing spending on zero-carbon power production; second, by reducing the need for carbon removal and sequestration; and third,

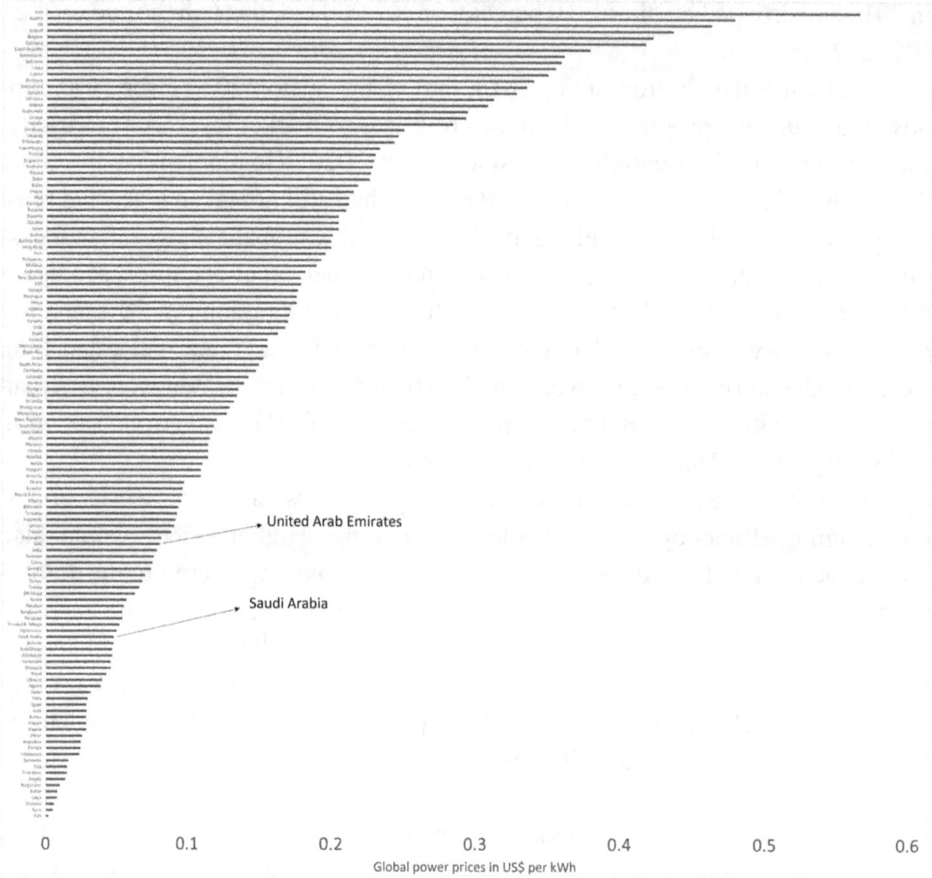

Figure 4.4 Power prices in US cents per kWh.

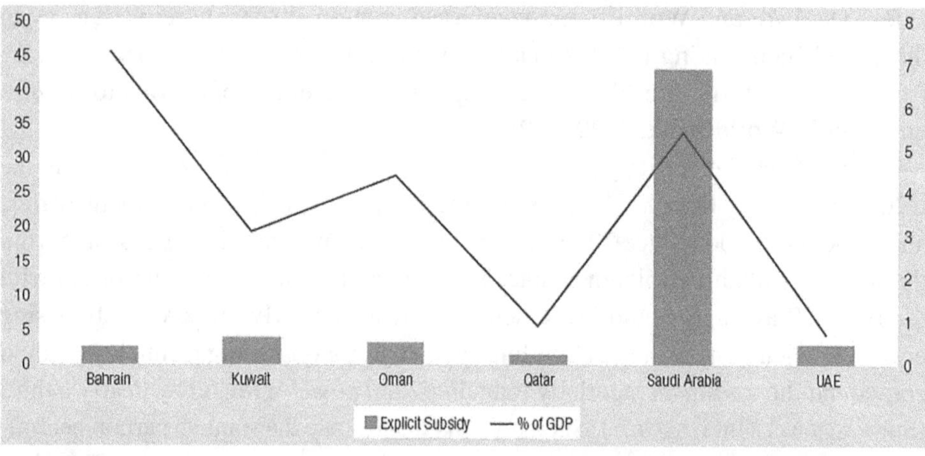

Figure 4.5 Subsidized energy products and services (in USD billions, left axis) accounted for more than 5% of 2020 Saudi GDP (in % of GDP, right axis).

by reducing the need for additional backup generation, since declining demand allows existing dispatchable generation to serve as backup, rather than requiring further investment for additional backup capacity to keep pace with increases in peak demand.

4.4.2 Power Sector Decarbonization

A sincere net zero plan would make an early effort to decarbonize the power sector, since zero-carbon generation options are widely available and produce power more cheaply than unsubsidized thermal generation. In Saudi Arabia, like the rest of the hot and humid Gulf region, the power sector is largely synonymous with what is described as the "buildings" sector elsewhere. Some 70 percent of power production in the kingdom and surrounding monarchies is used to cool buildings (World Bank, 2022). Electricity is by far the dominant household energy source except for cooking which is usually based on liquid petroleum gas (LPG).[5] Decarbonizing the power sector would ideally be done concurrently with a concerted shift in energy consumption away from direct fossil fuel combustion and toward electricity. As shown in Figure 4.2, 40 percent of the kingdom's emissions flow from power generation. Figure 4.6 shows the generation split between natural gas (61%) and oil-based fuels including crude oil and heavy fuel oil comprising nearly all the rest (BP, 2022).

Much of this decarbonization can be achieved from a massive expansion of renewables alongside oil-to-gas switching. Eventually, nuclear power could play

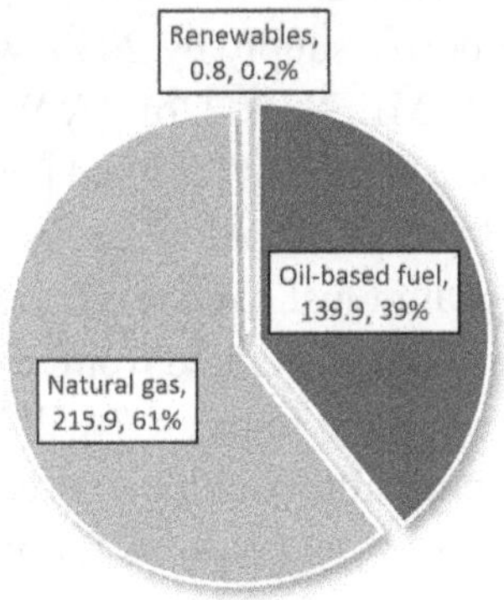

Figure 4.6 Saudi Arabia generated 357 terawatt-hours of power in 2021, less than 1 of which (about 0.2%) was generated using renewables.

[5] The 2017 Household Energy Survey showed that LPG was the primary cooking fuel for at least 90% of households in all Saudi regions except the Eastern Province, where electric stoves were used in about a quarter of households (Saudi Arabian Statistics Agency, 2017).

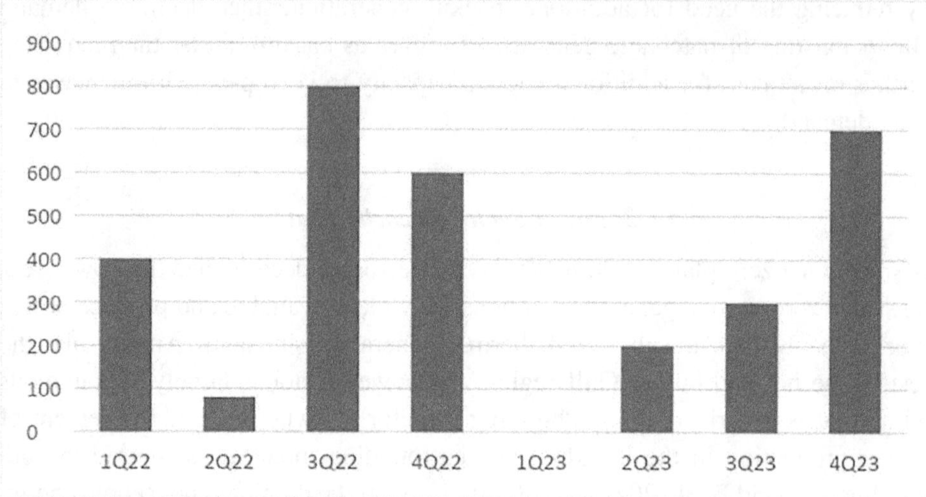

Figure 4.7 Saudi renewables capacity awards planned for 2022 and 2023, a total of 3.1 GW.

a role. The kingdom's comparative advantage in solar generation is well known. But Saudi Arabia is also home to uranium deposits that the government plans to leverage in a future nuclear power program (Reuters, 2023).

Solar power development is underway. Figure 4.7 documents announced contracts for nearly 5GW of renewables capacity had been awarded as of Spring 2022 and another 15 GW were to be granted by the end of 2023. These projects represent the initial stages of a pledged 58.7 GW renewables installation announced by Saudi energy minister Prince Abdulaziz bin Salman; part of a goal for renewables to generate half the national power supply by 2030, with natural gas covering the other half (Alshammari, 2021; MEES, 2022b). (A World Bank study projects an installation of 40 GW of solar PV, 16 GW of wind power, and 2.7 GW of concentrating solar power (World Bank, 2022).)

Reaching the 50 percent goal in just over seven years is unlikely. In 2021, just 0.2 percent of Saudi electricity was generated from renewable sources (BP, 2022). Investments far beyond those cited in Figure 4.7 will be required. While the kingdom's plans to deal with its emissions-rich power sector will help achieve its net zero target, there are rational economic reasons for replacing costly and dirty oil-fired generation with cheaper solar, wind and natural gas.

Saudi Arabia, like its GCC neighbors, enjoys the world's lowest-cost solar generation, due to copious solar radiation and large amounts of vacant land close to load centers. Recent power purchase contracts between developers and government-owned utilities have undercut the 2 US cents per KWh threshold. Daily peak demand corresponds relatively well with solar power production, particularly in inland areas. Coastal areas are more problematic for solar due to humid evenings encouraging consumption after dark. Wind generation appears less competitive, with the exception of consistent wind resources in western Saudi Arabia near 8 metres per second. Overall wind potential is low, with speeds averaging just over 5 m/s, well below the global average for windy regions of 11m/s (Global Wind Energy Atlas, n.d.).

Beyond just building out renewables to replace oil-fired generation, the kingdom will also need to neutralize the emissions of its remaining gas-fired power plants. This involves replacing gas with renewables (which allows gas to be used in higher value applications in petrochemicals, fertilizer, and hydrogen), or capturing the emissions of combustion gas. The energy minister also hinted at solutions for this as well. "We believe that carbon capture, utilization and storage, direct air capture, hydrogen and low-carbon fuels are the things that will develop the necessary ingredients," Prince Abdulaziz said in 2021 (Rathi, 2021).

The kingdom will also need to generate more electricity overall. That is because power demand, already growing at an average rate of nearly 5 percent per year over the last decade (BP, 2021) will expand further if price and efficiency measures (outlined above) are not imposed. Decarbonization by electrification increases the challenge by connecting new sources of demand to the power sector, particularly vehicles. Coping with intermittency will require backup generation and demand-side management tools such as load-shedding discounts. Backup generation candidates are natural gas with CCS, electricity storage systems like batteries, and – eventually – clean fuels like biogas or hydrogen. Nuclear power can also be paired with battery storage and used both as a replacement for thermal generation and a source of backup for renewables (Hartley, 2018).

4.4.3 Transport

The second most obvious candidate for decarbonization is the transport sector, responsible for 19 percent of the kingdom's CO_2 in 2020. Decarbonization of both power and transport sectors would eliminate roughly 60 percent of Saudi emissions. Light-duty vehicles, shown in Figure 4.8 as making up just over half of the kingdom's transport energy demand, represents the initial market for electrification. The kingdom and some of its neighbors had already embarked on electric vehicle strategies, including attracting manufacturers. Saudi Arabia's venture with Lucid Motors was expected to assemble 155,000 cars a year and sell 100,000 EVs to the Saudi government, while Saudi firm Electromin announced it had been contracted to install vehicle charging points (Sharma, 2022). The government's Saudi Green Initiative set a goal of 30 percent vehicle electrification in Riyadh by 2030 (Nereim, 2021). In the neighboring UAE, manufacturer M Glory began building

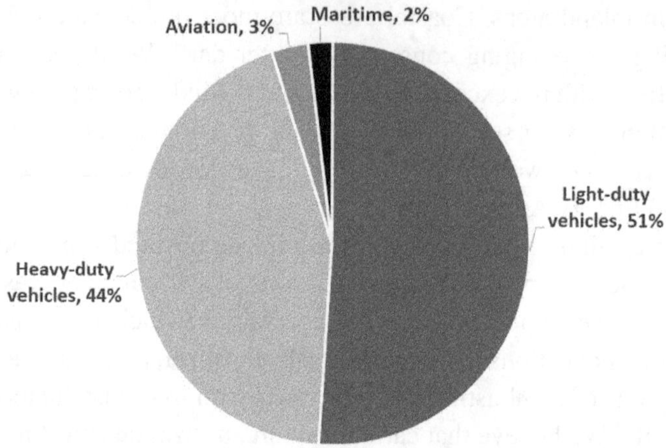

Figure 4.8 Energy demand in the Saudi transport sector.
Notes: Light-duty vehicles include sedan cars, sport utility vehicles (SUVs), minivans, and any other road vehicles that weigh less than 3,500 kilograms (kg); heavy-duty vehicles (also called commercial vehicles, i.e. trucks, buses, and other road vehicles that weigh more than 3,500 kg).

an assembly plant for 55,000 EVs per year in Dubai while China's NWTN agreed to build a similar-sized plant in Abu Dhabi (Cabral, 2022; The National, 2022).

Despite initial progress, decarbonizing the transport sector is more difficult than eliminating emissions from the electric power sector. While some transport modes work well with electrification – personal vehicles, public transport buses and trains, delivery fleet vehicles, and bicycles – others do not. Efficiency measures[6] can reduce emissions from long-distance freight transport, aircraft and shipping, but total elimination may require offsets. Research suggests some heavy transport modes may be more efficiently converted to hybrid (bio)diesel or hybrid gasoline systems, or perhaps hydrogen fuel cells or even compressed (bio)gas. Shifting between transport modes – for example, moving heavy diesel truck traffic to electrified rail – is another crucial component (Arioli et al., 2020). Air carriers are already experimenting with biofuels, while hydrogen (ammonia) and methanol (mainly from biomass) are among future potential sources in shipping.[7]

It bears noting that Saudi Arabia's net zero goal does not require it to concern itself with international aviation and shipping, which are tallied on external accounts. As Figure 4.8 shows domestic shipping and aviation represent small contributions to Saudi transport emissions.

[6] The 2021 Saudi NDC suggests phasing out inefficient used light-duty vehicles and implementing aerodynamic regulation for heavy-duty vehicles.

[7] Most methanol is made from natural gas via steam reformation. Low-carbon methanol can also be made from biomass such as crop and forestry residue. Maersk has twelve methanol-fueled container ships on order and intends to source more than 700,000 tonnes of biomass methanol by 2025 (see Maersk press release, 2022).

Subsidy reforms in 2016 and 2018 have reduced the average 7 percent yearly growth rate of Saudi fuel demand and improved fleet efficiency. Oil demand in the kingdom declined by an average of 1 percent per year between 2016 and 2021, BP data show.

4.4.4 Industry

Industrial emissions in Saudi Arabia – including the oil and gas sector itself – comprise the final 40 percent of the kingdom's emissions. Decarbonizing industry is well known as a challenging proposition. However, Saudi Arabia has already taken the initial step of launching the development of two of the most promising industrial decarbonization technologies, CCS and hydrogen.[8]

Saudi industrial emissions are dominated by four main industries: oil and gas, petrochemicals, cement, and metals. Petrochemicals is viewed as one of the more difficult industries to decarbonize. The petrochemical industry in Saudi Arabia is largely based around ethylene, a plastics precursor. Ethylene is produced using high-temperature steam to crack hydrocarbons derived from oil (naphtha) or gas (ethane). In one sense, petrochemical production represents a climate-compliant use for hydrocarbons. The oil and gas feedstocks are converted – usually to polymer and resin precursors to plastics – rather than combusted, and their carbon content is retained within the final product. Of course, any carbon sequestered can be released if plastics are incinerated. The process of cracking naphtha or ethane is the main emission source since it requires burning fossil fuels, mainly natural gas, to produce process heat. Creating a single kilogram of ethylene emits about 2 kg of carbon dioxide along with other pollutants. Globally, ethylene production was the No. 4 source of industrial emissions in 2020, emitting 230 million metric tonnes, nearly as much as Spain (Kapur, 2021).

Options for decarbonizing petrochemical plants include using clean electricity or hydrogen as heat sources, or capturing and sequestering emissions using CCS. Aramco is also experimenting with direct crude-to-chemicals conversion which would eliminate some energy-intensive processes. The geographic clustering of Saudi Arabia's industrial sector, along with advantageous geology, simplifies decarbonization. Most Saudi industry is concentrated in three regions, as depicted in Figure 4.9. Such clustering is ideal for capturing, gathering and storing emissions underground. Industrial clusters can become hubs for stripping carbon from flue gases, by reducing infrastructure requirements and costs for CCS, and for future refueling of plants with clean fuels like hydrogen.

[8] MEES (2022a, 2002c).

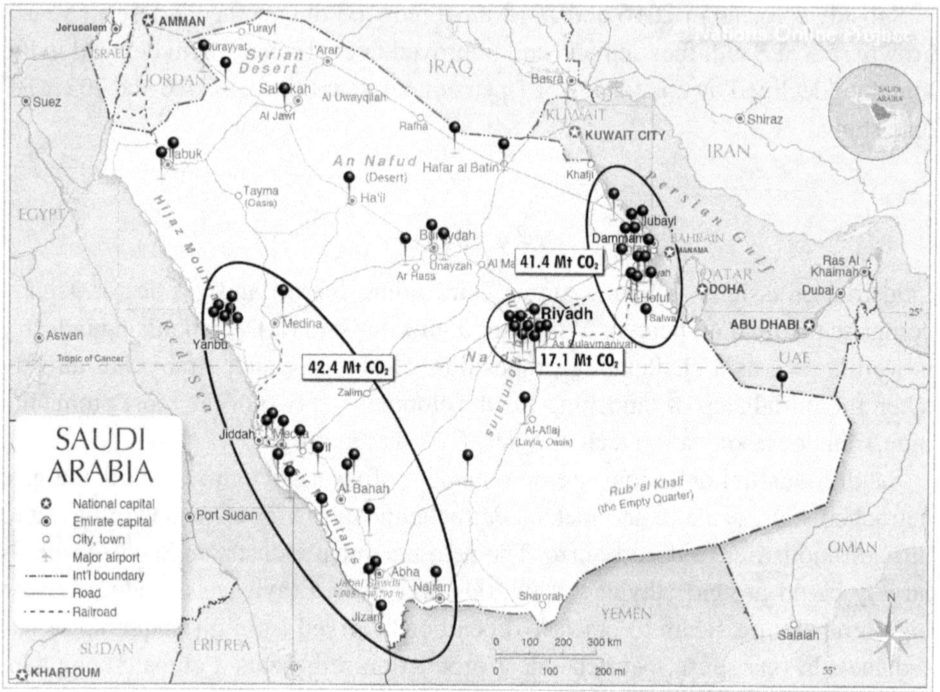

Figure 4.9 Large stationary emissions sources by type and cumulative emissions in Saudi Arabia. Sites include power generation, refining, cement, chemicals, desalination, and iron and steel.
Source: Brigid Krane using the map from Nations Online Project and plant data from Liu et al. (2012).

4.4.5 Carbon Capture and Storage

Saudi Arabia, like other fossil fuel-linked countries and firms, has been a proponent of carbon capture and storage. This is due to the technology's attributes as both a source of fossil fuel demand and a method for abating its emissions. Both attributes serve to preserve fossil fuels in a climate-compatible energy mix. Capturing and sequestering carbon is also a key component of Aramco's blue hydrogen and blue ammonia ventures.

The kingdom also has numerous physical characteristics rendering it an ideal location for CCS. Two capture projects already exist in the kingdom. Saudi chemical firm SABIC has captured CO_2 since 2015 at an ethylene glycol plant. The 500,000 metric tonnes of carbon captured per year is not stored underground but used as a feedstock for fertilizer, methanol, and liquefied CO_2 used in the food and drink industry (SABIC, 2022). A second facility operates at Uthmaniyah, which captures and sequesters up to 800,000 metric tonnes/year of CO_2 from a natural gas processing facility (Wright, 2021).

Saudi Arabia's 2021 UN climate pledge details plans to transform the emissions-rich industrial cities of Jubail and Yanbu into centers of carbon capture. Aramco plans to capture 11 million tonnes per year by 2035 en route to achieving the promised elimination or offsetting its direct and supply chain emissions (Scope 1 and 2). Aramco's 2021 sustainability report estimated Scope 1 emissions at 52.3 million tonnes of CO_2 equivalent, and Scope 2 emissions at 15.5 million tonnes, for a combined 68 million tonnes. This is depicted in Figure 4.10. Without CCS, Aramco's emissions would rise, given plans to increase oil production capacity to 13 million b/d, alongside expansions in refining and gas production.

Note that these totals include only emissions from wholly owned and operated facilities and do not include joint ventures. Adding in joint chemical and refining ventures would add as much as 28 million tonnes of additional yearly emissions, according to Bloomberg. Adding in Scope 3 emissions from combustion would increase the total by some 1.6 billion tonnes (Rathi & Martin, 2021).

Were the kingdom to pursue the capture of 11m tonnes of CO_2 per year at recent US cost estimates, initial capture costs in Table 4.1 reveal a range from USD200 million to USD2.2 billion per year, depending on the purity of the waste stream. High-purity CO_2 streams that do not require separation from other waste gases are the cheapest to capture. Transport and sequestration would add additional costs.

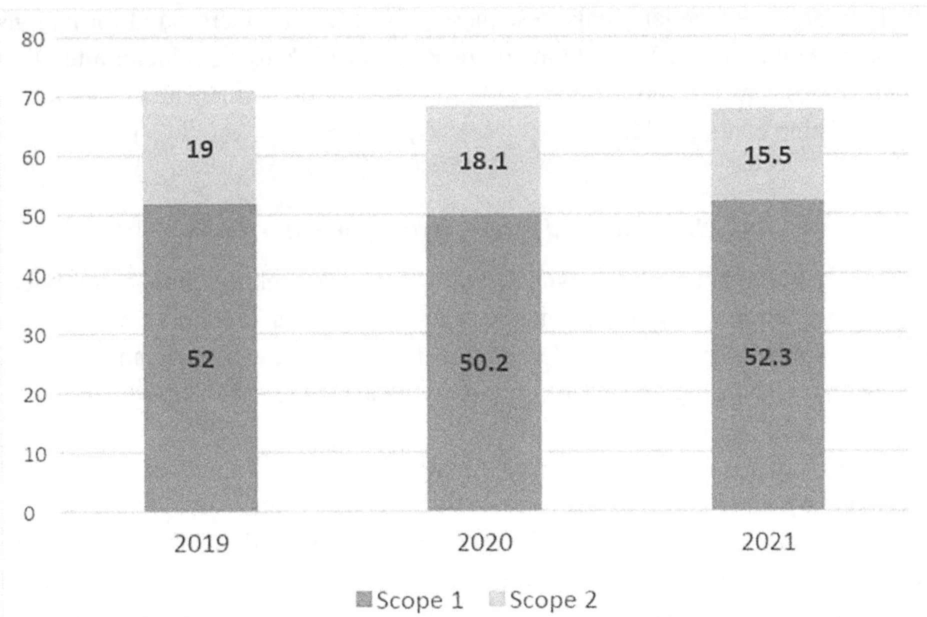

Figure 4.10 Saudi Aramco's 2020 Scope 1 and 2 emissions accounting from its 2021 sustainability report.

Table 4.1 *CCS costs in the US context for industrial carbon streams of various CO_2 concentrations. Estimates do not include the cost of transport or sequestration, cost reductions from learning by doing, efficiency improvements, or technological advances.*

	Ammonia production		Hydrogen production		Natural gas power plant		Cement production	
	Low	High	Low	High	Low	High	Low	High
Cost per tonne (USD/y)	22	32	65	136	49	150	19	205
Cost for 11m tonnes (mn USD/y)	242	352	715	1,496	539	1,650	209	2,255

One study estimated these costs at USD17–USD23/tonne in the US context (Moch et al., 2022).

Saudi geology and industrial expertise are ideally suited for capturing and storing waste products from oil and gas. The kingdom already holds the necessary expertise in pipeline and project engineering and is well supplied with geological pore space for storing captured carbon. Depleting oil fields are found throughout the Eastern Province, with others just southeast of Riyadh. The eastern half of the Arabian Peninsula contains multiple stacked aquifers with suitable structures for long-term CO_2 storage, while aquifers along the peninsula's western edge are also likely to provide excellent seals to sequester CO_2. Other underground formations in Saudi Arabia, the UAE and Oman are ideal for CCS using mineral alteration technologies that convert gaseous CO_2 into solids for permanent sequestration (Vahrenkamp et al., 2021).

4.4.6 Decarbonized Fuels (Hydrogen and Ammonia)

Hydrogen is another favored route for oil companies seeking climate-compliant approaches to preserving the profitable "fuel supply chain" model of energy provision. Exports of hydrogen or derivatives like ammonia and methanol are more compatible with the hydrocarbon commodity trade than renewables, which require no fuel.

Saudi Arabia is among the cheapest places in the world to develop hydrogen due to large natural gas reserves, copious solar radiation, ample geological storage, and unused surface land near population centers (Collins, 2022). Two types are of interest: "blue" hydrogen, which splits natural gas into hydrogen and a sequestered carbon stream; and "green" hydrogen, which uses renewable power to electrolyze water into hydrogen and oxygen. Hydrogen can be burned directly as a fuel in industrial boilers and power plants (and even vehicles) or used in fuel cells to power electric vehicles. Hydrogen gas can also be rendered more transportable if converted to liquid ammonia with the addition of nitrogen, and "cracked" back into hydrogen at the destination. A third type, turquoise, may also be relevant. Turquoise hydrogen is produced through pyrolysis using oil or natural gas as a feedstock. Rather than creating CO_2 emissions, the process creates solid carbon that could be converted into fibres for use in industrial and other applications to replace steel or aluminium (Rice University Carbon Hub, n.d.).

Zero-carbon hydrogen could be the industrial fuel for a decarbonized Saudi Arabia, as well as an export commodity for industrial or transportation use. Aramco has already announced its intent to produce large volumes of blue hydrogen and blue ammonia (up to 11 million tonnes/year by 2030) from domestic natural gas.

Meanwhile, a plan for green hydrogen in northwest Saudi Arabia suggests that costs, particularly on electrolysis, could be a short-run hurdle. The Helios Green Fuels project would invest USD5 billion to produce just 237,000 tonnes of hydrogen per year, which works out at USD2–USD3 per kilogram over ten years.[9] Perhaps as a result, Aramco's sustainability report notes a preference for blue hydrogen. "Despite the interest and possibility of producing hydrogen from multiple energy sources, in the short- and medium-term, hydrocarbons will remain the primary feedstock for the production of hydrogen," it states (Saudi Aramco, 2022, pp. 40–41).

4.5 Saudi Governance Advantages and Credibility

Saudi Arabia is starting the energy transition from a strong position. As outlined above, the kingdom has advantages in the low cost and carbon intensity of oil production, both of which augur for the sector's long-run survival, even in a declining market. The kingdom has advantages in decarbonization: a relevant knowledge base, ideal geology, and renewables-rich geography. It draws motivation for change from its front-line exposure to climate damage. Wealth is another advantage. Cyclical windfalls provide investment capital. Investments in future-oriented sectors represent an ideal way to share oil rents with the coming generations.

What about the advantages inferred by the kingdom's monarchical rule? Since governance is autocratic, there is no legislature or veto-wielders who can block the ruler's directives. The autocratic rule also reduces the government's need to tailor policy to short-term election cycles, which allows policymaking on a long-term horizon ideal for responding to climate change. Further, the Saudi system enjoys

[9] One person familiar with the Helios project suggested an equivalent amount of energy could be garnered by drilling two oil wells for roughly USD10 million, about 1/500th of the cost.

great continuity. Ruling sheikhs hold onto power until they die or are incapacitated, upon which power transitions to a son or brother. Streamlined successions help to ensure present-day initiatives will be shepherded by tomorrow's ruler, providing certainty for investors. Saudi Arabia's de facto ruler, Crown Prince Mohammed bin Salman, sees himself governing for the next half-century. The crown prince is preparing the groundwork for long-term rule, which includes setting the kingdom on a new energy path.

However, autocratic rule has disadvantages. It tends to be more capricious than democratic rule. Policymaking indeed tends to move more slowly in democratic systems than autocratic ones, since democratic policymakers contend with multiple veto points and representative institutions. The political economy literature on "credible commitment" in governance suggests that once decisions are made under a democratic system, such policy – enshrined in laws or legal rights – tends to be more durable and credible than the decrees or pronouncements made by an unelected sovereign. The lack of institutional oversight means autocrats can discard past priorities or even make strategic U-turns.[10]

Therefore, the commitments binding Gulf rulers to their own national policy goals are weak. It is difficult to oblige rulers to adhere to decisions if rewards from deviation outweigh those from compliance (Forder, 2001). As a result, credibility is an important consideration when evaluating present-day pronouncements about a thirty-nine-year process of emissions elimination.

4.6 Effects on Saudi Geopolitical Stature and Economy

Saudi Arabia's economy and governance exhibit a further weakness that shapes its climate policy. They depend on the survival of two key transport technologies: the internal combustion engine and the jet turbine. Those two technologies uphold oil's near-total monopoly on the transportation fuel market. The more the fuel monopoly comes under challenge by alternate fuels and technologies – whether EV batteries, fuel cells or biofuels – the less secure the Saudi governance model becomes.

High oil prices at the time of writing in spring 2023 were encouraging a gradual consumer shift away from oil, while major vehicle manufacturers were announcing the phase-out of gasoline and diesel engines. Governments, including those of China and the United States, already incentivize EV adoption, with China also supporting the phase-in of electric trucks (McKerracher, 2022). Continuation or strengthening of these trends will hasten the shift away from oil. Uncertainty around the future of oil is reflected in scenarios produced by the International Energy Agency (IEA).

[10] The "credible commitment" literature is substantial but an important work establishing this principle is North and Weingast (1989). A useful discussion of "credible commitment" in climate policy can be found in Brunner et al. (2012).

The IEA in 2021 projected world oil demand in 2040 ranging anywhere from 44 million barrels per day to 104 million b/d. Transition-driven losses are forecast to weigh heaviest on hydrocarbon exporters and carbon-intensive economies. As mentioned, however, the low-cost asset base in Saudi Arabia suggests an increasing share of a dwindling oil market (Wood Mackenzie, 2022). Even so, government finances would be strained if declining oil prices outweighed countervailing gains in market share.

The loss of oil's monopoly hold on transport portends an eventual decline in the geopolitical stature of oil producers, including Saudi Arabia, and the drifting apart of the United States and its partner regimes in the Gulf. Even if oil demand continues to grow in the developing world, those countries are unlikely to match the level of strategic backing on offer from Washington. For producer countries, new tactics and strategies will be needed to recapture the strategic interest of global powers and to cope with the transition away from fossil fuels (Krane, 2022, 2020).

4.7 Discussion: Saudi Opportunities from Net Zero

To summarize, this chapter has argued that Saudi Arabia's net zero 2060 pledge should not be considered an embrace of climate action, but a mission to seize upon natural resource advantages to shape future energy preferences in a way that extends the age of oil and preserves Saudi geopolitical stature. The chapter also argues that Saudi climate goals provide political cover for otherwise necessary but difficult energy sector reforms. Even so, any vow of climate action by Saudi Arabia should be treated with caution given a mixed track record in achieving prior environmental and clean energy goals. Other oil producers find themselves in similar positions. The UAE, Kuwait and Qatar share the greatest number of attributes with Saudi Arabia, while Iran, Iraq, Oman and oil producers in Central Asia and North Africa share similar advantages in renewable resources, geology, empty land, and low-cost oil and natural gas.

Given these findings, how should Saudi Arabia approach climate action? The Saudi strategy at climate talks has long been based on obstructing progress and removing draft treaty language deemed threatening to fossil fuel demand (Krane, 2021). As recently as the 2021 COP26 in Glasgow, delegates from Saudi Arabia, Australia and Japan urged a UN committee to temper language urging a swift transition to cleaner energy (Rowlett & Gerken, 2021). A few months earlier, the Saudi oil minister told a group of bankers that the kingdom would produce "every molecule" of its oil and gas reserves (Said & Faucon, 2021).

The Saudi government's declaratory embrace of domestic decarbonization does not necessarily signal a change in climate strategy. Policymakers in the kingdom appear comfortable advocating diverging climate policies for Saudi Arabia and the rest of the world. As discussed, decarbonizing the kingdom serves policy goals beyond those of the global climate action agenda. By contrast, *global* decarbonization – particularly a transition to renewables-led mass electrification – is viewed as economically harmful to the Saudi economy and its rent-distributive governance. Saudi policymakers espousing net zero for the kingdom have a national interest rationale for opposing hydrocarbon substitution elsewhere.

The Saudi net zero initiative sidesteps discussion of Saudi oil exports. That is ostensibly because exported oil would be consumed outside Saudi borders and appear on another country's carbon account. (Saudi Aramco might eventually tally those emissions in its Scope 3 accounting, however (Saudi Aramco, 2022, p. 39)) The Saudi regime may also require oil rents to fund government priorities in economic diversification and decarbonization.

Within the kingdom, the crown prince's declaration of intent to decarbonize signals that the public will be asked to relinquish long-held subsidies once considered fundamental rights. Such concessions from the public are considered difficult in the rentier autocratic setting, but opposition is more easily managed when heads of state can point to "outside pressure" to deflect blame (Krane, 2019). Implementing net zero allows Saudi policymakers to reduce domestic consumption of fossil fuels, particularly oil, which will be retained for higher-value use. The net zero goal also justifies continued improvements in the efficiency of buildings, appliances and vehicles.

Progress in these ventures allows Saudi Arabia to buttress its external influence. "Green economy" soft power could manifest itself in shaping the direction of the global energy transition. For instance, Saudi Arabia might steer climate action toward a more accepting role for CCS and modifying oil and gas infrastructure for fuels like hydrogen and green/blue ammonia. In that way, countries that import Saudi energy commodities might remain tethered to fuel-based energy systems with supply chains leading back to the Middle East, rather than shifting to renewable systems which need no fuel and connect to supply chains only during manufacturing (Krane & Idel, 2021).

Developing large-scale CCS might also lead to the creation of a "carbon management" services sector. Saudi firms could market subsurface pore space alongside negative emissions techniques like direct air capture or mineral alteration. Carbon disposal services could be sold to foreign firms and governments seeking to offset emissions.

Still, the CCS-hydrogen route to decarbonization remains uneconomic. The late entry of oil-producing countries and firms into the energy transition means that their preferences have been eclipsed by inexpensive renewables. Even so, the CCS-hydrogen path is more viable for industrial decarbonization and appeals to oil and gas producers, including those in the United States, who want to retain profitable fuel supply businesses (Greater Houston Partnership, 2021).

For Riyadh to gain credibility, it must demonstrate that it is more than a climate spoiler. Progress on the kingdom's net zero commitment serves as a demonstration of good faith. It also serves as a source of future trade advantage. At the moment, emissions-intensive economies are disproportionately exposed to emerging carbon border tariffs like those being formulated by the European Union. One recent estimate shows Saudi Arabia facing a major loss of income and exports from proposed EU tariffs (UNCTAD, 2021).

The lower the carbon footprint of the Saudi economy and its exports – whether manufactured goods or crude oil – the more competitive they will be when assessed in importing countries. A declining carbon footprint also enhances attractiveness for foreign investors seeking low-emission supply chains – minimizing their co-called Scope 2 and 3 emissions.

Finally, decarbonizing Saudi Arabia helps reduce risks in a region acutely exposed to climate damage. A 2°C warming scenario could bring average surface temperature increases of 4°C or 5°C in the Arabian Peninsula, essentially making parts of the region uninhabitable in summer (MacDonald, 2022; World Bank, 2022). For the viability of human settlement in the Gulf, mitigating climate change is imperative.

4.8 Conclusion

Saudi Arabia has a clearer path toward net zero than many countries. It has an enormous resource base in terms of renewable energy and feedstocks for clean fuels, as well as accessible geological pore space for carbon storage. It has concentrated emissions sources that are geographically clustered. It has an impressive reservoir of human engineering talent and demonstrated expertise in leveraging geology and deploying energy conversion and transportation infrastructure. High oil prices at the time of writing have replenished its currency reserves and provided investment capital. Riyadh has determined autocratic leadership without veto wielders in its governance system. Combined, these factors provide a strong competitive advantage in decarbonization.

There are also external factors. The kingdom faces a long but near-certain path to geopolitical obscurity and economic decline by continued reliance on petroleum and refined product exports. Retaining its stature on the international stage requires a major role in energy systems of the future, and demonstrating alternate pathways to decarbonize. It will be exceedingly difficult for Saudi Arabia to reach net zero by 2060. But the kingdom has the motivation, the money, and the tools to achieve it.

References

Abu Omar, A. (2022). Saudi Arabia's making $1 billion from oil exports every day. *Bloomberg News*.

Alshammari, H. (2021). Saudi Arabia aims to generate 50% of power from renewables by 2030. Arab News.

Arioli, M., Fulton, L., and Lah, O. (2020). Transportation strategies for a 1.5°C world: a comparison of four countries. *Transp. Res. Part Transp. Environ.* 87, 102526. Doi: 10.1016/j.trd.2020.102526.

BP (2021). *BP Statistical Review of World Energy 2021*. Statistical Report. London: BP.

BP (2022). *BP Statistical Review of World Energy 2022*. Statistical Report. London: BP.

Brunner, S., Flachsland, C., and Marschinski, R. (2012). Credible commitment in carbon policy. *Clim. Policy* 12, pp. 255–271. Doi: 10.1080/14693062.2011.582327.

Cabral, A. (2022). UAE company opens new electric vehicle manufacturing plant in Dubai industrial city. The National News.

Carpenter, C. (2022). Saudi Arabia set to double renewables tenders as Middle East growth may pick up. S&P Global. Commodities. Insights.

Climate Accountability Institute (2020). *Carbon Majors 2018 Data Set. Database*. Snowmass, CO: Climate Accountability Institute.

Collins, L. (2022). Green hydrogen now cheaper than blue in Middle East, but still way more expensive in Europe. *Recharge Magazine*. Available online: www.rechargenews .com/energy-transition/green-hydrogen-now-cheaper-than-blue-in-middle-east-but-still-way-more-expensive-in-europe/2-1-1173423.

EDGAR – Emissions Database for Global Atmospheric Research (2022). CO_2 Emissions of All World Countries. European Commission, Brussels. Government-sponsored research.

Financial Times (2021). Saudi Arabia 2060 net zero target keeps crude in the picture. 23 October.

Forder, J. (2001). The theory of credibility and the reputation-bias of policy. *Rev. Polit. Econ.* 13, pp. 5–25.

Fulton, L. M., Jaffe, A., and McDonald, Z. (2019). Internal combustion engine bans and global oil use. Academic paper. University of California-Davis, Davis, California.

Global Wind Energy Atlas (n.d.). *Global Wind Energy Atlas: Saudi Arabia*. Online database. Available online: https://globalwindatlas.info/en/area/Saudi%20Arabia.

GlobalPetrolPrices.com (2023). Global Gasoline, Diesel, and Electricity Prices. Internet database. GlobalPetrolPrices.com.

Government of Saudi Arabia (2021). Kingdom of Saudi Arabia – Updated First Nationally Determined Contribution. United Nations Framework Convention on Climate Change, Glasgow. UN climate pledge.

Greater Houston Partnership (2021). Greater Houston Partnership launches regional energy transition strategy. Greater Houston Partnership press release, June 29.

Hartley, P. R. (2018). The cost of displacing fossil fuels: some evidence from Texas. *Energy* 39 (2), pp. 233–258.

Holland, B. (2022). Path to net-zero: European, US oil and gas companies split on Scope 3 emissions. S&P Global Market Intelligence.

International Energy Agency (IEA) (2022). *World Energy Outlook 2022*. IEA, Paris. NGO report.

Kapur, S. (2021). *The Energy Transition and Decarbonization in the Ethylene Industry*. Petrochemical industry consultancy report. Houston, TX: Apex PetroConsultants.

Kennedy, R. (2021). 'Dangerous and delusional': critics denounce Saudi climate plan. Al Jazeera.

Kingdom of Saudi Arabia (2018). *Fiscal Balance Program: 2018 Update*. Vision 2030. Riyadh. Government report.

Krane, J., (2019). *Energy Kingdoms: Oil and Political Survival in the Persian Gulf, Center on Global Energy Policy Series*. New York: Columbia University Press.

Krane, J. (2020). Climate action versus inaction: balancing the costs for Gulf energy exporters. *Br. J. Middle East. Stud.* pp. 1–19.

Krane, J. (2021). Climate strategy for producer countries: the case of Saudi Arabia, in Luciani, G., and Moerenhout, T. (eds.), *When Can Oil Economies Be Deemed Sustainable?* Singapore: Springer Singapore, pp. 301–327. Doi: 10.1007/978-981-15-5728-6_12.

Krane, J. (2022). Last man standing: Saudi Aramco and global climate action, in Thompson, M. C., and Quilliam, N. (eds.), *Governance and Domestic Policymaking in Saudi Arabia: Transforming Society, Economics, Politics and Culture*. London: I. B. Tauris, pp. 257–289.

Krane, J., and Idel, R. (2021). More transitions, less risk: how renewable energy reduces risks from mining, trade, and political dependence. *Energy Res. Soc. Sci.* 82, p. 102311.

Liu, H., Tellez, B. G., Atallah, T., and Barghouty, M. (2012). The role of CO_2 capture and storage in Saudi Arabia's energy future. *Int. J. Greenhouse Gas Control* 11, pp. 163–171. Doi: 10.1016/j.ijggc.2012.08.008.

MacDonald, F. (2022). One of the world's wealthiest oil exporters is becoming unlivable. Bloomberg News.

Maersk (2022). *A.P. Moller-Maersk engages in strategic partnerships* across the globe to scale green methanol production by 2025. Press release, March 10. Available online: www.maersk.com/news/articles/2022/03/10/maersk-engages-in-strategic-partnerships-to-scale-green-methanol-production.

Martin, P., and Zhou, Y. (2022). *No Pain, No Gain: The Economic Consequences of Accelerating the Energy Transition*. Consultancy research report. London: Wood Mackenzie.

McKerracher, C. (2022). China's electric trucks may well pull forward peak oil demand. Bloomberg News.

Middle East Economic Survey (MEES) (2021). Saudi Arabia sets out its stall for net-zero 2060. October 29. Available online: www.mees.com/2021/10/29/opec/saudi-arabia-sets-out-its-stall-for-net-zero-2060/a244b9e0-38b4-11ec-abd8-bbf38d0cbd31.

MEES (2022a). Petro Rabigh signs up to CCUS. April 8.

MEES (2022b). *Saudi Arabia awards 1GW of solar projects*. 65.

MEES (2022c). Saudi Arabia urges colorblind approach to hydrogen. December 13.

MEES (2022d). Saudi May 2022 Key Oil Data. 65.

Moch, J. M., Xue, W., and Holdren, J. P. (2022). *Carbon Capture, Utilization, and Storage: Technologies and Costs in the U.S. Context*. Policy brief. Boston, MA: Belfer Center, Harvard University.

Nereim, V. (2021). Saudi Arabia to start electric-vehicle push in capital Riyadh. Bloomberg News.

North, D. C., and Weingast, B. R. (1989). Constitutions and commitment: the evolution of institutions governing public choice in seventeenth-century England. *J. Econ. Hist.* 49, pp. 803–832.

Pitel, L., and Kıraç, N. (2022). Turkey's new power plant exposes 'huge contradictions' of net zero pledge. *Financial Times*.

Rahman, F. (2022). Dubai's Hassyan power plant to be fueled by natural gas to reduce emissions. The National News.

Rathi, A., and Martin, M. (2021). Aramco's new disclosures still exclude vast majority of its emissions. Bloomberg, April 6. Available online: www.bloomberg.com/news/articles/2021-04-06/aramco-s-new-disclosures-still-exclude-vast-majority-of-its-emissions.

Rathi, A. (2021). How Saudi Arabia is planning to reach net zero by 2060. Bloomberg News.

Reuters (2023). Saudi Arabia plans to use domestic uranium for nuclear fuel. Reuters.

Rice University Carbon Hub (n.d.). *From Fuels to Feedstock*. Houston, TX: Rice University.

Rowlett, J., and Gerken, T. (2021). COP26: document leak reveals nations lobbying to change key climate report. BBC News.

SABIC (2022). Creating the world's largest carbon capture and utilization plant. SABIC press release. SABIC, Riyadh.

Said, S., and Faucon, B. (2021). Ahead of COP26, Saudi Arabia resists calls to cut oil investment. *Wall Street Journal*. October. Available online: www.wsj.com/articles/ahead-of-cop26-saudi-arabia-resists-calls-to-cut-oil-investment-11634911150.

Saudi Arabian Statistics Agency (2017). *Household Energy Survey*. Available online: www.stats.gov.sa/sites/default/files/household_energy_survey_2017en.pdf.

Saudi Aramco (2021). Aramco expands climate goals, stating ambition to reach operational net-zero emissions by 2050. Saudi Aramco press release. Saudi Aramco, Dhahran.

Saudi Aramco (2022). *Saudi Aramco Sustainability Report 2021: Energy Security for a Sustainable World*. Company report. Saudi Aramco, Dhahran.

Saudi Aramco (2023). Aramco announces record full-year 2022 results. Saudi Aramco press release. Saudi Aramco, Dhahran.

Sharma, A. (2022). PIF-backed EV maker Lucid to produce 150,000 cars a year at its Saudi factory. *The National*, May 18. Available online: www.thenationalnews.com/business/economy/2022/05/18/pif-backed-ev-maker-lucid-to-produce-150000-cars-a-year-at-its-saudi-factory/#:~:text=The%20plant%20will%20help%20the,to%20500%2C000%20EVs%20per%20year&text=Lucid%20Group%2C%20which%20is%20backed,of%20155%2C000%20units%20a%20year.

Soummane, S., and Ghersi, F. (2022). Projecting Saudi sectoral electricity demand in 2030 using a computable general equilibrium model. *Energy Strategy Rev.* 39, 100787. Doi: 10.1016/j.esr.2021.100787.

The National (2022). Abu Dhabi's Kizad signs lease with NWTN for electric vehicle assembly plant. Available online: www.thenationalnews.com/business/road-to-net-zero/2022/09/06/abu-dhabis-kizad-signs-lease-with-nwtn-for-electric-vehicle-assembly-plant/#:~:text=The%20facility%20will%20have%20an,capacity%20to%2050%2C000%20units%20annually.

United Nations Conference on Trade and Development (UNCTAD) (2021). *A European Union Carbon Border Adjustment Mechanism: Implications for Developing Countries*. NGO report. New York: United Nations Conference on Trade and Development.

Vahrenkamp, V., Afif, A., Tasianas, A., and Hoteit, H. (2021). The geological potential of the Arabian Plate for CCS and CCUS – an overview. *Proceedings of the 15th Greenhouse Gas Control Technologies Conference 15–18 March 2021*, pp. 15–18. Doi: 10.2139/ssrn.3822139.

Walt, V. (2022). Saudi energy minister says the country will pump more oil, despite net-zero goals. *Time*.

Wood Mackenzie (2022). *National Oil Companies: Strategies for the Energy Transition*. Consultancy research report. London: Wood Mackenzie.

World Bank (2022). *Gulf Economic Update: Achieving Climate Change Pledges*. NGO report. Washington, DC: World Bank.

World Nuclear Association (2022). *Nuclear Power in Saudi Arabia*. Industry association report. London: World Nuclear Association.

Wright, A. (2021). Challenges and opportunities for CCS in Saudi Arabia. *Natural Gas World*.

Part III

Infrastructure

5

Energy Efficiency and Carbon Neutrality Potentials for the Building Sector in the GCC Region

MONCEF KRARTI

5.1 Introduction

Bahrain, Kuwait, the Kingdom of Saudi Arabia (KSA), Oman, Qatar, and the United Arab Emirates (UAE) are countries located in the Middle East and form an alliance known as the Gulf Cooperation Council (GCC) based on economic and political agreements. The economy of the GCC region is dominated almost exclusively by the export of fossil fuels and depends on the prices of both oil and natural gas. Moreover, GCC countries utilise exclusively oil and natural gas products to power their economies. The main economic and energy indicators for the six GCC countries can be extracted based on reported data from the International Energy Agency (IEA, 2023), World Bank (2023), and Krarti et al. (2019). As expected, Saudi Arabia has significantly higher absolute values for both economic output and energy consumption among all the GCC countries due to its larger population. However, Qatar has the highest gross domestic product (GDP) and energy consumption per person. The GDP created by the unit of energy consumed, often referred to as the 'energy productivity indicator', is highest for the UAE (USD8,246/ton of oil equivalent, TOE) and lowest for Bahrain (USD4,248/TOE). The energy productivity indicates the energy efficiency of the country's economy. Energy policies in several countries have the goal of increasing the energy productivity of their economy through both energy efficiency programmes and economic diversification (Krarti et al., 2019).

All GCC countries rely mainly on oil products (54%) and natural gas (46%) to meet their primary energy needs (IEA, 2023). Unlike the case of the GCC region, coal has been used to meet a significant part of the energy needs of other regions in the world, contributing, respectively, 27% of the total primary energy supply (TPES). Nuclear, hydro, and renewables (i.e. sources with no carbon emissions) are also prominent in the world, serving up to 10% of TPES.

Over the last two decades, energy consumption in the GCC region has seen a steady increase due mostly to growth in population and economic activities. The GCC region has seen a significant increase in energy consumption with an average annual growth rate of 3.7% in TFEC for the period of 2000–2015, with a reduction of almost 6% between 2015 and 2020 driven primarily to the deployment of energy price reforms in some countries, including Saudi Arabia (IEA, 2023). During 2020, the GCC region consumed slightly more than 3,200 terawatt hours (TWh) of energy to meet its economy's needs. Most of these needs are met by using oil products, natural gas, and electricity representing, respectively, 52%, 29%, and 18%. As expected, Saudi Arabia is the dominant energy consumer in the GCC region and is responsible for over 57% of the total TFEC reported for the region during 2020.

This chapter will provide some specific guidelines for the potential to decarbonise the building sector in the GCC region through the implementation of various energy efficiency and renewable energy technologies. Indeed, the most effective strategies to reduce the carbon emissions of buildings, especially in the GCC region that relies heavily on the fossil fuels to operate its economy, including its building stock, it is crucial to lower energy demands first and then use renewable energy systems to meet these demands. First, the energy consumption attributed to the building sector is discussed for all GCC countries, including the energy end-use distributions for both residential and commercial buildings. Then, the status of the energy efficiency programmes is outlined for the GCC countries, ranging from energy efficiency codes and minimum energy performance standards (MEPS) for various energy intensive systems. Finally, the specific reductions of energy use and carbon emissions are quantified for various large-scale energy programmes for the GCC region, including more stringent energy efficiency codes and MEPS involving net zero energy and low carbon building designs and retrofits.

5.2 Energy Consumption in the Building Sector

The contribution of the building sector in the national total TFEC varies significantly between countries within the GCC region. As indicated in the IEA (2023) statistics, buildings represent 12–17% of TFEC specific to the GCC region for which the industry sector is dominant in terms of energy demands. Residential buildings consume almost double the amount of energy used by the commercial and public buildings.

Generally, the GCC countries utilise mostly electricity to meet the energy needs for both their residential and commercial building stocks. As expected, Saudi

Arabia consumes the highest energy for both residential and commercial buildings (Krarti, 2019). Indeed, buildings in Saudi Arabia consumed 269 TWh during 2020, representing more than half of the total final energy used by the building sector in the GCC region.

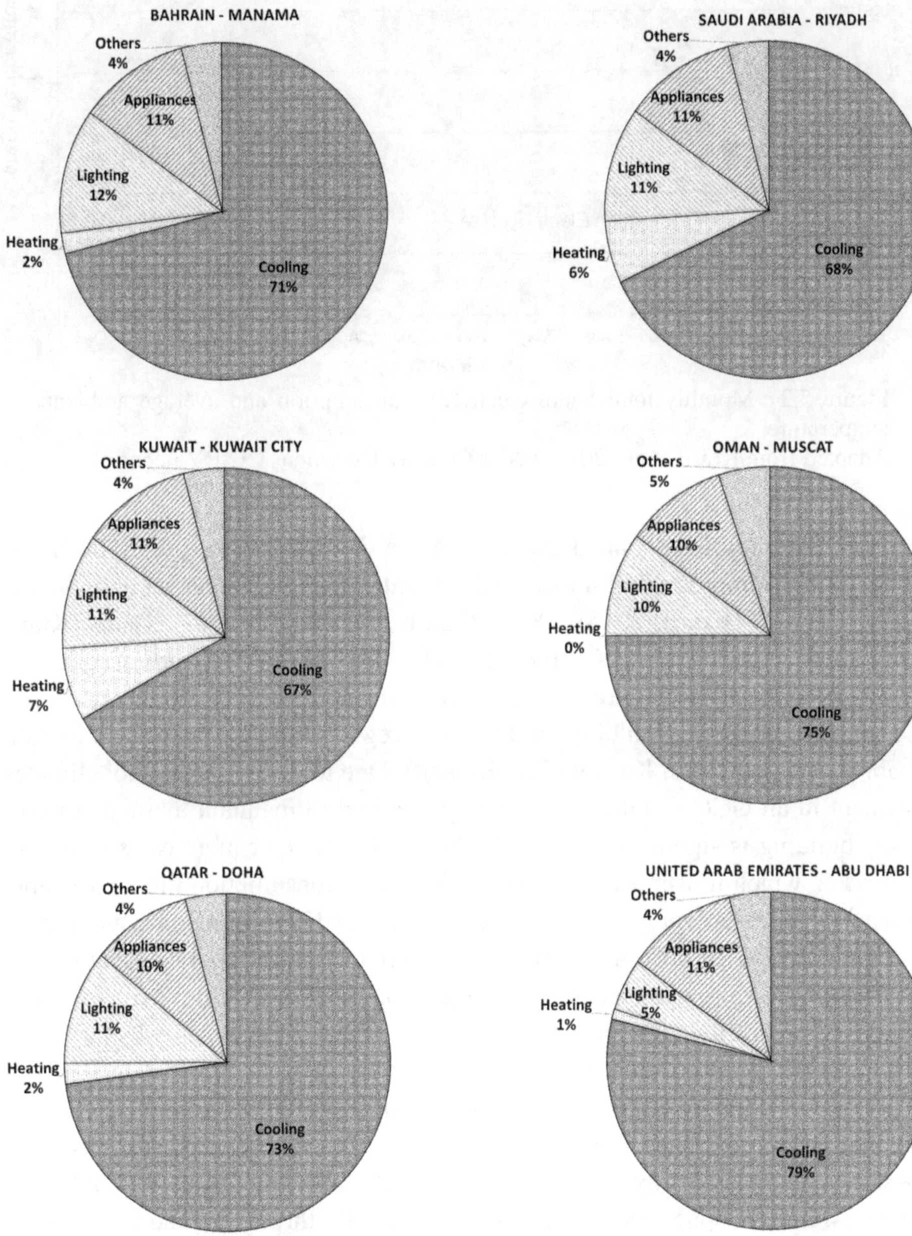

Figure 5.1 Annual energy end-use distributions for villas in six cities representing all GCC countries.

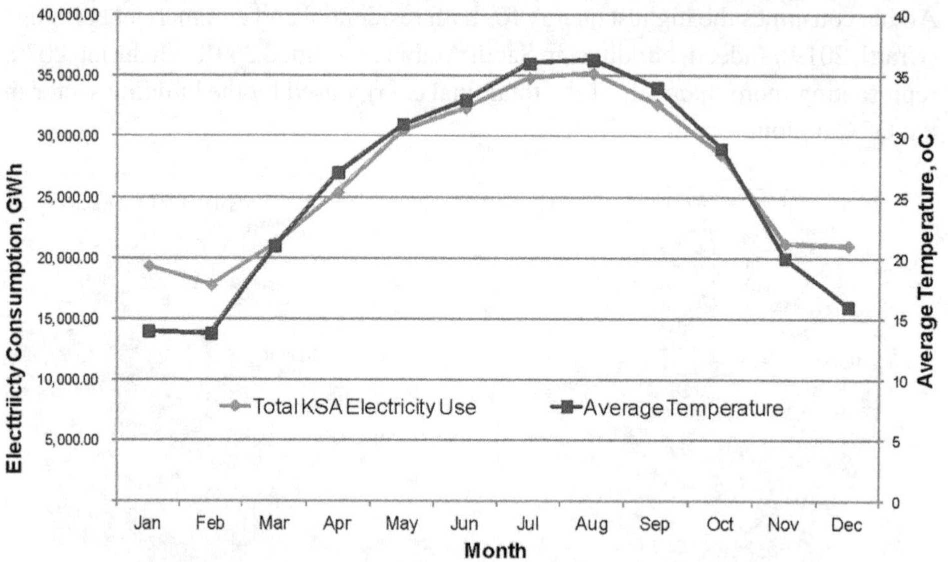

Figure 5.2 Monthly total Saudi electricity consumption and average ambient temperature.
Adapted from Krarti et al. (2017) under Creative Commons CC-BY license.

Figure 5.1 shows the annual energy end-use distribution for prototypical villas in six cities representing all the GCC countries: Bahrain (Krarti and Dubey, 2018a), Kuwait (Krarti, 2015), Oman (Krarti and Dubey, 2017), Qatar (Krarti et al., 2018), Saudi Arabia (Krarti et al., 2017), and the UAE (Krarti and Dubey, 2018b). As indicated in Figure 5.1, air conditioning represents the dominant energy end use for residential buildings in the GCC region, ranging from 79% in Abu Dhabi (UAE) to 67% in Kuwait City (Kuwait). Due to the extremely hot climates prevalent in all GCC countries, the energy required to maintain thermal comfort in any building is significant especially during the summer months, as shown in Figure 5.2, which illustrates the monthly electricity consumption in Saudi Arabia with an average outdoor temperature (Krarti et al., 2017). Indeed, air conditioning is responsible for the bulk of electricity consumption by the Saudi building stocks. After space cooling, appliances (i.e. refrigerators and cooling devices) followed by lighting are attributable for most of the energy consumed annually by the Saudi housing stock (Krarti et al., 2020).

The annual energy end-use distributions for office buildings for all GCC countries are shown in Figure 5.3 (Ashraf et al., 2020). As expected, space cooling consumes the most energy annually due to hot climates that characterise all GCC countries. Indeed, space cooling represents 44 to 49% throughout the GCC region (Ashraf et al., 2020).

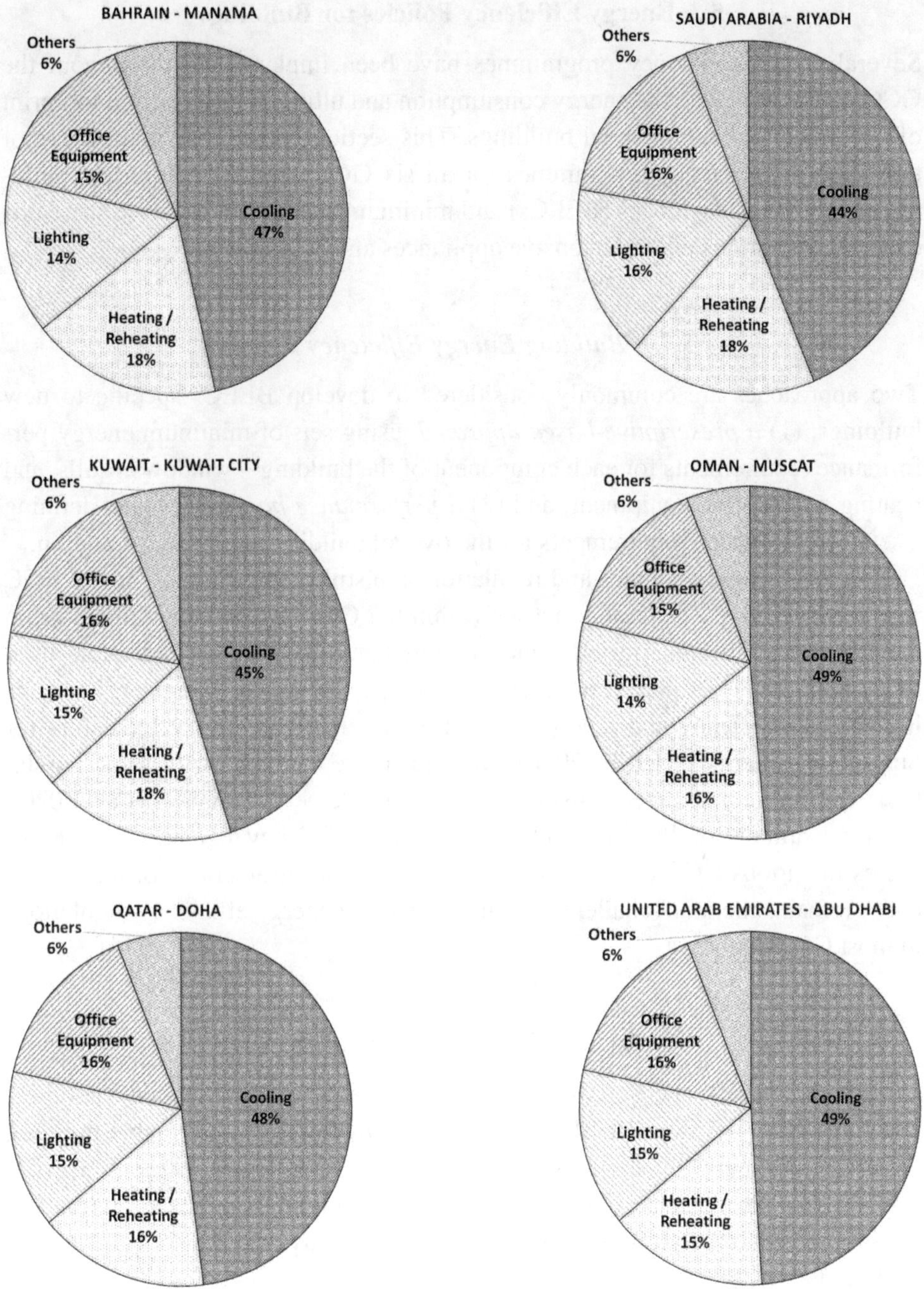

Figure 5.3 Annual energy end-use distributions for office buildings in GCC countries.
Adapted with permission from Ashraf et al. (2020).

5.3 Energy Efficiency Policies for Buildings

Several energy efficiency programmes have been implemented throughout the GCC region to reduce the energy consumption and ultimately the carbon footprint of residential and commercial buildings. This section outlines the main scope of these energy efficiency programmes for all six GCC countries, including building energy efficiency codes (BEECs) and minimum energy performance standards (MEPS) for various energy intensive appliances and equipment.

5.3.1 Building Energy Efficiency Codes

Two approaches are commonly considered to develop BEECs specific to new buildings: (1) *a prescriptive-based approach* using sets of minimum energy performance requirements for each component of the building – windows, walls, and heating and cooling equipment; and (2) *a performance-based approach* defining a set of performance requirements for the overall building energy consumption.

Energy efficiency policies and regulations are still in their infancy in the GCC region (Asif, 2016). Several countries within the GCC region have limited or no mandatory building energy efficiency requirements. One of the indicators used to assess a country's policy and regulatory support of sustainable energy including energy efficiency and renewable energy is called Regulatory Indicators for Sustainable Energy or RISE (2016). Even for those countries with some regulations, the enforcement mechanisms are not yet implemented (Ashraf et al., 2020). Table 5.1 summarises the status of building energy efficiency regulations and RISE scores in various GCC countries (Krarti, 2018a). The enforcement of mandatory codes remains the main challenge for implementing energy efficiency regulations in most GCC countries.

5.3.2 Building Rating Systems

In addition to some energy efficiency codes, some GCC countries have adopted, and some have developed building rating systems to foster sustainable building designs. Specifically, US Leadership in Energy and Environmental Design (LEED) certifications have been accredited to several new buildings in the GCC countries (Krarti, 2019). In addition, building rating systems have been developed in two GCC countries, including:

- Global Sustainability Assessment System (GSAS) developed in Qatar by the Gulf Organization for Research and Development in collaboration with the University of Pennsylvania (GORD, 2010). Like LEED, GSAS is a performance-based rating system to assist designers reduce the ecological impacts of buildings while

Table 5.1 *Status of building energy efficiency regulations in GCC countries.*

Country	Building EE regulation	Type of compliance	Mandatory/ voluntary	EE RISE score (max. 100)
Bahrain	Thermal Insulation Requirements for commercial buildings (1999) and other building types (2013)	Prescriptive	Mandatory	25
Kuwait	Energy Conservation Code of Practice No. R-6 (1983 updated 2014)	Prescriptive	Mandatory	30
Oman	None	NA	NA	NA
Qatar	Global Building Assessment System (GSAS): All new Public Buildings (2012) All new Commercial Buildings (2016) All new Residential Buildings (2020)	Sustainable Building Label System	Mandatory	50
Saudi Arabia	Thermal Performance Code (2014)	Prescriptive	Mandatory	49
United Arab Emirates	Thermal Insulation Requirements (2003) Green Dubai Building System (2020) Pearl Rating System (2010)	Prescriptive Elemental – Performance Performance	Mandatory Mandatory (Dubai) Mandatory (Abu Dhabi)	63

considering specific local environmental needs. Specifically, GSAS considers eight assessment categories with different weights: urban connectivity, site, energy, water, materials, indoor environment, cultural and economic value, as well as management and operation. Residential, commercial, and institutional buildings are rated relative to reference levels for both energy performance (expressed in kWh/m^2/year) and carbon emissions (expressed in kg CO_2/m^2/year). There are some flexibilities in meeting energy performance and carbon footprint requirements in the design and operating phases through improvements in the building envelope, lighting, and air-conditioning systems as well as human comfort. Since 2016, GSAS has been adopted as a mandatory rating system for all new governmental buildings in Qatar.

- The Pearl Rating System (PRS) is a green building rating certification system developed by the Abu Dhabi Urban Planning Council as part of its sustainable development initiative, Estidama (PBRS, 2022). PRS is developed using similar

LEED standards with several rating levels that depend on a scoring system with mandatory and optional credit points ranging from one to five pearls. PRS was developed specifically for designing buildings in hot and arid climates, with several categories covering: natural systems, resourceful energy, precious water, stewarding materials, livable villa/building/community, integrating development process, and innovating practice. PRS requires a minimum energy performance of buildings to be assured using either prescriptive or performance approaches. Any additional improvements from the minimum can be awarded credit points. Since 2010, a minimum certification of one pearl has been required for all new construction in Abu Dhabi. For new government buildings, a level of two pearls is required.
- Green Dubai Building System is a rating system that is required for any new buildings in Dubai (Al Safat, 2020). It has two compliance approaches consisting of an elemental method with specific set of required specifications and a performance method that is based on detailed modelling analysis and Appendix G of ASHRAE standard 90.1 (ASHRAE, 2018). The rating address various aspects of building sustainability as follows: (1) ecology and planning (i.e. access and mobility, ecology and landscaping, neighbourhood pollution, microclimate and outdoor comfort, as well as environmental impact assessment); (2) building vitality (i.e. ventilation and air quality, thermal comfort, acoustic comfort, hazardous materials, daylighting and visual comfort, water quality, as well as responsible construction); (3) energy efficiency (i.e. building fabric, building systems, commissioning and management, as well as on-site power generation and renewable energy systems); (4) water resources effectiveness (i.e. conservation and efficiency, commissioning and management, as well as on-site recovery and treatment); and (5) materials and water resources effectiveness (i.e. materials and resources as well as waste management).

5.3.3 Minimum Energy Performance Standards (MEPS)

Minimum energy performance standards or MEPS are proven to be effective instruments in transforming the markets for energy-consuming devices, including appliances, lighting, and air-conditioning systems. Deployment of MEPS stimulates the adoption of new and more energy efficient technologies and products. Products covered by MEPS include all end uses and fuel types with a focus on appliances, information and communication devices, lighting, heating and cooling systems, and other energy-consuming equipment. Table 5.2 and Table 5.3 provide the list of MEPS requirements for, respectively, household appliances and lighting systems in the GCC countries (Krarti, 2018a, 2019). Again, the enforcement of these regulations remains a challenge for most GCC countries and includes the

Table 5.2 *Status of minimum energy performance standards (MEPS) for air conditioning and appliances in the GCC countries.*

Country	Regulation type	Status of policy
Bahrain	Air conditioners	Under preparation
Kuwait	Air-conditioning systems	Adopted since 1983 as part of the Energy Conservation Code of Practice for Buildings. The Code of Practice has been since update in 2010 and 2014
Oman	Not available	Not available
Qatar	Air-conditioning systems	Adopted since 1983
Saudi Arabia	Air-conditioning systems, freezers, refrigerators, and washing machines	Adopted since 1983 and last revised in 2013
UAE	Air-conditioning systems, refrigerators, and washing machines	Adopted since 2013

Table 5.3 *Status of energy efficiency regulations for lighting systems in the GCC countries.*

Country	Building EE regulation	Status of policy
Bahrain	MEPS for household light bulbs based on the EU Commission Regulation No 244/2009	Adopted since 2009
Kuwait	Not available	Not available
Oman	Not available	Not available
Qatar	Ban of import for incandescent light bulbs (Tungsten). First phase of the ban includes 100W and 75W incandescent bulbs. The implementation of the regulation shall be effective starting from 2014	Adopted since 2014
Saudi Arabia	Regulations are being prepared to focus on the phase out of least efficient light sources in buildings	Under preparation
UAE	The Emirates Authority for Standardization and Meteorology (ESMA) has banned the import and sales of incandescent and low-quality energy saving bulbs since 1 January 2015	Adopted since 2014

lack of qualified testing facilities to ensure that appliances and lighting systems sold in the region meet the stated MEPS requirements (Asif, 2016). Saudi MEPS are among the first standards introduced not only in the GCC region but also in the Arab world and have been regularly revised (Al-Homoud and Krarti, 2021).

As detailed in the review study by Al-Homoud and Krarti (2021), Saudi Arabia has issued several updates for MEPS for appliances and air-conditioning systems over the last two decades (SASO, 2012, 2013, 2014, 2017, 2018a, 2018b, 2018c).

5.4 Energy Efficiency Potential for the Building Sector

As discussed in Section 5.3, there are several energy efficiency programmes implemented for the building sector in some GCC countries, including MEPS, energy conservation codes, and green building ratings. However, these programmes target mostly new buildings and in some countries are not enforced consistently. The potential for improving the energy performance of buildings in the GCC region remains significant for both new and existing building stocks for all GCC countries. Indeed, several opportunities are available to reduce energy consumption and enhance the sustainability of buildings in the GCC region through well-designed and targeted energy policies. In this section, some of these opportunities are evaluated based on detailed analyses and reported studies. In particular, the potential benefits of large-scale implementation of selected energy efficiency programmes are presented for both new and existing building stocks. The analysis is based on a bottom-up approach of the building stock to account for the characteristics of the building stock in the GCC region. The details of the bottom-up approach are outlined in the reported literature for each of the GCC countries (Krarti, 2015; Krarti and Dubey, 2017; Krarti et al., 2017; Krarti et al., 2018; Krarti and Dubey, 2018a; Krarti and Dubey, 2018b).

5.4.1 Benefits for Improved MEPS

The potential benefits of setting MEPS based on currently available energy efficiency equipment and appliances commonly used in buildings have been estimated by a recent analysis reported by United for Energy Efficiency (U4E, 2017). In particular, the analysis has considered energy-consuming products commonly used in residential buildings including air conditioners, refrigerators, and lighting. The potential annual savings in electricity consumption during 2025 and 2030 for all GCC countries are summarised in Table 5.4 for lighting, Table 5.5 for refrigerators, and Table 5.6 for room air conditioners based on the implementation of stricter MEPs (U4E, 2017). While refrigerators are specific to residential buildings, lighting and room air conditioners may affect the energy consumption of both residential and commercial buildings.

As noted in the results shown in Tables 5.4 through 5.6, the overall annual electrical savings that can be achieved by 2030 from updating, implementation, and enforcement of MEPs are highest for lighting (15.517 TWh/year), followed by

Table 5.4 *Potential annual benefits attributed to lighting MEPS in the GCC region adapted with permissions from (U4E, 2017).*

	Electricity use (TWh/year)		Energy cost (USD million/year)	
Country	2025	2030	2025	2030
Bahrain	0.305	0.316	7.0	7.3
Kuwait	1.571	1.618	15.7	16.2
Oman	0.725	0.746	37.7	38.8
Qatar	1.395	1.437	34.9	35.9
Saudi Arabia	8.000	8.200	400.1	412.4
UAE	3.100	3.200	361.1	367.3
GCC	15.096	15.517	856.5	877.9

Table 5.5 *Potential annual benefits attributed to MEPS for refrigerators in the GCC region adapted with permissions from (U4E, 2017).*

	Electricity use (TWh/year)		Energy cost (USD million/year)	
Country	2025	2030	2025	2030
Bahrain	0.047	0.090	1.1	2.1
Kuwait	0.180	0.325	1.8	3.3
Oman	0.069	0.137	3.6	7.1
Qatar	0.035	0.072	0.90	1.8
Saudi Arabia	0.800	1.500	40.4	77.20
UAE	0.400	0.700	40.9	85.7
GCC	1.531	2.824	88.7	177.2

room air conditioners (5.709 TWh/year), and then refrigerators (2.824 TWh/year). Based on Business as Usual (BAU) projections for 2030, these savings represent 2.1% (lighting), 0.8% (room air conditioners), and 0.4% (refrigerators) of the final energy consumption of the building sector in the GCC region.

Table 5.6 *Potential annual benefits attributed to improved MEPs for room air conditioners in the GCC region adapted with permissions from (U4E, 2017).*

	Electricity use savings (TWh/year)	
Country	2025	2030
Bahrain	0.021	0.033
Kuwait	0.055	0.091
Oman	0.117	0.200
Qatar	0.051	0.085
Saudi Arabia	2.200	3.600
UAE	1.100	1.700
GCC	3.544	5.709

5.4.2 Impact of EE Programs for New Buildings

Based on the reported literature, more effective building energy efficiency codes (BEECs) can be developed in all six GCC countries for all new buildings (Krarti, 2015; Krarti and Dubey, 2017; Krarti et al., 2017; Krarti et al., 2018; Krarti and Dubey, 2018a; Krarti and Dubey, 2018b). Figure 5.6 illustrates the optimised designs for villas in various cities and representatives of various GCC countries. The optimised designs are based on minimising life-cycle cost (LCC) as well as achieving net zero energy building (NZEB) status. As illustrated in Figure 5.4, throughout the GCC region, 70–75% savings can be achieved using LCC optimal designs for residential buildings. The benefits of integrated design-based BEECs applied to the new buildings are estimated and summarised as shown in Table 5.7 (Krarti, 2019).

Figure 5.5 illustrates the projections in annual energy demand in the GCC region due to the implementation starting in 2030 of stricter energy efficiency requirements including high performance building envelope, integrated building energy efficiency code (BEEC), and net zero energy buildings (NZEB) for new housing units. The impact of improving building envelope systems (i.e. through the addition of thermal insulation) is rather minimal since most of the GCC countries have already mandatory thermal insulation code requirements and are not included in the analysis. However, the deployments of stricter construction requirements for new residential buildings starting from 2030 using both integrated energy performance based BEEC and NZEB designs have the potential to substantially reduce

Table 5.7 *Economic and environmental benefits for implementing integrated BEECs for all new buildings in the GCC region.*

Building type	Annual energy use savings (TWh/yr)	Peak demand savings (MW)	Annual CO_2 emissions savings (million tons/yr)
Residential buildings	9.490	1543	2.960
Commercial and public buildings	3.249	528	1.014
Total	12.739	2071	3.974

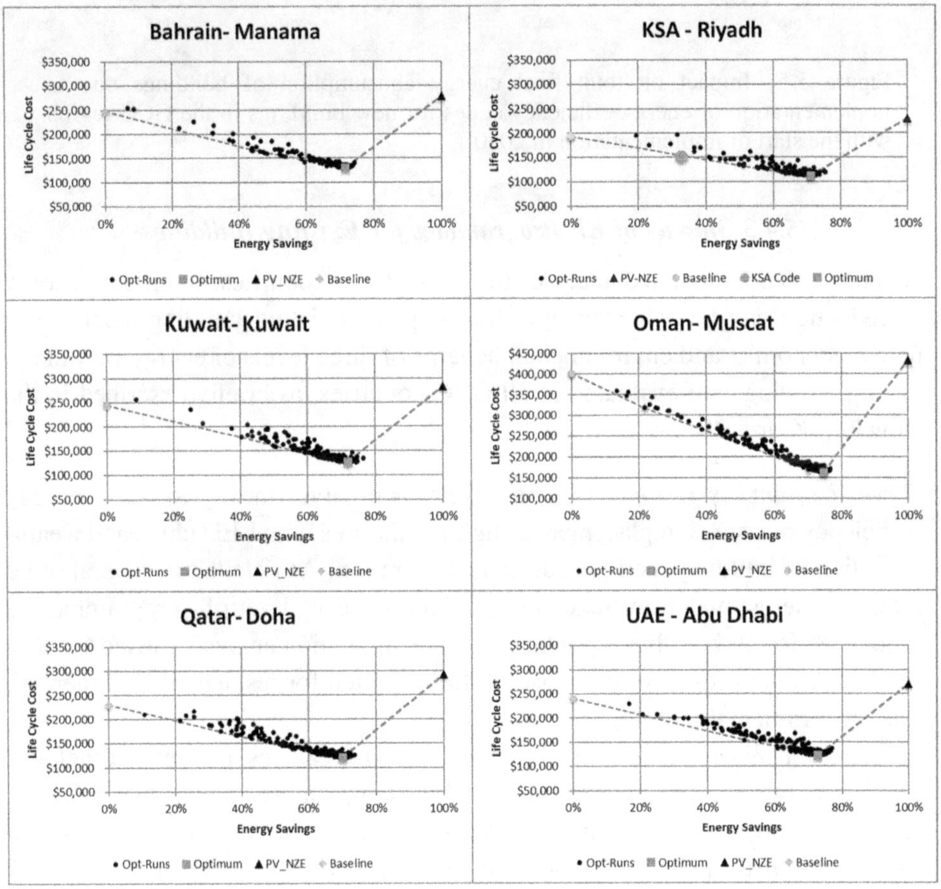

Figure 5.4 LCC-base optimised and NZEB designs for villas in six cities representing GCC countries.

energy demand in the GCC region. With the requirements, the annual energy use savings in the GCC region can reach 108 TWh and 198 TWh, for respectively integrated energy performance BEEC and NZEB designs and by 2050.

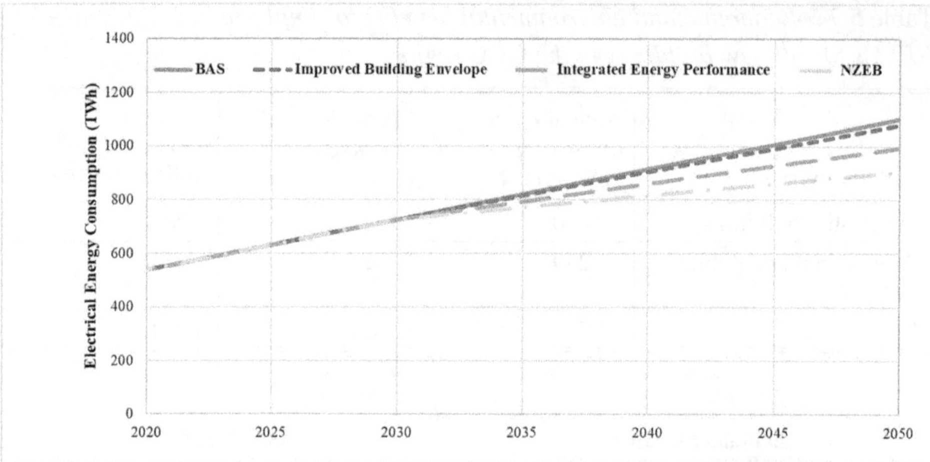

Figure 5.5 Impact on total final energy consumption of buildings due to implementation of energy efficiency codes for new buildings in the GCC region with the start of implementation in 2030.

5.4.3 Impact of EE Programmes for Existing Buildings

As documented by detailed analyses for all the GCC countries, significant energy use reduction can be achieved by retrofitting the existing building stocks. The energy, economic, and environmental benefits of three levels of energy retrofits of existing buildings are evaluated in all GCC countries, as briefly described in the following (Krarti, 2019):

- *Level-1 of energy retrofit*: This basic retrofit involves mostly low-cost energy efficiency measures, replacement of lighting fixtures with LED units, and weatherisation of building shell to reduce air infiltration. As detailed in several other studies, the estimated average savings from a Level-1 retrofit programme are about 8% for all building types based on the simulation analysis carried for several GCC countries as well as case studies reported for residential, commercial, and governmental buildings.
- *Level-2 of energy retrofit*: In addition to Level-1 measures, this retrofit includes use of energy efficient equipment as well as temperature and lighting controls. Based on reported studies in the Arab region as well as from the simulation results outlined in this study for Arab countries, average savings of about 23% can be achieved for Level-2 retrofits for all building types.
- *Level-3 of energy retrofit*: This type of retrofit, known as a 'deep retrofit', requires the implementation of capital-intensive measures, including the addition of roof thermal insulation, cooling system replacement, and installation of automated control systems. While deep retrofits are typically costly, they can provide

Table 5.8 *Energy and environmental benefits for three levels of building energy efficiency retrofit programmes for the GCC region.*

Retrofit programme	Level-1	Level-2	Level-3
Annual energy savings (TWh/year)			
• Residential buildings	26.914	76.576	165.421
• Commercial buildings	9.214	27.291	60.377
Total existing building stock	36.128	103.867	225.799
Peak demand savings (MW)			
• Residential buildings	4,135	11,175	23,586
• Commercial buildings	1,416	3,825	7,862
Total existing building stock	5,551	15,000	31,448
Annual CO_2 savings (tons/year)			
• Residential buildings	8.407	24.170	52.545
• Commercial buildings	2.862	8.230	17.891
Total existing building stock	11.270	32.400	70.436

significant energy use savings exceeding 50%, as noted in several reports and in the optimal analysis conducted for the Arab region.

Table 5.8 summarises the annual energy use, electricity peak demand, and carbon emissions savings for Level-1, Level-2, and Level-3 building energy efficiency retrofit programmes applied to the entire existing building stock in the GCC region. As the table clearly shows, significant energy and environmental benefits can be achieved for all the levels of the building energy retrofit programmes. While requiring higher implementation costs, higher benefits for Level-2 and Level-3 retrofit programmes can achieve larger savings and more benefits compared to Level-1 retrofit programmes. The economic and environmental benefits that can be realised for residential buildings are significantly higher than those obtained for commercial and public buildings for all energy retrofit levels. Indeed, over 74% of the overall benefits can be achieved by solely retrofitting residential buildings in the GCC region, as indicated in Table 5.8.

It is expected that implementation of the large-scale building energy retrofit programmes will be gradual, requiring several years due to two main reasons: (1) the significant investments needed for renovating the entire existing building stock; and (2) the lack of qualified energy efficiency contractors in most GCC countries, requiring at least a few years to develop and train more of them. However, any of the three energy retrofit programmes can result in significant economic and environmental benefits for the GCC region, even when only a small fraction of the existing stock is targeted, as shown in Table 5.8. The energy retrofit programmes for the existing building stock have significant impacts on final energy consumption, peak electrical demand, and carbon emissions in the GCC region, even when implemented gradually over ten years, starting from 2030. As expected, Level-3 retrofit has the highest impact, with an annual energy consumption reduction of 226 TWh, as well as a decrease in electrical demand of 31.5 gigawatt (GW) and 70.4 million tons per year of carbon emissions when the programme is fully implemented by 2030. Level-1 and Level-2 retrofit programmes would still save, respectively, 36 TWh and 104 TWh in annual final energy consumption without significant investment requirements (Krarti, 2019).

The retrofit programmes can start initially with non-residential buildings since they provide higher energy savings per unit floor area than residential buildings for the GCC region (Krarti, 2019). Moreover, it is easier to perform energy audits and retrofit for larger non-residential buildings through ESCOs than it is for smaller residential buildings. In addition, retrofitting residential buildings offers specific privacy and cultural sensitivity challenges in several countries within the GCC region (Krarti, 2019). As indicated in Figure 5.6, the potential benefits depend on when the programmes are initiated and the rate of the retrofit. The results of Figure 5.6 assume a 10% rate of retrofit (i.e. 10% of the existing building stock is retrofitted each year). If lower retrofit rates are considered, the potential benefits would be reduced accordingly.

The highest impact scenario for reducing the final energy use and peak demand would be to simultaneously: (1) implement integrated BEEC for new buildings; and (2) upgrade over ten years the entire existing building stock using Level-3 energy retrofit. Figure 5.7 shows that there is a significant potential saving of buildings energy consumption, especially when the Level-3 energy retrofit programme is implemented within ten years and new buildings are constructed using an integrated energy efficiency code. In this scenario and if the code and the retrofit programme is implemented by 2030, the total GCC region annual final energy consumption could be reduced by 334 TWh (or 30%) from a projected 1,101 TWh per year for the baseline scenario (BAS). Similar reductions in both electrical peak demands and carbon emissions can be achieved. While the required investments to implement these energy efficiency programmes can be significant as highlighted later for Saudi Arabia in Table 5.11, the economic benefits can be substantial for most countries as reported for several GCC countries (Krarti, 2015; Krarti and Dubey, 2017; Krarti et al., 2017; Krarti et al., 2018; Krarti and Dubey, 2018a; Krarti and Dubey, 2018b).

The costs of the retrofit programmes vary with the level and the country as summarised in Table 5.9, Table 5.10, and Table 5.11, for large-scale deployments of, respectively, Level-1, Level-2, and Level-3 retrofit programmes. Specifically, Table 5.9 through Table 5.11 summarise the required investment costs and the potential direct, environmental, and social benefits of the three retrofit levels for the entire existing residential and non-residential buildings in each of the six GCC countries. The analysis approaches for all the GCC countries are detailed in reported studies

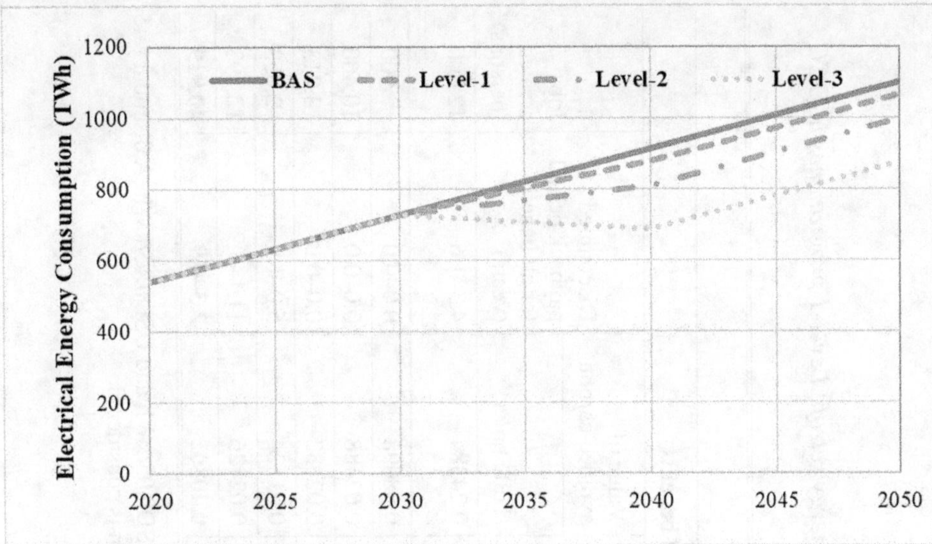

Figure 5.6 Impact on load profiles for electrical energy consumption due to implementation of energy retrofit programmes for the entire existing GCC building stock when the programmes start in 2030.

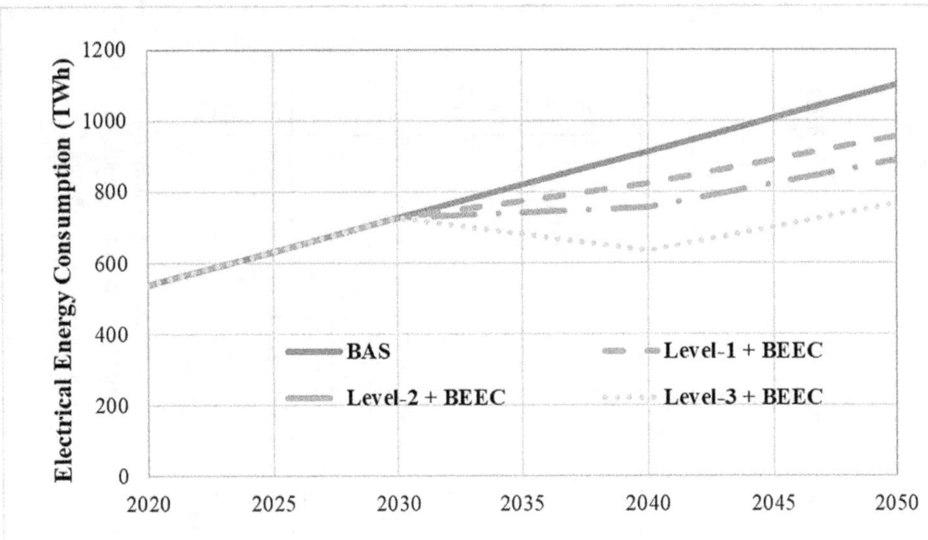

Figure 5.7 Impact on final energy consumption due to implementation of both comprehensive energy efficiency code for new buildings and energy retrofit programmes for the entire existing GCC building stock when the programmes start in 2030.

Table 5.9 *Investment costs and direct and wider social benefits for building energy retrofit Level-1 programmes in GCC countries.*

	Level-1 retrofits						
	Direct benefits			Wider social benefits			
Country	Investment cost (USD bn)	Value of avoided energy consumption (USD bn/year)*	Discounted payback period for direct benefits only (years)*	Value of avoided generation capacity (USD bn)	Value of avoided carbon (USD bn/yr)*	Discounted payback period for all benefits (years)*	Jobs created (persons)
Saudi Arabia	10.4	0.80–2.40	16.7–4.7	6.239	0.24384	4.3–1.6	12,000
UAE	2	0.38–1.13	5.9–1.8	2.397	0.08098	0.0–0.0	900
Kuwait	0.9	0.07–0.21	16.1–4.6	1.3855	0.02488	0.0–0.0	10,460
Qatar	0.3	0.09–0.27	3.6–1.2	0.7038	0.02382	0.0–0.0	3,213
Bahrain	0.6	0.04–0.13	18.1–5.0	0.34	0.01324	5.0–1.9	2,053
Oman	1.6	0.08–0.25	29.4–7.3	0.629	0.02126	11.1–3.9	12,293
GCC	**15.8**	**1.46–4.39**	**13.2–3.9**	**11.6943**	**0.40802**	**2.3–0.9**	**40,919**

* Value for avoided energy consumption assumes electricity price ranges of between USD0.05/kWh and USD0.15/kWh. A discount rate of 3% is used for estimating the discount payback periods. A carbon price of USD20/ton is considered.

Table 5.10 *Investment costs and direct and wider social benefits for building energy retrofit Level-2 programmes in GCC countries.*

	Level-2 retrofits						
	Direct benefits			Wider social benefits			
	Investment cost	Value of avoided energy consumption*	Discounted payback period for direct benefits only	Value of avoided generation capacity	Value of avoided carbon	Discounted payback period for all benefits	Jobs created
Country	(USD bn)	(USD bn/year)	(years)	(USD bn)	(USD bn/ year)	(years)	(persons)
Saudi Arabia	103.7	2.20–6.90	100–20.3	17.85	0.70102	66.1–14.0	123,000
UAE	10.7	1.08–3.26	11.9–3.51	6.8	0.26268	3.1–1.1	2,500
Kuwait	5.4	0.21–0.62	52.5–10.3	3.9916	0.0715	5.6–2.1	63,974
Qatar	1.7	0.26–0.77	7.5–2.3	2.0247	0.05048	0.0–0.0	20,290
Bahrain	3.2	0.13–0.37	49.5–10.0	0.9996	0.03806	17.6–5.9	15,856
Oman	8.8	0.24–0.71	100–15.7	1.8071	0.06554	39.9–10.6	71,817
GCC	**133.5**	**4.21–12.63**	**100–12.91**	**33.473**	**1.18928**	**27.5–8.3**	**297,437**

* Value for avoided energy consumption assume electricity price ranges of between USD0.05/kWh and USD0.15/kWh. A discount rate of 3% is used for estimating the discount payback periods. A carbon price of USD20/ton is considered.

Table 5.11 *Investment costs and direct and wider social benefits for building energy retrofit Level-3 programmes in GCC countries.*

	Level-3 retrofits						
	Direct benefits			Wider social benefits			
Country	Investment cost (USD bn)	Value of avoided energy consumption (USD bn/year)*	Discounted payback period for direct benefits only (years)	Value of avoided generation capacity (USD bn)	Value of avoided carbon (USD bn/ year)	Discounted payback period for all benefits (years)	Jobs created (persons)
Saudi Arabia	207.4	5.03–15.10	100–18.0	38.93	1.52398	49.8–12.3	247,000
UAE	21.4	2.36–7.08	10.7–3.2	14.96	0.57106	2.3–0.9	5,600
Kuwait	10.8	0.45–1.34	43.7–9.4	8.6785	0.15546	3.8–1.5	127,937
Qatar	3.4	0.56–1.67	6.9–2.1	4.403	0.10974	0.0–0.0	40,555
Bahrain	6.5	0.27–0.81	42.8–9.3	2.1726	0.08276	15.4–5.3	31,173
Oman	17.6	0.52–1.55	100–14.11	3.9287	0.14244	33.0–9.4	143,633
Total	**267.1**	**9.18–27.55**	**69.7–11. 6**	**73.0728**	**2.58544**	**23.1–7.3**	**595,898**

* Value for avoided energy consumption assumes electricity price ranges of between USD0.05/kWh and USD0.15/kWh. A discount rate of 3% is used for estimating the discount payback periods. A carbon price of USD20/ton is considered.

(Krarti, 2015; Krarti and Dubey, 2017; Krarti et al., 2017; Krarti et al., 2018; Krarti and Dubey, 2018a; Krarti and Dubey, 2018b). The payback periods using direct and all benefits from these retrofit programmes are estimated from two perspectives: (1) households and private entities using a subsidised electricity price of USD0.05/kWh; and (2) the government accounts for the actual costs of generating and distributing electricity at a rate of USD0.15/kWh. Moreover, the analyses assume that the cost of a power plant construction is USD1,700/kW, and the cost of carbon emissions is USD20/ton. Specifically, it is found that:

- Given the low electricity prices in most GCC countries, it makes little sense for households and other private organisations to invest in energy efficiency. The subsidies for energy prices need to be first reduced and ultimately eliminated for building owners and/or operators to cost-effectively invest in energy efficiency.
- When the economic benefits from avoided fuel consumption and reduced need for electricity generation capacity are considered, energy efficiency investments by the GCC governments for retrofitting existing buildings are highly cost-effective. For instance, a basic retrofit (i.e. Level-1) of all existing buildings can pay for itself in Kuwait, Qatar, and the UAE.
- Other benefits include stimulating employment in energy auditing and management and carbon mitigation. In particular, over 76 million tons of carbon emissions can be eliminated when the Level-3 retrofit programme is implemented for the existing KSA building stock. The same programme would avoid the construction of 22,900 MW in power plant capacity with an elimination of USD17.8 billion in construction costs. In addition, the Level-3 retrofit programme would create 247,000 new jobs per year over a ten-year implementation period for a total of 2.47 million job-years created.
- Innovative financing mechanisms will need to be developed to incentivise the private sector to undertake large-scale energy efficiency investments. For instance, the creation of energy service companies can be initiated by the government using the concept of performance contracting as a means of financing energy efficiency based on future savings.
- Successful implementation of any energy efficiency programme for both new and existing buildings will require the development of strong institutional and labour force capacity.

5.4.4 Impacts of Occupant Behaviour

The occupant behaviour on energy performance of buildings is well documented (Hu et al., 2020). However, the potential for occupant behaviour in GCC buildings has been the subject of limited studies (Alaidroos and Krarti, 2015; Alshahrani and

Boait, 2019). In particular, the results of analysis specific to Saudi residential buildings have indicated that space cooling energy end use can be lowered by up to 45% when occupants adjust the operation of air-conditioning systems (Alshahrani and Boait, 2019). These reductions in energy consumption are mostly due to turning off the air-conditioning systems when houses are unoccupied. However, several KSA housing units are occupied throughout the day limiting the option of turning off all air-conditioning units. Indeed, extended Saudi families with over seven members often live together within the same residential building. Other studies have shown that increasing the cooling set point by 1°C or 2°C can achieve a substantial reduction in energy use (Alaidroos and Krarti, 2015; Krarti, 2018b; Alshahrani and Boait, 2019). While the recommended cooling set point in KSA for maintaining indoor thermal comfort is 23–25°C (SEEC, 2022), most buildings are air-conditioned at lower temperatures as low as 18°C especially in housing units (Alshahrani and Boait, 2019). A more detailed evaluation of the impacts of indoor temperatures by occupants as well as the use of smart thermostats has been reported for the entire Saudi housing stocks (Krarti, 2018b). The study has indicated that occupant adjustments of the indoor temperature settings can have significant impacts on total energy consumption and electrical peak demand of Saudi residential buildings (Krarti, 2018b). Specifically, the analysis results have shown that when the indoor temperatures are setback during winter seasons, space heating needs require higher electrical power draws initially to bring low indoor temperatures to desirable and comfortable levels. Similarly, when indoor temperatures are set up for unoccupied spaces and/or periods during cooling seasons can cause indoor thermal discomfort during the initial hours of resetting the temperatures to desirable levels. Table 5.12 summarises the analysis results associated with various occupancy-based temperature control strategies evaluated in this study in terms of both energy efficiency and demand response performance for housing units located in three KSA cities (Krarti, 2018b). As noted in the table, the adjustments of indoor temperature settings during unoccupied periods such as set-up for cooling and set-back of heating save significant annual energy use for all Saudi locations. However, the same adjustments can result in high peak demand, especially for mild climates of Abha and Tabuk as highlighted by the grey colour in Table 5.12.

Using a bottom-up analysis approach to consider the make-up of existing Saudi residential building stocks (Krarti et al., 2019), the potential impacts on annual energy consumption, carbon emissions, and electrical peak demand for all Saudi regions and housing types have been estimated for a wide range of occupant temperature settings as well as the use of smart thermostats as summarised in Table 5.13. The indoor temperature settings range from simply increasing the cooling set point by 1°C and 2°C, to the use of temperature setup/setback settings (with a 4°C step or simply by shutting off the cooling

Table 5.12 *Impacts of temperature control strategies on annual energy consumption and peak demand of a prototypical villa in three KSA cities.*

Control strategy	Riyadh		Tabuk		Abha	
	Annual energy use	Peak demand	Annual energy use	Peak demand	Annual energy use	Peak demand
Baseline T_{cool}=24°C, T_{heat}=20°C	138.3 kWh	44.0 kW	112.4 kWh	37.2 kW	57.2 kWh	24.9 kW
Uniform temperature settings						
Cooling temperature	%	%	%	%	%	%
T_{cool}=25°C	5.3	3.1	6.0	2.2	7.7	0.0
T_{cool}=26°C	10.6	6.3	11.1	2.2	14.3	0.0
Heating temperature						
T_{heat}=19°C	2.3	0.0	5.7	0.3	9.2	12.6
T_{heat}=18°C	4.1	0.0	10.0	0.3	16.9	19.6
Limited-use spaces settings						
T_{cool}=26°C, T_{heat}=18°C	0.4	0.0	6.6	0.0	7.9	8.4
T_{cool}=28°C, T_{heat}=16°C	4.2	2.5	11.0	2.9	11.0	17.3
T_{cool}=30°C, T_{heat}=14°C	7.3	5.4	13.7	6.1	11.9	20.0
Unconditioned	12.6	18.8	16.2	18.5	12.0	20.0
Setup/setback settings						
T_{setup}=26°C, $T_{setback}$=18°C	6.4	3.5	9.7	−12.5	12.0	−10.2
T_{setup}=28°C, $T_{setback}$=16°C	11.7	7.3	16.7	−23.4	16.2	−26.8
T_{setup}=30°C, $T_{setback}$=14°C	16.6	7.1	19.9	−31.3	18.1	−27.2

Table 5.12 (*cont.*)

	Riyadh		Tabuk		Abha	
Control strategy	Annual energy use	Peak demand	Annual energy use	Peak demand	Annual energy use	Peak demand
Baseline T_{cool}=24°C, T_{heat}=20°C	138.3 kWh	44.0 kW	112.4 kWh	37.2 kW	57.2 kWh	24.9 kW
Off during unoccupied periods	25.6	12.2	24.7	−31.3	18.7	−27.2
Combined schedules						
T_{setup}=T_{cool} =26°C, $T_{setback}$=T_{heat}=18°C	9.1	4.4	12.9	−2.2	17.3	1.2
T_{setup}=T_{cool}=28°C, $T_{setback}$=T_{heat}=16°C	16.4	9.4	22.9	−8.2	24.2	−8.0
T_{setup}=T_{cool}=30°C, $T_{setback}$=T_{heat}=14°C	23.5	14.6	28.7	0.9	26.8	2.2
Unconditioned for limited-use spaces and system off for unoccupied periods	38.7	34.7	36.4	2.2	27.6	2.7

Table 5.13 *Reduction levels of annual energy consumption, carbon emissions, and peak demand of various temperature controls strategies when applied to the entire KSA housing stock.*

Temperature settings	Annual savings in electricity consumption (TWh/year)	Annual reduction in CO_2 emissions (million tons/year)	Electrical peak demand reduction (GW)
Increase cooling set point by 1°C (from 24°C to 25°C)	7.377	5.267	0.963
Increase cooling set point by 2°C (from 24°C to 26°C)	14.476	10.336	1.910
Setup/setback by 4°C for unoccupied rooms and periods	16.548	11.815	2.159
Shut off heating and cooling equipment for unoccupied rooms and periods	32.184	22.979	3.609
Use smart thermostats to optimise indoor temperature settings	48.247	34.448	10.385

and heating systems) and then to the installation of smart thermostats that able to detect when spaces are occupied. When installed for the entire KSA housing stock, smart thermostats have the potential to reduce annual electricity consumption by 48 TWh/year, that is, over 30% of the 2018 residential sector electricity consumption (Krarti, 2018b).

Moreover, when the indoor temperature settings match both spatial and temporal occupancy patterns of Saudi households can achieve up to 34 tons/year reduction in CO_2 emissions as indicated in Table 5.13. While some temperature setup/setback settings can increase electrical peak demand, all other indoor temperature adjustments have demand reduction benefits as noted in the table. Specifically, electrical peak demand could be 10 GW lower when smart thermostats are implemented for the entire existing Saudi housing stock. The reduced peak demand would result in operating more efficiently the existing power plants and ultimately lead to the reduction and even the elimination of constructing new power plants to meet future KSA electricity needs (Krarti, 2018b).

5.4.5 Carbon-Neutral Designs

Stricter than designing and retrofitting buildings to be net zero energy, the current trend is to achieve carbon-neutral communities and economies. Instead of designing individual buildings to be net zero energy, it is more effective to establish carbon-neutral communities through the deployment of both energy efficiency and renewable energy technologies. Most GCC countries have plans to generate electricity using renewable resources (i.e. solar and wind) to lower their carbon emissions. For instance, Saudi Arabia has a plan to deploy 60 GW of clean power sources to achieve a goal set for 2030 that 30% of the power mix is to be supplied by renewables (Amran et al., 2020). This goal would assist KSA in meeting the commitment to reducing its carbon emissions by 130 million tons in 2030 (Thomas, 2020). The design of carbon-neutral buildings is generally stricter and requires more investments than achieving net zero energy status (Krarti, 2018c). However, experiences documented in several countries have indicated that designing carbon-neutral communities instead of individual buildings can be more effective and impactful (Romero-Rubio et al., 2017, Lowitzsch et al., 2020).

For the GCC region, there are limited well-documented case studies and reported feasibility analyses for carbon-neutral communities and urban centres. Indeed, most of the reported studies involve the evaluation of the cost benefits of deployment of either standalone or grid-connected hybrid power generation systems involving several resources including fossil-fuel-powered generators and renewable systems such as wind turbines and PV systems (Alaidroos et al., 2012; Ramli et al., 2017; Rezk et al., 2020). A recent study provided some guidelines on designing carbon-neutral residential communities in Saudi Arabia using combinations of energy efficiency and renewable energy systems (Krarti and Aldubyan, 2021). Specifically, the study considered grid-connected communities of 100 housing units made up of 60 villas and 40 apartments that include both PV systems and wind turbines to generate sufficient electricity to ensure carbon-neutral operation as depicted in Figure 5.8.

A cost-benefit design analysis is carried out to minimise the life-cycle costs to deploy both energy efficiency as well as PV systems with inverters and wind

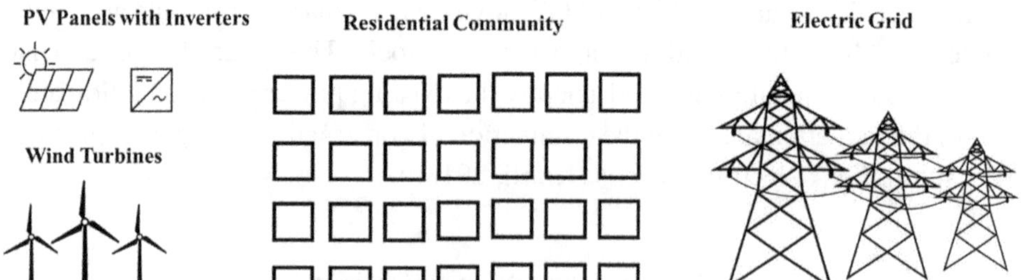

Figure 5.8 Basic components of grid-connected carbon-neutral residential community.

Table 5.14 *Capacities of renewable power systems and LCOE values for baseline and EE communities to achieve carbon neutrality designs.*

Location	Community type	PV size (kW)	Inverter size (kW)	Wind turbine capacity (kW)	LCOE (USD/ kWh)	Renewable fraction (-)
Riyadh	Baseline	3000	1800	0	0.163	0.70
	Energy efficient	2000	1600	0	0.133	0.67
Jeddah	Baseline	3000	1800	2500	0.142	0.69
	Energy efficient	1600	1000	1000	0.138	0.70
Dhahran	Baseline	3000	1600	2500	0.136	0.71
	Energy efficient	1700	1700	1000	0.133	0.71
Abha	Baseline	2500	1000	1000	0.160	0.77
	Energy efficient	850	600	500	0.135	0.72

turbines. The cost-effectiveness of hybrid renewable power systems is typically evaluated using their Levelised Cost of Energy (LCOE) values expressing the price (in USD/kWh) of the power they produce over their lifecycle period. Figure 5.9 illustrates the LCOE variations with the percent carbon reduction relative to grid-only option for several capacity combinations of PV systems and wind turbines represented by the solid dots. The lower solid lines in the figure show the Pareto paths of PV-wind design combinations that provide the minimum LCOE values for any desired reduction of carbon emissions. As noted for all the locations and both baseline and Energy Efficient (EE) communities, the LCOE values increase with higher reductions in carbon emissions due to the inclusion of larger capacities of PV systems and wind turbines in generating on-site electricity. A carbon-neutral community design is achieved when the reduction in carbon emissions reaches 100%. Table 5.14 summarises the capacities of renewable energy systems as well as LCOE values to achieve the carbon neutrality status for both baseline and EE communities. As expected, smaller capacities of the PV and wind systems are needed to reach carbon neutrality for the EE communities compared to the baseline communities for all Saudi sites considered in this study. Indeed, the EE communities have less electricity demand from the grid and thus induce less carbon emissions. Table 5.14 indicates that the LCOE values required to reach the carbon neutrality status are consistently lower for the EE communities than those needed for the baseline communities (Krarti and Aldubyan, 2021).

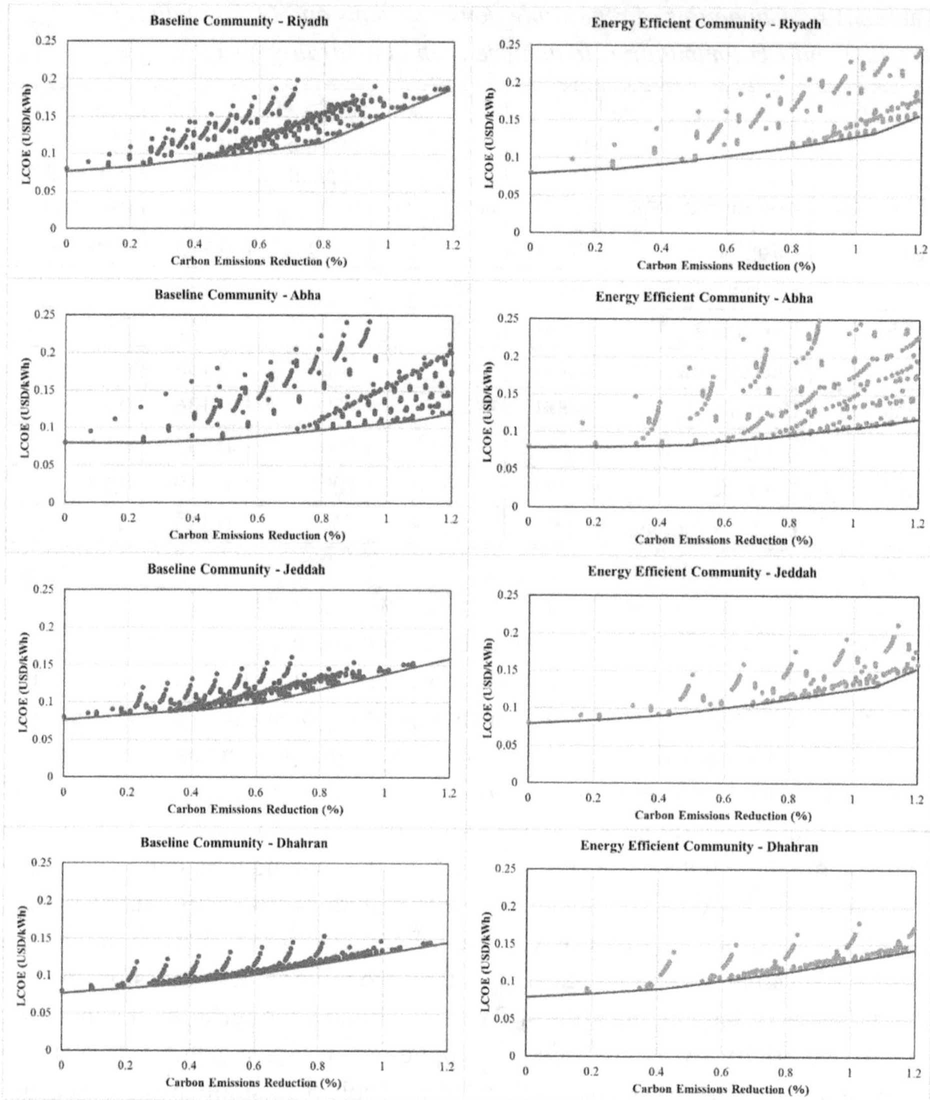

Figure 5.9 Optimal paths for carbon neutral design for baseline and EE communities in Riyadh, Abha, Jeddah, and Dhahran.

5.5 Summary

In this chapter, past and current energy consumption trends in the building sector are first analysed for the GCC region and countries. While the building sector contributes only 15% of the total final energy consumed in the GCC region, it has the highest growth rate during the last decade with the energy used by households having tripled between 2000 and 2015. One of the main challenges facing the GCC economies is to curb energy waste and improve the energy efficiency especially for the building sector. Indeed, energy efficiency will provide several benefits to the region including but not limited to reducing energy expenditures, lowering carbon emissions, and improving economic competitiveness. For the GCC countries, energy efficiency is a tool to reduce consumption of a significant part of national oil resources to generate additional income that could be utilised for improving economic productivity through diversification and investments in other sectors.

As presented in the chapter, one of the main factors aiding in the inefficient use of energy in the GCC region is the occurrence of rather high subsidies resulting in artificially low prices for electricity and fuels to the end users. While the subsidies were initially adopted in several GCC countries to share the wealth and assist the needy, they have some undesirable consequences, including: (1) an increase in social inequities since wealthy citizens benefit the most; (2) inefficient use of energy; and (3) a decrease in the cost benefits of investments in energy efficiency and renewable energy technologies.

This chapter summarises reported analyses for the benefits of the large-scale implementation of energy efficiency programmes for the building sector in all GCC countries. The analyses include strategies to improve the energy performance of both new and existing building stocks. The overview of current energy policies related to buildings has indicated that most GCC countries have only recently adopted either minimum energy performance standards (MEPS) for air conditioners, lighting fixtures, and appliances. Moreover, most GCC countries have adopted energy efficiency codes for new buildings. However, these energy efficiency codes are typically limited to prescriptive requirements and consist of thermal insulation addition to walls and roofs and use of double-pane glazing for windows. The enforcement of MEPS and building energy efficiency codes still pause challenges for the GCC region.

5.6 Conclusion

The results of the analysis presented in this chapter clearly indicate that there is a significant potential to improve the energy performance of buildings throughout the GCC region using proven energy efficiency measures and adequate energy policies. Specifically, implementing MEPS for energy intensive equipment in buildings (i.e. lighting, appliances, and air conditioners) is a good first step to take since it allows a reduction of about 20 TWh in annual electricity consumption. Moreover, the adoption and the implementation of an integrated and comprehensive energy efficiency code for both residential and commercial buildings can result in an additional reduction of 108 TWh/year in final energy consumption for the GCC region. Even higher savings of 198 TWh annually can be reduced when net zero energy designs are required for all new buildings. However, the analysis has clearly indicated that the most significant potential to save energy lies in retrofitting existing building stock. Indeed, even with a basic retrofit programme with no significant capital investments, about 85 TWh/year can be saved throughout the Arab region by 2030. A more aggressive retrofit programme can save up to 470 TWh or a third of the building sector's final energy consumption per year after 2030. Combining comprehensive energy efficiency codes for new buildings and extensive retrofit programmes for existing buildings would reduce the total final energy consumption of the building sector in the GCC region by 600 TWh by 2030. In addition, these programmes can create significant high-skilled jobs, avoid the need of additional future power plants, and substantially reduce carbon emissions. These energy efficiency programmes could be more effective when deployed in large communities rather than implemented for individual buildings.

References

Al Safat (2020). *Dubai Green Building System.* Abu Dhabi: Government of Dubai and Dubai Municipality. Available online: www.dm.gov.ae/wp-content/uploads/2020/11/Safat-English.pdf (accessed 4 April 2023).

Al-Homoud, M. S., and Krarti, M. (2021). Energy efficiency of residential buildings in the Kingdom of Saudi Arabia: review of status and future roadmap. *Journal of Building Engineering* 36, pp. 102143.

Alaidroos, A., and Krarti, M. (2015). Optimal design of residential building envelope systems in the Kingdom of Saudi Arabia. *Energy and Buildings* 86, pp. 104–117.

Alaidroos, A., He, L., and Krarti, M. (2012). Feasibility of renewable energy based distributed generation in Yanbu, Saudi Arabia. Proceedings for World Renewable Energy Forum, May, Denver, CO.

Alshahrani, J., and Boait, P. (2019). Reducing high energy demand associated with Air-Conditioning needs in Saudi Arabia. *Energies* 12, Article 87.

American Society of Heating, Refrigerating, and Air Conditioning Engineers (ASHRAE) (2018). *Standard 90.1, Energy Standard for Sites and Buildings Except Low-Rise Residential Buildings.* Atlanta, GA: American Society of Heating, Refrigerating, and Air Conditioning Engineers.

Amran, Y. H. A., Amran, Y. H. M., Alyousef, R., and Alabduljabbar, H. (2020). Renewable and sustainable energy production in Saudi Arabia according to Saudi Vision 2030: Current status and future prospects. *Journal of Cleaner Production* 247, Article 119602.

Ashraf, F., Park, B., and Krarti, M. (2020). Analysis of optimal energy performance for commercial buildings in the GCC region, in Bumajdad, A., Bouhamra, W., Alsayegh, O., Kamal, H., and Alhajraf, S. (eds.), *Gulf Conference on Sustainable Built Environment.* Cham: Springer. Doi.org/10.1007/978-3-030-39734-0_20.

Asif, M. (2016). Growth and sustainability trends in the buildings sector in the GCC region with particular reference to the KSA and UAE. *Renewable and Sustainable Energy Reviews* 55, pp. 1267–1273.

Dehwah, A. H., and Krarti, M. (2019). Optimal hybrid power Energy systems for residential communities in Saudi Arabia. *Journal of Solar Energy Engineering* 141 (6), Article 061002, pp. 1–10.

GAStat (2023). *Housing Survey Data*. General Authority for Statistics. Riyadh: Kingdom of Saudi Arabia. Available online: www.stats.gov.sa. (accessed 20 January 2023).

Gulf Organisation for Research and Development (GORD) (2010). *Qatar Sustainability Assessment System (QSAS)*. Doha: Gulf Organisation for Research and Development.

Hu, S., Yan, D., Azar, E., and Guo, F. (2020). A systematic review of occupant behavior in building energy policy. *Building and Environment* 175, Article 106807.

International Energy Agency (IEA) (2023). *IEA Statistics: World Energy Balances*. Paris: International Energy Agency. Available online: www.iea.org/statistics (accessed 15 February 2023).

Krarti, M. (2015). Evaluation of large-scale building energy efficiency retrofit program in Kuwait. *Renewable and Sustainable Energy Reviews* 50, pp. 1069–1080.

Krarti, M. (2018a). *Addressing Energy Sustainability Issues in the Buildings Sector in the Arab Region*. Report for United Nations Economic and Social Commission for Western Asia (ESCWA), Report No. E/ESCWA/SDPD/2018/TP.5, Beirut. Available online: www.unescwa.org/sites/default/files/pubs/pdf/addressing-energy-sustainability-issues-buildings-sectori-arab-region-english_0.pdf (accessed 15 January 2022).

Krarti, M. (2018b). Evaluation of occupancy-based temperature controls on energy performance of KSA residential buildings. *Energy and Buildings* 220, p. 110047.

Krarti, M. (2018c). *Optimal Design and Retrofit of Energy Efficient Buildings, Communities, and Urban Centers*. Oxford: Butterworth-Heinemann, Elsevier.

Krarti, M. (2019). Evaluation of energy efficiency potential for the building sector in the Arab region. *Energies* 12 (22), Article 4279.

Krarti, M., and Aldubyan, M. (2021). Role of energy efficiency and distributed renewable energy in designing carbon neutral residential buildings and communities: case study of Saudi Arabia. *Energy and Buildings* 250, Article 111309.

Krarti, M., and Dubey, K. (2017). Energy productivity evaluation of large-scale building energy efficiency programs for Oman. *Sustainable Cities and Society* 39, pp. 12–22.

Krarti, M., and Dubey, K. (2018a). Evaluation of high performance of residential buildings in Bahrain. *Journal of Building Engineering* 18, pp. 40–50.

Krarti, M., and Dubey, K. (2018b). Review analysis of economic and environmental benefits of improving energy efficiency for UAE building stock. *Renewable and Sustainable Energy Reviews* 82 (1), pp. 14–24.

Krarti, M., Ali, F., Alaidroos, A., and Houchati, M. (2018). Macro-economic benefit analysis of large-scale building energy efficiency programs in Qatar. *International Journal of Sustainable Built Environment*. Doi.org/10.1016/j.ijsbe.2017.12.006.

Krarti, M., Dubey, K., and Howarth, N. (2017). Evaluation of building energy efficiency investment options for the Kingdom of Saudi Arabia. *Energy* 134, pp. 595–610.

Krarti, M., Dubey, K., and Howarth, N. (2019). Energy productivity analysis framework for buildings: a case study of GCC region. *Energy* 167, pp. 1251–1265.

Krarti, M., Aldubyan, M., and Williams, E. (2020). Residential building stock model for evaluating energy retrofit programs in Saudi Arabia. *Energy* 195, Article 116980.

Lowitzsch, J., Hoick, C. E., and van Tuldera, F. J. (2020). Renewable energy communities under the 2019 European Clean Energy Package – Governance model for the energy clusters of the future? *Renewable and Sustainable Energy Reviews* 122, Article 109489.

Pearl Building Rating System (PBRS) (2022). *Pearl Building Rating System (PBRS)*. Abu Dhabi: Department of Municipalities and Transport. Available online: https://pages.dmt.gov.ae/en/Urban-Planning/Pearl-Building-Rating-System (accessed 15 December 2022).

Ramli, M. A. M., Sennoga, T., and Alghamdi, A. U. (2017). Energy production potential and economic viability of grid-connected wind/PV systems at Saudi Arabian Coastal Areas. *Journal of Renewable and Sustainable Energy* 9 (6), Article 65910.

Rezk, H., Kanagaraj, N., and Al-Dhaifallah, M. (2020). Design and sensitivity analysis of hybrid photovoltaic-fuel-cell-battery system to supply a small community at Saudi NEOM City. *Sustainability* 12 (3341), pp. 1–20.

Regulatory-Indicators-for-Sustainable-Energy (RISE) (2016). *Regulatory-Indicators-for-Sustainable-Energy (RISE)*. Report. Washington, DC: World Bank. Available online: http://documents.worldbank.org/curated/en/538181487106403375/pdf/112828-REVISED-PUBLIC-RISE-2016-Report.pdf. (accessed 15 January 2022).

Romero-Rubio, C., Ramónde, J., and Díaz, A. (2017). Sustainable energy communities: A study contrasting Spain and Germany. *Energy Policy* 85, pp. 397–409.

SASO (2012). Saudi Arabia Standards Organization, Energy Labelling and Minimum Energy Performance Requirements for Air-Conditioners. Standard No. 3459, Saudi Arabia.

SASO (2013). Saudi Arabia Standards Organization, Energy Labelling Requirements of Household Electrical Clothes Washing Machines. 2013. Standard No. 3569, Saudi Arabia.

SASO (2014). Saudi Arabia Standards Organization, Energy Performance Capacity and Labelling of Household Refrigerators, Refrigerator-Freezers, and Freezers. 2014. Standard No. 3620, Saudi Arabia.

SASO (2017). Saudi Arabia Standards Organization, Energy Labelling and Minimum Energy Performance Requirements for Dryers. Standard No. 2883, Saudi Arabia.

SASO (2018a). Saudi Arabia Standards Organization, Energy Labelling and Minimum Energy Performance Requirements for Air-Conditioners. Standard No. 2663, Saudi Arabia.

SASO (2018b). Saudi Arabia Standards Organization, Energy Labelling and Minimum Energy Performance Requirements for Washing Machines. Standard No. 2885, Saudi Arabia.

SASO (2018c). Saudi Arabia Standards Organization, Energy Labelling and Minimum Energy Performance Requirements for Refrigerators and Freezers. Standard No. 2892, Saudi Arabia.

SEEC (2022). *Buildings, Overview by Saudi Energy Efficiency Center*. Available online: www.seec.gov.sa/en/blog/buildings (accessed 26 December 2022).

Sharifi, A., and Murayama, A. (2013). A critical review of seven selected neighborhood sustainability assessment tools. *Environmental Impact Assessment Review* 38, pp. 73–87.

Thomas, G. (2020). *Energy Transition: Delivering Net Zero Carbon in Saudi*. Sustainable Finance, HSBC Bank Middle East. Available online: www.sustainablefinance.hsbc.com/carbon-transition/energy-transition-delivering-net-zero-carbon-in-saudi (accessed 26 December 2022).

U4E (2017). *United for Energy Efficiency, Country Assessments*. Available online: http://united4efficiency.org (accessed 26 December 2022).

World Bank (2023). *World Development Data*. Washington, DC: World Bank. Available online: http://databank.worldbank.org/data/home.aspx (accessed 27 February 2023).

6

Electrifying Public Transport Networks in Dubai

Environmental Benefits, Urban Improvements, and Social Challenges

GIOVANNA POTESTÀ AND MARIO TARTAGLIA

6.1 Introduction

The plan set up by United Arab Emirates (UAE Net Zero, 2024) to make public transport CO_2 free by 2050, is part of the initiatives promoted by the UN Climate Change Conference (COP26) in Glasgow. Although the UAE is not obliged to implement the greenhouse gases (GHG) reduction plan, they have accepted the commitment as a stimulus for diversification of production and development aiming at further economic growth. The government agenda of the UAE committed to the containment of harmful CO_2 emissions a long time ago, obtaining results that are significant in the context. Data from 1990 to 2010, a period when the decarbonisation policy was less aggressive and the population constantly growing, show in fact that the load of emissions decreased from 32.6 tons per year per individual to 21.9 tons (UAE Net Zero, 2024). Although essential for the planet, ecological sustainability alone does not represent an improvement if it does not come along with the other aspects of sustainability, namely economic and social sustainability. Considering the implication of a containment policy of CO_2 in the field of public urban transit and relating the technological improvements to the urban and social assets of UAE, the chapter offers a picture of possible challenges and benefits based on the experience that Europe has matured in the same sector. The foreseen picture considers and discusses differences emerging between Europe and UAE in terms of resources, available technology, impact on the built environment, and consequences for citizens and residents. The decarbonisation of public transport targets the reduction of greenhouse effects, whose presence is dangerous to human existence. Temperature rises is a worldwide experience, documented over several decades and confirmed by data of recent years. This phenomenon might be particularly worrying in hot climate regions like the Arab Gulf and specifically the UAE. Considering that, the cities of the Gulf, unlike European cities that grow in a denser form and at a slower pace, tend to occupy a larger portion of land, the provision of CO_2-free public transport is a priority for the safeguarding of people's well-being. Alternative energy sources have already been tested in the past years in Europe and in this sense, provisional experiences matured so far can help UAE and the other countries in the Gulf, to minimise dead ends in technological developments. An overview of the state of the arts in the field of decarbonisation vehicles, particularly in the field of public transit, introduces the European experience. The latter does not constitute a paradigmatic lesson but only a possibility of further knowledge and experience comparison. Factors to consider are in any case the geographical conditions, the climate, the structure of the city, and the availability of alternative energy sources. All of these aspects will be reviewed and critically analysed. The last factor to consider is that the research process is always dynamic and whatever is the most suitable goal in a limited time frame, might not be the best goal to consider in the short run. This implication is particularly poignant in the case of green hydrogen, whose potential benefits are currently in the limelight but whose real feasibility in terms of sustainable production is yet to be realised.

6.2 The Decarbonisation of Public Transport and Its Implications

6.2.1 Need for Action

The decarbonisation of public transport originates from the concept that CO_2 emissions are a pernicious agent for the environment and consequently for human well-being. Although CO_2 emissions are by themselves not dangerous for human health, their growth along with other gases creates a denser layer of greenhouse effects. The layer of gases can be penetrated by the sun's rays from the atmosphere to the earth's surface, but the same rays are trapped when bouncing back to the atmosphere. The consequence is an increase in temperature and the creation of an environment that is no longer suitable for human well-being. GHG emissions are produced by several human and non-human actions. Among human actions, transport contributes to a part of the total GHG emissions. Therefore, the decarbonisation of transport represents a contribution to the reduction of the greenhouse effect and consequently to temperature rises on earth. The containment of temperature rise is particularly important in hot climatic regions like the UAE. Among the GHG emissions, CO_2 is particularly determinant for its contribution to the creation of the greenhouse effect, although its chemical nature does not make it poisonous to human life.

Decarbonisation, beneficial for human presence on the planet, is challenged, however, by increased anthropogenic activity recorded in the last decades. The 2022 report of the Intergovernmental Panel on Climate Change (IPCC) confirms that global GHG emissions produced by anthropogenic activities not only did not stop increasing worldwide but that GHG emissions related to CO_2 from fossil fuel combustion and industrial processing are also rising. Transport vehicles moving on the earth's surface, and therefore not considering air traffic, can be privately or publicly managed. Car producers are investing in new technologies using alternative energy sources, but the production process and the utilisation of vehicles cannot keep apace as may be forecast in the public sector. For this reason, countries around the world are experimenting with the potential of new energies and the advantages of decarbonisation in public transport. The success of the operation is tied to technological research and the commercial feasibility of public transport projects, but it also depends on people's behaviour and their attitudes toward moving and the use of public transport. Not least the form of the built environment, the location of activities, and the behaviour of people can contribute towards the further success of public transport decarbonisation.

6.2.2 Alternative Energy Sources

The field of action to reduce CO_2 emissions is potentially vast and solutions, not yet commercialised, will be available in the future. Many studies and technological innovations are in the testing phase and it is not currently possible to define their hypothetical application. Transport and construction are the sectors in which it is more difficult to hypothesise a substantial reduction in CO_2 emissions, especially as a result of the ever-increasing demand from emerging markets. The acceleration towards the electrification of road vehicles in public transport, especially in short-term journeys, represents the greatest contribution to reducing emissions, although other solutions that include the use of hydrogen and natural gas are not completely set aside.

The electrification of transport involves the use of charged batteries supplying energy to the engine. Batteries will be charged by a power plant, which, in turn, can be powered by fossil fuels or non-traditional sources. In the first case, if the power plant is powered by traditional fossil fuels, the use of batteries for the vehicles will be mostly irrelevant, while in the second case, if the power plant is powered by alternative energy sources (solar, wind, geothermal, hydroelectric, etc.), CO_2 emissions can be highly contained. A different kind of energy, able to offer benefits concerning the containment of CO_2 reduction, is hydrogen. Hydrogen-fuelled vehicles, however, depend on the type of hydrogen used as a fuel, the adduction system of hydrogen, and the nature of hydrogen production plants (IEA, 2021).

The pledge towards CO_2 containment and GHG containment in general will be successful if GHG gases are not generated in all phases of the energy production process, including management, storage, and end-of-life. CO_2 emissions in electric vehicles and hydrogen vehicles also depend on the carbon intensity of power generation, for example the emissions from the construction and decommissioning of power plants and upstream emissions. IPCC (2022) specifies that a power generation plant modulated on low-carbon intensity should produce batteries with lower power and therefore have the engine performing more moderately (Sims, 2014). Environmental mitigation and containment of emissions are complex aspects of a productive circle that needs to be optimised throughout the entire phased sequence. Also, economic and social aspects cannot be considered in environmental mitigation.

6.2.3 Electrification and Its Limitations

With all the considerations mentioned above, electrification is the most promising strategy to achieve a considerable CO_2 reduction and satisfy energy efficiency in the public urban transport sector. Although not yet comparable to the traditional engines in terms of the entire management and performance, the effect on the containment of GHG is amply tested (IEA, 2021). Specifying that the effects on the environment will be relevant in countries where power parks are alimented by clean sources, transitioning from power plants alimented by oil or coal to power plants alimented by clean energy sources is expensive. In developing economies, most of the energy is still produced by coal plants and even in the years to come no major changes are expected, while in developed countries the use of coal, which is already significantly lower, will further decrease (IEA, 2021). On the other hand, the Stated Policies Scenario (STEP) estimates that the world demand for energy will grow by 30%, and in the next few years up to 2050, the biggest change in terms of energy use will be in the field of electricity (IEA, 2021). The Announced Pledge Case (APC) developed by the International Energy Agency (IEA) has formulated that over the next thirty years, electricity consumption will double the current, with more than half of the electricity being produced through the use of renewable energy such as solar panels, wind turbines, and hydropower (IEA, 2021). In this scenario, the final effect will be a consistent reduction of temperature due to GHG emissions but an overall rise of final temperature due to the heat highlands generated by a higher production of energy.

In reference to the problem of the use of electrified public urban transport it will be possible to contain CO_2 emissions and therefore contribute to a lower increase in temperature due to GHG emissions, but the augmented demand for transport vehicles induced by a growing population will not avoid heat islands and heat generation.

A downside of the different characteristics inherent in the electrification of public transport concerns the efficiency of the vehicle engines. The efficiency of a road vehicle powered by electric sources is comparable to a traditional one only in optimal conditions because its performance can be limited by factors such as excessive distance, orography of the road, frequency of availability of infrastructure for recharging the batteries, type of electrical grid, and the number of stops on the bus route (Carrilero et al., 2018). Also, the cost of energy, usually determined by national fares, impacts the use of electric vehicles, resulting in a trigger effect or producing an obstacle in the transition process. In terms of manufacturing then, the cost of batteries must be taken into account in the production of electric vehicles, which can be considered an extra cost in the production of a vehicle. Western production plants of engines were developed in the past century without considering the production of batteries. Nowadays, they are mostly manufactured in Eastern countries, where global market conditions made it more favourable to build plants. It cannot be set aside that China has almost the entire control of minerals necessary for the production of batteries. Consideration must also be given in the production of batteries to the wearing-down and dismantlement of the batteries during their life cycle (Carrilero et al., 2018).

One more deterrent to the wide electrification of vehicles is the need for frequent recharging stations. Public urban transport is one of the sectors that can better obviate the problem due to the nature of the trips, which are usually quite limited, and the fact that buses can be stored and frequently charged. Ongoing costs of batteries during their life cycle include their production, operation, and reuse or dismantlement. If one of these is not well conducted, the consequences, such as occasional fires and the dispersion of toxic substances, can be dangerous to life and the environment. Once discarded, batteries can pollute water basins and water faults through the process of acidification and eutrophication or may lead to air pollution through a photochemical process, inhibiting the growth of living organisms. Damaged batteries are also toxic to the huma nervous system and endocrine systems. By 2025, in the absence of efficient strategies for battery dismantlement in world economies, 11 million tons of lithium-ion waste will have accumulated with subsequent noxious effects.

Recycling is the first step for the correct minimisation of the risk. This is then followed by improved technologies able to provide the correct separation of the raw materials. Lithium-ion batteries can also be replaced by sodium-ion batteries, whose technology, however, is still improving. In any case, whatever the selected clean energy source, the transition implies costs, especially for the infrastructures that are demanded to make the new energy system operational. The cost of infrastructure can be supported by public or private stakeholders who have access to financial capital. In this sense, the cost of capital is a determinant in the success of the investment, avoiding potential risks due to an underestimation of the costs (IEA, 2021). In addition to the costs inherent to the transition from oil-dependent technology to electrification, other costs are include those determined by unforeseen geopolitical situations. Presently, the war in Ukraine is affecting gas imports from Russia. The shortage of gas may accelerate the transition to renewable energy but on the other hand, at least for the short term, the recourse to the restoration of fossil fuel sources currently in disuse will increase the percentage of GHG emissions, while in the meantime Russia and its satellite countries, which are taking progressively distancing steps from UN agreements, will continue using fossil fuels (Tollerson, 2022).

6.2.4 Decarbonisation, People's Behaviour, and Form of the City

People's behaviour and the form of built environment play a significant role in the amount of GHG emissions produced. Wherever a user's preference is for public transport, this contributes towards the containment of GHG emissions, and specifically CO_2 emissions, while short journeys or preference accorded to walking distances will increase the decarbonisation of the environment. In a city with a densely built area, a high density of population, and plentiful job opportunities, GHG emissions will be lower than in spread-out built-up areas (Masnavi, 2000). If additionally, an urban area presents a mix of uses and occasions, residents most likely will have fewer reasons to move to different areas, contributing to the minor impact of emissions. People's behaviour is influenced by the cultural and social environment, but in any context, the availability of public transport is a strong incentive to minimise the use of private vehicles. Consequently, public administrations and stakeholders will be more incentivised to provide public transport when the dimension of the urban environment consents to the highest possible number of users to reach the largest possible number of destinations. While in a sprawling city, the effort of providing integrated public transport will be extremely difficult in terms of infrastructure networking and economic costs, in a compact city, with limited sections of unbuilt space, the costs and provision of infrastructural support are manageable. To achieve a sustainable environment capable of supporting an adequate distribution of functions, and avoiding the risk of overcrowding, urban density should be contained to tall buildings that are not towering. A denser city shortens the travel distance of residents, acting positively on the perception of citizens, the emissions released into the environment and on the amount of energy consumed.

6.3 Public Transport in Europe

6.3.1 Strategies towards Decarbonisation

If substituting the use of private vehicles with the use of public transport to reach the same destination favours the reduction of GHG emissions, then the use of energy that is not provided by the combustion of fossil fuels is a step forward in the reduction of temperature caused by GHG emissions.

In Europe, the use of public transport is amply diffused and socially well accepted. The compactness of European cities has favoured the optimisation of public transport networks, making public transport preferable to private vehicles. Urban public transport in European cities is responsible for 10% of GHG emissions (Carrilero et al., 2018), while transport in general is responsible for about a quarter of GHG emissions. In 2011, the rising danger of GHG emissions set off alarm signals that caused the European Commission to take stringent measures, leading to the release of a white paper listing a roadmap of forty concrete initiatives aimed at creating a competitive transport system. The roadmap envisioned the extension of mobility, removal of obstacles, and growth of job opportunities.

Along with technological innovations, the containment of emissions requires a change in people's behaviour. The progress of European cities in achieving the decarbonisation of public transport is measured through a system of fifteen indicators, including affordability, safety, and accessibility for the fragile sectors of the population (Gudmundsson et al., 2016; EC, 2017). In 2017, the European Union (EU) launched the 'European Clean Bus Deployment Initiative', whose declaration of intent includes a commitment to cities, industrial sectors, and associations to accelerate the transition to 'clean' buses (EU, 2017).

Technological research, testing, and application may change according to contexts and time. However, in any case, the containment of GHG emissions needs the collaboration of people in the responsible use of resources. Changing people's behaviour and making the use of private vehicles less attractive compared to the use of public transport are priorities that need to be considered, whatever the energy source.

6.3.2 Considerations on Hydrogen-Fuelled Urban Buses

Although the electrification of public urban transport seems to be the most efficient containment strategy, presently in the world, hydrogen technologies are still used in this sector of transport. Natural gas has several pros and cons that impact differently according to the context of the application. Even though it does not solve the problem of emission of GHG either, natural gas has the advantage of being easily addressed to the adduction systems and being able to adjust its intensity according to the momentary needs. The disadvantages are represented by the high percentage of material losses during the transfer and by the highly reduced energy power that reaches the vehicle. Only a quarter of the thermal energy produced is used as a driving force, while three-quarters are dispersed into the environment as heat. As a result, operating a hydrogen vehicle requires a greater production of electricity than that required to power an electric battery, since the efficiency of a hydrogen engine is about a third of that of a traditional engine. In Europe, natural gas is available but not extracted. Natural gas reaches Europe transported through intercontinental pipelines or liquified and then transported in tankers (Staffel et al., 2019). Once in the destination site, natural gas can be used in liquid form or re-gasified. Constructing production plants in Europe could solve the problem of costs related to the transport and storage of gas, but it would add costs that would be calculated according to national fares of electricity production, usually much higher than those of the origin countries.

Hydrogen imported needs in any case, and according to the sophistication of the process it is classified in different categories, each depending on the amount of GHG that is emitted during its production. Hydrogen exists in different forms, each with a different range of emissions. Only green hydrogen has emissions lower than the standards set up by the EU. Green hydrogen, the most sophisticated form of hydrogen, does not present climate-altering emissions, while grey hydrogen, on the other extremity of the range, is produced through the combustion of fossil fuel and is therefore highly dangerous. Blue hydrogen is presently in use and represents a compromise between the quantity of GHG emissions and production costs (Ajanovic et al., 2022).

Hydrogen buses alimented by fuel cells use hydrogen that is stored inside the vehicle and generate electricity through the combustion of hydrogen with oxygen. This process generates water and heat which are considered zero-impact carbon-dioxide emissions. The electricity produced will be only partially used as a driving force while the rest will be dispersed into the air, contributing to the heat island effect (Logan, 2020). The advantage is that hydrogen can be easily stored and produced during times when electricity demand is lower, unlike electric vehicles which need to be charged on an as-needed basis (Patyk et al., 2013; Logan, 2020).

Where the regeneration of exhausted batteries and electric engines pose problems of reuse and dismantlement, hydrogen engines are unable to adapt their characteristics to the circular economy process due to the impossibility of reusing disposed engines (Howarth, 2021; Logan, 2020) Considering also that the emissions of electric buses and hydrogen buses in the context of the capacity of use, reveal that under 25% of the capacity of use, the emissions from hydrogen buses are 31.2g CO_2 km per 1 person, while the emissions of electric buses are 15.6g CO_2 km for 1 person, and that the cost is double for a hydrogen bus, it is clear why the choice of European cities is in favour of electric urban buses (Logan, 2020).

6.3.3 Current Trends in CO_2 Reduction

While in the past some cities like Madrid, Amiens, and Geneva, had adopted public transport services with natural gas engines, now European municipalities are increasingly adopting electric buses or hybrid to decarbonise the atmosphere and reduce local pollution The Municipal Transport Company of Madrid has been using hybrid buses since 2011 and this choice seems very advantageous because the power generated by the batteries can be stored up until the power supply station is available. If the power station is not available, the bus runs on the traditional engine. Despite the convenience of the system, to further reduce the emissions of CO_2, in 2017 Madrid launched the first fully electric bus journey. The electric induction system, comprising 42 stops, is recharged during the night when the buses are not in operation. In the same year, Amiens signed a contract for the supply of forty-three articulated electric buses, each 18 metres long, while Valladolid decided to replace the hybrid buses in the historic centre with electric buses. The refills take place through a system of inverted pantographs mounted on the vehicle. In France, a 2018 agreement between Île-de-France Mobilités and RATP promoted a tender for the supply of 1,000 electric buses needed to cover two bus lines (EC, 2019).

The adoption of electric urban bus fleets in European cities accelerated in 2021 when the greatest trend in their purchase was shown by local administrations (ACEA, 2022). In fact, in 2021, the registration of new electric buses in Europe grew by 78.7% compared to the previous year, with 3,000 buses purchased. Hybrid motor buses also recorded a 10% increase in 2021 compared to the previous year, with a total of just under 3,000 vehicles (IEA, 2021), although the development of hydrogen buses is momentarily set aside by European cities. This preference depends on multiple factors, such as deeper research in the field of electrification sponsored by manufacturers and governments, problems in manufacturing and structural development, and the urban environment conditions. Referring to this last aspect, the condition of European cities, characterised by a compact urban fabric, with a good mix of activities and density of population can sustain the modest autonomy of electric batteries between two charges. The same consideration, therefore, is not applicable to long-distance trucking and air travel, in particular, will remain difficult to decarbonise even further to the required levels, despite regulatory, technological, and operational advancements and an expected slowdown in demand growth (ITF, 2021).

The current European situation, with all the differences in the case, can work as an example for accelerating the process toward decarbonisation in the UAE. The limitations and advantages presented in the case of Europe will not have the same field of application for the UAE, but models already experienced in Europe may contribute to the faster achievement of goals in public transport policy. Along with technological achievements, the containment of GHG emissions in the sector of transport needs to have incorporated into the plan a wider strategy enhancing public transport effectiveness through people behaviour shifts and different city planning models.

6.4 Expected Results in the UAE

6.4.1 Decarbonisation in the UAE: Goals and the Present Situation

The strategies used by Europe toward decarbonisation imply a pathway that is not always linear but articulated and modified during the process. Public transport, particularly public urban transport, plays a pivotal role that will somehow condition the energetic transitions of other transport modes. Despite some initial uncertainties and downfalls, Europe consolidates its role model position in the energetic transition due to the completeness of the planned goals and political and economic consistency of the actions that have been taken. For these reasons, Europe could represent a best practice example, able to inspire the transition in other countries. Granting the fact that the transition to 'clean' transport relies on central government policies, technological development, and factors such as the environment, territory, and economic and social assets, certain characteristics are common throughout different models. From this perspective, GCC countries, and specifically the UAE, focus on values and conditions proper to the context. In the UAE, the main source of energy production is now natural gas, while other sources account for less than 5% (DEWA, n.d. [2021]). In general, compared to Europe, the transition to alternative energy sources in the UAE face differentiations and probably some facilitations. The use of hydrogen, although being a technology that at the present state of research is not highly performative, counts on the availability of the gas on site. For this reason, the costs of buying, shipping, and substance transformation are minimal. In terms of infrastructural projects of the networks, the expanding form of the city, which is not sedimented yet, facilitates the construction of new portions of cities equipped with the most convenient systems of transport, attracting investment from foreign capitals. Another consideration refers to the availability of materials that diverse geopolitical configurations and diplomatic policies make easier to obtain.

Decarbonisation in UAE is a stringent goal, considering that although the impact of CO_2 emissions contributes to a small share of global emissions, the emissions per capita are high. In 2021, the yearly amount of CO_2 emissions recorded inside the UAE, not including the international transport of people and goods, was around 140 million tonnes of GHG (Ritchie et al., 2022). Internal transport impacts with a production of 80.77 million tonnes of GHG, making this activity one of the most harmful (UAE Net Zero, 2024). To achieve the decarbonisation goal by 2050, the UAE is currently investing in the production of cleaner hydrogen, trying to achieve the production of green hydrogen (UAE Net Zero, 2024).

If investments in this direction are facilitated by the availability of gas in the region, questions about the real and efficient applicability of hydrogen persist. The first question concerns chronological issues, in other words when the green hydrogen will be ready for utilisation as a fuel. Momentarily green hydrogen is still in its initial phase of production and the possibility of using it as a powering force in vehicles is lingering, to the point that many industrialised countries have lost interest in this technology. The second question concerns the valuable containment of emissions. The use of the present forms of hydrogen in public transport, even the use of blue hydrogen, so far the 'cleaner' type of gas, is highly impacted by dispersions of methane. Along with the high dispersion of methane, scientists assume that the footprint of GHG emissions from blue hydrogen is 20% higher than the footprint of GHG emissions depending on burning natural gas or coal, and 60% higher the footprint caused by burning diesel oil (Howarth et al., 2021). These data need some caution and better reviewing, since the UAE plans to use hydrogen for 50% of transport needs by 2050, while the remaining 50% will be powered by batteries (Deloitte, 2021). The forms of hydrogens considered in the plan are specifically blue and green hydrogen, whose utilisation is problematic in the case of the first one, while it is not yet available in the case of the second. The use of electricity that will not involve the use of toxic or polluting fuels, is linked to the completion of the Mohammed bin Rashid Al Maktoum solar park, which is expected to be operational by 2030 with a capacity of 5,000 MW (RTA Sustainability Report, 2021).

6.4.2 Decarbonisation and Social Implications

In its effort to extend the use of low emissions vehicles in public transport, the UAE needs to take into account the effort required or people to change their habits and behaviour. In this way, different planning strategies can be calibrated for the expansion of the city. Planning awareness needs a comprehension of a better use of resources and considerate use of land, avoiding dispersed building settlements. People moving within the city contribute to GHG emissions. Reducing dependence on cars and increasing the use of public transport represents an important change. The RTA in Dubai has adopted a strategic plan which aims to increase the use of public transport from the current 14.7% to 30% by 2030, giving priority to connectivity and the integration of traffic solutions, thereby encouraging public transport (RTA Sustainability Report, 2021).

Shifting users' behaviour from private cars to public transport implies the use of effective attraction strategies in favour of public transport, measurable in terms of time, money, and social image. Despite the absence of numeric data, public transport in Dubai is mostly used by foreign residents and almost ignored by locals. The stigma of using public transport is a condition shared in different social contexts worldwide. Surveys conducted in the Middle East and North Africa (MENA) region on women's mobility confirm that women and men have different experiences in public transport, different challenges during their journeys, and different modal choices (Delatte et al., 2018). A common fact is the reluctance of the middle and upper classes to mingle with lower classes on the basis of factors that can differ from culture to culture (Tran et al., 2021). A recent study conducted in Saudi Arabia, based on questionnaires addressed randomly to the population of Dammam has detected factors that most probably can also apply to possible answers from the local population in Dubai. Factors acknowledged by the survey include: lack of efficiency, incomplete service not reaching the desired destinations, lack of safety inside the vehicle, lack of safety at the bus stop or when walking to the destination, lack of comfort and privacy, either inside the vehicle, during waiting times, or along walking paths to destinations. Gender issues are also particularly relevant in countries of the Middle East. Women feel uneasy sharing the same space with men and require comfort zones of privacy for themselves. Women seem also more attentive to the climatic and visual discomfort caused by bus stops not equipped with acclimatisation or poorly designed walkways to destinations (Nahiduzzaman Kh Md et al., 2021).

To make public transport stations more attractive and the streetscape more inviting, Dubai has managed the implementation of an environmental plan able to highlight the visual quality of city neighbourhoods. The increased chances of reaching the bus stops more comfortably have resulted in a higher satisfaction for users, who revealed they were more inclined to use public transport. The new stations designed by the Mobility Team and the upgrading of neighbourhood streets are encountering favouring visitors and residents, making them eager to use public transport (RTA Sustainability Report, 2021). The Road and Transport Authority (RTA) of Dubai has also assessed how good signage around public transport, accessibility for all people, pedestrian connections, pedestrian crossing, lanes for bicycles, and air-conditioned stations are beneficial for all the residents (RTA Sustainability Report 2021).

6.4.3 Decarbonisation and Form of the Built Environment

Urban transport management is dependent on urban form. Historical European cities are characterised by a dense centre, where narrow sections of streets and roads often make it difficult for the contemporary transition of several transport modes. On the other hand, the compactness of the urban fabric and the shortness of city drives facilitate the use of electric vehicles subject to recurring operations of charging. New cities, and specifically cities depending on global economies, such as Dubai and Abu Dhabi, expand into random portions of land, according to real estate conditions, with scarce planning controlled by the local administration. Neighbourhoods surrounded by unbuilt land are frequent, as frequent are urban design compositions favouring tall, isolated buildings surrounded by parking lots, roads, and expensive landscaping. Connecting these swatches of city requires higher planning energies whose effort is partially compensated by the fact that the environment is still mouldable. In any case, isolated areas of developing cities represent an unsustainable form of growth and only a comprehensive plan and a managerial approach can avert the collapse of the system once it is implemented.

Connecting urban parts that are disjointed represents a challenge for the sustainability of urban transport, whose goals along with decarbonisation and containment of construction and management costs, face the problem of making the public service desirable to a wider sector of the population, to limit traffic congestion and pollution caused by an intensive use of private vehicles (Gudmundsson, 2016). Sometimes, public transport authorities try to accelerate the duration of bus trips by conveying the vehicles along major roads or highways where the landscape is monotonous and less interesting. Highways, although more convenient for the management of transport services, lack proximity to the targeted scopes of the trip, making passengers less likely to use public buses. In the scenario of dispersed low-demand areas not sufficiently covered by public transport, on-demand transport can result from an interesting option to pursue, as the RTA in Dubai is actually doing. A transport operator controls the vehicles through a GPS application and in the same way, riders can locate the position of the vehicle closest to their location. The operator can combine similar requests, organising an itinerary based on user needs (Giuffrida, 2020).

Whereas the expanding form of the city is an advantage in terms of infrastructure construction, because building the infrastructural services along with the architecture of the city requires lesser effort and serving all citizens with the same infrastructures may turn out to be both difficult and expensive. The generation of new capital and the expansion of the 'creative class', will push citizens with a lower income to the peripheral parts of the built environment, in areas that are distant from basic services. The model of the globalised cities, cast upon the theory of modernism in urban planning, proved to be unsuccessful in Europe and the USA, but still leads the physical form of developing cities. This trend unfortunately contributes to an unsustainable use of resources and the management of services, where the decarbonisation of public transport can only contribute to a minimal part in the containment of GHG total emissions.

Guiding the transformation of developing cities from disorderly sprawl to high-density and compact development is conducive to carbon emission reduction Disorderly expansion would occupy a large amount of natural land, reduce natural carbon sinks, and result in longer commuting distances and greater commuting flow, thereby increasing urban energy consumption (Cirilli et al., 2014; Zhang, 2018) Urban sprawl leads to longer infrastructure service lines, resulting in massive demand for infrastructure investment, while compact development aims to slow the trend of urban sprawl and implement the intensive planning of urban form. It is generally assessed that compact development is negatively related to carbon emissions because a compact urban form helps reduce a city's erosion of the surrounding ecological environment and dependence on private cars. Improving the compactness of the urban environment, promoting the sharing of resources, services, and infrastructure, reducing land occupation, and reducing the energy and resource costs of urban operation are conducive to the sustainable development of a city(Sun, 2022).

6.5 Conclusion

The decarbonisation goals of public transport in the UAE align with the targets of most of the advanced countries engaged in the commitment to minimising GHG emissions by 2050. The experiments made by Europe in the specific sector of public urban transit may contribute to speeding up the process in the UAE. A review of some experiences that matured in recent years offers the framework of European pathways in the field. After a period of investments in hydrogen-fuelled technology for urban fleets, most European cities are addressing their interest in favour of the electrification of urban public transport. Some of the reasons are specifically dependent on the characteristics of the fuel. Hydrogen, at least in this phase of the research, is modest in performative capacities and represents several aspects of dispersion, not least the need to import from countries where it is produced. In the UAE, this last aspect is not influential, nevertheless the challenges posed by present hydrogen technology need scrutiny. Alternative energy sources and their successful use in public urban transport also face other challenges according to different geographical and cultural contexts. The engagement of users and their attitude towards public urban transport have a primary effect as well as the formal planning of the city, with particular reference to density.

The comparison with the experiences that European cities already have should not lead to the assumption that the concept has a status of a necessarily virtuous model, but the aspects that have been considered in the past and are presently experienced can provide some insights for the best profitable choices in the short run.

References

Ajanovic, A., Sayer M., and Haaset R. (2022). The economics and the environmental benignity of different colors of hydrogen. *Int. J. Hydrogen Energy* 47 (57), pp. 24136–24154. Doi: 10.1016/j.ijhydene.2022.02.094.

Carrilero I., González M., Anseán D., Viera J., Chacón J., and Pereirinha P. (2018). Redesigning European public transport: impact of new battery technologies in the design of electric bus fleets. *Trans. Res. Procedia* 33, pp. 195–202. Available online: www.sciencedirect.com (accessed 4 May 2022).

Cervero, R., and Kockelman, K. (1997). Travel demand and the 3Ds: density, diversity, and design. *Trans. Res. Part D Transp. Environ.* 2, pp. 199–219.

Cirilli, A., and Veneri, P. (2014). Spatial structure and carbon dioxide (CO_2) emissions due to commuting: An analysis of Italian urban areas. *Reg. Stud.* 48, pp. 1993–2005.

Crippa, M., Guizzardi D., Muntean M., Schaaf E., Solazzo E., Monforti-Ferrario F., Olivier J., and Vignati E. (2020). *CO_2 Emissions of all World Countries – 2020 Report. EUR 30358 EN*. Luxembourg: Publications Office of the European Union.

Delatte, A., Baouni, T., Belwal, R., Daou, L., Imam, R., Zitoun, M. S., and Smadi, A. (2018). Understanding the needs of MENA public transport customers: culture of service and gender-responsive recommendations. *Tema: J. Land Use, Mobility, and Environ.* 1, pp. 7–30.

Deloitte (2021). *Enablers to Become the Hydrogen Economy Superpower: Closing the Hydrogen Capabilities Gap in the GCC*. London: Deloitte. Available online: www2.deloitte.com (accessed 27 April 2022).

Dubai Electricity and Water Authority (DEWA) Fact Sheet 2021. (n.d.). Dubai Supreme Council of Energy, carbon footprint eduction measures. Available online: https://dubaisce.gov.ae/en/carbon-footprint/ (accessed 27 April 2022).

European Automobile Manufacturers Association (ACEA) (2022). *Fuel Types of New Buses: Electric 10.6%, Alternative Fuels 10.5%, Hybrid 10.1%, Diesel 68.8% Share in 2021*. Brussels: ACEA. Available online: www.acea.auto/fuel-cv/fuel-types-of-new-buses-electric-10-6-alternative-fuels-10-5-hybrid-10-1-diesel-68-8-share-in-2021/ (accessed 4 May 2022).

European Commission (EU) (2016). *White Paper Roadmap to a Single European Transport Area – Towards a Competitive and Resource Efficient Transport System*. Brussels: European Commission. Available online: www.eesc.europa.eu/ (accessed 7 May 2022).

European Commission (EU) (2017). *Sustainable Urban Mobility Indicators (SUMI)*. Brussels: European Commission. Available online: https://transport.ec.europa.eu (accessed 10 May 2022).

European Commission (2019). *Transport and the Green Deal*. Brussels: European Commission. Available online: https://ec.europa.eu/ (accessed 7 April 2022).

European Environment Agency (EEA) (2016). *Air Quality in Europe – 2016 Report*. Copenhagen: European Environment Agency. Available online: www.eea.europa.eu (accessed 10 May 2022).

Fang, C., Wang, S., and Li, G. (2015). Changing urban forms and carbon dioxide (CO_2) emissions in China: a case study of 30 provincial capital cities. *Appl. Energy* 158, pp. 519–531.

Giuffrida N., Le Pira M., Inturri G., Ignaccolo M., Calabrò G., Cuius B., D'Angelo R., and Pluchino A. (2020). On-demand flexible transit in fast-growing cities: the case of Dubai. *Sustainability* 12, p. 4455. Doi: 10.3390/su12114455.

Gudmundsson, H., Marsden G., and Zietsman J. (2016). *Sustainable Transportation: Indicators, Frameworks, and Performance Management*. Heidelberg: Springer.

Howarth, R., Jacobson M. (2021). How green is blue hydrogen? *Energy Sci. Eng.* 9, pp. 1676–1687.

International Energy Agency (IEA) (n.d.). *Trucks and Buses*. Paris: IEA. Available online: www.iea.org/reports (accessed 4 May 2022).

International Energy Agency (IEA) (2021). *The Cost of Capital in Clean Energy Transitions*. Paris: IEA. Available online: www.iea.org/articles/the-cost-of-capital-in-clean-energy-transitions (accessed 23 January 2023).

International Panel Climate Change (IPCC) (2022). *International Panel Climate Change Report*. Geneva: IPCC. Available online: www.ipcc.ch/ (accessed 4 April 2022).

International Transport Forum (ITF) (2021). *Decarbonising Transport in Europe. The Way Forward.* Brussels: ITF. Available online: www.itf-oecd.org/sites/default/files/docs/decarbonising-transport-europe-way-forward.pdf (accessed 2 May 2022).

Lander L., Tagnon C., Nguyen-Tien V., Kendrick E., Elliott R., Abbott A., Edge J., and Offer G. (2023). Breaking it down: a techno-economic assessment of the impact of battery pack design on disassembly costs. *Appl. Energy* 331, p. 120437.

Lee, S., and Lee, B. (2014). The influence of urban form on GHG emissions in the US household sector. *Energy Policy* 68, pp. 534–549.

Logan K., Nelson J., and Hastings A. (2020). Electric and hydrogen buses: shifting from conventionally fueled cars in the UK. *Transportation Research Part D: Transport and Environment* 85, p. 102350.

Lv, F., and Qi, X. C. (2013). The urban planning strategies research of decreasing traffic carbon emissions. *Adv. Mat. Res.* 671, pp. 2402–2405.

Masnavi, M. R. (2000). The new millennium and the new urban paradigm: the compact city in practice, in Williams, K., Burton, E., and Jenks, M. (eds.), *Achieving Sustainable Urban Form.* Abingdon: Routledge, pp. 64–73.

Ministry of Climate Change and Environment (MOCCAE) (2018). *UAE 4th National Communication Report.* Abu Dhabi: MOCCAE. Available online: www.moccae.gov.ae/en/reports-listing/23/4/2018/4th-uae-national-communication-report-2018.aspx (accessed 20 April 2022).

Ministry of Infrastructure and Sustainable Mobility (MIMS) (2022). *Decarbonising Transport: Scientific Evidence and Policy Proposals.* MIMS. Available online: https://mit.gov.it (accessed 20 March 2023).

Nahiduzzaman, K. M., Campisi, T., Shotorbani, A. M., Assi, K., Hewage, K., and Sadiq, R. (2021). Influence of socio-cultural attributes on stigmatizing public transport in Saudi Arabia. *Sustainability* 13, p. 12075.

Ou, J., Liu, X., Wang, S., Xie, R., and Li, X. (2016). Investigating the differentiated impacts of socioeconomic factors and urban forms on CO_2 emissions: empirical evidence from Chinese cities of different developmental levels. *J. Clean. Prod.* 226, pp. 601–614.

Patyk A., Bachmann T., and Brisse A. (2013). Life cycle assessment of H2 generation with high-temperature electrolysis. *Int. J. Hydrogen Energy* 38 (10), pp. 35–48.

Ritchie, H., Roser M., and Rosado P. (2022). CO_2 and greenhouse gas emissions: our world in data. Our World in Data. Available online: https://ourworldindata.org (accessed 15 April 2022).

Road and Transport Authority (RTA) (2021). *Sustainability Report 2020.* Abu Dhabi: RTA. Available online: www.rta.ae/wps/portal/rta/ae/home/open-data (accessed 18 May 2022).

Scarlat, N., Prussi, M., and Padella, M. (2021). Quantification of the carbon intensity of electricity produced and used in Europe. *Applied Energy.* 305, p. 117901.

Sclar, R., Camron, G., and Castellanos S. (2019). *Barriers to Adopting Electric Buses.* Washington, DC: World Resources Institute (WRI)/Ross. Available online: https://wrirosscities.org/sites/default/files/barriers-to-adopting-electric-buses.pdf (accessed 15 May 2022).

Shi, K., Xu, T., Li, Y., Chen, Z., Gong, W., Wu, J., and Yu, B. (2020). Effects of urban forms on CO_2 emissions in China from a multi-perspective analysis. *J. Environ. Manag.* 262, p. 110300.

Sims R., Schaeffer R., Creutzig, F., Cruz-Núñez, X., et al. (2015). Transport, in Edenhofer, O., Pichs-Madruga, R., Sokona, Y., Farahani E., et al. (eds.), *Climate Change 2014: Mitigation of Climate Change.* Contribution of Working Group III to the Fifth

Assessment Report of the Intergovernmental Panel on Climate Change (IPCC) in Cambridge University Press, Cambridge, United Kingdom and New York, NY, USA. Cambridge and New York: Cambridge University Press, pp. 599–670.

Staffel I., Scamman, D., Velazquez Abad, A., Balcombe, P., Dodds, P., Ekins, P., Shah, N., and Ward, K. (2019). The role of hydrogen and fuel cells in the global energy system. *Energy Environ. Sci.*, 12, 463–491.

Sun, C., Zhang, Y., Ma, W., Wu, R., and Wang, S. (2022). The impacts of urban form on carbon emissions: a comprehensive review. *Land* 11, p. 1430.

Tollerson J. (2022). What the war in Ukraine means for energy, climate, and food. *Nature* 14, pp. 232–233.

Tran, H. A., and Schlyter, A. (2010). Gender and class in urban transport: the cases of Xian and Hanoi. *Environ. Urban.* 22, pp. 139–155.

Tritto C., and Poggio, A. (2021). Il ruolo dell'idrogeno nel trasporto terrestre (Hydrogen role in land transport). *Legambiente*. Available online: www.legambiente.it/wp-content/uploads/2021/05/ruolo-idrogeno-nel-trasporto-terrestre_2021.pdf (accessed 25 March 2022).

United Arab Emirates (UAE) *National Climate Change Plan of UAE*. Abu Dhabi: UAE. Available online: https://u.ae/en/about-the-uae/strategies-initiatives-and-awards/federal-governments-strategies-and-plans/national-climate-change-plan-of-the-uae (accessed 23 April 2022).

United Arab Emirates (UAE) (2024) *UAE Net Zero 2050*. Abu Dhabi: UAE. Available online: https://u.ae/en/information-and-services/environment-and-energy/climate-change/theuaesresponsetoclimatechange (accessed 12 April 2022).

United Nations Climate Action (2021). *COP26: Together for Our Planet*. [Glasgow]:United Nations Climate Action. Available online: www.un.org/en/climatechange/cop26 (accessed 6 April 2022).

WAM – The Emirates News Agency (2021). UAE announces Hydrogen Leadership Roadmap, reinforcing nation's commitment to driving economic opportunity through decisive climate action. WAM. Available online: www.wam.ae/en/details/1395302988986 (accessed 23 April 2022).

Wan T., and Wang Y. (2022). The hazards of electric car batteries and their recycling. *IOP Conference Series: Earth and Environmental Science* p. 1011 012026. Available online: https://iopscience.iop.org/article/10.1088/1755-1315/1011/1/012026/pdf (accessed 12 April 2023).

Zero Emission Urban Bus System (ZeEUS) (2017). *eBus Report #2: An Updated Overview of Electric Buses in Europe*. ZeEUS. Available online: https://zeeus.eu/uploads/publications/documents/zeeus-report2017-2018-final.pdf (accessed 4 May 2022).

Zhang, Y., Wu, Q., and Fath, B. D. (2018). Review of spatial analysis of urban carbon metabolism. *Ecol. Model.* 371, pp. 18–24.

7

Net Zero Emissions in the GCC Region

Challenges and Opportunities for Green Hydrogen Applications

AHMED BADRAN

7.1 Introduction

In the past three decades, the world has become aware of the dangers of relying solely on depleted energy sources, including coal, oil, and gas. Concerns about the effects of climate change have influenced the quest for a low-carbon energy transition in recent years. Climate change concerns have resulted in the Paris Climate Agreement in 2015 that sharpened the focus on renewable clean energy. The agreement aims to stop rising pollution levels from industries, transportation, and other sources that have led to significant environmental problems and an overall increase in temperatures. To achieve this goal, the Paris Agreement contains provisions mandating signatory nations to cut their carbon emissions. The agreement also urges wealthier nations to give underdeveloped countries the technical support they need to pursue carbon-reduction strategies (Badran, 2021; Constable, 2021).

The scientific community has carried out a number of tests and research studies in an effort to identify and test new technologies that provide energy continuously without having an adverse effect on the environment. Innovations in clean energy sources, such as solar and wind energy, ground energy, bio energy, and gravity energy, are the consequence of these efforts. In response to these advances in the energy sectors, many governments all around the world are revamping their energy policies to boost the share of renewable energy in their energy supply mix. By 2050, Europe intends to eliminate its dependency on fossil fuels. Several countries, particularly those in the GCC, have made commitments to cut back on carbon emissions. In this context, a novel method for producing ecologically friendly energy is focusing on extracting hydrogen by using energy generated from renewable sources has arisen and is known as green hydrogen (Cho, 2021). This novel energy source has piqued the interest of energy and environmental academics since its inception. Green hydrogen has also sparked a slew of questions, the answers to which will necessitate further research into this new type of ecologically friendly energy source. As a result, the researchers concentrated their efforts on learning more about this new energy source, as well as its possible implications in various economic and environmental domains. In addition to such scientific efforts, several governments are looking into the potential of hydrogen in decarbonised energy systems (Esily et al., 2022).

The debate over the future of energy systems and the part that green hydrogen can play in decarbonising the energy industries has moved to the centre of the green hydrogen policy discourse. Worldwide demand for green hydrogen produced with reduced CO_2 emissions is predicted to reach 530 million tonnes by 2050. This amount should substitute nearly 10.4 billion barrels of oil equivalent to 37% of pre-Covid-19 pandemic global oil production. Green hydrogen exports are expected to be worth USD300 billion yearly, generating 400,000 jobs in renewable energy and hydrogen manufacturing around the world (Anouti et al., 2021; IRENA, 2020a).

Despite the growing interest in green hydrogen, oil and gas corporations in the GCC do not place a high focus on hydrogen generation. It is important to note that several GCC countries have begun the initial steps in developing this sort of energy. Due to their advantages, these states are leading the way in harnessing hydrogen as a sustainable energy source. In this context, it can also be noted that the countries of the region enjoy a comparative advantage in terms of producing and exporting green hydrogen. In comparison to other countries such as China and the United States, the export possibilities of the GCC countries are higher. In other words, the ability of China and the United States to export to international energy markets are constrained by strong local demand. The GCC countries, on the other hand, have sufficient access to cheap renewable energy while yet being able to export a significant percentage of their green hydrogen. Due to the GCC region's favourable conditions for the use of this new clean energy source, particularly the availability of renewable energy sources, the transition to a green hydrogen economy will signal a transformation in the region. In other words, adopting green hydrogen and incorporating it into the mix of renewable energy sources helps minimise carbon emissions and the negative environmental effects of all pollutants. In turn, this will enable these nations to achieve the net zero emissions target. As stated by van Renssen (2020) theoretically, green hydrogen can assist in achieving net zero emissions by three means: storing excess renewable energy when the grid is unable to handle it, decarbonising hard-to-electrify industries like heavy industry and long-distance transportation, and substituting fossil fuels as a zero-carbon feedstock in the manufacture of chemicals and fuels.

Given the dearth of studies on hydrogen energy in the GCC, this chapter seeks to address the problem by examining the notion of 'green hydrogen' and its implications in the GCC region. The degree to which the GCC states may profit from this new clean energy source is determined with the help of such a knowledge of the nature and applications of green hydrogen as well as the difficulties associated with their implementation. The GCC countries' capacity to rely on green hydrogen as a sustainable energy source depends also on such a deep understanding of this novel clean energy source. In light of this, the purpose of this chapter is to address a significant research question: Would the Arabian Gulf's use of green hydrogen energy create new opportunities or will it be constrained by technical and economic factors?

7.2 Green Hydrogen and the Decarbonisation of Energy Systems

Prior to conceptualising green hydrogen, it is crucial to comprehend the molecular properties of hydrogen. Understanding hydrogen's production process, as well as its applications, is equally important. This explanation will make the green hydrogen notion simpler to understand. Early in the sixteenth century, when a gas was found as a by-product of a reaction between sulphuric acid and iron, molecular hydrogen was first mentioned. Henry Cavendish identified this gas as a distinct substance in 1776; nevertheless, it was not named until 1788 by Antoine Lavoisier, who derived the term from the Greek words 'hydro' (water) and 'genes' (creator). Hydrogen has been extensively explored and used for a variety of applications since then (Bockris, 2013; IRENA, 2020a).

As a chemical element, hydrogen is located at the beginning of the periodic table and is characterised by its simple structure, lightweight, and many isotopes. As such, hydrogen (atomic ratio 53 pm and atomic mass 1.008) is the smallest and lightest element in the periodic table, and it is the most prevalent element in the universe. It is the tenth most abundant element on earth (0.14%) and may be found in our atmosphere (0.6 ppm), water, organic molecules, and other chemical substances. Hydrogen is mainly found in moderate conditions of temperature and pressure in the gaseous state. Nonetheless, hydrogen can be converted to a liquid by subjecting it to very low temperatures and pressures. As for its source, hydrogen is not available unilaterally but is found in chemical compounds with other elements, whether in water, gaseous compounds, fossil fuels, or even plants (Germscheidt et al., 2021).

Regarding the ways by which hydrogen can be produced, it can be noticed that hydrogen can be extracted from nature by separating it from the compounds with which it is combined. This can be done by using chemical processes and reactions. For example, hydrogen can be obtained by combining two chemicals and producing pure hydrogen because of the reaction. Furthermore, numerous chemical processes for hydrogen synthesis, such as displacement, thermal disintegration, electrolysis, and other commercial procedures, bear names attributed to their creators, such as the Bush and Len methods. Since ancient times, hydrogen has been used for a variety of reasons, and it is currently produced and used extensively around the world. It is used in military applications, where the hydrogen bomb is known for its capacity to destroy, and it is used as a missile fuel. Ammonia, hydrogenated oils, ethanol, methanol, and certain acids are all related to the hydrogen industry. The hydrogen is used in nuclear fusion and fission processes due to its chemical characteristics. Because of the diversity of its isotopes, it is also useful in biology and chemistry. According to a 2018 estimate, 51.70% of total hydrogen is used for refining, 42.62% for ammonia manufacture, and just 5.68% for other purposes including the usage as a clean and sustainable fuel (Germscheidt et al., 2021: 1).

From an energy perspective, hydrogen's application in the energy sector is nothing new. Hydrogen is an energy carrier and transferor that can be utilised to save and store energy. Hydrogen energy is extremely adaptable, as it may be utilised as a gas or liquid, transformed into power or fuel, and produced in a variety of ways. Every year, over 70 million metric tons of hydrogen are produced for use in oil refining, ammonia production, steel production, chemical and fertiliser manufacture, food processing, metallurgy, and other applications (Cho, 2021). According to the International Renewable Energy Agency (IRENA), around 120 million tonnes of hydrogen are produced each year around the world, with two-thirds being pure hydrogen and one-third being a mixture of other gases. Hence, hydrogen is not only found in the composition of fossil fuels but it has also been extracted for use in numerous scientific applications over the years (IRENA, 2019).

Recent studies, however, have revealed that hydrogen may be created and used for energy in a variety of ways. Different hydrogen extraction technologies can be recognised, which are colour-coded according to the severity of the production processes' environmental impact (Constable, 2021; IRENA, 2020a). A distinction can be made between *grey*, *blue*, *yellow*, *turquoise*, and *green hydrogen*. The grey hydrogen is created by separating hydrocarbons, such as those found in fossil fuels. The most common way for manufacturing grey hydrogen is to use natural gas or coal as a feedstock, which is then mixed with steam at high temperatures and pressures to produce synthesis gas, which consists primarily of hydrogen and carbon monoxide. The synthesis gas is then treated with additional water to produce pure hydrogen and carbon dioxide. These are well-known reactions, although they produce a substantial amount of CO_2 (Anouti et al., 2021). As a result of the amount of carbon emissions originating from the separation process that are not captured and create air pollution, the grey colour has been given to this type of hydrogen (Sarathi, 2021).

The GCC countries utilise a significant amount of grey hydrogen generated from natural gas 8.4 megatonnes (Mt)/year, about 7% of global consumption. Carbon capture, utilisation, and storage (CCUS) could be used to retrofit some of this (Babonneau et al., 2021). Refineries, steel mills, and petrochemical industries are where the majority of hydrogen units are found. As reported by Qamar Energy, Gas-to-Liquids (GTL) accounts for around 39% of hydrogen use in the region, followed by oil refining (27%), ammonia production (21%), methanol production (9%), and steel manufacturing (4%) (Qamar Energy, 2020: 2).

Blue hydrogen, the second most common technique, uses the same basic mechanisms as grey hydrogen, but it uses carbon-capture equipment to absorb up to 90% of greenhouse gas emissions. In certain circumstances, the carbon is kept underground, which entails a high initial investment. Alternatively, it can be recycled as a feedstock for industrial purposes but CO_2 is still discharged into the atmosphere (Anouti et al., 2021). In other words, the blue hydrogen is produced from fossil fuels as well but by sequestering carbon to prevent it from being emitted into the atmosphere. As noted by van Renssen (2020), the account of capture and storage (CCS) is being revived by blue hydrogen. It is the process of producing 'decarbonised' hydrogen by combining CCS with the standard method of producing hydrogen by steam methane reforming. According to IRENA, (2020a: 9), blue hydrogen has drawbacks that have limited its adoption thus far: it requires finite resources, is vulnerable to fluctuating fossil fuel prices, and does not serve energy security goals. Furthermore, social acceptance of blue hydrogen is hampered by the fact that it incurs additional expenditures for CO_2 delivery and storage and necessitates CO_2-storage monitoring. Additionally, CCS capture efficiencies are projected to be 85–95% at most, implying that 5–15% of CO_2 will still be discharged. Moreover, these high capture rates are still a work in progress.

In comparison to grey and blue hydrogen, yellow hydrogen can be produced in a relatively small proportion. The electrolysis process, also known as water splitting, which employs water as a raw material-produces yellow hydrogen. An electrolysis cell consists of an electrolyte (the ion conductor), active layers for redox reactions, and a current and material collector (the electronic conductor), which allows for the delivery and collection of reactants and products as well as the supply and collection of electricity. Gas-cooling, filtration, compression, and hydrogen storage capacity are also required by electrolysis systems. In addition, to condition the power from the power source, safety and control systems are implemented. Depending on the feed contaminants, purity required, and scale of application, mechanical vapour compression, reverse osmosis, or electrodialysis are used to pre-treat the feed water (Rouwenhorst et al., 2021). The process's final environmental impact is determined by the energy input. The yellow hydrogen is obtained using a nuclear-powered electrolysis process, but the hydrogen is produced with a mix of fossil and renewable fuels. This type of hydrogen is known for its complete purity and is produced from uranium, but it is not very effective and is not used much due to the dangers of dealing with uranium (Germscheidt et al., 2021).

According to Philibert (2020), the turquoise hydrogen can be added to aforementioned types of hydrogen. This kind combines the utilisation of natural gas as a feedstock with the elimination of CO_2 emissions. The carbon in methane is converted to solid carbon black by the pyrolysis process. There is already a market for carbon black, which provides an extra revenue source. Carbon black has the potential to be more powerful. CO_2 in liquid form is easier to store than CO_2 in gaseous form. Turquoise hydrogen is at present still in the pilot stage (Philibert, 2020).

Finally, green hydrogen – the focus of our chapter – has been of great importance recently because of its efficiency in storing and transmitting energy. Green hydrogen is created by splitting water molecules into their essential constituents of hydrogen and oxygen using renewable energy to power electrolysis. This technique produces a clean energy source that can be stored for a long time and transferred over vast distances. Consequently, this type of hydrogen is distinguished by the fact that it is produced using renewable energy sources. In other words, green hydrogen is hydrogen produced with renewable energy rather than fossil fuels. It has the ability to provide clean energy for industrial, transportation, and other applications, with water as the only result (Cho, 2021). In that sense, green hydrogen is a promising method since it uses renewable energy to fuel the electrolysis that separates water molecules into hydrogen and oxygen. This type of hydrogen is green since the energy comes from renewable sources (Anouti et al., 2021; Rouwenhorst et al., 2021).

In conclusion, it can be noted that the search for clean, renewable, and environmentally friendly hydrogen sources has led to the use of water as a feedstock. Green hydrogen's significance stems from the idea of using it to produce clean energy and consequently addressing environmental problems brought on by carbon emissions from the burning of fossil fuels. In order to save vast amounts of energy that would otherwise be lost, green hydrogen offers the possibility of storing energy produced from sustainable sources.

In that sense, green hydrogen can be defined as a technology for extracting hydrogen by using energy generated from renewable sources in operating electrolysis devices that analyse and separate water molecules into oxygen and hydrogen (van Renssen, 2020). After the separation process, the hydrogen is either compressed into tubes or cooled to temperatures as low as –258°C. The hydrogen produced can be stored in liquid form and used as a clean energy source (Thapa & Thapa, 2020). Currently this technology is known in the production of pure hydrogen. The available research in this area has also indicated that technologies for producing pure hydrogen are constantly evolving and limitless through environmentally friendly methods.

As noted by Fraile et al., there are different techniques that can be used to produce hydrogen from renewable sources. That includes biomass pyrolysis and gasification, raw biomass reforming, thermochemical water splitting, photo electrochemical cells, fermentation in the dark, and supercritical water gasification biomass are the six ways. Testing and evaluating these technologies from technical and economic standpoints indicate that they are among the most efficient methods for hydrogen production (Fraile et al., 2016). A multistep process, which includes biogas reforming, water–gas–shift reaction, and hydrogen separation, can also be used to manufacture green hydrogen from biogas as a sustainable resource. Steam reforming, dry reforming, dual reforming, and tri-reforming are four methane-reforming processes. Only steam methane reforming (SMR) has been commercialised, but it is well known as a high-energy process (IRENA, 2018). As a result, new techniques are being developed, including dry, dual, and tri-reforming. Because of their high carbon dioxide concentration, which can be utilised as an oxidant, these solutions are particularly appealing for biogas reforming.

7.3 The Case for Green Hydrogen in the GCC Region

At the outset, the case for green hydrogen can be supported by many advantages of hydrogen as a clean energy source. Hydrogen is abundant in nature and easy to extract using renewable energy sources. Hydrogen has also proven its efficiency in storing energy for long periods, as is the case in hydrogen fuel cells. Moreover, in comparison to hydrocarbon sources of energy, hydrogen is more energy efficient as it contains energy equal to three times the energy stored in fossil fuels. Considering green hydrogen, the case is becoming even stronger by taking account of the developments in the green hydrogen markets. In this regard, the low variable renewable energy (VRE) electricity costs is illustrative. The cost of electricity is a primary cost driver for green hydrogen. In recent decades, the cost of electricity generated by solar photovoltaics (PV) and onshore wind farms has dropped dramatically. In various GCC countries, new low prices were set in 2019 and 2020. In the United Arab Emirates (UAE), for example, solar PV was contracted at USD13.5/MWh (Shumkov, 2020). In Saudi Arabia, onshore wind was contracted at USD21.3/MWh (Masdar, 2019).

From a technological perspective, as production prices fall, scaling up green hydrogen technologies could make future paths more appealing for the countries of the region. Several components of the hydrogen value chain have previously been tested on a small scale and are ready for commercialisation; however, scaling up will require investment. The capital cost of electrolysis has decreased by 60% since 2010 (Hydrogen Council, 2020). This decline has resulted in a reduction in hydrogen costs from a range of USD10–15/kg to as low as USD4–6/kg.

The case for green hydrogen can also be advocated by considering the flexibility, system efficiency, and cost-effectiveness of power systems. Existing power systems require additional flexibility as the share of VRE grows in diverse regions throughout the world, including the GCC region. By reacting to electricity pricing, the electrolysers used to make green hydrogen can be built as flexible resources that can swiftly adjust to fluctuations in VRE output.

The importance of hydrogen in the global energy transition is becoming acknowledged, sparking interest in a fully integrated hydrogen economy. Many countries, particularly GCC states, created an ambitious hydrogen strategy that asks for large hydrogen deployment as well as imports from regional and worldwide markets to reach its 2050 net zero carbon target and hydrogen strategy by 2030. This, on the other hand, has a stipulation. Policy, pricing, and infrastructure issues are all key factors to consider (Qamar Energy, 2020). In this context, it would be reasonable to ask how much hydrogen contributes to the GCC region's carbon neutrality. What are the advantages and disadvantages of moving to a green hydrogen economy?

At present, there is increased interest in green hydrogen because of the availability of appropriate conditions for its application (Sturm, 2018). In this context, many countries, including the Gulf States, have concluded partnerships and signed agreements with relevant energy companies and businesses specialised in technological development to invest in hydrogen projects. The aim is to achieve global goals in reducing greenhouse gas emissions. For example, the Kingdom of Saudi Arabia is well known for its dominance in the fossil energy sector. However, the Kingdom today aspires to be one of the world's leaders in the clean energy industry. The growing investments in green hydrogen projects attest to this. The Kingdom is also working to support and enhance research efforts to develop production technologies through experimental research at King Abdullah University (Sarathi, 2021). In this context, the Kingdom emphasised the importance of the partnership between universities and research centres on the one hand, and the 'NEOM' project. As reported by Qamar Energy (2020: 2), the USD5 billion, 237,000 tonne/year Neom Helios project in North-West Saudi Arabia, developed by Acwa Power and Air Products, is the only advanced large-scale green hydrogen generation facility in the GCC. This green project aims to build a city powered by renewable energy, especially green hydrogen.

The UAE has gone the same way to keep pace with the world in shifting to renewable energy and fulfilling international commitments related to reducing carbon emissions as well as aiming for carbon neutrality (Al-Ain news, 2021a). In this context, the UAE was keen to establish a pilot project to produce pure hydrogen supported by solar power plants. The UAE government also signed an agreement between the UAE Investment Mubadala and Sanam International Company, with the aim of developing the green hydrogen sector (Al-Ain news, 2021b; Mataluci, 2021). As for the Sultanate of Oman, the Omani government has concluded an agreement between the Oman Authority for Special Economic Zones and Free Zones and the Indian company ACME specialised in the field of solar energy. Based on this agreement, a specific area was selected in Oman with the appropriate climatic conditions for the production of pure hydrogen (Oman News Agency, 2021).

For the state of Qatar, hydrogen energy is a hedge issue for the future (Constable, 2021). The beginnings of Qatar's interest in the field of green hydrogen was in an agreement with the British Shell Company to invest in green hydrogen projects in the United Kingdom (Pekic, 2021). In order to intensify efforts towards decarbonising the transportation and other industrial sectors, Qatar signed a cooperation agreement with the Korean Hydrogen Alliance with the aim of expanding the circle of cooperation in developing the sector for the two countries. Such an agreement with Qatar Energy was signed in the presence of the Minister of State for Energy Affairs. The agreement stressed the need to expand the production and export of hydrogen (Al Sharq, 2021).

In this context, an expert working at the Qatar Environmental and Energy Research Institute of Hamad Bin Khalifa University confirmed that the State of Qatar has capabilities to help it increase the production and use of hydrogen produced from renewable energy sources such as green hydrogen. The expert explained that if Qatar does not use the developments in the field of production and use of green hydrogen, it would lose the opportunity to form diversified industries in the Qatari economy (Constable, 2021). In other words, participating in the green hydrogen economy is an opportunity for the state of Qatar to start looking beyond liquefied natural gas. On the one hand, this field will allow the Qatar to enhance its economic position regionally by diversifying the economy and reducing dependence on fossil fuel resources as a major source of income. Additionally, the green hydrogen economy will help reduce the environmental impact of the combustion of hydrocarbon fuels, along with helping the Qatari government build a long-term strategy to ensure that prosperity continues for decades.

7.4 Green Hydrogen in the Balance: Opportunities and Challenges for GCC Countries

The observed growth in the use of green hydrogen applications in the GCC region should not be taken to imply that this process is without obstacles. Several scientists and scholars have questioned the benefits that these countries will receive from implementing these modern applications. Another difficulty for the adopted countries is the comparatively high cost of the application process. In addition, the research in this field highlights a number of logistical issues that would need to be resolved before hydrogen could be transported to international energy markets.

Having said that, the chapter here does not entirely discount the chances and benefits that the GCC nations may experience from using this cutting-edge, ecologically friendly technology.

On the bright side it can be noticed that the GCC region is well positioned to become a green hydrogen producer due to its abundant low-cost land, cheap cost of capital, existing industrial capacity, good solar and (in some cases) wind resources, and geographic closeness to growth markets. Similarly, it can produce cost-competitive blue hydrogen thanks to its low-cost natural gas and ease of carbon capture, utilisation, and storage (CCUS). Many studies have agreed that the Arabian Gulf has all the advantages that make it a strategic area for green hydrogen production and export (Cho, 2021; Sturm, 2018).

As noted by Anouti et al. (2021: 4), the global market for green hydrogen exports for the GCC countries will be worth around USD300 billion per year. Given their significant energy use in the heating, industrial, and transportation sectors, as well as the high cost of importing fuel, European and East Asian countries will have the highest demand for green hydrogen. In this context, the opportunities available to the Gulf countries to produce and export green hydrogen are twofold. The first is the opportunities currently available to continue the transition to the hydrogen economy. The other is the opportunities that will be provided by the transition to green energy in the form of positive returns resulting from the application of green hydrogen technology.

The availability of the key inputs to the production process is one of the most essential aspects that qualifies the GCC region to activate green hydrogen technology and to produce green hydrogen at scale and at low cost (Anouti et al., 2021). As previously mentioned, one of the prerequisites of the manufacturing process is the availability of renewable energy sources, as well as the necessity for wide areas to develop renewable energy generation facilities and hydrogen production electrolysis plants. When we look at the situation in the Gulf countries, we can see that they have sunny weather all year round and that winds blow over different parts of the Gulf. Therefore, clean sources of energy generation are available, which enhances the applicability of green hydrogen technology (Sturm, 2018).

Producing green hydrogen at a lower cost will benefit a variety of industries especially those known as hard-to-electrify and therefore hard-to-abate sectors, including steel, chemicals, and power generation (IRENA, 2020b). Such an expansion in the production and utilisation of green hydrogen will also advance the objective of making countries and businesses more environmentally sustainable by reducing the carbon emissions. This will apply to both existing and new green hydrogen uses. As a result, green hydrogen consumption is expected to increase dramatically. Hydrogen, for example, is utilised as a chemical feedstock in the synthesis of ammonia and methanol in the chemical industry. Accordingly, the chemical industry's demand for hydrogen should expand in tandem with the ammonia and methanol industries. A considerable number of new ammonia and methanol production plants will switch to green hydrogen as green hydrogen becomes more cost-competitive.

Climate change regulations will also likely push steel producers to abandon their traditional methods in favour of more ecologically friendly ones that utilise hydrogen as a reducing agent. The need for green hydrogen could increase because of this modification to industrial operations. In the power generation sectors, conventional power, derived from the combustion of hydrocarbons, now accounts for the majority of global electricity generation. Countries with limited renewable energy and hydrocarbon resources are heavily reliant on costly, polluting, imported fuels. Green hydrogen, on the other hand, offers an option. Countries that currently import hydrocarbons might instead import low-cost green hydrogen and convert it to energy in domestic power plants using large-scale fuel cells. As a result, green hydrogen could serve as a bridge between expanding and sustainable renewable energy output and hard-to-electrify industries (IRENA, 2018).

Another conducive factor to the application of green hydrogen technology is the strategic location that characterises the GCC states. One of the advantages of hydrogen when produced is that it can be stored and transported in the form of a cooled liquid in tankers, ships across the sea, or in tankers via land freight or pipelines in the event of export to nearby countries. Hence, the geographical location of the countries of the GCC region and their control over several waterways with several countries makes exporting hydrogen from the GCC region to all parts of the world easy. It is worth noting in this regard that the Gulf States possess a natural gas infrastructure that can be exploited for hydrogen transportation (IRENA, 2020a). However, some warn against using natural gas pipelines to transport hydrogen, as this may lead to the fragility of steel pipes, causing cracks to occur (Cho, 2021). Hence, those holding this view believe that the use of natural gas transportation networks in hydrogen transportation operations will require many modification and maintenance operations for the existing pipelines. Hence, proponents of this view favour the creation of a special infrastructure for hydrogen transportation.

The Arabian Gulf has held a strong position in international energy markets for decades thanks to its abundant natural resources such as oil and natural gas. The GCC states are able to keep control over hydrogen production and export because of their prestigious status and good reputation. If a global market for pure hydrogen exists, the GCC states can gain from their strong trading ties with many other energy-importing countries across the world. The Gulf countries have enjoyed the trust of importing countries as energy suppliers for decades. Hence, they can build on that trust to strengthen ties so that it will be the first port of call for those consuming countries, whether in Europe or East Asia. The GCC countries will reap several economic gains because of this. In other words, the success of the Gulf countries in transitioning to a green hydrogen economy in terms of production and export will give them several opportunities to achieve development in all its aspects, while also enabling them to achieve the reduction of carbon emissions and the goal of net zero emissions. The countries of the region can advance in the field of local industries and achieve economic prosperity by creating new job opportunities in the hydrogen sector. This, in turn, will help in improving the living and social conditions of many individuals in the GCC region. At the same time, the application of green hydrogen technology will reduce the carbon footprint of countries in the region and help them reach a state of carbon neutrality.

From an energy security perspective, by providing another energy carrier with various supply chains, suppliers, and markets, hydrogen can help to increase energy security in the region by diversifying the energy mix and improving system resilience. When hydrogen is utilised in fuel cells, it produces no emissions other than water, which helps to reduce pollution. Given the significant investment required to develop it as an energy carrier from an industrial feedstock, it has the potential to stimulate economic growth and job creation (IRENA, 2020a).

Despite the opportunities and benefits that the GCC region has, these countries confront a number of obstacles in the field of green hydrogen economy. These issues could hamper the success of some countries in the region in implementing green hydrogen technologies. Among these challenges is *the high cost of application processes*. Green hydrogen is currently more expensive than other forms of hydrogen, costing nearly twice as much as traditional manufacturing methods. As noted by Cho (2021), the multiple challenges that green hydrogen faces can be boiled down to just one: cost. In comparison to grey and blue hydrogen, green hydrogen production cost is the highest. As noted by van Renssen (2020), grey hydrogen costs roughly €1.50 euros (USD1.84) per kilogramme, blue hydrogen costs €2 to €3 per kilogramme, and green hydrogen costs €3.50 to €6 per kilogramme. Consequently, green hydrogen's significant problem is its cost as green hydrogen is currently three times the price of natural gas in some countries, including the United States.

Green hydrogen is also significantly more expensive to produce than grey or blue hydrogen due to the high cost of electrolysis, though prices of electrolysers are falling as manufacturing scales up. Furthermore, the application of hydrogen technology is carried out through a number of stages, all of which require huge financial resources. For instance, the construction of electrolysis stations, in addition to electrolysis devices, and the requirement to build hydrogen storage facilities all require a significant amount of financial resources. It might be challenging to advance in this area given the economic difficulties the region's countries are facing. Hence, the cost of manufacturing hydrogen, especially low-carbon green hydrogen, will be a crucial factor in the long-term viability of hydrogen-powered technologies (Dodds, 2015).

Given the high cost of green hydrogen, it is worth noting that developments in electrolysis technology, lower renewable energy costs, and increasing economies of scale should lower the cost of production and make hydrogen extraction a financially feasible option. The efficiency of various electrolysis systems have improved, as has the process's operational lifetime. Furthermore, using new and less expensive materials will cut the overall capital cost of equipment, lowering the capital cost per kilowatt. The operational costs of electrolysis procedures include a significant amount of electricity. More low-cost solar photovoltaic and wind power plants installed around the world, on the other hand, will produce the required electricity at a lower cost. Annual increases in electrolysis capacity, along with higher average project sizes, are resulting in increased economies of scale and lower project capital costs.

The complexity of supply chains is also among the challenges facing the GCC countries in the field of producing and exporting green hydrogen. Technically and geopolitically, hydrogen supply chains are highly complex. This complexity in supply chains results from the complexity of production and transportation processes, which in turn may lead to a significant loss of energy and resources. Hence, in order for the GCC countries to reach the hydrogen economy and benefit from its applications, the governments of those countries and the relevant companies should cooperate with each other. It is also necessary to develop policies and legal frameworks and ensure the integration of national strategies, in addition to working to improve aspects related to production technology (IRENA, 2020a).

The *shortage of water resources* necessary to conduct electrolysis operations to obtain hydrogen poses additional difficulties on top of the ones mentioned above. Due to climate change, a lack of rainfall, and the aridity of the Arabian Gulf's climate – deserts make up a significant portion of the region – the world as a whole, and the GCC countries in particular, suffer from a shortage of water resources. Moreover, electrolysis technology can only analyse clean freshwater. Nonetheless, it is worth noting in this regard that countries such as Saudi Arabia carry out tests and research in order to develop electrolysis techniques that can directly analyse seawater (Sarathi, 2021). The GCC countries have little access to freshwater, but lots of seawater, therefore coastal arid zones would present a large opportunity for hydrogen production from seawater. In this context, the use of saltwater as a feedstock for hydrogen production can benefit a variety of communities around the world, especially those in the GCC region (Germscheidt et al., 2021). Added to this, if successful, these efforts will reduce the complexity of the production chain, which currently depends on desalinating seawater first, then using the desalinated water in electrolysis to extract hydrogen. The question that arises here is whether the cost of achieving this goal will be high or low. Given the limited fresh water in the Gulf countries, where most countries depend on seawater desalination, dependence on freshwater resources available in those countries and the use of water in hydrogen extraction threatens water security in the Arabian Gulf.

Considering the competitiveness in global energy markets, the *high cost of transporting hydrogen* may reduce the competitive advantage of the GCC countries once they succeed in producing and exporting hydrogen. Nevertheless, it should be noted here that the technology for transporting and exporting hydrogen to global energy markets is not much different from that currently used to export and transport natural gas. Then, pipelines can be built to transport hydrogen in the event that the geographical distance between the producing countries in the Gulf and the importing countries is close, or using hydrogen liquefaction technology and transporting it by sea through tankers designated for that.

Finally, *the lack of clear policies*, specific goals and carefully drawn plans regarding the transition to a green hydrogen economy is one of the most important challenges facing the Gulf States. The establishment of a clean hydrogen economy is reliant on regulation, and the most difficult problem is putting in place the correct regulations (Badran, 2012). The absence of these policies and legal and regulatory frameworks makes it difficult to assess and follow up on developments in this path (Badran, 2013, 2017, 2022). Hence, failure to develop appropriate policies for the transition towards a hydrogen economy negatively affects the ability of countries in the region to identify deficiencies that need to be worked on and to calculate the appropriate cost of current hydrogen projects. It is also useful in this regard, in addition to setting policies and goals, to develop a common vision among the Gulf States for cooperation in order to ensure the success of hydrogen projects and to develop technologies necessary for production and export operations. As put by IRENA (2020a) to overcome initial resistance and reach a minimum threshold for market penetration, an integrated policy approach based on four central pillars is required: developing national hydrogen strategies, identifying policy priorities, establishing a governance system and enabling policies, and developing a system for green hydrogen guarantee of origin.

To sum up, the Gulf States should seize this opportunity to transition to a green hydrogen economy. These countries have the potential to be among the top exporters of green hydrogen. Three fundamental actions can be taken to accomplish this: at the beginning, a pilot project should be created in association with well-known companies in the area of green hydrogen production technology. Additionally, hydrogen strategies should be shaped as theoretical scenarios fall short in terms of assisting in the identification and eradication of problems. Moreover, national governments should start implementing energy policies to increase domestic consumption, which includes setting time-bound, explicit goals that are both clear and measurable. After the domestic hydrogen sector has expanded sufficiently, the GCC countries should be able to continue exporting and competing on international markets. (Anouti et al., 2021). There is also the need to consider environmental factors and to ensure that green hydrogen is produced with renewable energy sources. In addition to this, it is necessary to motivate business owners to support national plans with ambitious goals in line with decarbonisation and the intensification of the use of renewable energy. It is also useful to introduce tax structures for green hydrogen projects to stimulate growth and competitiveness.

7.5 Conclusion

This chapter investigated the potentials of green hydrogen for meeting the net zero emissions goal in the GCC region. The discussion has indicated that for the GCC countries, green hydrogen signifies a promising possibility to reach the net zero emissions goal and reducing their carbon footprints. The main reason for it is that in comparison to other parts of the world, the GCC countries have favourable conditions, including the availability of oil and other sources of fossil fuels in addition to renewable energy sources. Nonetheless, in order to transform green hydrogen from a niche player to a mainstream energy carrier, specific policies will be needed at each stage of technology readiness, market penetration, and market expansion. Despite the fact that many countries have ambitious plans for green hydrogen applications, the GCC states have distinct advantages that could position them as leaders in the hydrogen economy. They also have a financial incentive to abandon fossil fuels. The GCC countries can establish the groundwork for economic growth in a decarbonised world and assure their continued influence in the global energy markets by grasping the green hydrogen potential.

References

Al Sharq (2021). Qatar Energy and the Korean Hydrogen Alliance sign an agreement for cooperation in the field of hydrogen. Available online: www.qatarenergy.qa/en/MediaCenter/Pages/newsdetails.aspx?ItemId=3687.

Al-Ain news (2021a). Green hydrogen is the UAE's vision to shift towards a sustainable economy. Available online: https://al-ain.com/article/green-hydrogen-uae-vision-transition-economy.

Al-Ain news (2021b). Mubadala enhances hydrogen economy efforts in the midst of a global agreement. Available online: https://al-ain.com/article/an-understanding-between-mubadala-and.

Anouti, Y., Kombargi, R., Elborai, S., and Hage, R. (2021). The dawn of green hydrogen: maintaining the GCC's edge in a decarbonized world (Strategy&). Available online: www.strategyand.pwc.com/m1/en/reports/2020/the-dawn-of-green-hydrogen/the-dawn-of-green-hydrogen.pdf.

Babonneau, F., Badran, A., Benlahrech, M., Haurie, A., Schenckery, M., and Vielle, M. (2021). Economic assessment of the development of CO_2 direct reduction technologies in long-term climate strategies of the Gulf countries. *Climatic Change* 165 (3–4), p. 64. Doi: 10.1007/s10584-021-03058-4.

Badran, A. (2012). The rationale behind the creation and diffusion of independent regulatory agencies: the case of the telecommunications sector in Egypt. *International Journal of Public Administration* 35 (3), pp. 204–213. Doi: 10.1080/01900692.2012.638521.

Badran, A. (2013). Understanding the Egyptian regulatory state: independent regulators in theory and practice, in Dubash, N. K., and Morgan, B. (eds.), *The Rise of the Regulatory State of the South*. Oxford: Oxford University Press, pp. 53–74. Doi: 10.1093/acprof:oso/9780199677160.003.0003.

Badran, A. (2017). Revisiting regulatory independence: the relationship between the formal and de-facto independence of the Egyptian telecoms regulator. *Public Policy and Administration* 32 (1), pp. 66–84. Doi: 10.1177/0952076716643381.

Badran, A. (2021). Energy resilience and climate change in the GCC. Başkent Congress on Physical, Social and Health Sciences.

Badran, A. (2022). Independent regulators in the Middle East, in *Handbook on Regulatory Authorities*. Cheltenham: Edward Elgar Publishing.

Bockris, J. O. M. (2013). The hydrogen economy: its history. *International Journal of Hydrogen Energy* 38 (6), pp. 2579–2588. Doi: 10.1016/j.ijhydene.2012.12.026.

Cho, R. (2021, 7 January). Why we need green hydrogen. *State of the Planet*. Available online: https://news.climate.columbia.edu/2021/01/07/need-green-hydrogen/.

Constable, M. (2021). Are we really close to using hydrogen energy? Available online: www.hbku.edu.qa/ar/news/hydrogen-energy-fast.

Dodds, P. (2015). *Compendium of Hydrogen Energy*. Sawston: Woodhead Publishing, Elsevier. Doi: 10.1016/C2014-0-02671-8.

Esily, R. R., Chi, Y., Ibrahiem, D. M., and Chen, Y. (2022). Hydrogen strategy in decarbonization era: Egypt as a case study. *International Journal of Hydrogen Energy* 47 (43), pp. 18629–18647. Doi: 10.1016/j.ijhydene.2022.04.012.

Fraile, D., Altmann, M., & Barth, F. (2016). Study on hydrogen from renewable resources in the EU: Final report. Publications Office. Available online: https://data.europa.eu/doi/10.2843/28276.

Germscheidt, R. L., Moreira, D. E. B., Yoshimura, R. G., Gasbarro, N. P., Datti, E., dos Santos, P. L., and Bonacin, J. A. (2021). Hydrogen environmental benefits depend on the way of production: an overview of the main processes production and challenges by 2050. *Advanced Energy and Sustainability Research* 2 (10), p. 2100093. Doi: 10.1002/aesr.202100093.

Hydrogen Council (2020). *Path to Hydrogen Competitiveness a Cost Perspective*. Available online: www.hydrogencouncil.com/wp-content/uploads/2020/01/Path-to-HydrogenCompetitiveness_Full-Study-1.pdf.

International Renewable Energy Agency (IRENA) (2018). *Hydrogen from Renewable Power: Technology Outlook for the Energy Transition*. Available online: www.irena.org/-/media/files/irena/agency/publication/2018/sep/irena_hydrogen_from_renewable_power_2018.pdf.

International Renewable Energy Agency (IRENA) (2019). *Hydrogen: A Renewable Energy Perspective*. 30 September. Available online: www.irena.org/publications/2019/Sep/Hydrogen-A-renewable-energy-perspective.

International Renewable Energy Agency (IRENA) (2020a). *Green Hydrogen: A Guide To Policy Making*. Available online: www.irena.org/publications/2020/Nov/Green-hydrogen.

International Renewable Energy Agency (IRENA) (2020b). *Reaching Zero with Renewables: Eliminating CO_2 Emissions from Industry and Transport in Line With the 1.5°C Climate Goal*. Available online: www.irena.org/-/media/Files/IRENA/Agency/Publication/2020/Sep/IRENA_Reaching_zero_2020.pdf.

Masdar (2019). Dumat Al Jandal. Available online: https://masdar.ae/en/masdar-clean-energy/projects/dumat-aljandal.

Mataluci, S. (2021). The Hydrogen Stream: Italy's Eni lays out plans in Algeria and Egypt, UAE joins race with help from Japan. *PV Magazine*. Available online: www.pv-magazine.com/2021/07/09/the-hydrogen-stream-hydrogen-arrives-in-long-island-eni-lays-out-plans-in-algeria-and-egypt-uae-joins-race/.

Oman News Agency (2021). Signing the land reservation agreement for the green hydrogen and ammonia project in progress. Available online: https://omannews.gov.om/.

Pekic, S. (2021, October 19). Qatar Energy and Shell team up for hydrogen solutions. *Offshore Energy*. Available online: www.offshore-energy.biz/qatarenergy-and-shell-team-up-for-hydrogen-solutions/.

Philibert, C. (2020). Methane splitting and turquoise ammonia. *Ammonia Energy Association*. Available online: www.ammoniaenergy.org/articles/methane-splitting-and-turquoise-ammonia/.

Qamar Energy (2020). *Hydrogen in the GCC: A Report for the Regional Business Development Team Gulf Region*. Available online: www.rvo.nl/sites/default/files/2020/12/Hydrogen%20in%20the%20GCC.pdf.

Rouwenhorst, K. H. R., Krzywda, P. M., Benes, N. E., Mul, G., and Lefferts, L. (2021). Ammonia production technologies, in Valera-Medina, A., and Banares-Alcantara, R. (eds.), *Techno-Economic Challenges of Green Ammonia as an Energy Vector*. London: Academic Press, Elsevier, pp. 41–83. Doi: 10.1016/B978-0-12-820560-0.00004-7.

Sarathi, M. (2021). Green hydrogen is the energy source of the future. Available online: www.kaust.edu.sa/ar/news/green-hydrogen%E2%80%99s-time-is-now.

Shumkov, I. (2020). Record low bid for 2-GW solar project shines in Abu Dhabi. Available online: www.renewablesnow.com/news/record-low-bid-for-2-gw-solar-project-shines-in-abudhabi-696804/.

Sturm, H. (2018). Hydrogen economy for Arab Countries. Available online: www.researchgate.net/publication/326827521_aqtsad_alhydrwjyn_lldwl_alrbyt.

Thapa, B. S., and Thapa, B. (2020). Green hydrogen as a future multi-disciplinary research at Kathmandu University. *Journal of Physics: Conference Series* 1608 (1), p. 012020. Doi: 10.1088/1742-6596/1608/1/012020.

van Renssen, S. (2020). The hydrogen solution? *Nature Climate Change* 10 (9), pp. 799–801. Doi: 10.1038/s41558-020-0891-0.

Part IV

Policy and Data Transparency

8

GCC Carbon Neutrality and Net Zero Policy Tracker

Framing, Methodology, and Findings

ANDREAS RECHKEMMER, LOGAN COCHRANE, AND NOUREDDINE RADOUAI

8.1 Introduction

Our point of departure is the general insight and theorem that any present or future climate policy framework aiming at greenhouse gases (GHG) emission reductions and carbon neutrality ought to fit and mirror the realities – real or anticipated – and the real-world policy-making challenges for which it is designed. Since climate change realities and the ensuing policy challenges tend to play out at and affect various geographic scales and governance levels, not just the global one, global policy solutions must also address regional, national, and local issues simultaneously in so far as these are linked to the global problems at hand.[1] As we move deeper into the twenty-first century, it becomes clear that problems, challenges, and opportunities that global and multilevel policies have been and will have to be designed for are more and more characterised by unprecedented complexity and multicausality, often paired with high levels of ambiguity and uncertainty (Chapman et al., 2017; Kovacic & Di Felice, 2019). Furthermore, non-linear case trajectories and the cascading of unfolding hazardous climatic events and developments of note seem to become the rule rather than the exception, as the phenomenology of climate change, but also of biodiversity loss, or the Covid-19 pandemic has shown. Thus, the academic literature speaks of *wicked problems* and *grand challenges* when such a phenomenon is described (Head, 2008, 2019; Head & Alford 2015).

To illustrate the above scenario we provide three broad examples: (1) Anthropogenic climate change, in itself completely unprecedented in the history of humanity and the planet, highly complex and unfolding in a non-linear fashion with many cascading effects, comes with an urgent need for rapid decarbonisation, drastic GHG emission reductions, disruptive energy transitions and technological regime shifts, massive adaptations and emergency measures, and

[1] The authors wish to thank Professor Leslie A. Pal for his precious advice and intellectual input regarding the genesis and ontology of worldwide policy trackers, indexes, and governance indicators.

large-scale behavioural and societal changes – all of which have to be combined coherently and implemented urgently and simultaneously in an integrated way. Has there ever been a more daunting challenge to international cooperation and global policy action? (2) The novel coronavirus Sars-CoV-2 and the Covid-19 pandemic illustrated how vicious and complex the multi-scalar occurrence of a global policy problem can be and how intersectional and networked global crises in the twenty-first century may look like. At the same time, the pandemic powerfully illustrated the need for and the added value of global policy coherence and action as no country, region, or even continent was in a position to effectively tackle this crisis alone. From targeted, science-based internationally concerted policy action and novel public–private partnerships via the tackling of questions of supply chains, trade, and finance, to the need for North–South cooperation in a spirit of solidarity, Covid-19 literally touched upon the very notions of policy effectiveness, policy coherence, and policy diffusion. (3) Threats to peace, security, democracy, the rule of law, and the autonomy and integrity of long-established global norms and multilateral institutions have become more complex, intricate, multilayered, and challenging in the twenty-first century. Over the past two decades, there has been a steady paradigmatic shift away from the textbook type of interstate wars that the UN Charter was established to prevent in the first place, toward an unprecedented and proliferating array and range of intrastate wars, internal conflict, violence, insurgencies, and domestic institutional fragmentation paired with inherent governance fragility and failing statehood. Moreover, various types of novel global challenges – for example, climate change as a threat to international peace and security – are now being seen in direct combination and correlation as the wars in Sudan and Syria have demonstrated (Tiitmamer et al., 2018).

8.1.1 Overcoming Both Nation-Centred and 'Overly Global' Approaches

The famous Rio Earth Summit of 1992 (United Nations Conference on Environment and Development, UNCED) became the first 'playground' on which so-called *global governance* concepts were brought in and tested, and subsequently mainstreamed and reflected in UNCED's official conference outcomes, that is to say, the Rio Declaration, Agenda 21, and the Rio Conventions – United Nations Framework Convention on Climate Change (UNFCC), United Nations Convention on Biological Diversity (UNCBD), and United Nations Convention to Combat Desertification (UNCCD)[2] – as well as in the entire Rio follow-up process

[2] UN Framework Convention on Climate Change, UN Convention on Biological Diversity, UN Convention to Combat Desertification.

(Rechkemmer, 2006). Thus, global governance concepts led to a new approach in international law, adding more non-binding treaties and instruments, and establishing the mandatory consensus principle in global environmental policy-making. These elements were certainly well intentioned, aiming to overcome the traditional national interest-based power politics *à la* 'political realism' and its inevitable stalemates in international diplomacy, and replacing that paradigm with a consensual process based on scientific evidence and shared normative convictions. And yet, thirty years later, it is obvious that non-binding treaties based on voluntary contributions and 'pledges' combined with the notorious need to have every single country party agree to whatever the outcome of a conference or policy-making draft represents, have not done the trick of tangibly advancing effective global environmental legislation and policy implementation in a measurable, meaningful way. Climate COPs,[3] in particular, have become a perennial ritual that routinely leads to peak emissions and hollow PR shows, but not to deep decarbonisation (Climate Justice Alliance, 2022, Harris, 2022).

Before Rio and, therefore, before UNFCCC, the primary focus of environmental and climate-related policy-making was on the nation-state and its dominion-based law-making, policy-making, and enforcement capabilities. Then, in the 1990s, the unfolding discourse on global environmental governance emphasised the supranational sphere as the only legitimate and promising place and means to address global sustainability issues and therefore, climate change. Sustainability issues were now supposed to be addressed through problem formulation, agenda setting, multilateral negotiations, 'deals' to bring about new energy regimes, and an iterative process of consensus building and institutionalisation (Rechkemmer, 2006). The hope was to get a critical mass of nation states committed to taking effective collective legal, political, and social action to curb GHG emissions, reduce waste and pollution, protect biodiversity, freshwater and marine resources, and so forth. The price to pay, however, was the move away from legally binding and enforceable treaties as the gold standard of international law in favour of softer, non-binding agreements (such as, ultimately, the Paris Agreement). Also, the Rio Earth Summit deliberately triggered a process of multiple parallel negotiation streams aiming to address a wide array of environmental issues in separate topical law- and policy-making processes. However, these negotiation streams were poorly interrelated thematically and badly orchestrated institutionally, resulting in an eclectic collection of somewhat disjointed legal agreements and fragmented policy frameworks (Rechkemmer, 2005a, 2005b). In hindsight – more than thirty years after Rio – the global governance theory-inspired paradigm shift did not deliver on its promise. GHG

[3] Conferences of the Parties under the UNFCCC.

emissions have been rising since the 1970s in a steady fashion, and 27 COPs under the UNFCCC regime so far have not changed this trajectory at all – an inconvenient but undeniable fact (Chan et al., 2022).

8.1.2 The Regional Prerogative

Neither unilateral, nationally dominated, nor full-scale multilateral, that is to say 'overly' global, approaches to climate change mitigation law- and policy-making have proven to be effective enough to lead to measurable progress toward the clear objectives of the UNFCCC, the Kyoto Protocol, and the Paris Agreement. Meanwhile, the most severe climate impacts play out at a regional scale and resolution. They typically occur across and beyond the borders of nation states but also show characteristics that correlate with the unique geographical, topographical, morphological, and sociocultural ontologies of the world's regions. Hence, the default scale and level of governance interventions, through law and policy frameworks and processes, should be the regional one. Second, climate change is a global threat of completely unprecedented magnitude and severity. Its impacts, effects, and consequences are now present and cascade into literally every single sustainability issue of our time. Both ontologically and methodologically, it was a mistake to classify and address climate change as a mere subset of the large global environmental issues cluster, allocating just one among many international conventions to it and following a 'one-size-fits-all' approach. Rather, climate change requires to be understood and conceived of as the 'mother of all sustainability challenges' – and thus a far more comprehensive and robust governance approach is needed. In sum, a major shift in our thinking on legal and policy frameworks, instruments, and resources is required to increase the intensity and the efficacy of law and policy efforts if we want to even have a remote chance of success in dealing with climate change *and* other sustainability grand challenges of the twenty-first century (Andonova et al., 2009).

Since Rio, multilateral cooperation has experienced a redefinition of its genuine connotation. Multilateral cooperation now incorporates non-state actors; the scientific community; and non-hierarchical and alternative regulatory and networking patterns. International cooperation has become a more complex and non-linear system of structures and agents that govern at multiple levels and through multiple means. This system includes, but is not limited to, formal and intergovernmental negotiation processes under the aegis of the UN, which are based on or produce legal agreements and regimes on single issues. Nation states are still important as principal actors, among many others. Many scholars have highlighted the role of non-governmental organisations (NGOs) along with the need for a more formalised legitimacy model for the same.

For example, in their article '*The Role of NGOs and Civil Society in Global Environmental Governance*', Gemmill and Bamidele-Izu identify five major roles for civil society to play in sustainability governance: collecting, disseminating, and analysing information; providing input to agenda-setting and policy development processes; performing operational functions; assessing environmental conditions and monitoring compliance with environmental agreements (a so-called 'watch-dog' function); and advocating environmental justice (Gemmill & Bamidele-Izu, 2002). Still, governments remain in charge of devising policies, laws, and related measures regarding climate change mitigation. Given the aforementioned insights, however, there is ample reason for expecting such laws, policies, and measures to be more effective if they are orchestrated and diffused regionally, and anchored in civil society.

In this chapter, we examine and analyse if and how governments in the Gulf Cooperation Council (GCC) have responded to the unprecedented challenges of climate change ever since the adoption of the Paris Agreement in December 2015. In particular, our interest has been on the mitigation policy side, and, within this policy field, on carbon neutrality and net zero related laws, policies, and government measures. The methodology that we used for our research is 'policy tracking', a relatively recent addition to the mixed-methods field of assessing policy based on rigorous accounting for government activity, gaining valuable insights regarding stringency, intensity, and the allocation of public resources within a given policy field. Our policy tracker has allowed us to literally count, and account for, carbon neutrality related policy measures in the GCC member states since 2015, and analyse the respective commitments or lack thereof. This method allows for a preliminary comparative assessment of 'real' ambition beyond strategic communication and pledges made at international conferences. For the purpose of this chapter, we focused on ambition rather than 'action', that is to say, physical interventions evidently leading to an immediate curb of GHG emissions. Our chapter first highlights the commonalities and unique traits that influence GCC countries' respective climate policy approaches. We then turn to the methodology aspect, introduce the overall approach, and situate it within governance effectiveness and indexing research, and finally we describe how we tracked climate policies across the region. We then present the results of our study and discuss future research directions.

8.2 The Climate Policy Context in the GCC Region

While many existing and projected impacts of climate change are similar across the GCC region, some of the climate risks and threats facing the GCC member states are specific or pose particular or even unique challenges that require adaptation and resilience-yielding responses that are conceived of and tailored accordingly. Well noted in much of the scholarship is the accelerated rise of temperatures and with it, prolonged heatwaves, which will affect the region even more in years to come. This will have impacts not only on human well-being, livelihoods, food security, and biodiversity (terrestrial and marine) but also on the economy as, for instance, rapidly increasing demands for cooling will place more demands on energy, which at present increase hydrocarbon utilisation and, in turn, carbon emissions and air pollution. Less discussed in the literature is the impact of sea level rise (and associated impacts, such as storm surges, extreme swell waves, salination of underground water sources, and coastal flooding), which is of critical importance as many of the major cities and industrial complexes in the GCC are in the low-lying coastal zone (Cochrane & Al-Hababi, 2023; Hababi, 2023). Water scarcity is already a serious issue in the GCC, with a heavy reliance upon desalination (which is energy-intensive and dirty and increasing demands place even greater demands on energy production). Increasing populations and rapid economic development are resulting in greater demands not only for energy but also water, and thereby more energy. Without effective work to reduce consumption and enhance efficiency, these demands will continue to rise, and without serious investments in green and renewable sources, these demands will continue to be met with hydrocarbons. Due to some geographic traits of the region (being arid and largely desertic) as well as being a region processing hydrocarbons, air quality is low and stands to worsen if the status quo continues. From a macroeconomic and geopolitical perspective, as the GCC countries' economic well-being has historically been relying almost entirely on hydrocarbon resources, these demands may become less in the long term, however, even the most optimistic global energy mix scenario predictions expect oil and liquified natural gas (LNG) to continue to be used well beyond 2060. Within more pragmatic assessments, LNG demand may continue to rise beyond 2060, which is a problem unless economies are sufficiently diversified (Cochrane & Al-Hababi, 2023).

The GCC member states share common risks related to climate change. These risks need to be considered with regard to country-specific capacity and readiness to adapt. Drawing upon data from the World Bank Data Bank (2022; Table 8.1), the GCC member states have similar and unique traits, which alter their respective ability to respond to the risks associated with climate change. The member states have relatively small populations (less than 10 million, with the exception of Saudi Arabia), with populations that are not as youthful as the global average (only Saudi Arabia is on par with the percentage of the population being 0–14, however, temporary immigration in some of these countries needs also to be taken into account). The countries have relatively high levels of gross domestic product (GDP) per capita (all member states exceed the global average of USD10,916), the latter being enabled by hydrocarbon resources in most member states. The extraction, processing, and export of those resources have contributed to very high CO_2 emissions per

Table 8.1 *Demographic and economic data for GCC member states.*[4]

Member state	Population (millions)	Population% aged 0–14	GDP per capita (current USD)	CO_2 emissions per capita (metric tonnes)	Electricity production from renewable sources (% of total)*
Bahrain	1.7	18	20,410	19.6	0.0
Kuwait	4.3	21	24,812	21.6	0.0
Oman	5.1	22	14,485	15.2	0.0
Qatar	2.8	14	50,124	32.4	0.0
Saudi Arabia	34.8	25	20,110	15.3	0.0
UAE	9.9	15	36,285	20.8	0.2

* Excluding hydroelectric, data for most countries from 2015 (most recently available).

capita, alongside high levels of economic development and associated consumption. Qatar, Kuwait, and the UAE are listed as having the highest CO_2 emissions per capita by the World Bank. According to the ND-GAIN Index (considering both vulnerability and readiness), demographic and economic differences (as well as sociopolitical and institutional factors), contribute to divergences despite similar challenges. On the global ranking, the countries rank (in order of most ready to least) as: UAE (30), Qatar (44), Saudi Arabia (56), Oman (58), Kuwait (65), and Bahrain (71) (World Bank Data Bank, 2022; Table 8.1).

Given the abundant solar resources in the region, by the time the Paris Agreement was adopted, no member states of the GCC were leaders in investing in solar energy (or any other renewable energy) for diversifying their energy mix to include non-hydrocarbon renewables. The World Bank data used in Table 8.1 is from 2015 and reflects the situation just prior to the Paris COP. The world average for electricity production from renewables in 2015, for comparative purposes, was 6.8%, which was also remarkably low given the collective recognition of the need to make this transition for decades. However, after the adoption of the Paris Agreement, an interesting change emerged. While the percentage of domestic renewable energy capacity in Bahrain, Kuwait, Oman, and Qatar between 2016 and 2020 remained basically flat, a slight uptick could be noticed for the Kingdom of Saudi Arabia (KSA) and even a very significant rise for the UAE, as shown in Figure 8.1. By the end of 2020, the UAE was by far the regional leader in terms of installed renewable energy capacity. However, as the International Renewable Energy Agency (IRENA) notes, renewable

[4] World Bank, 2022 (using most recently available data).

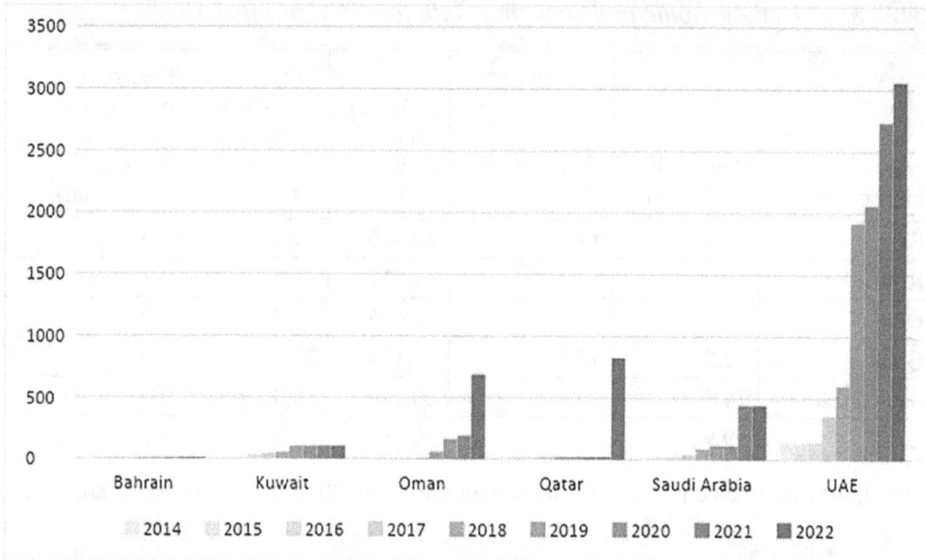

Figure 8.1 Total renewable energy in megawatts (MW), 2014–2022.

power projects in Saudi Arabia are expected to grow more rapidly than in the UAE so that by 2030, Saudi Arabia is expected to overtake the UAE with an installed capacity nearly twice that of the UAE if the current trajectory continues.

8.3 Policy Tracking Methodology

The tracking and mapping of *policy-relevant statistics* is by now routine – interest rates, financial markets, unemployment, government expenditures and economic stimulus packages, trade balances, and so on – but the tracking of *public policy initiatives and measures is less* so. And note that 'tracking' and 'mapping' are different from annual or periodic indices like the Worldwide Governance Indicators or the Corruption Perceptions Index (to name two of the most prominent). To 'track' and 'map' *policy* means to register government actions in real-time, in the sequences in which they occur. Over longer periods of time, this can accumulate to a more or less comprehensive 'profile' of sorts on the character, phenomenology, and tilt of a given government's policies in specific policy fields or areas. For example, tight budgets year after year are reasonable evidence of a contractionary fiscal policy stance (Raudla et al., 2015). The accumulation over time of various policies in health, education, and social protection allows us to classify welfare states into various ideal types (Esping-Andersen, 1990; Armingeon & Beyeler, 2004; Schelkle, 2012). Covid-19, similar to the 2008 financial crisis, provided another laboratory case of a single, global disastrous event that demanded rapid public health, economic, and social policy responses, as well as coordination at the regional and international levels. Events and hazards of this type and magnitude provide an unparalleled opportunity to track and map a rapid series of policy responses and measures that may vary by national circumstance and context, sociocultural norms, institutional traditions, or political ideology. Tracking government actions on climate and the environment allows us to judge fidelity to the UNFCCC Paris Agreement (New Climate Institute, n.d.) or other multilateral environmental agreements (MEAs). In this case, apart from the methodological enticement, there is genuine interest in comparing government policies to understand what works, what works best, and what are action-oriented measures.

Policy trackers and governance indicators have grown in large numbers in the last decades (Arndt & Oman, 2008; Pal & Ireland, 2009; Buduru & Pal, 2010) and by now number in the hundreds (Rotberg & Bhushan, 2015). Some of the most prominent include the Worldwide Governance Indicators (Kaufmann et al., 2010), the Corruption Perceptions Index and related measures (Mungiu-Pippidi, 2015; Mungiu-Pippidi & Dadašov, 2016; Mungiu-Pippidi & Johnston, 2017), and happiness indexes (Global Happiness Council, 2018; Stiglitz et al., 2018; Helliwell et al., 2019). This is a well-established field but with virtually no examples tailored specifically for the GCC region.

The intense interest in government policy responses, actions, and measures to the Sars-CoV-2 pandemic rapidly yielded an unusual number of new 'policy trackers' and 'dashboards' from different organisations and research entities, focusing on either specific policy fields or geopolitical regions. This chapter focuses on one that was developed by the authors for the GCC region, looking at climate policy measures and announcements by the six GCC states (Bahrain, Kuwait, Oman, Qatar, Saudi Arabia, and the UAE). Methodological details and some of the most interesting preliminary findings are provided in this chapter. We briefly present the data-gathering and analytical approaches, methods, and techniques, some of the key results, and discuss observations and speculations on those results regarding the prevalence, character, and intensity of carbon neutrality relevant climate policy measures.

We discuss some of the methodological choices in constructing a 'tracker' below, but at the moment, will simply note that trackers fall squarely within a solid tradition of governance and policy indicators (Pollitt, 2011; Davis et al., 2012; Karabell, 2014; Bradley, 2015; Merry et al., 2015; Rottenburg et al., 2015; Bouckaert & Van Dooren, 2016; Maggetti & Gilardi, 2016). A recent development in the field has been the construction of various 'indexes' that combine data and indicators into some more evaluative ranking or measure – Oxford University's Blavatnik School of Government 'Coronavirus Government Response Tracker', for example, tried to measure the 'stringency' of policy responses to Covid-19.

The country selection comprised, as noted earlier, of all six of the GCC states. Data collection initially focused on the main areas of governments' climate policy announcements. For each of these areas, further subcategories of policy measures and interventions were identified. Ultimately, this 'taxonomic' categorisation allowed us to focus on those policies and measures immediately relevant to carbon neutrality and net zero goals and objectives under the Paris Agreement. Researchers gathered qualitative and quantitative data on policy interventions in each relevant area and subcategory for each country, by harvesting data from official intergovernmental bulletins and datasets (e.g. the European Union (EU), Organisation for Economic Co-operation and Development (OECD), International Monetary Fund (IMF), various UN agencies, and World Bank), official government bulletins, announcements, social media accounts, and websites (for each of the six countries), trusted news sources traced back to official sources, policy briefs and documents, and academic publications (using information in English, French, and Arabic). Data were collected for the period 1 October 2015, through 31 December 2022, to amount to a day-to-day comprehensive and comparative tracker dataset.

The methodology was deliberately agnostic. Our approach was simply to track each relevant measure taken by each of the six governments over the period under examination and thereby produce an interactive profile for each country as well as various comparative datasheets. No single initiative or policy response is weighted more than others, and while the raw data will allow the construction of indexes our work did not attempt to do this. However, by tracking each measure across numerous climate policy subfields, it is possible to see patterns and trajectories of responses over time, and also the relative balance within and across policy subareas, and, of course, compare all of these across the country sample.

Our database of policy initiatives, measures, and interventions was constructed in two phases. The first drew on existing policy trackers and datasets. The second phase relied more heavily on official government websites and social media outlets, reports, media articles, and academic literature to provide a more finely grained and continuous reading of the stream of policy announcements coming from the respective governments (in three languages, English, Arabic, and French). The range of available and reliable sources varied by country. This reflected both a mix of the freedom of the press in each country and the intensity of international interest in different countries. Manual data collection was the main methodology used. The data were collected in Excel spreadsheet software with each sheet representing a separate country. As data were manually collected for each country they were entered in a new row in a cell under specific categories with a date and description of the headline, along with a hyperlink attached that could be accessed by clicking on the cell leading to the original data source. The collected data were checked for mistakes and several quality check iterations were performed to ensure consistency in collection methods. Table 8.2 provides generic examples of policy trackers (Table 8.2) and our proprietary tracker's data entry workbook format, both for the field of Covid-19-related policy analysis in the GCC.[5]

[5] Interested readers may obtain our dataset (API) by contacting us by email at: info@rcp-futures.com.

Table 8.2 *Generic examples of comparative policy trackers (for Covid-19 measures).*

Name	Sponsor	Link	Content (as of October 2020)
Country Policy Tracker	OECD	www.oecd.org/coronavirus/country-policy-tracker/	Fiscal and monetary, employment and social, and health. However, it also includes data on country responses in educational policy, science and innovation, tax policy, and supply of disinfectants. The scope of countries is different for each policy field, but the core consists of OECD member states and G20 non-OECD members.
OPSI COVID-19 Innovative Response Tracker	OECD	https://oecd-opsi.org/covid-response/	Innovative policy responses (submitted by governments). 434 entries, including information and practice sharing with public and/or internal; public service delivery under new circumstances; real time data collection, sharing, and analysis; crowdsourcing responses; health and safety of responders; patient care; etc.
Social Protection Responses to Covid-19 Crisis Around the World	ILO	www.social-protection.org/gimi/ShowWiki.action?id=3417	206 countries and 1,496 measures, of which unemployment protection, income protection, housing and special allowances account for over 50%. Health and food security are also included.
Policy Responses to Covid-19	IMF	www.imf.org/en/Topics/imf-and-covid19/Policy-Responses-to-COVID-19	Comprehensive, and includes the key economic responses of 196 countries in fiscal policy (spending on health measures, support for households and firms, tax measures), monetary and macrofinancial policy (interest rates, bond markets, liquidity provisions, bank credit, and lending facilities), and exchange rate and balance of payments (currency devaluations, foreign exchange marked interventions to mitigate volatility).
Coronavirus Government Response Tracker	Blavatnik School of Government, Oxford University	www.bsg.ox.ac.uk/research/research-projects/coronavirus-government-response-tracker	The Oxford tracker (OxCGRT) assembles 17 indicators for data from more than 160 countries, in three areas: (1) containment and closure (e.g. school and workplace closing, public transport, international and domestic travel), (2) economic (e.g. income support and fiscal measures), and (3) health systems (e.g. testing, contact tracing, investment in Covid-19 vaccines). The data are assembled into four composite indexes on overall government response (which includes all the indicators and provides an index whether responses have become ‘stronger’ or ‘weaker’ over the pandemic), ‘stringency’ (the strictness of lock-down measures), containment and health, and economic support.

Table 8.2 (*cont.*)

Name	Sponsor	Link	Content (as of October 2020)
Covid-19 Observatory in Latin America and the Caribbean	Economic Commission for Latin America and the Caribbean (UN)	www.cepal.org/en/topics/covid-19	Monitors movement restrictions, health, economy, employment, social protection, education and gender. It does so for the countries in the region, chronologically, and in terms of 'actions' taken (with a narrative record of those actions for each country). 'Social protection' include cash transfers, food transfers/in-kind transfers, guarantee of basic services, and other social protection. The labour index include actions on labour protection (e.g. teleworking, paid work leave, paid sick leave, unemployment insurance, prevention of discrimination based on Covid-19, labour policies for low-wage and/or informal workers), elective work leave, reduction of working hours, and prohibition of dismissal from work. For each of the seven tracking indicators, 'story maps' are generated showing the number of 'actions'.
Daily Clock for Covid-19 in Arab Countries	UN Economic and Social Commission for Western Asia (ESCWA)	www.unescwa.org/covid-19-prevalence-arab-countries	ESCWA draws on World Health Organization (WHO) and Ministries of Health data to provide a 'daily clock' of the prevalence of Covid-19 in the Arab region, which includes (in declining order of number of cases): Saudi Arabia, Qatar, Egypt, UAE, Kuwait, Oman, Iraq, Bahrain, Algeria, Morocco, Sudan, Djibouti, Somalia, Mauritania, Lebanon, Tunisia, Jordan, Yemen, Palestine, Libya, Comoros, and Syria.
Coronavirus Disease (Covid-19) Dashboard	WHO	https://covid19.who.int/	Health impact data (confirmed cases, new cases, deaths) across the world, by country and by WHO region (Americas, Europe, Eastern Mediterranean, South-East Asia, Western Pacific, and Africa), similar Johns Hopkins University and the Coronatracker, though it presents the data in different ways. In addition, however, it provides 'country guidance' and so is a source of global policy standards, benchmarks, and guidelines.

Policy Tracker of Government Responses (PTGR) to the Covid-19 crisis for the MENA region	College of Public Policy, Hamad Bin Khalifa University	www.menatracker.org	This site presents government responses to the coronavirus pandemic across the middle east and north Africa (MENA). The tacker assembles policy responses into three broad areas: (1) health (physical and social distancing/workplaces; physical and social distancing/schools; physical and social distancing/mass gatherings; physical and social distancing/public spaces and transportation; movement measures; special protection measures/ persons at risk, vulnerable persons, and others; special protection measures/ health workers); (2) economic (fiscal responses; monetary responses; support to labour market; trade and supply chain; support to key sectors; support to other countries; reopening of the economy); and (3) social (access to education; care/healthcare/maternity care/childcare; children and family/maternity/parental leave; food and nutrition; housing/basic services; income/jobs protection/unemployment benefits/injury benefits/sickness/benefits paid for loss of earning; pensions; special allowance/grant targeting vulnerable groups: women, refugees, disability).

8.4 Discussion of Results and Findings

The first observation is that all GCC countries adopted and disseminated a national 'vision' strategic plan in the fields of energy, water, climate change, and the environment more broadly. Although all of these issue areas represent a critical short-term priority in these nations' economic and development policies, until recently, GCC governments seemed to be obsessed with having long-term 'national visions' identified instead (Hvidt, 2013). As the fossil fuel industry is the backbone of the economy in these countries, stated climate policies are typically strongly linked to national economic diversification plans, through which the more ambitious GCC countries seek to inch closer toward a 'post-fossil fuel world'. Yet this presents a conundrum. For instance, all GCC countries rely on desalination plants for their freshwater supply, which is either free or heavily subsidised for citizens. This leads to high pressure regarding the securing of energy sources to run these plants, which typically does not bode well for decarbonising this critical sector – unless governments decide on game-changing policies and bold action, for example, phasing out subsidies on fossil fuel-based consumption or even introducing tax instruments, which is a real challenge for rentier states. As a small common denominator, all GCC governments have by now taken steps in the direction of decarbonising at least certain sectors – albeit to highly varying degrees, as our comparative analysis shows.

Similarly, all six states have started policy work to render the production of energy and water more efficient, again, to very varying degrees. This includes diversifying electricity sources, which are still primarily generated from oil. To produce electricity, most countries announced that they plan to rely more on natural gas, nuclear power stations, solar plants, and hydrogen going forward. For instance, the UAE has already established nuclear plants aiming to reduce the dependency on oil in electricity production, while Saudi Arabia is working to construct several stations. On the other hand, Qatar, as the world's leading LNG exporter, has advocated for the use of natural gas as being less harmful to the earth's climate compared to coal or oil – a position that is controversial given the undeniable fact that natural gas is still a fossil fuel resulting in GHG emissions. Moreover, like the European Commission, Qatar states that gas can be a transitory solution toward truly green, environmentally friendly, and carbon-neutral energy production. However, most GCC countries so far have made very limited investments in domestic renewable energy production, particularly solar plants, due to political, economic, and, in part, technical reasons (e.g. conventional solar plants are not able to deal with the extreme heat and dust in the Gulf region). More recently, however, R&D has led to novel solar technology more suitable for the Gulf environment. The following section tables and discusses government measures relevant to carbon neutrality in the six GCC countries that our tracker unveiled and documented.

In Bahrain in 2015, just in time for COP21 in Paris, the government adopted a six-year plan to scale back subsidies for the domestic consumption of electricity, water, and petrol along with an 'Energy Efficient Lighting Initiative', which sought to replace energy-inefficient incandescent lamps (ILs) with more efficient CFLs in the short term and with LED-based lamps in the medium term, and new 'Motor Vehicles Standards' and related technical regulations to reduce emissions from gasoline and diesel engine vehicles. Also, the Civil Aviation Authority's 'Emission Management Plan for Sustainable Aviation Growth' was launched along with the 'Kingdom of Bahrain Energy Efficiency Programme' (KEEP), which targets public, residential, and commercial buildings and the industrial sector and calls to improve energy efficiency and reduce cumulative electricity consumption by 2030. On the corporate side, Bahrain Petroleum Company's (BAPCO) 'Energy Conservation Policy' promoted the more efficient use of natural resources through enhancing heater efficiency and condensate recovery, and reducing mass loss. Also, BAPCO's 'Carbon Recovery Plan' utilises runoff CO_2 for industrial applications, and its 5 MW photovoltaic (PV) grid-connected plant demonstrated PV solar technology under local conditions. The Gulf Petrochemical Industries Company's (GPIC) 'Carbon Recovery Project' captures CO_2 in the runoff gases of the GPIC Methanol Plant, and Bahrain National Gas Company (Banagas) completed a retrofit project of gas turbines which yields an average reduction of 44% nitrogen oxides (NOx) emissions from the power generation stations. Finally, the government and Tatweer Petroleum jointly announced multiple efficiency projects including flare reductions, gas compression, and oilfield electrification, to reduce CO_2 emissions, but failed to provide verifiable quantitative information. Note that all of the above initiatives and measures were kick-started in the margins of COP21, presumably as part of a bold campaign to showcase the country's commitment to UNFCCC and the Paris Agreement. Our tracker unveiled that after COP21, however, very few new policies were adopted until 2021, which was in sharp contrast to the initial 'demonstration of ambition'. At COP26 in Glasgow, Scotland, Bahrain pledged to reach net zero by 2060 and to reduce emissions by 30% by 2035 through decarbonisation, efficiency initiatives, and a doubling of the deployment of renewables. However, our tracker did not find sufficient evidence for tangible carbon neutrality ambition in Bahrain since 2016.

Since 2015, Kuwait's government has introduced more efficient district cooling systems in new residential areas, increased the production of electricity from solar power, planted Avicennia to absorb gas emissions and launched multiple energy efficiency programmes. However, we did not find independent verifiable data to quantify the scope and effect of these changes. In 2019, Kuwait pledged to produce 15% of its energy from renewable sources by 2030 and adopted the 'National Adaptation Plan 2019–2030', which, despite the title, included some mitigation elements also. In 2020, the country updated its nationally determined contributions (NDCs) to concretise earlier pledges and demonstrate increased ambition. At COP26 in 2021, Kuwait presented updated its commitments and, for the first time, submitted a quantitative emission reduction goal, namely to lower annual GHG emissions by 7.4% by 2035, by adopting a circular economic model. Then, at COP27 at Sharm El Sheikh, Egypt, the country for the first time submitted a carbon neutrality pledge for its oil and gas sector by 2050. More recently, there have been several new technological initiatives implemented by the government, such as carbon capture and storage (CCS) projects and an increase in new wind and solar plants, although concrete numbers regarding capacity and net emission reductions could not be found by the tracker. In sum, sufficient government action underpinning the stated ambition appears to be still lacking. For instance, by the end of 2021, renewable energy accounted for less than 1% of domestic grid capacity, which is in contrast to Kuwait's pledged target of 15% by 2030 (see Figure 8.1). Indeed, our tracker did not find evidence yet for tangible action that would put the country on a credible pathway to reach carbon neutrality by 2050.

In 2015, the Sultanate of Oman launched its 'National Strategy for Adaptation and Mitigation of Climate Change' for an initial period of five years, along with its 'National Energy Strategy'. Then, in 2018, the country submitted its second NDC report to the UNFCCC Secretariat, part of which was a new strategic framework for engagement with the Green Climate Fund (GCF) through the GCF's 'Readiness' programme. In October 2019, Oman adopted the 'National Strategy for Adaptation and Mitigation to Climate Change 2020–2040', which foresees that renewable energy capacity shall be more than 2,600 MW by 2025, which would reduce about 6,000 tonnes of CO_2 equivalents, an abatement of about 6% of the total GHG emissions of 2015. Also in 2019, the sultan announced the 'Million Date Palm Plantation Project', which is geared toward reducing CO_2 in the air. In 2021, the first wind farm in the country and also in the Gulf region, Dhofar I, went online and immediately reached 7% of the installed power generation capacity (50 MW). In the same year, the government adopted the '2030 Carbon Control Target Plan', part of which is the government's pledge that solar power would generate 21% and wind and waste power together another 9% of the total energy required domestically in Oman by 2030. In 2022, the country opened its first large-scale solar photovoltaic farm, located in Ibri, with a capacity of up to 500 MW. The government also announced a policy to produce 2,450 MW of renewable energy by 2025, mainly from solar energy, and pledged net zero emissions for the domestic oil and gas industry by 2050. Note that all of these pledges were made very recently, and so, it is too early to tell whether or not the government is tangibly following through with implementation. In sum, however, given its relatively modest economic power (in comparison to other GCC states), Oman has surprised with a number of actual hands-down mitigation projects potentially putting the country on a more credible carbon neutrality path compared to the two aforementioned countries. Indeed, as Figure 8.1 shows, IRENA independently reported a spike in domestic renewable energy capacity in Oman for 2022.

For the period between 2015 and 2018, our tracker did not reveal the implementation of significant governmental projects of scale that would tangibly demonstrate an immediate net emission reduction effect in Qatar. Rather, due to the rapid economic development of the country and the approaching 2022 FIFA World Cup in Qatar, a substantial rise in the production of GHG emissions, primarily due to unprecedented activity in the construction, transportation, and infrastructure sectors, occurred. On the other hand, in the same period, the country made significant investments in the field of carbon mitigation R&D, including next-generation PV technology suitable for harsh desert climates, water efficiency, flare reduction, emission reduction from LNG processing, and CCS technology. Also, in 2015, Qatar had announced steps toward more efficient forms of desalination, however, progress has been slow and most of the desalination plants are operating at a high-emission pace. The country made rapid progress though in public transportation including a state-of-the-art metro system and several smaller smart and efficient tramway systems. In 2019, Qatar announced the launch of the largest CCS facility in the Gulf region, with a capacity of 2.2 megatonnes at launch and 5 megatonnes of CO_2 equivalent per year to be achieved by 2025. Then, in 2021, the government adopted the 'National Climate Change Action Plan 2030' with the target of a 25% reduction in GHG emissions by 2030, a 37 megatonnes (Mt) CO_2 equivalent. By the same token, the country announced the Al Shaheen flare reduction project at a projected 2 Mt CO_2 equivalent per annum, a jetty boil-off gas recovery initiative at 1.6 Mt CO_2 equivalent per annum, and a large-scale tree planting and greenspace extension project, much of which was verifiably achieved by the end of 2022, as IRENA data show as well (see Figure 8.1). The country also opened the Al Kharsaah solar PV plant with an 800 MW capacity. Finally, at COP27, the government pledged to achieve net zero emissions by 2050. In sum, the country's mastery of the art of strategic communication makes it difficult to discern between symbolic announcements and tangible action. However, there has been significant progress in very recent years regarding laws, policies, ambition, and action toward GHG emission reduction and environmental sustainability more broadly. As Figure 8.1 shows, IRENA independently reported a significant uptick of renewable energy capacity in Qatar for 2022. On the other hand, given Qatar's planned and in part already implemented extension of LNG production, conventional tourism, and the infrastructure, transportation, and building sectors, it would appear that much of the emission reduction effect is eclipsed by these activities.

Hence, despite the progress made on renewables, our tracking did not provide any evidence for assuming that the country is yet on a credible path to carbon neutrality.

In 2015, Saudi Arabia's COP21 pledge stated that it aims for 50% of electricity to be generated with renewable energy and 50% with natural gas by 2030. While this remains to be seen, the country's Uthmaniyah CCS facility was opened in July 2015. It is capable of capturing around 0.8 Mt per annum of CO_2 from the Hayiwah LNG recovery plant. In 2016, the country presented Vision 2030, which contains a roadmap for economic diversification and the aim of reducing the country's dependence on oil in favour of an alternative, diversified economy. In 2017, Saudi Arabia announced the doubling of its natural gas production to displace the direct burning of crude oil in power generation and water desalination. In 2018, the KSA started to implement the establishment of a tangibly greater share of energy production from gas, solar, wind, and nuclear sources and made major investments in more efficient technologies. In 2019, a national programme was announced to rationalise water consumption in the Kingdom. In 2020, the 400 MW Dumat Al-Jandal wind farm was opened as the country's first utility-scale wind power project and one of the largest wind farms in the Middle East. In 2021, the Kingdom launched the 'Saudi Green Initiative' (SGI) and the 'Middle East Green Initiative' (MGI), which aim to reduce carbon emissions in the Middle East by more than 10% of the current global contributions. At COP26, the KSA pledged to reduce CO_2 eq. emissions by 278 million tonnes per year by 2030, and to reach net zero by 2060 through the 'Circular Carbon Economy' (CCE) framework. The country also announced joining the Global Methane Pledge, which aims at limiting methane emissions by 30% compared to 2020 levels, as well as establishing a 10 billion dollar fund for deploying CCS technologies in the Middle East and Africa. The KSA also launched a large afforestation project.

In 2021, the Sakaka Solar Power Plant consisting of 1.2 million solar panels arranged over 6 km^2 of land was opened. In 2022, the government announced to target carbon capture of 44 million tonnes by 2035 and to reach 70% of Saudi Arabia's renewable energy target of 58.5GW capacity by 2030 through the establishment of a new green financing framework under the Public Investment Fund. In sum, while the aforementioned projects were independently confirmed, the KSA government has flooded the global carbon community since 2015 with a plethora of announcements and PR campaigns, making it somewhat difficult to assess real ambition. Also, the country is notorious for its efforts to water down outcome documents at UNFCCC COPs, similar to China, India, and Russia. On the other hand, since 2015, Saudi Arabia has no doubt made massive new investments in the R&D and also in the physical establishment of green technologies and renewable energy plants, especially solar, but also wind and hydrogen, and CCS facilities – not only in the KSA itself but also abroad through joint ventures. Major new green infrastructure initiatives have been announced such as the NEOM project. However, the country has also increased its fossil fuel production and processing since 2015, while at the same claiming to be diversifying its economy. As Figure 8.1 indicates, Saudi Arabia's real renewable energy installed capacity in 2022 was significantly lower than that of Qatar and even Oman, rendering the political rhetoric somewhat moot so far. Likewise, our tracker has not provided any evidence that the country is yet on a path toward carbon neutrality.

In 2015, the UAE introduced a fuel pricing reform, linking gasoline and diesel prices to international market prices. In 2016, a target to increase the share of clean energy in the national energy mix to 27% by 2021 was announced along with a renewed commitment to build a railway network in the country to provide faster and cleaner mobility options. Also, the UAE implemented the 100 MW Shams 1 concentrated solar power project along with the Mohammed bin Rashid Solar Park which leverages both photovoltaic and concentrated solar technologies and is set to generate 5,000 MW of electricity. The UAE was the first Gulf state to announce a national climate strategy in 2017 and was also the first to link its climate strategy with its economic development plans, for which the UAE Green Agenda 2015–2030 was established as an overarching implementation framework. Also in 2017, the Al Reyadah CCS project opened, which captures CO_2 at an iron and steel factory (the world's first such plant), and compresses, dehydrates, and transports it through a pipeline for injection into oil wells for enhanced oil recovery applications. The 200 MW phase two of the Mohammed bin Rashid Al Maktoum Solar Park was commissioned in March 2017. The UAE's 'National Energy Strategy 2050', released in 2017, aims for 50% of renewable and nuclear energy in installed electric capacity by 2050, while substantially reducing final electricity demand. Also, the UAE announced plans for implementing upper limits of 12% of coal and 38% of natural gas-based capacity. In 2019, at the launch of a new sustainable building programme dubbed Barjeel, Ras Al Khaimah's municipality said it would start to build 600 MW of rooftop solar and 600 MW of utility-scale solar projects. Also in 2019, the UAE launched the 'Regional Collaboration Centre Dubai', a collaboration with UNFCCC and the World Green Economy Organization (WGEO) dedicated to advancing the goals of the Paris Agreement in the MENA region, and launched the 'National Framework for Action on Climate Change and Health 2019–2021' in partnership with the WHO. Also, the 'Circle Coalition' was established to develop a circular economy model to combat the issue of plastic and packaging waste pollution in the country. In 2020, the UAE pledged to reduce its GHG emissions by 23.5% by 2030, relative to the business-as-usual (BAU) scenario. The 'National Energy Strategy 2050' envisages a 50% share of renewables and nuclear energy in the installed power capacity mix by 2050. Also, the Abu Dhabi National Oil Company (ADNOC), UAE's largest oil and gas producer, announced a target to decrease its GHG emissions intensity by 25% by 2030. All of these announcements and pledges, as in other GCC countries, remain rhetorical as long as they are not implemented and independently verified.

In 2021, the UAE scaled up independent water projects based on reverse osmosis (RO) technology to expand the share of renewable energy in desalination. Dubai's Department of Tourism and Commerce Marketing laid down a set of sustainability guidelines that hotels are required to comply with, along with monthly reporting of their carbon emissions. The Al Dhafra project broke ground with a projected capacity of 2 GW. Once operational, the Solar PV IPP is expected to be the world's largest single-site solar power plant, using approximately 3.5 million solar panels to generate enough electricity for approximately 160,000 homes across the UAE, mitigating 2.4 Mt of CO_2 eq. annually. The government also presented the 'UAE Sustainable Finance Framework'. At COP26, the UAE pledged to become net zero by 2050 and announced a USD1 billion fund to accelerate the rollout of renewable energy technologies in developing countries in partnership with the International Renewable Energy Agency. In 2020 and 2021, the third and fourth phases of the Mohammed bin Rashid Al Maktoum Solar Park were inaugurated. In 2022, the new Taweelah reverse osmosis (RO)-based desalination plant in Abu Dhabi was launched with a maximum production capacity of 909,200 cubic metres of water per day. At COP27, the UAE launched the 'National Net Zero by 2050 Pathway', which announced the timeframe and mechanisms of implementing the 'UAE Net Zero by 2050 Strategic Initiative', introduced at COP26. The pathway defines the country's emission reduction target of 18% compared to the UAE's updated second NDC under the Paris Agreement by 2030, 60% by 2040 and 100% by 2050, compared to 2019 levels. In the real world, based on our tracking methodology, the UAE has made significant progress and stands out by far as the GCC countries' clear leader in tangible, verifiable climate change mitigation policies and ambition. This result corroborates the IRENA data presented in Figure 8.1. The country has demonstrated action on the ground along with ambition. In our judgement, the UAE is the only GCC country at this point that is on a trajectory that could potentially lead to carbon neutrality by 2050 or 2060.

8.5 Conclusion

Our chapter started from the premise that given a concerning decarbonisation policy gap, the need to document and account for measurable policies, laws, and government actions for carbon neutrality has never been greater, specifically in the GCC region. As a methodological strategy to establish such accounting and to raise GCC governments' accountability levels, we introduced policy tracking, a technique that has gained traction in empirical and comparative policy analysis. The chapter presented and discussed the results from a methodologically rigorous tracking of domestic climate policies of GCC countries since 2015 in response to pledges and obligations under the Paris Agreement. This includes government policies, laws, government actions and measures toward the mitigation goals of the Paris Agreement, and internationally established carbon neutrality and net zero targets. We situated our tracker in the wider landscape of policy metrics and indexes, discussed its features, and presented results on mitigation and energy policy responses to the climate crisis in the Gulf. Our chapter included a detailed discussion of the evidence that our tracker found, comparing the six GCC countries with one another. We corroborated our data and findings with pertinent literature and data from IRENA and the World Bank. Our main conclusion is that stringency, intensity, projected effectiveness, credibility, and sustainability of government policies and measures in the fields of water, energy, and decarbonisation vary widely across the sample and over time. Specifically, the decarbonisation-necessary macroeconomic, fiscal, technological, and social policy measures vary greatly in terms of their intensity and the public investments made. Our comparative analysis found that the UAE is the region's outlier and is the only Gulf country that has made investments in renewable energy production a top priority to this date, putting the country on a credible decarbonisation pathway. We found that the KSA, relative to its geographic, population, and economic size and multiple high-powered PR campaigns, is less decarbonising than expected, and that Qatar and Oman have finally started to catch up with the UAE in 2022. However, in most GCC countries, policy measures taken so far appear to be disproportionate to the challenges linked to both reaching the goals of the Paris Agreement and the Gulf countries' very own NDCs.

References

Andonova, L. B., Betsill, M. M., and Bulkeley, H. (2009). Transnational climate governance. *Global Environmental Politics* 9 (2), pp. 52–73.

Armingeon, K., and Beyeler, M. (2004). *The OECD and European Welfare States*. Cheltenham: Edward Elgar.

Arndt, C., and Oman, C. (2008). *The Politics of Governance Ratings*. Working Paper MGSoG/2008/WP003. Maastricht: Maastricht University, Maastricht Graduate School of Governance.

Bouckaert, G., and Van Dooren, W. (2016). Performance measurement and management in public sector organizations, in Bovaird, T. and Loeffler, E. (eds.), *Public Management and Governance*. 3rd ed. London: Routledge, pp. 148–161.

Bradley, C. G. (2015). International organizations and the production of indicators: the case of Freedom House, in Merry, S. E., Davis, K. E., and Kingsbury, B. (eds.), *The Quiet Power of Indicators: Measuring Governance, Corruption, and Rule of Law*. Cambridge: Cambridge University Press. pp. 27–74.

Buduru, B., and Pal, L. A. (2010). The globalized state: Measuring and monitoring governance. *European Journal of Cultural Studies* 13 (4), pp. 511–530.

Chan, S., Hale, T., Deneault, A., Shrivastava, M., Mbeva, K., Chengo, V., and Atela, J. (2022). Assessing the effectiveness of orchestrated climate action from five years of summits. *Nature Climate Change* 12, pp. 628–633.

Chapman, D. A., Lickel, B., and Markoqitz, E. M. (2017). Reassessing emotion in climate change communication. *Nature Climate Change* 7, pp. 850–852.

Climate Justice Alliance (2022). Frontline leaders decry lack of progress for real climate justice at COP27. Press release, 20 November.

Cochrane, L., and Al-Hababi, R. (eds.) (2023). *Sustainable Qatar: Social, Political and Environmental Perspectives*. Singapore: Springer.

Davis, K. E., Fisher, A., Kingsbury, B., and Merry, S. E. (eds.) (2012). *Governance by Indicators: Global Power through Classification and Rankings*. Oxford: Oxford University Press and the Institute for International Law and Justice, New York University School of Law.

Esping-Andersen, G. (1990). *The Three Worlds of Welfare Capitalism*. Cambridge: Polity Press.

Folke, C., Hahn, T., and Olsson, P. (2005) Adaptive governance of social-ecological systems, annual review of environmental, *Resources* 30, pp. 441–473.

Gemmill B., and Bamidele-Izu, B. (2002) The role of NGOs and civil society in global environmental governance, in Esty, D. C. and Ivanova, M. H. (eds.), *Global Environmental Governance: Options & Opportunities*. Forestry and Environmental Studies Publications Series 8. New Haven, CT: Yale School of Forestry & Environmental Studies, pp. 77–100.

Global Happiness Council (2018). *Global Happiness Policy Report 2018*. Dubai: World Governance Summit.

Harris, P. (2022). COP26: The eternally weak pulse of climate diplomacy, and what needs to change, *PLOS Climate* 1 (3) (e0000019).

Head, B. W. (2008). Three lenses of evidence-based policy. *Australian Journal of Public Administration* 67 (1), pp. 1–11.

Head, B. W. (2019). Forty years of wicked problems literature: forging closer links to policy studies. *Policy and Society* 38 (2), pp. 180–197.

Head, B. W., and Alford, J. (2015). Wicked problems: implications for public policy management. *Administration and Society* 47 (6), pp. 711–739.

Helliwell, J., Layard, R., and Sachs, J. (2019). *World Happiness Report 2019*. New York: Sustainable Development Solutions Network.

Karabell, Z. (2014) *The Leading Indicators: A Short History of the Numbers That Rule Our World*. New York: Simon and Schuster.

Kaufmann, D., Kraay, A., and Mastruzzi, M. (2010). *The World Wide Governance Indicators: Methodology and Analytical Issues*. Washington, DC: World Bank.

Kovacic, Z., and Di Felice, L. J. (2019). Complexity, uncertainty and ambiguity: Implications for European Union energy governance. *Energy Research & Social Science* 53, pp. 159–169.

Maggetti, M., and Gilardi, F. (2016). Problems (and solutions) in the measurement of policy diffusion mechanisms. *Journal of Public Policy* 36 (1), pp. 87–107.

Merry, S. E., Davis, K. E., and Kingsbury, B. (eds.) (2015). *The Quiet Power of Indicators: Measuring Governance, Corruption, and Rule of Law*. Cambridge: Cambridge University Press.

Mungiu-Pippidi, A. (2015). *The Quest for Good Governance: How Societies Develop Control of Corruption*. Cambridge: Cambridge University Press.

Mungiu-Pippidi, A., and Dadašov, R. (2016). Measuring control of corruption by a new index of public integrity. *European Journal on Criminal Policy Research* 22 (3), pp. 415–438.

Mungiu-Pippidi, A., and Johnston, M. (eds.) (2017). *Transitions to Good Governance: Creating Virtuous Circles of Anti-corruption*. Cheltenham: Edward Elgar.

New Climate Institute (n.d.). Climate Action Tracker.

Pal, L. A., and Ireland, D. (2009). The public sector reform movement: Mapping the global policy network. *International Journal of Public Administration* 32 (8), pp. 621–657.

Pollitt, C. (2011). Performance blight and the tyranny of light?: Accountability in advanced performance measurement regimes, in Dubnick, M. J. and Frederickson, H. G. (eds.), *Accountable Governance: Problems and Promises*. Armonk, NY: M. E. Sharpe, pp. 81–97.

Raudla, R., Douglas, J. W., Randma-Liiv, T., and Savi, R. (2015). The impact of fiscal crisis on decision-making processes in European governments: dynamics of a centralization cascade. *Public Administration Review* 75 (6), pp. 842–852.

Rechkemmer, A. (2005a). International cooperation and environmental politics after Rio and Johannesburg: synchronicity of realities in a post-postmodern world? *Sicherheit und Frieden/ Security and Peace* 23 (1), pp. 40–44.

Rechkemmer, A. (2005b). *UNEO – Towards an International Environment Organization: Approaches to a Sustainable Reform of Global Environmental Governance*. Baden-Baden: Nomos.

Rechkemmer, A. (2006). *International Environmental Governance. Issues, Achievements and Perspectives. UNU-EHS Source 3/2006*. Tokyo and Bonn: United Nations University Press.

Rechkemmer, A., Ozturk, O., Brik, A. B., and Pal, L. A. (2020). COVID-19 Policy Tracker: MENA Government Responses to the Crisis.

Rotberg, R. I., and Bhushan, A. (2015). The indexes of governance, in Rotberg, R. I. (ed.), *On Governance: What it Is, What it Measures and its Policy Uses*. Waterloo, Ont.: Centre for International Governance Innovation, pp. 55–89.

Rottenburg, R., Merry, S. E., Park, S.-J., and Mugler, J. (eds.) (2015). *The World of Indicators: The Making of Governmental Knowledge through Quantification*. Cambridge: Cambridge University Press.

Schelkle, W. (2012). Collapsing Worlds and Varieties of Welfare Capitalism: In Search of a New Political Economy of Welfare. LSE Europe in Question Discussion Paper Series No. 54/2012. London: London School of Economics.

Stiglitz, J. E., Fitoussi, J.-P., and Durand, M. (2018). *Beyond GDP: Measuring What Counts for Economic and Social Performance*. Paris: OECD.

Tiitmamer, N., Mayai, A. T., and Mai, N. J. H. (2018). *Climate Change and Conflicts in South Sudan*. Juba: Sudd Institute.

UN-HABITAT (2007). *Tools to Support Participatory Urban Decision Making. Urban Governance Toolkit Series*. Nairobi: United Nations.

United Nations Development Programme (UNDP) (1997). *Governance for Sustainable Human Development*. New York: United Nations.

World Bank (2022). World Bank Data Bank, Washington, DC: World Bank.

World Health Organization (WHO) (2020). Clinical Management of COVID-19: Interim Guidance, 27 May 2020, Geneva: World Health Organization.

9

Data Policies and Governance for Greenhouse Gases Reports and Initiatives

HESHAM M. AL-AMMAL

9.1 Introduction

The United Nations Framework Convention on Climate Change (UNFCCC) was established in 1992 and a secretariat was formed to manage its programmes facilitating intergovernmental climate change negotiations. The secretariat today supports a complex architecture of bodies that serve to advance the implementation of the Convention, and the Kyoto Protocol and the Paris Agreement extending the Convention on climate change. Part of the duties of the secretariat includes receiving periodical national communications (NC) which is a 'report that each Party to the Convention prepares periodically in accordance with the guidelines developed and adopted by the Conference of the Parties (COP)' (UNFCCC, 2009).

The data collection and reporting process for the UNFCCC National Communications involves a systematic approach to gather and report information on national climate change activities, greenhouse gas emissions, and mitigation and adaptation measures. This process is crucial for assessing global progress in combating climate change and facilitating international cooperation. The following outlines the key steps involved in this process, referencing relevant sources:

1. *Inventory of Greenhouse Gas Emissions*: Countries are required to compile comprehensive inventories of their greenhouse gas emissions and removals, covering various sectors such as energy, industry, agriculture, forestry, and waste. This involves collecting data on emissions sources, activity data, and emission factors. The Intergovernmental Panel on Climate Change (IPCC) provides guidelines and methodologies for conducting these inventories, ensuring consistency and comparability across countries (IPCC, 2006).
2. *Vulnerability and Adaptation Assessment*: National Communications also include an assessment of a country's vulnerability to climate change impacts and the measures taken to adapt to these impacts. This involves gathering data on climate projections, vulnerability assessments, and adaptation strategies and

actions. The UNFCCC provides guidelines and methodologies for conducting vulnerability and adaptation assessments, supporting countries in their reporting efforts.

3. *Mitigation Measures and Actions*: Countries report on their mitigation efforts, including policies, measures, and actions aimed at reducing greenhouse gas emissions. This involves collecting data on energy efficiency measures, renewable energy deployment, emission reduction targets, and other relevant information. The reporting guidelines provided by the UNFCCC guide countries in reporting their mitigation actions (UNFCC, 2010).
4. *National Communication Submission*: After the data collection process, countries prepare and submit their National Communications to the UNFCCC secretariat. These reports undergo a review process by expert review teams, ensuring the accuracy and completeness of the reported information. The review process also facilitates knowledge sharing and capacity building among countries (UNFCC, 2023a).

As part of any NC, an inventory of greenhouse gases (GHG) must be submitted by each nation. This inventory of GHG must follow the guidelines of the IPCC, which were published in 2006 and then subsequently had amendments published that covered gaps in the guidelines (Eggleston et al., 2006). Greenhouse gas inventories are data intensive and contain emission statistics and accounting that are developed for a variety of reasons, including monitoring the country's progress toward reduction of emissions. Scientists also use inventories of natural and anthropogenic (human-based) emissions as tools to develop atmospheric models, forecast changes, and provide overall analysis.

This chapter aims at reflecting on the experience gained by Bahrain's successive National Communications and the process for collecting the data for the GHG inventory. After reviewing three successive cycles from over almost two decades, the chapter will present a case study of the past cycles to identify the challenges and highlight the data governance and data openness issues for achieving such a national data driven project.

The study will adopt a qualitative research method which starts by stating the research question and objectives. The case selection will be the data collection process for the GHG inventory for the Kingdom of Bahrain and the chapter will carry out a qualitative analysis of the remarks related to data procedures and uncertainty in the three past NCs (2005, 2012, and 2020). Then an analysis of the data will be presented, especially with respect to the challenges identified during these three cycles; and to remedy these challenges, a proposed data governance framework designed for GHG inventory reporting for Bahrain's and other national inventory efforts will be presented. The framework is adopted from a popular and well-tested data governance framework originally suggested by Khatri & Brown (2010). The chapter will also present some triangulation with data best practice cases, present lessons learned from the document analysis, and conclude with some remarks and conclusions.

9.2 The Role of Data Transparency

The Paris Agreement which was adopted in 2015 clearly aimed at enhancing transparency of the monitoring and evaluation of the parties' nationally determined contributions (NDCs), which constitute each nation's actions to reduce greenhouse gas emissions. It should be stressed here that transparency and data play a big role in the developed framework from 2015. Observers analysing the treaty note that as nations are not obliged to achieve their pledges, the transparency framework provided by the treaty is 'the main mechanism to hold states accountable for doing what they say' (Bodansky, 2016).

This approach ultimately places 'international review and peer pressure [as] the main multilateral tool for countries to strengthen the credibility of their pledges'. (Kawanishi & Fujikura, 2020) As each party has to submit the GHG inventory for a vast amount of activities, data processes play a big role in the preparation of such a national inventory. The past decade witnessed growing experience in managing data that led to a field called 'data governance' (Khatri & Brown, 2010).

9.2.1 The Importance of Data Transparency

The IPCC reporting process relies on comprehensive and accurate GHG inventories to assess the global climate change scenario. Data transparency is a key factor in building reliable inventories that enable informed decision-making and policy development. Later in this chapter, I will discuss some of the implications and interactions between data governance and the GHG collection process.

Data transparency enhances the credibility and trustworthiness of GHG inventories by allowing stakeholders to access, verify, and evaluate the data. It facilitates international cooperation, fosters accountability, and promotes a shared understanding of the climate change challenge.

9.2.2 Challenges Facing Data Transparency

Several challenges hinder data transparency in the IPCC reporting process context. These include data availability, data quality assurance, data management, data accessibility, and institutional and legal barriers. Overcoming these challenges is crucial for improving transparency. Several obvious strategies exist for facing the transparency challenges, including:

(1) *Open Data Practice*: Encouraging countries to make their data publicly available promotes transparency and allows for independent verification and scrutiny.
(2) *Standardised Methodologies*: Adopting standardised methodologies and reporting frameworks ensures consistency and comparability of GHG inventories across countries and time periods.
(3) *Data Quality Assurance*: Implementing robust quality assurance and quality control processes helps identify and rectify errors, ensuring accurate and reliable data.
(4) *Stakeholder Engagement*: Engaging relevant stakeholders, including scientific experts, civil society organisations, and the private sector, fosters transparency, inclusivity and collective ownership of the reporting process.

Clearly these strategies require considerable effort and continuous monitoring to ensure correct implementation and reliable impact. Dealing with a wide number of stakeholders within the country makes them more challenging. However, there are best practice examples around the world, including the European Union's Emissions Database (EDGAR, https://edgar.jrc.ec.europa.eu/), the United States Environmental Protection Agency's Greenhouse Gas Reporting Program (GHGRP, www.epa.gov/ghgreporting), and the Greenhouse Gas Protocol's Corporate Standard (UNFCC, 2023b). Many smaller countries can learn a lot from studying these examples and adopting some of the best practices within.

9.2.3 Research Question and Objectives

The chapter will attempt to answer the following research questions: What are the primary challenges encountered in the GHG inventory data process in the Kingdom of Bahrain? and What is a recommended implementation of robust data governance practices that can enhance the accuracy, reliability, and transparency of the IPCC GHG inventory data collection process?

As the Kingdom of Bahrain is currently attempting to build an online system for future GHG inventory projects which aims to avoid past shortcomings and provide better and more accurate information, the research objectives for the chapter are to:

- Provide background information on the IPCC reporting process for National Communications and Bahrain's experience in the past three cycles.
- Analyse the comments and recommendations regarding the data process for the past three GHG inventory reporting for the Bahrain.
- Identify the main shortcomings and challenges in the data process.

- Identify the role of transparency and open data on the GHG inventory data collection process.
- Propose/adapt a data governance framework suitable for the GHG inventory process that can ameliorate these challenges.

The aim is also to transfer the experience and knowledge related to these challenges and the proposed solution to other countries within the region that are making similar endeavours.

9.3 A Brief History of Bahrain's Three National Communications

After the UNFCCC was adopted in 1992, all parties to the agreement were obliged to announce their GHG inventories periodically and to submit their National Communications. These NCs also contain mitigation actions to reduce emissions. Developed countries (Annex I) during COP1 were also requested to submit their GHG inventories. Then the Kyoto Protocol adopted at COP3 in 1997 set binding emission targets for developed countries. These targets were to take effect in 2005, but the COP3 agreement emphasised regular compliance assessment and the need for accountability and verification (Kawanishi & Fujikura, 2020). This was superseded by the Paris Agreement in 2015, which established an enhanced transparency framework. The approach adopted by the UNFCCC 2015 was 'a bifurcated system that placed differing transparency requirements on developed and developing countries' (Rajamani, 2016).

Bahrain, along with 150 other countries, endorsed the UN Framework Convention on Climate Change at the Earth Summit in Rio de Janeiro, Brazil, in 1992. The Kingdom ratified the Framework Convention in the same year. Subsequently the Kingdom submitted three NCs for the UNFCCC in March 2005, February 2012, and finally in July 2020. The first NC determined 1994 to be the base year for the inventory of GHG emissions and did the calculations subsequently.

Preparation of the GHG inventory in the Bahrain was submitted to the UNFCCC three times, namely in 2006, 2015, and in 2020 as part of the National Climate Change Communication report. The data collection and calculation process are quite data intensive and require considerable effort to collect and process the required data based on the IPCC guidelines. These calculations and analysis were conducted for four main sectors; namely the *Energy*, *Industrial Processes and Product Use*, *Waste*, and finally the *Agriculture, Forestry and Other Land Use* sector. As can be noted from the way data is used by this process, data retention, quality, and verification are necessary over a long span of time (ideally a decade or more). This usually encompasses several administrations and requires rigorous actions.

9.3.1 IPCC Data Collection Guidelines

Data used for preparing GHG inventories follows the guidelines put forward by the IPCC (2006). The IPCC provides guidelines and methodologies for the preparation of GHG inventories, which serve as the basis for assessing and reporting GHG emissions. These guidelines ensure consistency, comparability, and accuracy in the data used for preparing the inventories. The key IPCC guidelines for data used in preparing the GHG inventory include:

1. IPCC Guidelines for National Greenhouse Gas Inventories (IPCC, 2006): provide detailed methodologies for estimating and reporting GHG emissions and removals. The guidelines cover various sectors, including energy, industrial processes, agriculture, forestry, and waste. They outline standardised approaches for data collection, activity data estimation, emission factor selection, and calculation procedures.
2. IPCC Good Practice Guidance and Uncertainty Management in National Greenhouse Gas Inventories (IPCC, 2019): supplements the inventory guidelines by providing additional guidance on improving the quality and transparency of GHG inventories. It offers methods for uncertainty assessment, quality assurance and quality control procedures, and approaches for addressing data gaps and uncertainties in the inventory preparation process.
3. IPCC Emissions Factors Database: serves as a valuable resource for selecting appropriate emission factors for different sectors and activities (www.ipcc-nggip.iges.or.jp/EFDB/main.php). The database provides a wide range of emission factors based on regional and technological variations.
4. IPCC Software Tool: This is an invaluable tool for preparing data and calculating factors. Designed by the IPCC this software tool supports the calculation and reporting of GHG inventories (found at: www.ipcc-nggip.iges.or.jp/tools/index.html). It includes tools, such as the IPCC Inventory Software and the Agriculture, Forestry, and Other Land Use (AFOLU) Calculator, to assist countries in organising and analysing their data according to the IPCC guidelines.

It is important to note that the specific guidelines and methodologies may be periodically updated by the IPCC to incorporate the latest scientific knowledge and advancements. Therefore, it is crucial for countries and practitioners to refer to the most recent IPCC publications and updates when preparing GHG inventories.

The most common approach outlined by the IPCC is to combine information on the extent of human activity (called activity data or AD) with coefficients that quantify the contribution of this activity toward emissions of GHGs (called emissions factors or EF). Then the GHG inventory would calculate the emissions for this country as = AD × EF.

For developing countries (including Bahrain), it is often difficult to maintain data on activities with high accuracy, if available at all. This led to the use of so-called 'default values' set by the IPCC. Unfortunately, in many cases these default values may not reflect the actual national values or circumstances and the IPCC guidelines do not offer any means of declaring the amount of the adopted default values in a GHG inventory.

The other major issue with the calculation of national emissions is the need for developing 'country specific' emissions factors. The aim here is to match the national circumstances to the model used for emission estimation to produce a more accurate GHG inventory (Kawanishi & Fujikura, 2020).

9.3.2 Remarks from Data Collection Procedures and Uncertainty in Past Inventories

The following is a summary of the three NCs submitted by Bahrain with emphasis on data collection and other procedural aspects. The section will also compare the reference versus the sectoral approach. After presenting the remarks, the section will present an analysis and identify the main recurring deficiencies.

9.3.2.1 Bahrain's Initial Communication to the UNFCCC, March 2005

The initial national communication was produced by intergovernmental bodies concerned with the environment within the Kingdom, along with the Arabian Gulf University in Manama, which had academic expertise and programs in Arid Climate Environments as well as other scientific disciplines. The report started with a section describing the national environmental profile and circumstances; followed by a GHG inventory which chose 1994 as a base year; then a chapter on vulnerability and adaptation assessment; and finally, a chapter on GHG mitigation initiatives and a strategy to raise public awareness on climate change (General Commission, 2005).

Energy data were mainly derived from the Central Statistics Organization and directly from private sector organisations. Alternative Emissions Factors were occasionally used. The Initial NC stated clearly that: 'A program to enhance the accuracy of Bahrain national GHG emissions inventory is necessary and important.' It continued, 'A reliable and verifiable GHG emissions database is a prerequisite for compliance and is relevant to Bahrain's ability to identify opportunities for achieving emissions reductions.' The report mentioned specific actions with regard to data and enhancing future GHG inventory reporting efforts:

- *Strengthening Institutional Infrastructures*: The 1st NC recommended establishing a permanent secretariat to coordinate period updates for the national inventory data. One of its main tasks is to update and maintain the data in a continuous manner. This Secretariat is also responsible for verification activities.

- *Improving Accuracy of Local Factors*: The report called for nationally developed and verified local emissions factors.
- *Address Gaps in the Data*: The report recommended that 'national surveys be conducted to better represent consumption levels and patterns of various sub sectors of the economy'.
- *Better Collection of Industrial, Waste and Agricultural Data*: Based on being a developing country and due to its small size, the report recommends addressing the gaps in the industrial, waste, and agricultural sectors.

These initial communication concerns seem to cover data issues in the data collection, maintenance, and verification phases. Relevant to this chapter's topic, it is worth noting that the initial communication (*c*. 2005) described the following methodology used for data collection:

1. The year 1994 was selected as the base year for all sectors.
2. The inventory used the latest IPCC guidelines.
3. Data on emissions-generating/sequestering activities were collected mainly from secondary sources, statistical reports, related studies, publications of the international groups, and periodical government reports.
4. The format of the available data was mostly suited for government planning and did not cover all the required information by the IPCC methodology.
5. The communication highlighted '*a future need for establishing reliable data banks within each sector, to provide complete standardised information*'.
6. For missing values, emissions and default values were taken from IPCC guidelines.

9.3.2.2 Bahrain's Second National Communication to the UNFCCC, February 2012

In the second NC, Bahrain reiterated its commitment to steep reductions in GHGs. As the report states, 'prepared by a group of national experts from many national institutions and universities with a view to incorporate stakeholders' comments and building local capacities to incorporate the contribution and follow-up for future tasks in this area' (Public Commission for the Protection of Marine Resources, Environment and Wildlife, 2012).

The report covered the period from 2000 to 2006 and had a similar structure like the initial NC, with a detailed GHG inventory as the second chapter. It should be noted that the second NC incorporated more national organisations and stakeholders in the preparation of the report, which stated: 'the national steering committee widened participation processes in the Second National Communication to include more public and private involvement discussions in all topics addressed in the report'.

The second NC states clearly that: 'enhancing the availability of detailed and high-quality activity data will increase confidence in the inventory results'. It continues its analysis of data issues as follows, 'problems arose in obtaining activity data at a level of detail in which aggregate emission factors can be applied'. This led to many factors with medium uncertainty (10–50%) due to the fact that it did not use multiple sources with a variety of origins in estimating the emission factors.

9.3.2.3 Bahrain's Third National Communication to the UNFCCC, March 2020

The third NC had a similar but expanded structure to the previous NCs and covered the period from 2007 to 2015, inclusive for the GHG inventory part. The report covered the national circumstances in detail, a GHG inventory, vulnerability and adaptation (covering mangrove habitats, coastal zones, and water resources), GHG mitigation actions, and finally a section on other information such as climate change awareness and educational initiatives.

The GHG inventory section relied on several guidance documents including: The 2006 IPCC Guidelines for National Greenhouse Gas Inventories, the Good Practice Guidance and Uncertainty Management in National Greenhouse Gas Inventories manual, and so on. The study also utilised the IPCC Inventory Software (version 2.54) to assemble activity and emission factor data.

Activity data were mainly obtained from the Central Statistics Organization and other data supplied by the Supreme Council for the Environment (SCE). However, other GHG data for the energy sector was obtained directly by the researchers from Bapco (Bahrain's main petroleum company) and other large industrial companies in Bahrain.

The GHG inventory's main finding was that there was an increase in GHG emissions associated with energy activities over the period from 2006 to 2015, as shown in Figure 9.1. The latest report showed that over the 2006 to 2015 period total emissions increased by 38%. Energy remains the main component responsible for the overall increasing trend in GHG emission levels.

The report states that: 'While Tier-1 approach of the IPCC guidelines were primarily utilised in the calculations for all reporting categories, Tier-2 and Tier-3 methods were used where warranted by adequate data availability and data quality.' This again raises the issue of data availability in a quantity that enables the use of approaches other than Tier-1. The GHG inventory part of the NC also mentions the need for a 'National Information System', which was under construction to better maintain the data in a centralised database.

But perhaps the most poignant observation in the third NC is in the Challenges section is where it states that: 'the primary challenge to the development of the current GHG inventory is data-related; namely the availability, accuracy, and consistency of data'. The report indicates the causes of these data gaps, which include

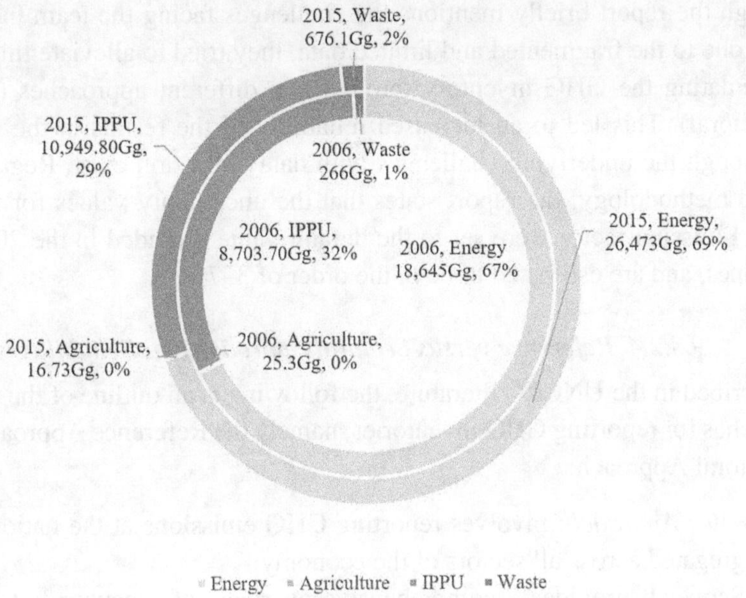

Figure 9.1 GHG emissions associated with Bahraini activities from 2006 and 2015.

'administrative and institutional barriers that impact the application of locally available technical capacity to collect, manage, and analyse pertinent data'. These challenges led to the following recommendations:

- Establish and enforce a national data collection system that covers the public and private sectors.
- Involve the Supreme Council for the Environment and relevant public organisations to maintain an online National Inventory System (Supreme Council for the Environment, 2021).
- Hold capacity building workshops to train experts and raise awareness.
- Institutionalise a GHG inventory committee.
- Manage data collection early in the reporting cycle.

At the conclusion of the Third GHG inventory exercise prepared by a team from the University of Bahrain (Alnaser et al., 2018), the following were the main comments regarding data:

- The calculation process was data intensive and required sizable efforts to collect and process the required data.
- Although the provided data were limited and fragmented to a certain degree, the CO_2 equivalent in the energy sector in the year 2015 was found to reach 26,473 Gg when taking the Sectoral Approach, while it reaches 25,174 Gg for the Reference Approach (i.e. a difference of 1.8%).

Although the report briefly mentions the challenges facing the team in data collection due to the fragmented and limited data, they tried to alleviate this concern by calculating the GHG inventory through two different approaches (reference and sectoral). This led to an increased reliability of the results in the third NC, even though the underlying challenges with data collection exist. Regarding the adopted methodology, the report states that the uncertainty values for the activity and Emission factor were set to the default value provided in the 2006 IPCC Guidelines, and are estimated to be in the order of 3–7%.

9.3.2.4 Reference versus Sectoral Approach and Reliability

As described in the UNCCC literature, the following is an outline of the main two approaches for reporting GHG inventories, namely the Reference Approach versus the Sectoral Approach:

Reference Approach: involves reporting GHG emissions at the national level, aggregated across all sectors of the economy:

- Scope: It provides a comprehensive overview of a country's total GHG emissions, including emissions from all sectors, such as energy, industry, agriculture, forestry, and waste.
- Data Collection: The Reference Approach requires compiling data from various sources and sectors to calculate the overall GHG emissions for the country.
- Use: This approach is primarily used for international reporting, comparison, and monitoring of GHG emissions across countries.
- Benefits: It allows for a comprehensive assessment of a country's overall contribution to global GHG emissions. It facilitates international negotiations and policy development by providing a basis for understanding each country's emission profile.

Sectoral Approach: involves reporting GHG emissions at a *sector-specific level*, focusing on individual sectors or industries within a country:

- Scope: It provides detailed information on GHG emissions within specific sectors, such as energy, transport, manufacturing, agriculture, and others.
- Data Collection: The Sectoral Approach requires collecting sector-specific data, including activity data, emission factors, and other relevant information, to calculate emissions within each sector.
- Use: This approach is valuable for sector-specific analysis, identification of emission trends, and formulation of targeted mitigation strategies within particular sectors.
- Benefits: It allows policymakers and stakeholders to identify sectors with high emissions and develop sector-specific mitigation measures. The

Sectoral Approach helps improve the effectiveness of mitigation efforts by providing more detailed and focused information.

The adoption of the two approaches may result in an overestimation or underestimation of the emissions. The Reference Approach and the Sectoral Approach often give different results because the Reference Approach is a top-down approach using a country's energy supply data and has no detailed information on how the individual fuels are used in each sector. The Reference Approach provides estimates for CO_2 to compare with estimates derived using a Sectoral Approach. Theoretically, it indicates an upper bound to the Sectoral Approach '1A fuel combustion' because some of the carbon in the fuel is not combusted but will be emitted as fugitive emissions (as leakage or evaporation in the production and/or transformation stage).

In general, the gaps between the two approaches are more than the expected limit (5% or less), this large difference maybe occur due to many reasons and the following indicate those significant to the Bahrain 2020 GHG report:

1. The collection of data from different fuel flow stages, which will result in large statistical differences between the energy supply and the energy consumption in the basic energy data (Alnaser et al., 2018). Collecting data from different fuel flow stages in the context of GHG inventory preparation can lead to dangers such as incomplete and inconsistent data, double counting or underestimation of emissions, challenges in data quality and reliability, and difficulties in data integration and aggregation. To mitigate these dangers, it is important to establish robust protocols for data collection, harmonise methodologies, improve coordination among stakeholders, and implement quality assurance procedures. Ensuring consistency, completeness, and accuracy in data collection throughout the fuel flow stages is crucial for reliable GHG inventory preparation.
2. The use of approximate net calorific and carbon content values for primary fuels which are converted rather than combusted (Alnaser et al., 2018). Using approximate net calorific and carbon content values for primary fuels that undergo conversion processes in GHG inventory calculations can lead to inaccuracies in emission estimates, distorted sectoral comparisons, misrepresentation of fuel efficiency, and compliance and reporting challenges. It is crucial to gather accurate and specific data on net calorific values and carbon content for converted primary fuels to ensure the reliability and accuracy of GHG inventory calculations. Collaborative efforts among stakeholders are necessary to improve data availability and enhance the effectiveness of emissions reporting, policy development, and climate change mitigation monitoring.
3. Missing information on combustion of certain transformation outputs (Alnaser et al., 2018), which refers to the absence or lack of data and details regarding

the process of burning or incinerating specific products or by-products. It means that there is incomplete or insufficient information on the emissions resulting from the combustion of these outputs in the context of greenhouse gas (GHG) inventory reporting. In GHG inventories, it is essential to account for the emissions associated with the combustion of various materials or substances. However, if specific transformation outputs are not adequately documented or monitored, key data such as the quantity of materials burned, combustion efficiencies, emission factors, or the resulting greenhouse gas emissions may be missing or unknown. This missing information on combustion can create gaps in understanding the overall emissions profile of a country, sector, or specific processes. It hinders accurate accounting, assessment, and reporting of emissions, leading to incomplete and potentially inaccurate GHG inventory reports.

9.3.3 Major Remarks of the 2020 NC

The preceding analysis of the remarks of the 2020 Bahrain NC team clearly shows the effects of missing and fragmented data and the adoption of default values on the reliability of the final inventory results. This can be avoided by adopting better data governance practices to increase reliability and fill out the missing values.

The inventory report by (Alnaser et al., 2018) further emphasises the need for a systematic and sustainable method for data collection in the following quotation. They suggest a national data bank that integrates the data from all data producers and reporting stakeholders:

> The greenhouse gas emissions from the energy sector are calculated using the IPCC Reference Approach (only for CO_2 emission) and Sectoral-Tier 1 approach for CO_2, CH_4 and N_2O. The Supreme Council for Environment provided the activity data used to prepare this report for the Kingdom of Bahrain. In fact, the data are those published by the Central Informatics Organization (CIO). It is imperative for the Supreme Council to build for future reporting a national data bank and review values with related users. (Alnaser et al., 2018)

The report further identifies the effects of missing contributions of stakeholders (another sign of lack of data governance procedures), namely, '*in this regard, it would be recommended, for future reports, to involve the Office of Assistant Undersecretary for Industrial Development in the Ministry of Industry, Commerce and Tourism to assist with the market survey and data collection*' (Alnaser et al., 2018, my emphasis).

A final remark from the Inventory team regarding the challenges of data collection concludes that data were collected from the industries mainly through the Supreme Council for Environment, but some data were also obtained through direct communication with the industries and from the CIO Annual Statistical Yearbooks.

The Department of Environmental Policies and Planning in the Supreme Council for Environment was very effective with collecting the required data after specifying for them the name of the company/sector to be contacted along with the specific questions. In general, the companies were very conservative with providing the requested data directly to the university team. This indicates again the need for sustainable practices for data collection for future GHG inventories. The same remark was reflected in Bahrain's National Communication (2020) under the section entitled Quality Control of the Greenhouse Gas Inventory chapter. It stated that:

> Other quality control measures were undertaken at the sector and category level through consultations between and among local experts. While feedback from local reviewers was not formally documented during the process, the inventory does incorporate their feedback and the final result offers the best possible estimates of emissions given the current state of scientific knowledge and regulatory and institutional framework in Bahrain.

The section concluded: 'For future inventories, *the National Information System – currently under development* – should greatly improve quality control aspects of the process' (Alnaser et al., 2018, my emphasis). This single statement reflects two huge gaps in the approach toward periodic GHG inventory tracking: First, the data collection and quality problem is always viewed as a data management or an IT system problem; and second, the definition of the underlying data governance policies and processes is still missing.

9.3.4 Analysis of Main Remarks and Challenges

From the above collection of remarks after each cycle, the following seem to be recurring themes regarding the data process:

(1) Data was mainly collected from secondary (non-primary) sources.
(2) Data formats did not adhere to the required information by the IPCC methodology.
(3) The need for '*establishing reliable data banks within each sector, to provide complete standardised information*' (my emphasis).
(4) Establish and enforce a national data collection system that covers the public and private sectors.
(5) Several missing values and emissions led to default values taken from IPCC guidelines.
(6) The calculation process was data intensive and required sizable efforts to collect and process the required data.

Considering the severity of these challenges toward achieving a good GHG inventory, one immediately notices their direct relationship with the principles and issues addressed by data governance. In the context of data governance, the main challenges in the data collection process are missing values, reliance on data from secondary sources, unspecified data custodians, lack of systematic data storage, and non-adherence to the IPCC format. Data governance principles address these challenges by emphasising data quality, transparency, and standardisation. They promote the implementation of protocols for handling missing values, verifying data credibility from secondary sources, establishing organised data repositories, and ensuring compliance with specific reporting formats like the IPCC format. By adhering to data governance principles, countries can overcome these challenges and achieve more accurate, reliable, and transparent data collection processes for greenhouse gas inventory reporting.

The identified challenges can be grouped into the following main areas within the data governance field.

(1) *Data Availability and Accessibility:* Obtaining the necessary data for GHG inventories can be a significant challenge. Data may be dispersed across different sectors, agencies, and sources, making it difficult to access and collect. Limited availability of data, especially in developing countries or specific sectors, can hinder comprehensive reporting. Based on the comments of all three NC teams, building and enforcing a *national data collection system* is the first priority. For such a large IT project, data governance practices (such as the ones outlined in this chapter) are essential to ensure overall project success.
(2) *Capacity and Expertise*: This is another priority as outlined by the remarks of the three national teams. Lack of capacity and expertise within country teams can hinder data collection and quality assurance processes. Insufficient knowledge of data collection methodologies, emission estimation techniques, and quality control procedures can impact the accuracy and reliability of GHG inventories.
(3) *Data Consistency and Standardization*: Achieving data consistency and standardisation across different sectors and data sources can be challenging. Diverse reporting formats, measurement units, and methodologies used by various sectors can complicate the process of aggregating data and ensuring consistency across the inventory. The GHG inventory being a periodic exercise that was performed over approximately two decades makes it necessary to standardise data formats across all stakeholders.
(4) *Institutional Coordination and Collaboration*: Effective coordination and collaboration among different institutions and agencies involved in data collection are essential. Challenges may arise due to fragmented institutional structures, limited communication channels, and varying levels of data sharing and cooperation, making it difficult to harmonise data collection efforts.

Addressing these challenges requires building capacity within country teams, strengthening institutional coordination, promoting data sharing mechanisms, and providing technical support and training. Enhancing data management practices, standardising methodologies, and investing in quality assurance measures can contribute to improved data collection and higher quality GHG inventories and national communications.

9.4 A Proposed National Data Governance Framework

With all of the challenges and recommendations from the Bahrain NCs over the past two decades, it is pertinent to establish some context within the data governance field that may elevate these structural challenges. Creating a national electronic or online database for GHG related activities is not a magical solution that will solve all of the recurring problems with continuity, availability, and so on of the needed data. Most such projects require public policy guidelines and compliance in order to be successful. In order to ensure sustainability, the committee responsible for implementing a GHG inventory project must ask the following questions (Mazmanian & Sabatier, 1983):

(1) Tractability of the problem: What are the technical difficulties, diversity of target group goals, and so on?
(2) Ability to structure the implementation: Clear objectives, allocation of financial resources, decision rules, formal access by outsiders, and so on.
(3) Other variables affecting the implementation: Public support, available technology, attitudes and resources of constituency groups, support from sovereigns, commitment to implementation officials.

The implementation of data governance at a national level in the context of public policy brings several key takeaways. First, data is recognised as a strategic asset, emphasising the need for its careful management, protection, and utilisation to drive evidence-based decision-making. Second, data governance enhances data quality and integrity, establishing standards and processes for accurate and reliable data that supports transparency and public trust.

Additionally, data governance promotes data sharing and collaboration, facilitating interoperability and the integration of diverse data sources for a comprehensive understanding of policy challenges. It also emphasises privacy protection and ethical use of data, ensuring adherence to legal frameworks and ethical considerations. Stakeholder engagement and citizen participation are crucial, fostering transparency and public support for data-driven policies. Data security and cybersecurity measures are implemented to safeguard against unauthorised access or breaches. Organisational culture and leadership play a vital role, promoting a data-driven mindset and assigning clear roles and responsibilities. Finally, continuous improvement and adaptation are essential, as data governance evolves with technological advancements and changing policy needs. Overall, implementing data governance at the national level empowers governments to harness data's potential for effective governance and improved outcomes.

9.4.1 Differences between Data Management and Data Governance

Because of the amount and importance of data being generated and used in modern times, dealing with data is no longer a question of creating a database or an online repository. From simple data management the field has grown into data science and data governance with major breakthroughs in methodologies and approaches. This has often led to a misunderstanding about the differences between data management and data governance. Table 9.1 attempts to summarise these differences.

Data management and data governance are distinct but interconnected concepts in the realm of data governance practices. Data management focuses on the technical aspects of data handling, encompassing operational activities like data storage, integration, and retrieval. Its primary goal is to ensure data is efficiently managed for day-to-day business operations. In contrast, data governance takes a broader strategic perspective, focusing on establishing policies, frameworks, and decision-making processes that align data activities with organisational objectives. It addresses issues such as data ownership, stewardship, privacy, and compliance to ensure data is governed effectively and used as a strategic asset (DAMA International, 2009).

While data management is primarily IT-centric and operational, data governance involves cross-functional collaboration and encompasses a wider organisational perspective. It includes stakeholders from executive management, business

Table 9.1 *Basic differences between data management and governance.*

Data management	Data governance
Involves the design and implementation of systems and processes that manage the organisation's data lifecycle	Involves creating the set of policies, processes, and protocols that govern how data is created, stored, and managed.
Includes systems for data preparation, cleaning, transformation, flow, security, and storage.	Handles aspects such as data ownership, content authorisation, privacy policies, data source management, assigning metadata, transparency, and security.

departments, data stewards, and compliance officers. Data governance ensures that data-related decisions and processes align with organisational goals, policies, and regulatory requirements. Together, data management and data governance work hand-in-hand to ensure data is well-managed, governed, and utilised in line with strategic objectives.

As was noted from the initial NC's team: data was available but ultimately it lacked consistency and integration. The data governance era was heralded as organisations became more serious about their data and started regarding it as one of their most important assets (Khatri & Brown, 2010).

9.4.2 Framework Domains, Roles, and Data Lifecycle

In order to handle a national effort such as a GHG inventory and maintain relevant and consistent data, the following framework proposes various aspects that have to be met, as shown in Figure 9.2, adopted from Khatri & Brown (2010). The authors outline the increasing importance of data governance in contemporary organisations, emphasising the challenges associated with data management and the need for strategic governance structures. As discussed through the Kingdom of Bahrain experience in Section 9.3, experience from the GHG inventory data collection process highlights the potential risks and negative impacts of poor data governance, including data inconsistency, regulatory non-compliance, and compromised decision-making processes.

To this end, Khatri and Brown (2010) propose a comprehensive data governance framework consisting of five key components: data governance drivers, data governance domains, data governance processes, data governance organisation, and data governance infrastructure. These components collectively form the basis for developing a robust data governance structure tailored to an organisation's specific needs. Figure 9.2 outlines the process describing the data lifecycle for the GHG inventory data, including the different roles of the participants; as well as the data ingest, transform, store, and visualise phases.

The framework identifies five fundamental data governance drivers, namely regulatory compliance, operational efficiency, data quality, strategic alignment, and risk management. Each driver is discussed in detail, highlighting its significance and impact on effective data governance. Furthermore, data governance domains focus on categorising data governance activities into distinct domains, namely data architecture, data stewardship, data quality, data integration, and data security. The authors provide an overview of each domain and discuss its role in achieving the overarching goals of data governance.

Khatri and Brown (2010) describe the essential processes required for effective data governance, including data definition and classification, metadata

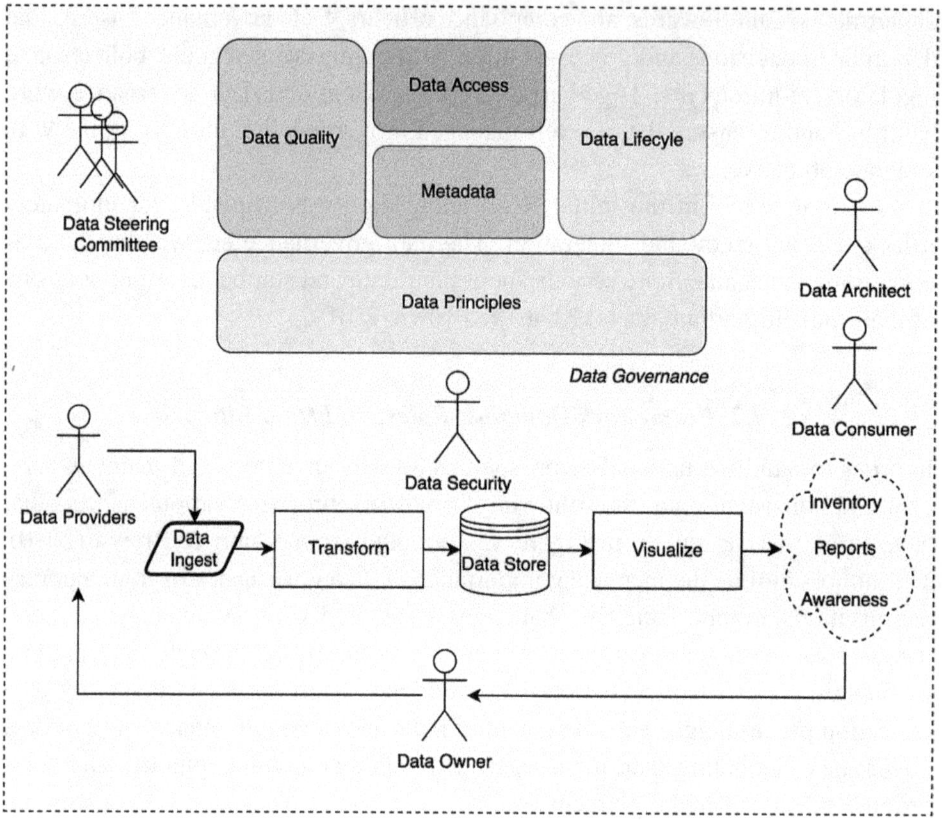

Figure 9.2 Decision domains, roles, and inventory data lifecycle.
Adapted for GHG Inventory Data from Khatri & Brown (2010).

management, data access and security, data lifecycle management, and data quality management. The authors emphasise the iterative and continuous nature of these processes, emphasising the need for ongoing monitoring and improvement.

Based on the framework adopted from Khatri & Brown (2010) and presented in Figure 9.2, Table 9.2 outlines decisions and roles may be assigned toward establishing the GHG inventory data governance. The questions in Table 9.2 must be clearly answered and defined before establishing the technical part (IT infrastructure) for the GHG inventory project. The roles in the summary were identified as: data owner/custodian, data provider/producer, data consumer, data oversight committee, subject matter expert, data quality manager, data architect, and data security officer.

The proposed framework emphasises the importance of establishing a dedicated data governance entity within an organisation, led by an executive sponsor and supported by a cross-functional data governance council. The roles and responsibilities of key stakeholders, such as data stewards, data owners, and data custodians, are defined, ensuring clear accountability and effective decision-making.

Table 9.2 *Framework for data decision domains.*

Data governance domain	Domain decisions	Potential roles for accountability
Data principles • Clarifying the data assets and maintaining transparency and accountability	• What are the uses of available activity data based on the IPCC guidelines? • What are the mechanisms for communicating the activity data on an ongoing basis? • What opportunities exist for sharing the data for research and reuse? • How do regulations influence the use of the data?	• Data provider/ producer • Data owner/ custodian • Data consumer • Data oversight committee
Data quality • Establishing the requirements based on intended use of the activity data	• What are the required IPCC standards for quality of data including accuracy, timeliness, completeness, and credibility? • What is the program for establishing and communicating data quality?	• Data owner • Subject matter expert • Data quality manager
Metadata • Establishing the semantics of data so that it is interpretable	• What are the codes for documenting the semantics of the data based on IPCC guidelines? • How to integrate all data sources consistently?	• Data owner • Data architect • Data oversight committee
Data access • Specifying access requirements for inventory data	• What are data access procedures and standards? • What are the risks involved in data availability and quality? • What is the policy for access to data, reports, and visualisations? • How will provider compliance audit and monitoring be conducted? • How will a security audit be conducted? • What is the program for data backup and recovery?	• Data owner • Data consumer • Data security officer • Data oversight committee
Data lifecycle • Determines the definition, production, retention, and retirement of the data	• How is data inventoried? • What are the standards for data definition, production, retention, and retirement? • What is the follow-up procedure for data compliance? • What are the mechanisms for MOUs with data providers?	• Data architect • Data oversight committee

Adopted from Khatri & Brown (2010).

The application of data governance in the environmental information systems sector is by no means a theoretical possibility. The following is a brief description of some of the best practice cases that incorporated data governance successfully:

- European Environment Agency (EEA): The EEA has implemented robust data governance principles and frameworks for environmental data collection and reporting. Their data governance practices involve establishing clear data management procedures, metadata standards, and data quality assurance processes. The EEA's Data and Information Management Framework ensures consistency, reliability, and accessibility of environmental data for reporting, analysis, and policy-making (European Environment Agency, 2020)
- Greenhouse Gas Protocol (GHGP): The GHGP, a collaboration between the World Resources Institute (WRI) and the World Business Council for Sustainable Development, has developed data governance principles and frameworks for greenhouse gas inventories. The GHGP's Corporate Standard provides guidelines for businesses to establish robust data management practices, including data collection, calculation methodologies, and data quality assurance processes. The framework ensures consistency, transparency, and accuracy in reporting GHG emissions (WRI, 2022).
- The United States Environmental Protection Agency (EPA): The EPA has implemented data governance principles for greenhouse gas inventories through its GHGRP. The program establishes data collection and reporting requirements for various sectors, including power plants, oil and gas facilities, and industrial processes. The EPA's data governance practices ensure data quality, consistency, and transparency, enabling accurate and reliable GHG inventory reporting (Congressional Research Service, 2023).

These success stories demonstrate the effects of applying data governance principles in the context of greenhouse gas inventories and environmental data collection. They emphasise the need to establish clear data management procedures, data quality assurance processes, and standardised reporting frameworks to ensure accurate, reliable, and transparent reporting of environmental data.

9.5 Discussion and Conclusions

The ultimate aim in any GHG inventory project is to ensure the following elements are met and satisfied by the stakeholders and the data submitted to the database. The project ultimately must be science-based, data-driven, ensures data integrity and security, and efficiently implements data integration. This is quite an undertaking at the national level and requires the collective cooperation of several key agencies and stakeholders.

However, it is also vital to consider data openness and transparency in such a project. Researchers have identified the following main opportunities for data-driven climate change and mitigation projects (Kaack, 2019):

- *Data Science:* The advances in data lifecycle design and management can contribute greatly to a data drive approach to climate change management. Technologies such as big data can also offer scientists an opportunity to deal with sensor data and huge amounts of gathered information in an efficient way.
- *Artificial Intelligence and Machine Learning:* Advances in forecasting, deep learning, and classification offer many opportunities for a data-driven approach to climate change monitoring and mitigation. However, the availability of the data and its quality are the main challenges in this area.
- *Remote Sensing:* Several technologies such as Internet of Things (IoT) and remote sensing offer opportunities for gathering more data on climate change. These can often be automated, and data can flow on a very high frequency.

This chapter started by considering three National Communications (2005, 2012, and 2020) by the Kingdom of Bahrain and then analysed the challenges faced by each cycle with regard to data. The main research of this study was aimed at conducting a qualitative case study of the three NCs in order to answer the following questions: What are the primary challenges faced in the greenhouse gas (GHG) inventory data process in the Kingdom of Bahrain? and What is a recommended implementation of robust data governance practices that can enhance the accuracy, reliability, and transparency of the IPCC GHG inventory data collection process? Based on the analysis, the main challenges facing Bahrain's periodic inventory projects are:

- *Data availability*: Lack of data specifically collected for the GHG inventory (mainly with regard to collecting activity data). A firm commitment at the leadership level is needed to ensure all stakeholders are reporting their data to the central committee preparing the GHG inventory. Data governance frameworks can help in building the required infrastructure and processes to make this smooth and sustainable. This was shown to be possible by best practice cases such as those by the USA and EU examples reported above.
- *Poor Data Quality*: The absence of data governance practices can lead to poor data quality, including issues with completeness, timeliness, integrity, and relevance. Poor data quality hampers the reliability and usefulness of the collected data, hindering effective analysis and decision-making processes.
- *Default Factors*: The problem with using default values and emission factors that are not calculated by Annex I countries. Country inventories often resort to default values within the IPCC software, but this should be done as an absolute last resort to decrease uncertainty in the results.

- *Lack of Openness*: Open data from both the private and public sectors are essential for the inventory of GHGs. This probably needs legislative intervention at a country level. As with any major IT project, it also needs support and commitment from the leadership to prevent failure.
- *Disregarding Data Governance*: Several GHG data collection efforts skip answering data governance questions in terms of domains, process, and stakeholders and jump directly to building an IT system or a database. This often leads to unreliable data or increased uncertainty in the reporting due to bad practice, especially those related to human factors in data collection. Without proper data governance practices, there is a greater likelihood of data inconsistencies and inaccuracies arising. Inadequate data validation, lack of standardised data formats, and insufficient data quality controls can result in erroneous or incomplete data, leading to unreliable insights and decision-making.
- *Lack of Data Consistency and Integration*: In the absence of data governance practices, integrating data from different sources or systems can become challenging. Incompatible data formats, inconsistent data definitions, and poor data documentation can impede data integration efforts, hindering comprehensive analysis and reporting.

To mitigate these challenges, it is crucial to incorporate robust data governance practices from the outset of designing the proposed Information Management System (Kawanishi & Fujikura, 2020). This involves defining data standards, implementing data quality controls, ensuring data security measures, establishing data access and privacy protocols, and aligning with relevant regulatory requirements. By prioritising data governance, GHG inventory projects can enhance data reliability, accuracy, security, and compliance, leading to better project outcomes and decision-making processes. Building a good foundation for data integration will enable the smooth task of reporting National Communications periodically, as well as increasing public awareness of climate change factors among the public and private sector.

Furthermore, adopting a data governance framework such as the one outlined above will enhance compliance among stakeholders and data producers and will clarify the roles and responsibilities of each member in the data lifecycle. This must also be enforced by a determined and clear leadership in order to achieve the sustainability and reduction goals outlined in the treaty. Ultimately, a clear and operational data governance structure also enables trust among stakeholders and ensures the smooth adoption of such a huge task.

It is unfortunate that many large environmental information systems are designed without taking into account these principles (i.e. transparency, accountability, integrity, collaboration, integration) and are often built with total disregard for the various questions needed toward setting up a huge data lifecycle at the national level. This often leads to the failure of large data projects and loss of both funding and human efforts. Often this is caused by such projects paying attention merely to technology and technical considerations, while ignoring setting data governance practices that ensure sustainability and maintenance of the data and take into account the human factors.

In conclusion, the proposed framework above can guide GHG data collection efforts but is in need of a top-management decision that emphasises successful data governance, careful consideration of organisational context, executive support, and an iterative approach to improvement. The framework also provides a valuable resource for organisations aiming to establish robust data governance structures to reap the associated benefits of improved data management and informed decision-making.

References

Alnaser, W. et al., (2018). Third Report on the GHG in the Kingdom of Bahrain, Sakheer: UOB.

Bahrain National Communication (2020). Available online: https://unfccc.int/documents/256562 (accessed 15 January 2022).

Bodansky, D. (2016). The Paris climate change agreement: a new hope? *American Journal of International Law* 110, pp. 228–319.

Congressional Research Service (2023). *EPA's Greenhouse Gas Reporting Program*. Washington, DC: Congressional Research Service.

DAMA International (2009). *The DAMA Guide to the Data Management Body of Knowledge (DAMA-DMBOK) Guide*. (N.p.): Technics Publications.

Eggleston, H. et al. (2006). *2006 IPCC Guidelines for National Greenhouse Gas Inventories*. (N.p.): IPCC (Intergovernmental Panel on Climate Change).

European Environment Agency (EEA) (2020). *EEA Data Policy*. Copenhagen: EEA. Available online: www.eea.europa.eu/legal/eea-data-policy (accessed 2023).

General Commission for the Protection of Marine Resources, Environment and Wildlife (2005). *Bahrain's Initial Communication to the United Nations Framework Convention on Climate Change*. March. Manama: General Commission for the Protection of Marine Resources, Environment and Wildlife.

Intergovernmental Panel on Climate Change (IPCC) (2006). *2006 IPCC Guidelines for National Greenhouse Gas Inventories, Kanagawa: National Greenhouse Inventory Program*, ed. Eggelston, S., Buendia, L., Miwa, K., Ngara, T., and Tanabe, K. Hayama: Institute for Global Environmental Strategies.

Intergovernmental Panel on Climate Change (IPCC) (2019). *2019 Refinement to the 2006 IPCC Guidelines for National Greenhouse Gas Inventories*. Geneva: IPCC. Available online: www.ipcc.ch/report/2019-refinement-to-the-2006-ipcc-guidelines-for-national-greenhouse-gas-inventories/ (accessed 2023).

Kaack, L. (2019). *Challenges and Prospects for Data-Driven Climate Change Mitigation*. (N.p.): Carnegie Mellon University.

Kawanishi, M., and Fujikura, R. (2020). Assessment for the implementation of a national greenhouse gas inventory: the case of Japan. *Management of Environmental Quality: An International Journal* 32 (2), pp. 359–379.

Khatri, V., and Brown, C. (2010). Designing data governance. *Communications of the ACM*, pp. 148–152.

Mazmanian, D. A., and Sabatier, P. A. (1983). *Implementation and Public Policy*. Glenview, IL: Scott Foresman.

Public Commission for the Protection of Marine Resources, Environment and Wildlife (2012). Bahrain's Second National Communication for the UNFCCC. Manama: Public Commission for the Protection of Marine Resources, Environment and Wildlife.

Rajamani, L. (2016). Ambition and differentiation in the 2015 Paris Agreement: interpretative possibilities and underlying politics. *International and Comparative Law Quarterly* 65 (2), pp. 493–514.

Supreme Council for the Environment (SCE) (2021). *Insourcing IT Developers for Developing an Information Systems*. Available online: www.tenderboard.gov.bh/tenderdetails/?id=2/2021/SCE(RFP/INT/SCE/2021/02) (accessed 15 January 2022).

United Nations Framework Convention on Climate Change (UNFCC) (2009). *UNFCCC Resource Guide Module 1: The Process of National Communications for Non-Annex Parties*. Bonn: UN.

United Nations Framework Convention on Climate Change (UNFCC) (2010). *Reporting Guidelines on Annual Inventories (Decision 14/CP.11)*. UNFCC. Available online: https://unfccc.int/resource/docs/2010/sbi/eng/17.pdf (accessed 2023).

United Nations Framework Convention on Climate Change (UNFCC) (2023a). *National Communications*. Bonn: UNFCC. Available online: https://unfccc.int/non-annex-I-NCs (accessed 10 January2023).

United Nations Framework Convention on Climate Change (UNFCC) (2023b). *National Inventories Submissions*. Bonn: UNFCC. Available online: https://unfccc.int/ghg-inventories-annex-i-parties/2023 (accessed 25 June 2024).

World Resource Institute (WRI) (2022). *The Greenhouse Gas Protocol: A Corporate Accounting and Reporting Standard*. Washington, DC: WRI.

10

Key Issues for Long-Term Climate Policy Design in GCC Countries with a Focus on Qatar

FREDERIC BABONNEAU, AHMED BADRAN, MAROUA BENLAHRECH, ALAIN HAURIE, MAXIME SCHENCKERY, AND MARC VIELLE

10.1 Introduction

The Gulf Cooperation Council (GCC) Countries, and in particular Qatar, were parties to the COP21 that has led to the Paris Agreement. Because they are so much exposed to climate change threats these countries must participate actively in the forthcoming climate negotiations that will define the regime leading to the fulfilment of the 1.5°C or 2°C objective. This gives rise to three key issues that are interrelated questions: (1) how can the GCC economies adapt to the worldwide transition to a decarbonised regime and how will their policy adapt to this global socioeconomic stress; (2) how can GCC countries adapt their own energy system to reduce GHG emissions drastically; (3) what outcome could GCC countries expect from negotiations leading to a fair international agreement on burden sharing in the drive of the world economy to a net zero emission regime by 2070 (the ultimate goal in the Paris Agreement).

Currently, of the energy used in the world, 34% comes from burning oil, 27% from coal, and 2% from gas. Nuclear power, hydroelectric power and all other renewables combined provide just 15%. The result of all of this fossil fuel use is an annual flow of 10 gigaton (Gt) of carbon (36.7 Gt of CO_2) out of the ground and into the atmosphere. The Paris Agreement of 2015 calls for increases to the atmospheres of carbon-dioxide level caused by fossil fuels to end by the second half of this century. The Intergovernmental Panel on Climate Change Fifth Assessment Report (IPCC AR5) defines the limit for total cumulative emissions since the onset of the industrial era, if humanity is to have a 66% chance of avoiding dangerous climate change (2°C of warming), as 1,000 Gt of carbon (3,670 Gt of CO_2) and notes that the world has already used up to 52% of this budget (see Stocker et al., 2013). Since some fossil fuel emissions may be very hard to eliminate from the economy, they could be counterbalanced by negative emissions that take carbon dioxide out of the atmosphere at a similar rate.

In several integrated assessment models recently developed, this appears as the only way to meet the Paris goal of stopping any further increase to the carbon-dioxide level. Two methods have emerged as the most effective in achieving this. One is Direct Air Capture (DAC), which involves trapping carbon dioxide from the atmosphere by drawing air through an absorbent material. The other is Bioenergy with Carbon Capture and Storage (BECCS), where absorption is done by trees and crops as they grow. This biomass is then burned to produce energy and the resulting carbon dioxide is captured. In both cases, the carbon dioxide is stored underground, permanently removing it from the atmosphere.

Two key drivers in the energy transition, worldwide as well as for GCC countries, will thus be: (1) the introduction of carbon capture and sequestration (CCS) in industry, associated with CO_2 direct removal (CDR); and (2) the advent of smart cities (SCs), associated with the emergence of smart energy systems (SESs) leveraging the development of the Internet of Things (IoT). Indeed, CCS in industry (APS, 2011) with renewables penetration (Bhutto et al., 2014; Doukas et al., 2006) fostered by SCs and SESs will enable Gulf region economies to become low emission and sustainable. At the same time, these game-changing developments will modify worldwide the economy of fossil fuels on which GCC states currently heavily depend. In the forthcoming climate negotiations, the share of a global safety carbon budget (Mainshausen, 2009; Babonneau et al., 2020) that could be claimed by GCC countries is related to unburnable fuel risk (Luomi, 2014). In the very long term, GCC countries could count on comparative advantage in harnessing DAC technologies. These technologies producing negative emissions will be of high economic value when the price of permits reaches very high levels, in a range USD500–USD1,000 per ton of CO_2 (tCO_2) after year 2050, as envisioned in recent integrated assessment models (Marcucci & Kypreos, 2017).

To answer these questions, the rest of the chapter is organised as follows: Section 10.2 provides an assessment of the exposure of GCC states to climate change damages in the long term and the possibility to adapt to the economic disruption due to global decarbonisation of the economy. Section 10.3 gives a macroeconomic evaluation of the possible welfare loss for these countries that could occur if a stringent abatement policy were adopted worldwide along a 2°C pathway (Babonneau et al., 2020). The section provides an exploration of the possible advantages that the GCC states could obtain from actively participating in the governance of climate negotiations in order to obtain an appropriate compensation through the allocation of emissions rights. Section 10.4 is a discussion of the necessary change in the energy policy in this region in order to be able to deal with this game-changing transition (Reiche 2010; Salahuddin & Gow, 2014; Luomi 2012; Abdmouleh et al., 2015; Al-Maamary et al., 2016; McGlade & Etkin, 2014; Al Shidi et al., 2016), In Section 10.5, we conclude our discussion.

10.2 Climate Change Impacts in GCC Countries

Climate change will have a double impact on Gulf countries: first, directly through a severe distortion of the climate in their own territory; and second, indirectly through a big disruption of their economic model based on the production and export of hydrocarbons and derivative products. Given that the Gulf countries' environment is already very engineered, the main impact is through the transformation of their business model, the resulting decrease of revenue, and the risk of stranded assets. The energy transition induced by international agreement and technical progress will have a large impact on the economies of the Gulf countries but they only just started to address the issue comprehensively. These two-pronged threats should motivate GCC member countries to participate actively in the coming climate negotiations to push for a fair burden sharing in a strategy aimed at containing the temperature increase to less than 2°C, or even 1.5°C.

The key physical impacts from climate change are variations in temperature (Elmesr et al., 2010) and precipitation and a rise in sea level. This creates water stress and increased surface temperature in GCC countries (Verner, 2012). There is also an acute dust issue in these countries that could be amplified by climate change (Prakash et al., 2015; Kalenderski et al., 2013). Water scarcity increases agricultural production cost, food import bills, and overall food insecurity given the highly subsidised domestic agriculture and high dependency of GCC countries on foreign food products (Depledge, 2008). Furthermore, to continue enjoying a comfortable lifestyle, cooling capacity will need to increase in line with the rising temperatures. Apart from physical impacts, climate change imposes a stress on resources and on their distribution among the populations in GCC countries. This will multiply the pre-existing socioeconomic tensions in the Gulf monarchies (Luomi 2012 & 2014). For example, Qatar's economic competitiveness is largely dependent on the relevance of its energy policy. Its energy industry is facing internal challenges as it must cope with one of the world's fastest -growing economies as well as external issues with the emergence of a new paradigm on the demand side where Asia has become the fastest-growing region for natural gas consumption. Also, unconventional gas sources continue to reshuffle global gas supplies as local shale gas and other unconventional production perspectives and competition grow stronger both from the US side and Asia Pacific. As indicated in the long-term 'national vision 2030', Qatar wants to build new competitive advantages beyond fossil fuels. To achieve this objective, the country has to challenge the basic building blocks of its current energy policy. Also, it faces new challenges to achieve sustainable development by integrating, in particular, the goals of the Paris Agreements. Energy choices need to be mapped out, quantified, and then simulated to clarify the long-term consequences of today's energy choices.

The substantial increase of consumption of low-priced gas in the Gulf countries is pushing Qatar to reconsider its regional energy policy (Krane, 2021). Another driver for drastic change in the use of fossil fuels in the regional energy system will be the possible trend toward a low-carbon economy fostered by an international climate regime resulting from post COP21 negotiations (see, e.g. the *Intended Nationally Determined Contributions* (INDC) document submitted by the State of Qatar Ministry of Environment for COP21 Paris 2015).

Currently, the GCC states, and in particular Qatar, are the largest per capita emitters of greenhouse gases (GHGs) as CO_2 emissions are linked to the economic growth of these countries (Salahuddin & Gow, 2014). The tradition of free or quasi-free access to fossil fuel energy makes it very difficult to implement a policy based on economic incentives. A solution to this quandary could be provided by the development of Smart Cities (SCs) associated with Smart Energy Systems (SESs), whereby, through the advent of the IoT, the technologies of use, like appliances, cooling systems, Plug-in Hybrid Electric Vehicles (PHEVs), and so on, will communicate with energy producers and distributors and use virtual energy prices to implement demand response, provide reserve, and participate efficiently in the system service duties. In so doing and without extra charge to the consumers, the penetration of variable renewable energy will be fostered.

Worldwide, the expected energy transition leads to a peak in fossil fuel demand. In a competitive market, the rent collected by each oil barrel sold will disappear and be replaced by a normal return on investment (real interest rate) (Hotelling, 1931). The revenue of Qatar and the Gulf countries will drastically decrease. All the subsidised economic activity will begin disappearing as well. The energy transition puts at risk the way of life enjoyed in Qatar and in other surrounding oil- and gas-producing countries. Some countries (Norway, Qatar, UAE) have constituted a sovereign fund to share the wealth created by hydrocarbons with the future generation. These countries are also looking to diversify their economy towards other value-creation activities. However, none of these changes will create as much revenue as the oil and gas business has generated over the previous years. The pace of transition will determine the effort and speed that oil and gas countries need in order to develop in their move towards diversification.

Oil- and gas-producing countries have important stakes in the forthcoming energy transition as they have among the most impacted economies. They face some strategic dilemmas: should they invest in domestic renewable energies to increase the export of oil and gas; will oil and gas reserves and infrastructure investment get stranded? Will they be able to diversify their economies in time? Should they invest massively in negative emission R&D? Is natural gas a transition or a destination fuel? Is liquified natural gas (LNG)-to-power a competitive option? What should be their positioning and proposals in COP agreement discussions? And there are many other questions that arise regarding the uncertain outcomes of energy transition.

Several analysts highlighted that to reach the 2°C target by the end of the twenty-first century, perhaps as much as 50% of the oil reserve should not be burnt (Luomi, 2014). Even with Carbon Capture and Sequestration (CCS) the question of unburnable oil remains at the top of the agenda of the energy transition (McGlade & Etkin, 2014). Within the framework of the United Nations Framework Convention on Climate Change (UNFCCC), the matter of receiving compensation for oil left in the ground was raised the first time by Ecuador in 2012. This idea is starting to gain momentum as GCC states have understood that revenue losses from reduced demand, low prices, oil rent loss, and trade barriers are only the near-term consequences of a loss of wealth from the potentially stranded oil and gas assets. Worldwide Energy transition leads to a significant shrinkage of the oil rent. New energy sources like solar- or wind-power generation are increasingly competitive with fossil fuel-power generation (IEA 2016) Electric vehicles threaten oil demand in the new needs for mobility and may lead to a peak oil demand as soon as 2030 (OPEC, 2017) The electric vehicle transition could be a matter of one or two decades only (Seba, 2014) if the value added for the end user is significant. Autonomous vehicles pilot experiments in smart cities demonstrate that urban users could unload significant value in time-saving and safety (EU Commission, 2017). An inherent dichotomy exists between the vast oil and gas wealth of GCC states and international potential climate change mitigation objectives (Luomi 2012 & 2014). Meanwhile, the Gulf countries are hesitant to fully embrace the 'Green Growth' concept. Despite their announced INDCs, many GCC countries are not yet committed to a drastic transformation of their economies, where energy efficiency, climate resilience, and sustainable economic development are combined. In recent years, the GCC countries recognised the synergy between climate action and economic diversification. 'Green Growth' plans have been drawn up in the UAE, Qatar, Saudi Arabia, and Oman. Following the drop in oil prices, every GCC country took the opportunity to increase the price of energy domestically (Verner, 2012) and are experimenting with a new approach in combining partial subsidy programmes and partial fossil fuel price adjustments. This could gradually move towards market-based efficient pricing over the medium to long term, when energy subsidies are eventually phased out (Poudineh et al., 2018). A low-carbon transition will require not only a reduction in emissions from the fossil fuel sector but also a transformation in the GCC countries' economic activities. As such, at COP18 in Qatar, some GCC countries proposed to add economic diversification as a climate change mitigation instrument. The effort to introduce national components into international agreements is now a well-established strategy to mitigate the impact of energy transition and climate policies.

10.3 A Macroeconomic Analysis of a Climate Agreement to Contain a Temperature Rise to 2°C

We refer to Babonneau et al. (2020 & 2021) for more details about our approach, which is based on the computable general equilibrium model GEMINI-E3, a world-wide macroeconomic modelling tool. The model describes ten countries/regions that are listed further on. Among them we find the GCC countries. In these simulations, we have introduced the possibility of producing negative emissions using CDR technologies, specifically DAC and BECCS. We use a recent description and assessment of an operational DAC process (Keith et al., 2018). The process requires either 8.81 gigajoules (GJ) of natural gas or 5.25 GJ of gas and 366 kWh of electricity per ton of CO_2 captured. For each ton of CO_2 captured, the process delivers 1.48 tons of dry CO_2 which must be sequestered. The extra 0.48 tons come from the burning of natural gas to provide electricity and heat. If the electricity is obtained from zero-emission technology, such as nuclear or solar power plants, the ratio of CO_2 sequestered to CO_2 captured from the air drops to 1.29. We therefore consider in this chapter, two levelised costs for DAC technologies, that is to say, USD300/t-CO_2 and USD350/t-CO_2, in order to differentiate among groups of countries with access to the most efficient solar power plants and/or with less opposition to new nuclear power plants that would lead to the lowest DAC operating cost. In the latter group, we find only the USA and European countries. Those figures are in line with the estimates mentioned in the literature. The levelised cost computed by Keith et al. (2018) is USD232/t-CO_2 captured, whereas the study by the America Physical Society (APS, 2011) proposed a levelised cost of USD550/t-CO_2. In House et al. (2011), the cost of powering a DAC plant using a natural gas-fired plant with CCS was USD396/t-CO_2 avoided. The extra energy cost of DAC was estimated to be around USD232/t-CO_2 captured, based on (Lackner, 2009). The storage cost was evaluated in (Rubin et al., 2015) to be in the range of USD6–USD13/t-CO_2 stored. For BECCS, we consider the standard technology of generating electricity from biomass while capturing and injecting CO_2 into geological formations. We use a unique worldwide levelised cost of USD60/t-CO_2 that is consistent with the IEA estimates (Koornneef et al., 2011).

The total quantity of CO_2 captured by DAC and other carbon capture technologies is constrained by the CO_2 storage capacity in the different groups of countries considered in this chapter. Estimates of these storage potentials, including deep saline aquifers, hydrocarbon fields, and coal beds are derived from Marcucci & Kypreos (2017). We assume that only 25% of these potentials can be used for DAC and BECCS technologies by 2100, as reported in Table 10.1. We also assume that these technologies will be mature enough for massive deployment in 2040, with a linear deployment trend after that.

Table 10.1 *Carbon storage potential per region in Gt CO_2.*

USA	24.0
European Union (EU)	37.5
China	30.5
India	20.0
Russia	126.5
Gulf Cooperation Council	86.0
Other energy exporting countries	23.0
Rest of Asian countries	46.0
Latin America	40.5
Rest of the World	23.0
World	**447.0**

In addition to storage capacities, BECCS potentials may also be limited in some countries by restricted access to biomass, which is the case in the Gulf countries. We calibrate those potentials of biomass based on the average of Shared Socioeconomic Pathways simulations.

A Business as Usual (BAU) scenario has been simulated by GEMINI-E3 for the 2017–2050 time span and extended to the 2100 horizon. It has been calibrated on the 'New Policies' scenario of the World Energy Outlook (IEA, 2016). The demographic assumptions are based on the 'median variant' scenario done by the (United Nations, 2017). Figures 10.1a and 10.1b shows the population, gross domestic product (GDP) and resulting CO_2 emissions at a global level for the BAU scenario. The world's population increased by 50% between 2016 and 2100, reaching 11.2 billion inhabitants by 2100. Over the same period, the world GDP has multiplied by 7, representing an annual growth rate of 2.4%. In our BAU scenario, global CO_2 emissions peak at 48.3 billion tons of CO_2 in 2070 and then decline to 46.8 billion tons of CO_2 by the end of our century. This decrease in CO_2 emissions can be interpreted by the scarcity of fossil energies in the second part of the twenty-first century. In the BAU scenario, more than 4.107 Gt of CO_2 were emitted during the twenty-first century and 6.327 Gt of CO_2 from 1876 to the end of our century. This would result, with 66% probability, in an increase of global surface atmospheric temperature (SAT) of more than 3.5°C since 1850–1900 (Rogelj et al., 2018).

Mitigation scenarios were simulated by imposing a safety cumulative emissions budget (SCEB) of 1,170 Gt of CO_2 that limits future global emissions. Figure 10.2 shows the global trajectory of CO_2 emissions and net emissions without and

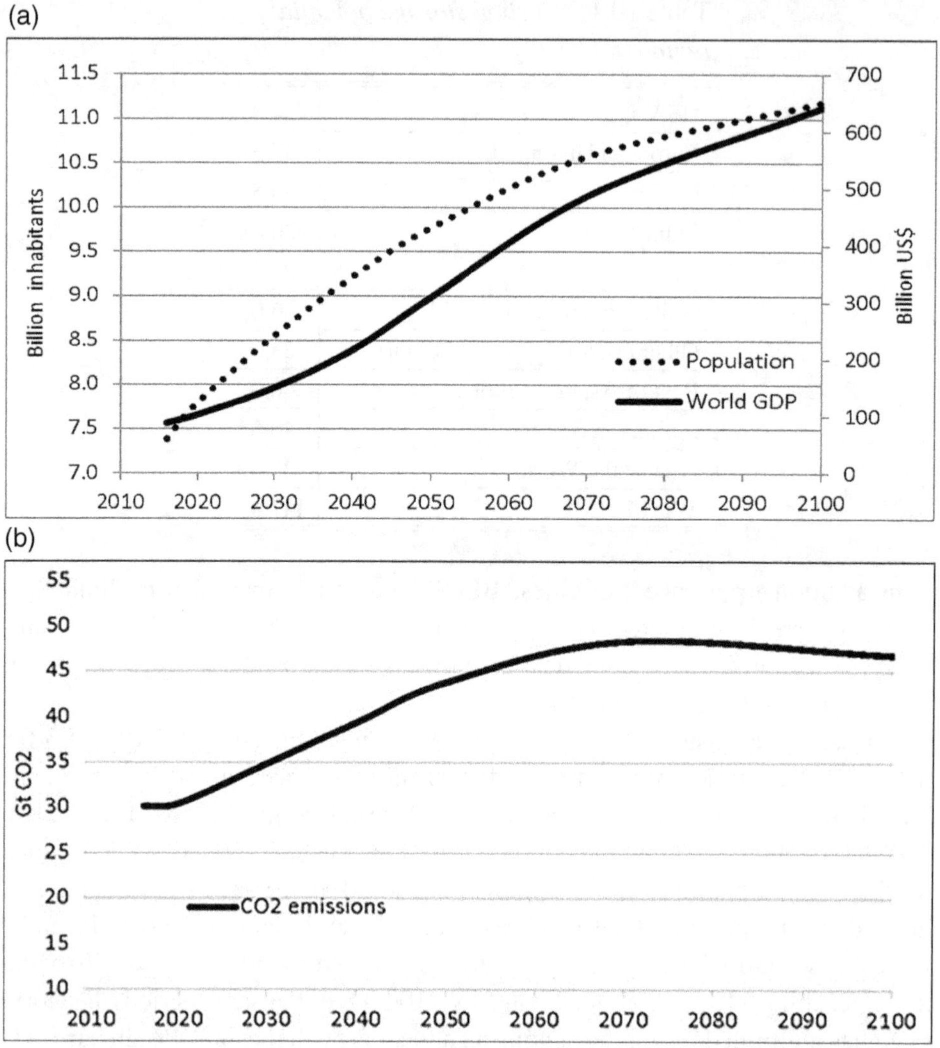

Figure 10.1 (a) Population and GDP in the BAU scenario at global level. (b) CO_2 emissions in the BAU scenario at global level.

with DAC/BECCS. Net emissions are equal to CO_2 emissions minus the emissions sequestered by DAC and BECCS. Figure 10.3 shows the contribution of DAC and BECSS in the mitigation scenarios. Figure 10.4 shows how the global welfare loss varies with the size of the SCEB. It shows that the 1.5°C objective seems to be very challenging (Rogelj et al., 2018) with a cost multiplied by 3.6 compared to a global warming limit of 2°C.

Table 10.2 gives the CO_2 price and the worldwide welfare cost. Without CO_2 sequestration, more abatements are needed and CO_2 emissions must converge to zero by the end of the twenty-fist century. The welfare cost is significant and is

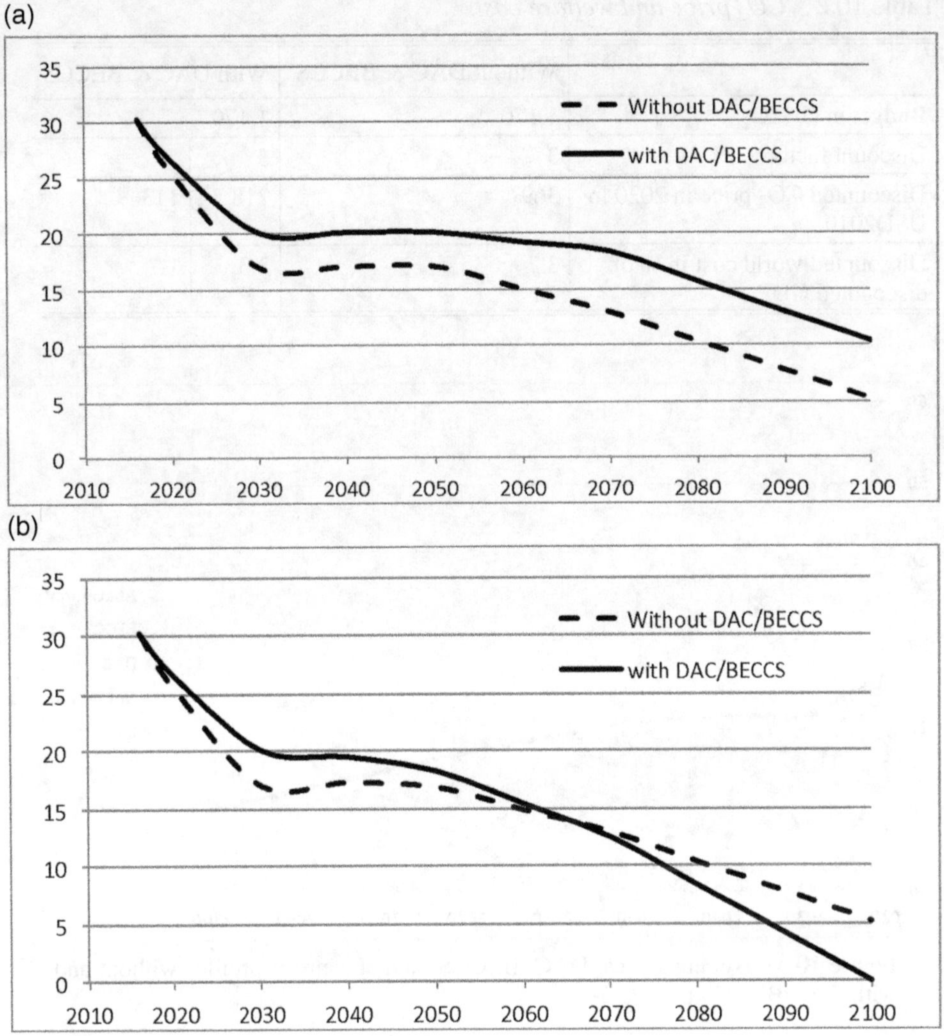

Figure 10.2 (a) Emissions trajectories in Gt CO_2 at global level. (b) Net emissions trajectories in Gt CO_2 at global level.

equal to 3.7% of the discounted GDP (assuming a 3% discount factor), with a CO_2 price equal to USD369 in 2020. When DAC and BECSS are used, the global welfare cost is reduced to 2.3% and the CO_2 price equals USD218. CDR contributes to the CO_2 mitigation mostly in the second part of the twenty-first century, as shown in the net emissions trajectories. With DAC and BECCS, our results are consistent with the figures of the mitigation scenarios given in the special report of global warming of 1.5°C carried out by IPCC (Rogelj et al., 2018). Indeed, under a 2°C mitigation pathway with greater than 66% likelihood, IPCC reports a median value of carbon price discounted at a 5% discount rate equal to USD75 per ton of

Table 10.2 *CO_2 price and welfare cost.*

	Without DAC & BECCS	With DAC & BECCS	
Budget in Gt CO_2	1,170	1,170	
Discount factor	3	3	5
Discounted CO_2 price in 2020 in USD2010	369	218	113
Discounted world cost in % of discounted GDP	3.7	2.3	1.7

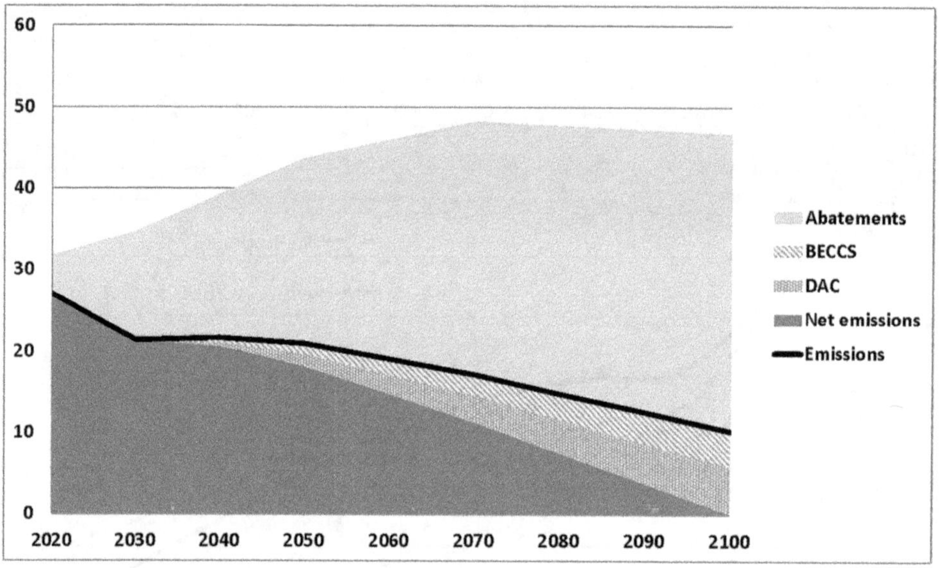

Figure 10.3 Net emissions, DAC, BECCS, and abatement profiles without and with DAC/BECCS in Gt CO_2.

CO_2. (Rogelj et al., 2018). With a scenario using a 5% discount factor, we find a USD113 CO_2 price (see Table 10.2).

In this stylised modelling framework, we introduce an international carbon market and let the different coalitions of countries, the GCC being one of them, exploit optimally the part of the SECB that has been allocated to them. One can then search for a 'fair allocation' of the carbon budget. Global climate justice is a thorny issue (see the survey by Pottier et al. (2017)) and several different fairness criteria can be invoked. First, we use two common rules that have been widely analysed in the literature: grandfathering and equal individual emission rights (per capita). Table 10.3 gives the results of these two allocations. The first rule considers the allocation of quotas to be proportional to emissions over the entire period

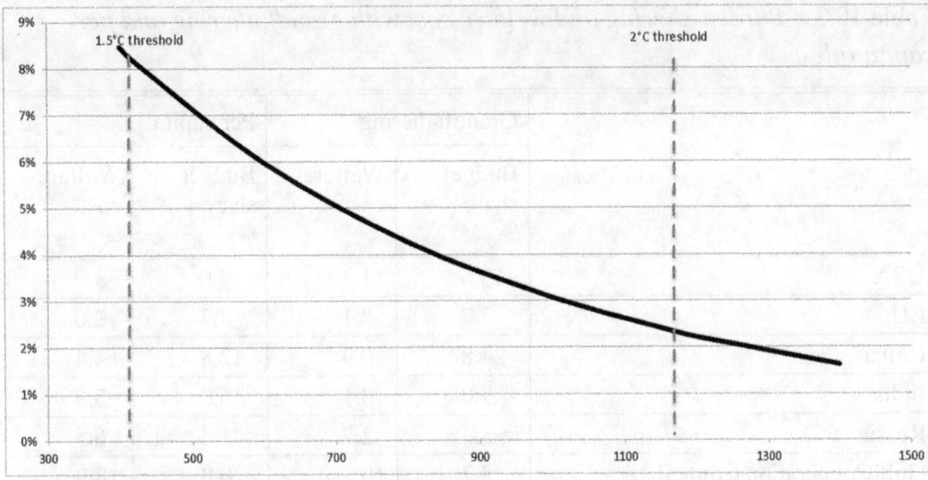

Figure 10.4 Discounted global welfare cost in % of discounted GDP with respect to carbon budget in Gt CO_2.

(i.e. 2016–2100) in the BAU scenario. This sovereignty principle is usually proposed as a starting point for environmental negotiations, considering the existing situations. Energy-exporting countries (such as Russia and the GCC) and the rest of the world support a very high burden, while India, Latin America, and China largely benefit from this allocation.

The second rule assumes that the budget share is proportional to population over the period 2016–2100. This equalitarian rule leads to many extreme welfare impacts. The most populous countries earn significant revenues from the sale of emissions. As a result, India, the rest of the world and Latin America experience welfare improvement after the implementation of the climate change mitigation policy. On the other hand, energy-exporting countries, but also China and the USA, bear a huge welfare cost.

We now design a burden-sharing rule that equalises the welfare loss across countries and groups of countries. We name this rule the 'Rawlsian' allocation in reference to Rawls' (1971) theory of justice. Table 10.4 shows the results of this game. It is interesting to compare this burden-sharing with those computed from grandfathering and per capita rules. Through this allocation, energy-exporting countries receive significant allowances to compensate their loss in terms of trade. The USA, Europe, China, and the rest of the world receive allowances that are between the grandfathering and per capita rules. In contrast, India, the rest of the Asian countries, and Latin America receive lower allowances than those computed from grandfathering and per capita rules. Table 10.4 also gives the components of the welfare cost. They confirm that energy-exporting countries are suffering from a considerable loss in terms of trade. On the other hand, they receive significant revenue from emissions trading.

Table 10.3 *Burden-sharing and welfare cost with grandfathering and per capita rules.*

	Grandfathering		Per capita	
	Budget share %	Welfare cost[a] %	Budget share %	Welfare cost[a] %
USA	13.6	1.4	4.0	3.9
EU	7.7	2.1	4.2	3.0
China	24.8	0.9	12.8	4.4
India	9.0	0.1	16.0	–5.9
Russia	3.3	2.7	1.3	6.5
Gulf Cooperation Council	3.7	10.4	0.8	18.9
Other energy-exporting countries	10.9	4.3	12.9	3.6
Rest of the Asian countries	13.0	2.2	16.8	1.4
Latin America	2.9	0.8	4.4	–1.2
Rest of the World	11.1	5.3	27.0	–2.9
World	**100.0**	**2.3**	**100.0**	**2.3**

[a] Discounted welfare cost in % of discounted GDP.

In terms of abatement costs, DAC and BECSS are relatively low-cost abatement options compared to 'traditional' CO_2 emissions abatement. There is an exception in Russia and the GCC countries where the huge amounts of CO_2 captured induce high abatement costs (above 3% of GDP), which are compensated by selling emission rights (-9% for the GCC countries). Figure 10.5 shows the contribution of each mitigation option at the global level. DAC and BECSS account for 18% of the global abatement.

10.4 A Scenario of Transition to Zero Net Energy for Qatar

In this section, we use the technology-rich bottom-up modelling tool ETEM-Q to create a scenario of a transition to Zero Net Energy (ZNE) for Qatar. We refer the reader to Babonneau et al. (2022) for the detailed description and calibration of ETEM-Q. The ETEM-Q model is driven by a forecast of useful demands that is summarised in Table 10.5. The other set of important drivers of the model, that is to say, the evolution of imported/exported energy prices are the ones given in Babonneau et al. (2022).

Figure 10.6 shows the desired emissions profile (target), which converges to ZNE by 2070 and the emissions path that is realised (actual). Significant negative

Table 10.4 *Burden-sharing and welfare cost with Rawlsian rule.*

	Budget share %	Welfare cost[a] %	CO_2 Abatement %	DAC %	BECCS %	GT %	Emissions Trading[b] %
				Components of welfare cost[a]			
USA	10.16	2.32	1.86	0.11	0.04	−0.01	0.32
EU	6.75	2.32	0.79	0.18	0.04	−0.46	1.78
China	19.84	2.32	3.72	0.11	0.03	−0.66	−0.87
India	6.34	2.32	3.40	0.19	0.08	−1.37	0.02
Russia	3.51	2.32	3.19	2.48	0.25	2.01	−5.60
GCC	5.78	2.32	3.26	2.42	0.04	5.69	−9.08
Other energy-exporting countries	16.69	2.32	1.73	0.12	0.03	1.05	−0.60
Rest of the Asian countries	12.30	2.32	1.42	0.12	0.03	−0.72	1.48
Latin America	1.69	2.32	1.83	0.79	0.19	0.13	−0.62
Rest of the world	16.93	2.32	2.59	0.17	0.04	0.34	−0.82
World	**100.0**	**2.32**	**2.05**	**0.26**	**0.05**	**0.00**	**0.00**

[a] Discounted welfare cost in % of discounted GDP. [b] + means buying – selling.

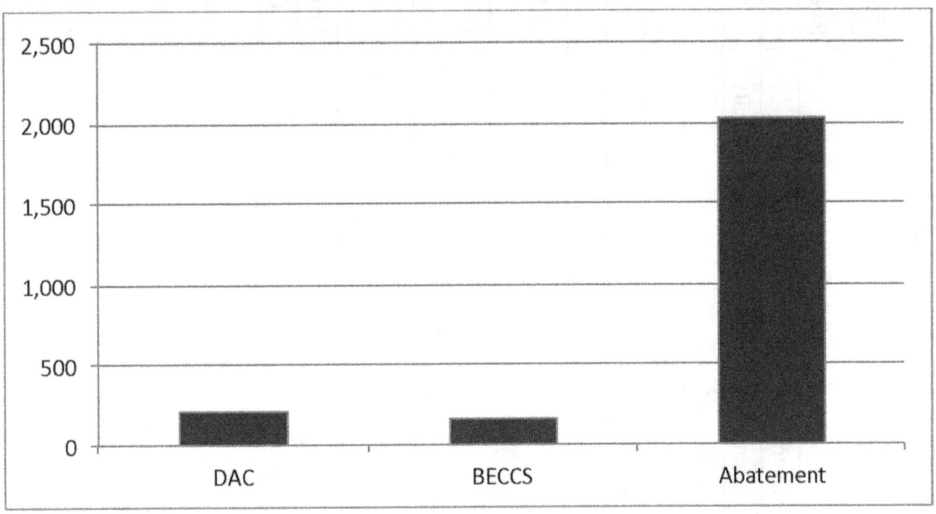

Figure 10.5 Worldwide contribution of mitigation options in Gt CO_2.

Table 10.5 *Useful demands.*

	2020	2030	2040	2050	2060	2070	2080	2090	2100
	Energy demand in petajoules (PJ)								
Residential/commercial cooling	88	93	99	104	106	110	117	120	123
Residential/commercial captive electricity	45	48	51	54	55	57	61	63	64
Industry – gas	364	368	379	390	402	414	427	439	453
Industry – electricity	58	59	61	62	64	65	67	69	71
Industry-oil	83	84	86	89	91	94	97	100	103
Aviation	136	137	141	146	150	154	159	164	169
	Water demand in million cubic meters (Mm3)								
Water desalination	605	650	695	740	746	784	840	863	881
	Transport demand in thousand kilometers per day **(kkmp/d)**								
Private	29,526	31,713	33,900	36,087	36,381	38,246	40,972	42,114	42,965
Metro	10,017	10,017	10,017	10,017	10,017	10,017	10,017	10,017	10,017
Bus	1,500	1,611	1,722	1,833	1,848	1,943	2,082	2,140	2,183
	Transport demand in thousand kilometer (kkm)								
Truck	9,600	9,696	9,987	10,286	10,595	10,913	11,240	11,578	11,925

Table 10.6 *Carbon price evolution (USD/t CO_2).*

2020	2030	2040	2050	2060	2070	2080	2090	2100
0	100	300	350	1,000	1,000	1,200	1,200	1,200

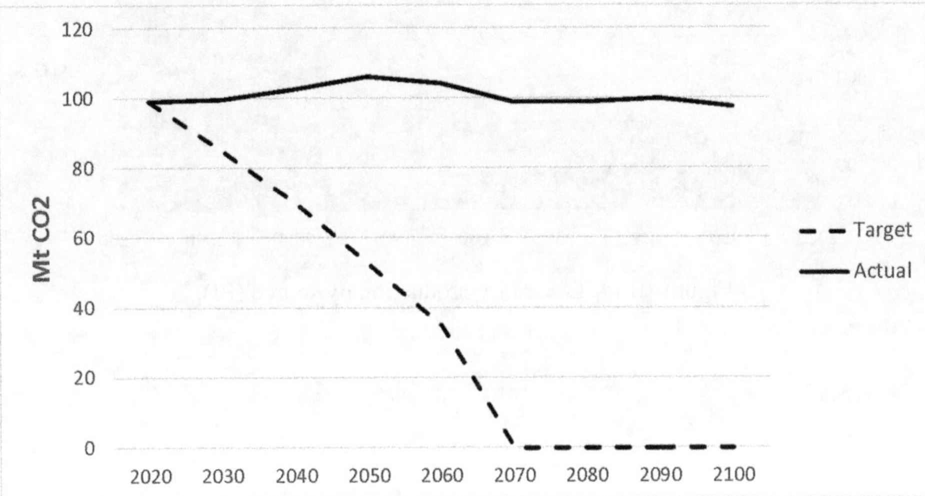

Figure 10.6 Emissions profile (megatonnes (Mt) CO_2).

emissions activity develop from 2070 onwards due to the high price of carbon on the international market. In the model, one represents a possibility to buy or sell emission permits on an international carbon-trading market with a cap-and-trade system imposed on each country. The price of carbon reported in Table 10.6 is consistent with the macroeconomic simulations reported in Babonneau et al. (2021). In the actual scenario, no climate constraints are imposed on the Qatar economy and the exports of fossil fuels remain at a business-as-usual level for the extended future. In the following, we present in detail the evolution of the Qatar energy system for the ZNE scenario.

Figure 10.7 shows that, to reduce emissions, electricity generation uses less gas and develops solar sources, mainly photovoltaic and concentrated solar power plants. The intermittency of photovoltaic generation is compensated by CSP and the installation of 3 GW of lithium batteries in the ZNE scenarios. To reach the ZNE objective, production from gas is halved by 2060. The development of negative emission technologies, hydrogen, and electric mobility are the main reasons for this electrification of the Qatar economy.

For private transport, the petrol cars are abandoned after 2050 and replaced by gas-powered hybrid cars and mainly by electric cars as they contribute to emissions

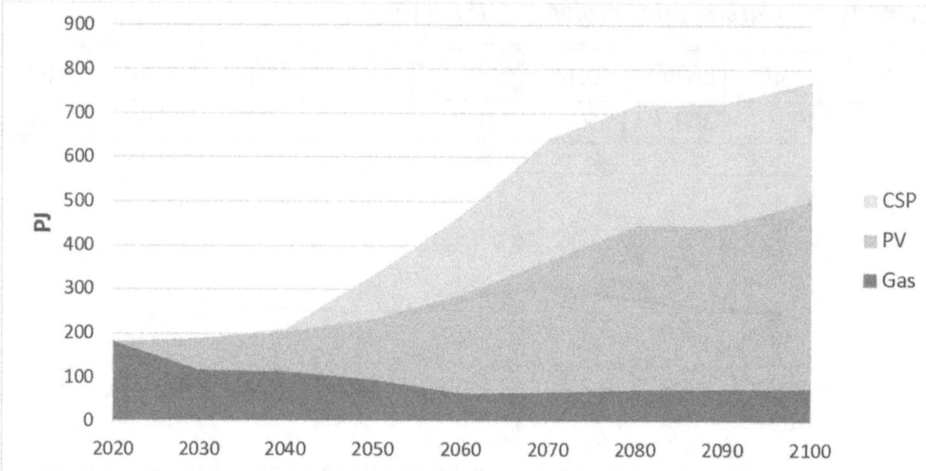

Figure 10.7 Electricity production by source (PJ).

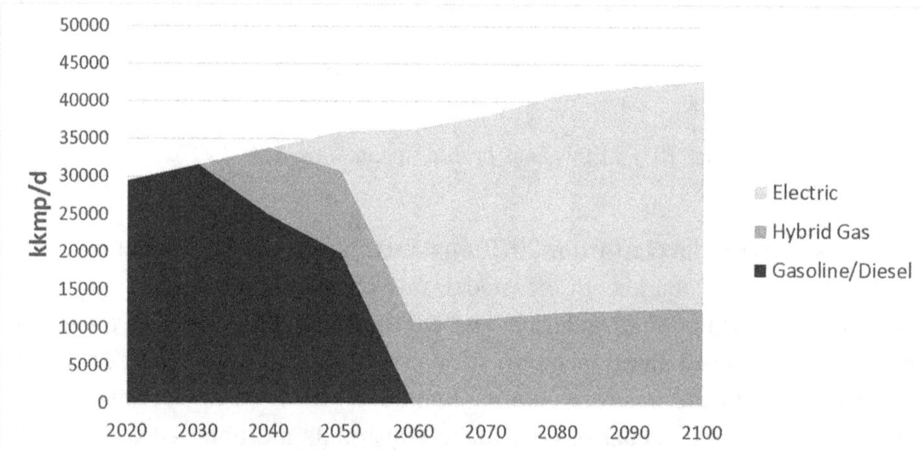

Figure 10.8 Usage technology for private transport (kkmp/d).

reduction (Figure 10.8). Regarding the other transport activities, the model shows the transformation of public and freight transport to hydrogen energy.

Figure 10.9 shows the penetration in the residential and commercial sectors of district cooling which are more efficient and competitive, but most of the demand is still met by distributed electric chillers.

Figure 10.10 indicates that the industrial hydrogen production sector is developing strongly, with the electrolysis option and especially the SMR gas option with CCS. Most of the hydrogen production is exported in the form of ammonia, which could partly compensate for the loss of revenue from LNG exports in a global ZNE context.

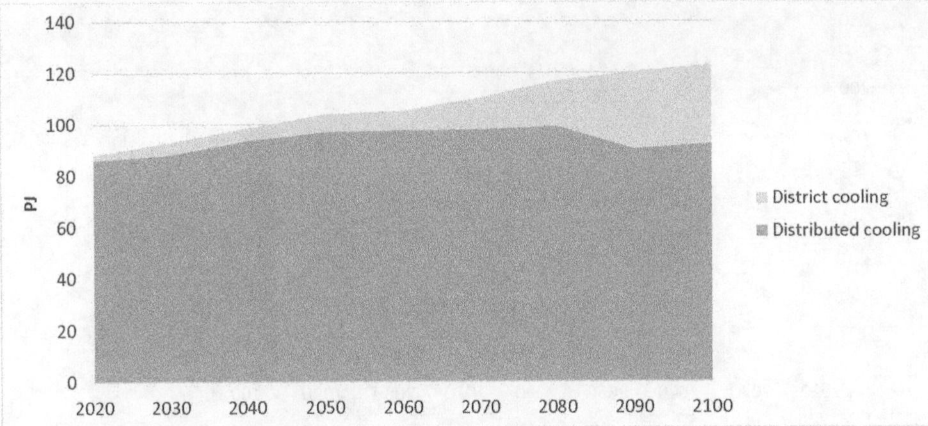

Figure 10.9 Usage technology for residential and commercial cooling.

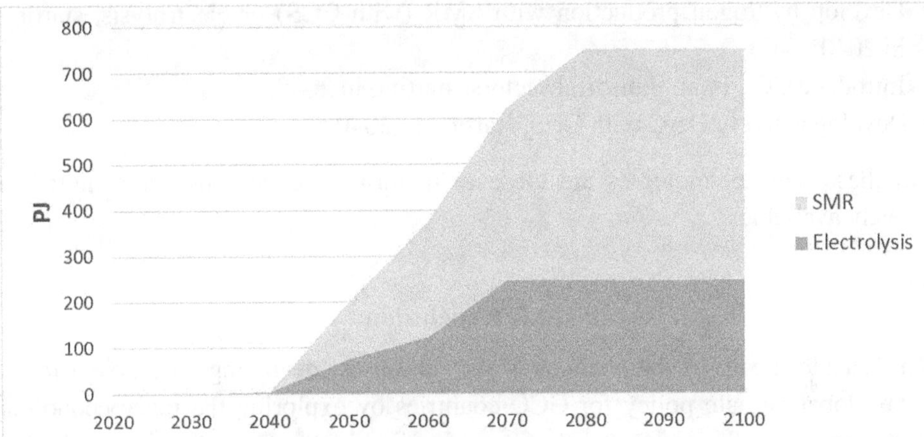

Figure 10.10 Hydrogen production by source (PJ).

In Figure 10.11, one sees that the storage of CO_2 in depleted oil and gas reservoirs develops significantly. Starting in 2050, DAC activity develops and reaches a high level at the end of the century (around 150 Mt of CO_2 captured and sequestered per year). This consumes 1,000 PJ of gas each year. Once the cap-and-trade targets are met, Qatar can sell emission permits on the international carbon market. This could be a second source of compensation for the loss of revenue from LNG exports.

In summary, to reach a ZNE regime by 2070 and exploit the resources offered by DAC technologies, this ZNE scenario proposes Qatar to:

- Start immediately to foster the use of hybrid and electric cars.
- Develop electricity generation from solar sources.

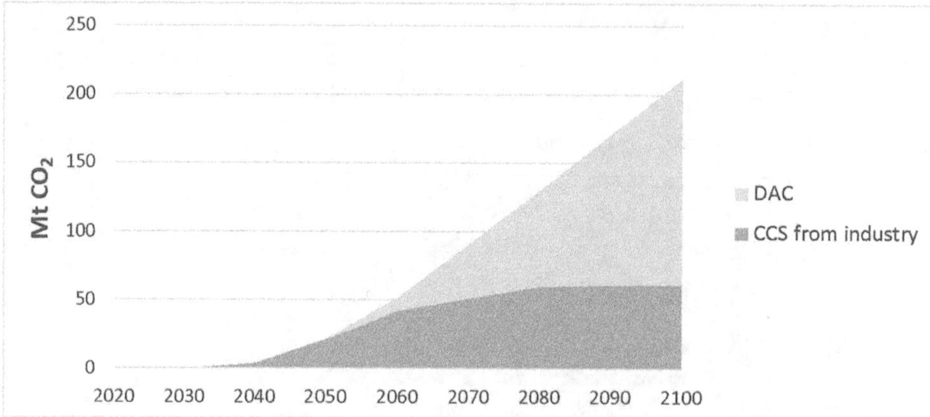

Figure 10.11 CO_2 storage (Mt CO_2).

- Develop district cooling.
- Develop hydrogen production with SMR (with CCS) or electrolysis, starting in 2040.
- Introduce CCS in all industrial sectors, starting in 2040.
- Develop actively DAC with CCS, starting in 2040.

All these new technologies are close to maturity and demonstration units are already available.

10.5 Conclusion

This chapter analyses the challenges and options of designing an efficient long-term global climate policy for GCC countries by exploring the macroeconomic cost of realising the emissions abatement implied by the Paris Agreement. It also evaluates the possibility of balancing the burden through an allocation of emissions permits in an international emissions trading system. Focusing on Qatar, the chapter conducts a bottom-up analysis to see how this country could drastically reduce its GHG emissions.

Our research has led to the following conclusions. The options offered by CCS, DAC, and a hydrogen economy tend to foster a mixed strategy, whereby on one side work is done to preserve the economic value of fossil fuels, while on the other side the local economy is entirely decarbonised and the opportunities offered by the international carbon markets are exploited. CCS and CCD technologies are essential to achieving the ZNE regime both globally and locally. In the scenarios studied in our research, the cumulative emissions budget was not allowed to be exceeded. Hence, there was no incentive to adopt a 'throw-in' strategy.

To summarise, GCC countries must be proactive in the coming negotiations. They should aim at defining a governance based on equalising the relative welfare losses among groups or coalitions of countries. GCC countries should develop their programs of clean fossil fuels, in particular CCS and hydrogen extraction. These countries must prepare for the change in oil and gas demand patterns caused by the advent of electric mobility and SCs. GCC countries should push forward their policies in favour of SCs and SESs. SCs and SESs will develop in GCC states only if a new energy policy, exploiting the opportunities offered by IoT, is put in place.

References

Abdmouleh, Z., Alammari, R. A. M., and Gastli, A. (2015). Recommendations on renewable energy policies for the GCC countries. *Renewable and Sustainable Energy Reviews*, 50, pp. 1181–1191.

Al Shidi, H., Sulaiman, H., and Amoatey, P. (2016). Shifting to renewable energy to mitigate carbon emissions: Initiatives by the states of Gulf Cooperation Council. *Low Carbon Economy* 7, pp. 123–136.

Al-Maamary, M. S. H., Kazem, H. A., and Chaichan, M. T. (2016). Changing the energy profile of the GCC states: a review. *International Journal of Applied Engineering Research* 11, pp. 1980–1988.

American Physical Society (APS) (2011). *Direct Air Capture of CO_2 and Climate Stabilization: A Model-Based Assessment with Chemicals: A Technology Assessment for the APS Panel on Public Affairs*. Technical report, April 15. College Park, MD: American Physical Society.

Atalay, Y., Biermann, F., and Kalfagianni, A. (2016). Adoption of renewable energy technologies in oil-rich countries: explaining policy variation in the Gulf Cooperation Council states. *Renewable Energy* 85, pp. 206–214.

Babonneau, F., Benlahrech, M., and Haurie, A. (2022). Transition to zero-net emissions for Qatar: the role of hydrogen and direct air capture. *Energy Policy* 170, p. 113256.

Babonneau, F., Haurie, A., and Vielle, M. (2016). Assessment of balanced burden-sharing in the 2050 EU climate/energy roadmap: a metamodeling approach. *Climatic Change* 134 (4), pp. 505–519.

Babonneau, F., Haurie, A., and Vielle, M. (2020). Assessment of climate agreements over the long term with strategic carbon dioxide removal activity. WP 2020-1, EPFL/ENAC/LEURE.

Babonneau, F., Badran, A., Benlahrech, M., Haurie, A., Schenckery, M., and Vielle, M. (2021). Economic assessment of the development of CO_2 direct reduction technologies in long-term climate strategies of the gulf countries. *Climatic Change* 165, p. 64.

Bhutto, A. A., Bazmi, G., Zahedi, G., and Klemes, J. J. (2014). A review of progress in renewable energy implementation in the Gulf Cooperation Council countries. *Journal of Cleaner Production* 71, pp. 168–180.

Birol, F. (2017). *World Energy Outlook 2017*. Technical report. Paris: International Energy Agency.

Daniel, M., James, R., Forster, P. M., Betts, R. A., Shiogama, H., and Allen, M. (2016). Realizing the impacts of a 1.5°C warmer world. *Nature Climate Change* 6 (8), pp. 735–737. Advance online publication, June.

Depledge, J. (2008). Striving for no: Saudi Arabia in the climate change regime. *Global Environmental Politics* 8 (4), pp. 9–35.

Doukas, H., Patlizianas, K. D., and Psarras, J. (2006). Renewable energy sources and rational use of energy development in the countries of the GCC: myth or reality. *Renewable Energy* 31, pp. 755–770.

Elmesr, M. N., Abu-Zreig, M. M., and Alazbi, A. A. (2010). Temperature trends and distribution in the Arabian Peninsula. *American Journal of Environmental Sciences* 6, pp. 191–203.

European Academies' Science Advisory Council (EASAC) (2018). *Negative Emission Technologies: What Role in Meeting Paris Agreement Targets?* February. Policy report. ISBN: 978-3-8047-3841-6. Available online: www.easac.eu.

European Commission (2017). *Autonomous Cars: A Big Opportunity for European Industry*. Technical report. Brussels: European Commission.

Gross, S., and Matsuo, Y. (2017). *Towards More Pragmatic Global Climate Goals and Policies*. Technical report. Riyadh: KAPSARC (King Abdullah Petroleum Studies and Research Center).

Hotelling, H. (1931). The economics of exhaustible resources. *Journal of Political Economy* 39 (2), pp. 137–175.

House, K. Z., Baclig, A. C., Ranjan, M., Nierop, E. A., Wilcoxx, J., and Herzog, H. J. (2011). Economic and energetic analysis of capturing CO_2 from ambient air. *PNAS Early Edition*, pp. 1–6.

International Energy Agency (IEA) (2016). *World Energy Outlook 2016*. Paris: International Energy Agency.

International Energy Agency (IEA) (2019). *The Future of Hydrogen: Seizing Today's Opportunities*. Technical report. Paris: International Energy Agency.

International Renewable Energy Agency (IRENA) (2018). *Global Energy Transformation: A Roadmap to 2050*. Technical report. Abu Dhabi: International Renewable Energy Agency.

Kalenderski, S., Stenchikov, G., and Zhao, C. (2013). Modeling a typical winter-time dust event over the Arabian Peninsula and the Red Sea. *Atmos. Chem. Phys.* 13, pp. 1999–2014.

Keith, D. W., Holmes, G., St. Angelo, D., and Heidel, K. (2018). A process for capturing CO_2 from the atmosphere. *Joule* 2 (August), pp. 1573–1594.

Keywan, R., van Vuuren, D. P., and Kriegler, E., et al. (2017). The shared socioeconomic pathways and their energy, land use, and greenhouse gas emissions implications: An overview. *Global Environmental Change* 42, pp. 153–168.

Koornneef, J., can Breevoort, P., Hendricks, C., Hoogwijk, M., and Koops, K. (2011). *Potential for Biomass and Carbon Dioxide Capture and Storage*. Technical report. Paris: International Energy Agency.

Krane, J. (2021). Climate strategy for producer countries: the case of Saudi Arabia, in Luciani, G., and Moerenhout, T. (eds.), *When Can Oil Economies Be Deemed Sustainable? The Political Economy of the Middle East*, Abingdon: Palgrave Macmillan, pp. 301–328.

Lackner, K. (2009). Capture of carbon dioxide from ambient air. *European Physical Journal Special Topics* 176, pp. 93–106.

Leeson, D., Mac Dowell, N., Shah, N., and Fennel, P. S. (2017). A techno-economic analysis and systematic review of carbon capture and storage (CCS) applied to the iron and steel, cement, oil refining and pulp and paper industries, as well as other high purity sources. *International Journal of Greenhouse Gas Control* 61, pp. 71–84.

Luomi, M. (2012). *The Gulf Monarchies and Climate Change*. London: Hurst Publishers.

Luomi, M. (2014). *Mainstreaming Climate Policy in the Gulf Cooperation Council States*. February. Technical report. Oxford: Oxford Institute for Energy Studies.

Mainshausen, M. (2009). Greenhouse-gas emission targets for limiting global warming to 2oC. *Nature*, pp. 1158–1162.

Marcucci, V. P., and Kypreos, S. (2017). The road to achieving the long-term Paris targets: energy transition and the role of direct air capture. *Climatic Change* 144, pp. 181–193.

McGlade, C., and Etkin, P. (2014). Un-burnable oil: an examination of oil resource utilization in a decarbonated system. *Energy Policy* 64 (C), pp. 102–112.

Meinshausen, M., Meinshausen, N., and Hare, W., et al. (2009). Greenhouse-gas emission targets for limiting global warming to 2°C. *Nature* 458, pp. 1158–1162.

Mondal, M. A. H., Hawila, D., Kennedy, S., and Mezher, T. (2016). The GCC countries RE-readiness: strengths and gaps for development of renewable energy technologies. *Renewable and Sustainable Energy Reviews* 54, pp. 1114–1128.

Nordhaus, W. (2018). Projections and uncertainties about climate change in an era of minimal climate policies. *American Economic Journal* 10 (3), pp. 333–360.

OPEC (2017). *World Oil Outlook—2017*. Technical report. Vienna: OPEC.

Pottier, A., Méjean, P., Godard, O., and Hourcade, J. C. (2017). A survey of global climate justice: from negotiation stances to moral stakes and back. *International Review of Environmental and Resource Economics* 11, pp. 1–53.

Poudineh, R., Abdallah Sen, A., and Fattouh, B. (2018). Advancing renewable energy in resource-rich economies of the MENA. *Renewable journal* 123, pp. 135–149.

Prakash, P. J., Stenchikov, G., Kalenderski, S., Osipov, S., and Bangalath, H. (2015). The impact of dust storms on the Arabian Peninsula and the Red Sea. *Atmos Chem Phys* 15, pp. 199–222.

Rawls, J. (1971). *Theory of Justice*. Cambridge, MA: Harvard University Press.

Reiche, D. (2010). Energy policies of Gulf Cooperation Council (GCC) countries- possibilities and limitations of ecological modernization in rentier states. *Energy Policy* 38, pp. 2395–2403.

Rogelj, J., Luderer, G., Pietzcker, R. C., Kriegler, E., Schaeffer, M, Krey, V., and Riahi, K. (2015). Energy system transformations for limiting end-of-century warming to below 1.5°C. *Nature Climate Change* 5 (6), pp. 519–527.

Rogelj, J., Riahi, K., and Forster, P., et al. (2018). *Global Warming of 1.5°C*. An IPCC Special Report on the impacts of global warming of 1.5°C above pre-industrial levels and related global greenhouse gas emission pathways, in the context of strengthening the global response to the threat of climate change, sustainable development, and efforts to eradicate poverty, chapter Mitigation pathways compatible with 1.5°C in the context of sustainable development. Geneva: Intergovernmental Panel on Climate Change (IPCC).

Rubin, E. S., Davison, J. E., and Herzog, H. J. (2015). The cost of CO_2 capture and storage. *International Journal of Greenhouse Gas Control* 40, pp. 378–400.

Salahuddin, M. and Gow, J. (2014). Economic growth, energy consumption and CO_2 emissions in Gulf Cooperation Council countries. *Energy* 73, pp. 44–58.

Seba, T. (2014). *Clean Disruption of Energy and Transportation*. Silicon Valley, CA: Clean Planet Ventures.

Sgouridis, S., Griffiths, S., Kennedy, S., Khalid, A., and Zurita, N. (2013). A sustainable energy transition strategy for the United Arab Emirates: Evaluation of options using an integrated energy model. *Energy Strategy Reviews* 2, pp. 8–18.

State of Qatar Ministry of Environment (2015). *Intended Nationally Determined Contributions (INDCs) Report*. Submitted for COP21 Paris 2015. Available online: https://unfccc.int/files/focus/indc_portal/application/pdf/qatar_to_zimbabwe.pdf (accessed 15 January 2022).

Stocker, T. F., Qin, D., Plattner, G.-K., et al. (2013). *Climate Change 2013: The Physical Science Basis. Summary for Policymakers*. Working Group I Contribution to the Fifth Assessment Report of the Intergovernmental Panel on Climate Change. Cambridge: Cambridge University Press/UNEP (United Nations Environment Programme).

United Nations. (2017). *World Population Prospects: The 2017 Revision*. New York: Population Division, Department of Economic and Social Affairs.

Ustadi I., Mezher, T., and Abu-Zahra, M. R. M. (2017). The effect of the carbon capture and storage (CCS) technology deployment on the natural gas market in the United Arab Emirates. *Energy Procedia* 114, pp. 6366–6376.

Verner, D. (2012). *Adaptation to a Changing Climate in Arab Countries*. Technical report. MENE Development Report. Washington, DC: World Bank.

Wogan, D., Pradhan, S., and Albardi, S. (2017). *GCC Energy System Overview*. Technical report. Riyadh: Kapsarc.

Part V

Behavioural Aspects and Human Factors

11

Energy Transition in Oil-Rich Countries

The Role of Resource Nationalism

SUSAN KURDLI AND RENATO LIMA-DE-OLIVEIRA

11.1 Introduction

The energy industry continues to be one of the major industries in the world. In new capital investments alone, it is responsible for about USD1.8 trillion per year (IEA 2018). This industry has traditionally been dependent on fossil fuels, which make up over 80% of the world energy consumption (BP 2020). In oil- and gas- (O&G) exporting countries, it is also a significant source of jobs, export earnings, and fiscal revenues. However, this pattern of energy consumption and its associated economic activities have been under intense threat. Environmental political pressures and international agreements such as the Paris Agreement of 2015 have highlighted the damage to the planet associated with burning fossil fuels and the dire consequences to climate change. More recently, the growing competitiveness of renewable-based energy sources such as solar and wind energy have made renewables more economically attractive than carbon-heavy sources. Together, these factors can seriously affect the economic survival of the fossil fuel industry – and the economies which are dependent on the exports of coal, oil, and gas.

If the challenge of tackling emissions is global, the local economic impact is unevenly distributed. Oil-rich countries that have benefited from exports of fossil fuel are particularly vulnerable as the world transitions to cleaner energy sources. It becomes imperative for them to develop new energy sources and domestic business opportunities in renewables. This move has been invariably supported by policy instruments that are a mix of carrot and stick, varying in terms of how much it discourages carbon-heavy sectors and promotes alternative energy sources. Such a policy frequently collides with existing players and policies designed around the supremacy of fossil fuels.

Yet there is no uniform response to how governments deal with climate change and energy transition – not even within oil-rich countries. Table 11.1 shows data from four substantive oil producers, two from the Middle East (the United Arab

Table 11.1 *Share and growth of renewables in selected countries and O&G production.*

Country	Electricity installed capacity megawatts (MW) (2020)	Share of renewables (2020)	Growth of solar and wind capacity megawatts (MW) (2010 to 2020)	Total O&G production (in kboe/d) (2020)
Brazil	180,885	0.83	24,150	3,362
Mexico	87,969	0.32	13,223	2,225
UAE	35,227	0.07	2,528	4,421
Kuwait	20,259	0.01	106	2,974

Emirates (UAE) and Kuwait) and two from Latin America (Brazil and Mexico). They are amongst the most comparable set of countries in their regions. All have important O&G sectors with national oil companies (NOCs) as leading firms in each country. Despite this, not only do we observe substantive historical differences in the share of current renewables in the power sector (particularly for Brazil and Mexico), but also in the rate of growth of solar and wind (as exemplified by the UAE's twenty-four-fold increase in comparison to Kuwait between 2010 and 2020).

What accounts for these puzzling differences? Varying technical factors such as solar and wind potential cannot explain these striking differences between countries of the same region. Unlike a point-source resource like O&G, modern renewables like solar and wind are more diffuse and technically viable to generate power from a much greater variety of countries (Carbon Tracker, 2021).

Instead, and in-line with a growing strand of the energy transition literature, we call attention to political economic factors to account for these differences. More precisely, this chapter shows the importance of resource nationalism and domestic political institutions in explaining the local development of alternative fuel sources. Market failures and the expectation placed on states to intervene and lead energy transition highlight the need to look at the role played by political institutions. In this regard, NOCs have an important role to play in the transition to cleaner sources of energy. Yet, according to the International Energy Agency's (IEA, 2020) report on energy transition in the O&G industry, none of the NOCs have been given an official mandate to lead energy transition and O&G companies have spent less than 1% of expenditure on renewable energy.

Increased international awareness of climate change risks and changing regulations create clashing demands on NOCs. On the one hand, they are expected to meet domestic energy needs and fund government expenses, and on the other hand, they need to follow international demands to transition to cleaner non-hydrocarbon energy sources. Given this challenge, it is important to understand the incentives and constraints that sway the pendulum in the transition to renewable energy.

This chapter argues that in spite of technological cost reduction and availability of renewable energy sources, domestic political factors have influenced the type of resource nationalism policies pursued, pitting incumbent interest groups and other beneficiaries against broader national policies aimed at reducing carbon emissions and developing the renewables sector. Therefore, governments that have pursued social-based resource nationalism have found it more difficult to transition to renewables, while governments that have pursued market-based resource nationalism have been able to incorporate higher rates of renewables into their energy mix in spite of being oil exporters.

To elaborate further on the argument presented, the chapter proceeds in the following manner: Section 11.2 discusses the determinants of renewable energy transition. Next, Section 11.3 discusses the theoretical frameworks through which we can understand the political economy of renewable energy transition. Resource nationalism, in particular, is relevant as it captures the variables this chapter aims to explore. This is followed by Section 11.4 on methodology. Then, the four cases are examined comparatively in Section 11.5 through 11.8, and a discussion of the results is presented in Section 11.9. Finally, the chapter concludes and recaps the main argument and results in Section 11.10.

11.2 Determinants of Renewable Energy Transition

In the early stages of the development of renewable energy sources, technological factors dictated the pace at which these new sources could be adopted, garnering numerous studies on the topic. For example, technological advancement was seen as a leading factor in price reduction and the subsequent increase in investment in renewable energy sources, especially in developed markets (Gatzert & Kosub, 2017; Alam & Murad, 2020; Bamati & Raoofi, 2020). However, the impact of political and institutional factors on the transition to cleaner sources of energy remains understudied in social sciences, with only 17.2% of articles tackling renewable energy in the social sciences between 1998 and 2017 in which political determinants were examined (Sequeira & Santos, 2018). Political determinants deserve special attention as renewables such as energy and wind are fairly abundant across the world, making the reasons to develop them, or not, mainly political, not technological. Moreover, 'technological advancement is a key factor in facilitating energy transition. However, policy-making does not often evolve as quickly. Therefore, policy change remains critical for transition to take place' (Arent et al., 2017, p. 8).

In the research that looked at political factors, the ideology and rhetoric used by various interest groups received attention. For example, the beliefs of politicians regarding climate change can heavily influence the type of energy policies promoted. More specifically, populist parties tend to be opposed to renewable energy policies and can mobilise their voters to oppose these policies (Kammermann and Dermont, 2018). Additionally, lobbying by manufacturers, right-leaning political parties, and low governance quality do significantly impede renewable energy policy (Cadoret & Padovano, 2016).

As far as case selection is concerned, most of the literature on renewable energy in general has focused on developed countries such as the US, UK, and Germany (Sequeira & Santos, 2018). China is the only developing country in the list of the top-five most researched countries. This leaves a wide gap in our understanding of renewable energy dynamics in terms of different regions, government types, and political institutions. A notable exception is Hochstetler (2021), who identifies four types of political economies of energy transition (climate change, industrial policy, siting policy, social policy) in her analysis of the energy policy of South Africa and Brazil.

Developing countries present a set of challenges different from those faced by developed countries as:

> The political economy of energy transition differs between developing and developed countries. The former faces the challenge of fulfilling developmental objectives while reducing carbon footprint, while the latter must meet the expectation that they lead energy transition in spite of incumbent interest groups. Additionally, developing countries will most likely continue to grow rapidly, placing upward demand on energy sources. (Arent et al., 2017, p. 9)

This highlights the urgency to understand transition determinants, especially political factors, in oil-rich developing countries, which continue to fuel their growth and other reliant energy-scarce countries through their hydrocarbon exports.

11.3 Resource Nationalism and Energy Transition

Resource nationalism is a useful conceptual framework that helps researchers capture the wide-ranging energy policies of oil-rich countries. Traditionally, these policies have covered how hydrocarbon revenues are used. But as discussed in earlier sections, the energy landscape is quickly changing. As a result, the importance of designing a nationwide renewable energy policy has become more pressing. This research aims to expand the concept of resource nationalism to account for these recent developments in the energy sector and the policy responses required to address them.

Resource nationalism can be broadly defined as the attempt by resource-rich states to increase control of and returns from their resources by implementing policies that could include a variety of forms of ownership, operation of upstream and downstream activities, and rent management (Stevens, 2008; Bremmer & Johnston, 2009; Andreasson, 2015; Wilson, 2015). As this definition illustrates, it is an umbrella concept that covers many aspects of energy policy with ample room to contribute and further polish existing arguments.

For example, according to Bremmer and Johnston (2009), there are four types of resource nationalism, depending on domestic political conditions. They categorise these policies based on the effect of contract changes with foreign oil companies. The first type is revolutionary resource nationalism, which occurs after political upheaval and results in radically altering previous contracts with foreign oil companies. The second type is economic resource nationalism whereby the change in pre-existing contracts is not as drastic as the first type. The third type is legacy resource nationalism, which is rooted in the social and cultural perception that resource ownership belongs to the people. The authors use the example of Kuwait and Mexico as two countries where the nationalisation of oil companies has been central to 'national politics and cultural identity' (Bremmer & Johnston, 2009, p. 151). They also add that this type may have the deepest impact in shaping the domestic energy industry. The fourth type is similar to Wilson's (2015) categorisation that occurs in liberal markets. Bremmer and Johnston (2009) label this as soft resource nationalism. In this category, states seek to enhance revenue by readjusting tax and royalty earnings without altering contracts, as ownership of resources in this type remains private. The authors use the example of OECD countries and Brazil. In these cases, resource nationalism is more market-based.

Wilson (2015) expands on the framework and categorises resource nationalism based on how rents are used. Accordingly, there are three types of resource nationalism pursued. The first is the rentier state where leaders distribute rent to augment popular support without an expansive economic policy. The second type can be likened to the developmental policies of East Asia where the leaders' tenure is highly linked to economic legitimacy. This link leads them to adopt industrialisation and diversification policies that result in economic development. The third type can be observed in liberal market-driven economies where states limit themselves to a regulatory role.

For the purpose of offering a parsimonious argument, this chapter divides resource nationalism policies into two categories based on the objectives of their policies. The type and objective of resource nationalism pursued, in turn, determines the speed in transitioning to renewable energy. The first type is distributive social-based policies aimed at welfare provision and job creation. This category fits the traditional categorisation of oil-rich countries as rentier states. The second type is market-oriented market-based policies aimed at boosting business activity and strengthening the private sector. This category considers how a group of oil-rich countries do not fit the rentier categorisation of rentier states and have managed to establish effective political institutions and robust industrial policies.

The key element in determining which policy is pursued lies in which body is capable of making decisions and the amount of autonomy they have. Consequently, due to these differing domestic political factors, some governments have adopted social-based resource nationalism and have found it harder to transition to renewable energy sources due to opposition from incumbent interest groups. Other governments have implemented market-based resource nationalism and have been able to transition relatively more easily. Kuwait and Mexico belong to the former group and the UAE and Brazil belong to the latter one. The aforementioned four case studies will attempt to trace the process from decision-making to implementation.

11.4 Methodology

Before delving into the case study, this section explains why these four case studies were selected and the method in which they will be analysed. As Sequeira and Santos (2018) state, most works on renewable energy rely on quantitative techniques and only few attempt to use the method of historical process tracing as this chapter does, they therefore offer little in the way of understanding causal mechanisms. Our chapter aims to fill this gap by using a qualitative method. To test the argument presented, a qualitative case study will be used relying on process tracing and cross-case analysis to compare two countries from the Middle East and North Africa (MENA), Kuwait, and the UAE, and two countries from Latin America, Mexico and Brazil. These two sets of case studies were chosen after controlling for country size, regime type, and regional subgrouping. Brazil and Mexico are both large democratic developing countries in Latin America. The UAE and Kuwait are both small monarchic developing Gulf countries. We use process tracing for its ability to uncover the causal mechanism linking the explanatory variable to the outcome variable (Bennett & Checkel, 2015). In this study, we aim to examine how the adoption of different types of resource nationalism policies influences the transition to renewable energy. Thus, we look closer at evidence of processes and sequence of events within each case and then compare these processes and events to one another in order to test our hypotheses and eliminate alternative explanations.

11.5 Energy Policy in Kuwait

Kuwait remains heavily dependent on oil for its economy. In 2019, 42% of Kuwait's GDP came from oil rents and fuel exports accounted for 94% of all exports (World Bank, 2021). Kuwait also relied on fossil fuels for 93.7% of its energy use and practically 0% came from renewable sources in the year 2014 (World Bank, 2021). While the majority of Kuwait's oil is destined for export, domestic consumption has been on an upward trajectory due to higher electricity demand oftentimes causing electricity cuts (EIA, 2016). Kuwait currently uses mostly hydrocarbons for electricity generation. However, electricity shortages have been so severe that downstream plants were shut down to divert natural gas use for electricity generation (EIA, 2016).

Although the electricity sector has often failed to meet peak demand, the country has not ventured into cleaner energies such as solar. Nor has it been able to lift energy subsidies significantly. Instead it has opted to invest in exploration and production of non-associated gas fields raising natural gas' contribution to the electricity to 43% in 2015 (EIA, 2016). The boost in natural gas production would be employed for water desalination, enhanced oil recovery processes, and petrochemical production (EIA, 2016). This strategy is aimed to meet rising demand without sacrificing oil that's slated for exports or importing more natural gas.

In addition to ongoing dependence on hydrocarbons for electricity generation, Kuwait continues to spend a considerable amount of its oil revenue on various subsidies, which remain particularly difficult to reform. For example, total fuel subsidies constituted 4.1% of its GDP (IEA, 2021). In 2020, the state declared that it would have to cut its budget due to the compound effects of lower oil prices and the pandemic; however, these planned cuts would not affect subsidies or welfare provided to Kuwaiti citizens (Saba, 2020). These expenses make up 73% of state expenditure (MacDonald, 2020).

Compared to other countries in the region, Kuwait has faced considerable challenges in its attempt to fulfil clean energy goals. Although Kuwait is situated in a prime location that could allow it to cheaply utilise abundant solar and wind energy to diversify its electricity mix – especially since solar power costs have decreased more than 80% of its price over the last ten years (Butler, 2019), the country embarked in 2009 on developing its nuclear capacity which was planned to be operational three years later. The Fukushima accident in 2011, however, shelved these plans permanently and the National Nuclear Energy Committee was disbanded in its aftermath (EIA, 2016). The only exception to an otherwise entirely hydrocarbon-based energy source is a recent contract issued by Kuwait National Petroleum Company to develop 1.5 gigawatts (GW) of solar power for its use (Butler, 2019).

The Kuwaiti state is acutely aware that diversifying energy sources and scaling back subsidies is necessary. However, this remains a complex challenge due to the unique political structure of Kuwait, especially when compared to other neighbouring Gulf countries. The overarching body that decides on energy policy is the Supreme Petroleum Council (SPC), which is headed by the prime minister and is composed of six ministers and six members from the business community. The SPC represents, therefore, the interests of the executive and large businesses to a lesser degree, pitting it against the parliament, the majority of which is elected by Kuwaiti voters and, thus, represents their interests. The Ministry of Oil oversees the way in which these policies are executed (EIA, 2016). The Kuwaiti NOC, Kuwait Petroleum Corporation, and its various subsidiaries are responsible for implementing these policies as well as all upstream and downstream activities. The Kuwait Investment Authority is responsible for replenishing the state budget and investing oil revenues abroad (EIA, 2016).

The National Assembly, Kuwait's legislative body, equivalent to a parliament, has opposed any measures that would reduce the welfare provided to Kuwaiti citizens. Unlike other Gulf countries, members of the National Assembly are all elected, with the exception of the sixteen ministers who sit in the Assembly, the total of whom can reach up to fifty members. Kuwait's political structure is unique among the Arab Gulf countries as it is the only country that has an autonomous legislative body, which often clashes with the executive branch represented by the emir and the cabinet he appoints, who often are members of the royal family. While political parties are officially banned, political currents do exist in Kuwaiti civil society and these leanings are often reflected in the National Assembly.

This structure has a direct impact on economic policy in Kuwait as the populist National Assembly has often blocked attempts by the executive to reduce spending on welfare and subsidies as a response to volatile oil prices and international pressure to transition to renewable energy. For example, following the drop in oil prices in 2014, the executive branch sought to reduce state spending and raise taxes. However, most proposals were blocked by the National Assembly. In August 2016, the executive branch raised gasoline prices to reflect international market prices as Kuwait offered the lowest prices at a global level (Shehabi, 2020). The National Assembly objected to this attempt by challenging the legality of the decision, as they argued that the government was not allowed to partake such measures unilaterally without parliamentary approval. The standoff resulted in the Assembly being dissolved by October the same year. Gasoline subsidies have not been reinstated.

Another example of a stalled energy project is that of the Clean Fuels Project. While the project did not aim to aid the country into transitioning to renewables, it was meant to upgrade the existing two refineries, enhance energy efficiency, and reduce environmental damage (Kuwait National Petroleum Company, 2021). The project, however, faced parliamentary opposition and requests for additional scrutiny slowing down progress (Etheridge, 2009). As the *Financial Times* reports, 'Kuwait's hydrocarbon sector is no longer the sole territory of energy technocrats. Projects have become political weapons in a long-running stand-off between parliament and government' (Etheridge, 2009).

The stalled transition to renewable energy could be traced to the so-called 'social contract' between Gulf governments and their citizens whereby the former distributes oil revenue in the form of welfare such as energy subsidies, employment, healthcare, education, and so on, while the latter cedes political activism. In the case of Kuwait, the autonomous National Assembly has proved itself a stalwart in guarding the social contract and ensuring the government delivers on its promises to provide welfare with the unintended consequence of lagging in renewable energy transition.

Energy subsidy is emblematic of other fiscal challenges the state has to contend with. For example, transfers and subsidies to citizens and local companies account for over half the state's expenditure (Shehabi, 2020). Moreover, the public sector, that is, government departments and state-owned enterprises (SOEs), remain the main source of growth. It is estimated that the public sector accounts for over 60% of the GDP in spite of privatisation plans aimed at spurring the private sector (Shehabi, 2020). This imbalance can be seen in employment figures for the public sector where 70% of employees are Kuwaitis, while the private sector employs only 5% in spite of incentives offered by the state to the private sector to boost Kuwaiti salaries and make them comparable to those in the public sector.

When analysing how some SOEs can overcome social-based demands such as employment in favour of market-based objectives such as profitability, Hertog (2010) argues that pockets of efficiency can be created bypassing traditional distributive rentier state mechanisms when two necessary but insufficient factors exist: lack of populist history and executive autonomy. This argument can be expanded to the renewable energy sector in Kuwait as decision-makers are often faced with populist demands to maintain social-based welfare energy policies at the expense of transitioning to cleaner sources of energy.

11.6 Energy Policy in the UAE

The UAE is one of the pioneers of renewable energy transition among oil-producing and oil-exporting countries, which seems counterintuitive considering that it has the seventh largest oil reserve in the world (EIA, 2020a). The emirate of Abu Dhabi, in particular, has taken the lead in taking steps to develop renewable energy sources through Mubadala Investment Company (Butler, 2019). In comparison to Kuwait, the UAE relies a lot less on oil revenues in its GDP, which accounted for 16% of GDP in 2019 and 77.9% of all exports (World Bank, 2021). In 2014, 86.1% of the UAE's energy consumption was derived from fossil fuels and 0.1% from renewable sources (World Bank, 2021). Total fuel subsidies made up 1.6% of its GDP (IEA, 2021). While these numbers are still high in absolute terms, they are much lower compared to other rentier oil states.

The main energy source of electricity in the UAE is natural gas, making up 98% in 2018 (EIA, 2020a). The UAE's 'Energy Strategy 2050' was launched in 2017 and aims to decrease reliance on hydrocarbons by deriving 44% of electricity from renewable sources, 6% from nuclear, 12% 'clean' coal, and 38% gas by 2050 (UAE Government Portal, 2021). To fulfil this strategy, the country plans to invest the equivalent of USD163 billion (UAE Government Portal, 2021). The strategy also targets a reduction of residential consumption by 40% through consumer behavioural change (UAE Ministry of Energy and Infrastructure, 2017). Some of the clean energy projects include a nuclear plant that would be operational in 2030 and Muhammad bin Rashid Al Maktoum Solar Park, which will be the largest solar facility in the world when it is scheduled to be completed in 2030 and will supply 25% of Dubai's energy (EIA, 2020a).

Similar to Kuwait, the Supreme Petroleum Council was responsible for setting energy policy and overseeing the operations of Abu Dhabi NOC, ADNOC. However, in 2020, the president of the UAE, Sheikh Khalifa bin Zayed, announced the establishment of a new government entity, the Supreme Council for Financial and Economic Affairs, which as the name implies, will have a wider authority, covering energy and economic matters and will conjunctively work with investment bodies such as Mubadala, ADIA, and ADQ, as well as with energy producers such as ADNOC (Hussein, 2020). The newly formed body is chaired by the president and its board members include the influential Mohammed bin Zayed, Minister of Industry and Advanced Technology and CEO of the sovereign wealth fund Mubadala (Saadi, 2020). This new body reflects the government's plan to integrate energy policy with economic, rather than distributive, interests.

In comparison to Kuwait, UAE's political structure is considerably less populist. Moreover, its political institutions do not allow for populist discourse in a fashion similar to Kuwait. All political parties are banned in the UAE and political activism is strictly suppressed. The UAE government is composed of a federal government and seven emirates-level governments. Almost all positions in the government are appointed. The only exception is the Federal National Council (FNC), which is a legislative branch equivalent to a parliament composed of forty members. Each emirate is responsible for choosing delegates to the FNC. Half of these members are directly appointed by the head of the emirate and the other half is elected by an electoral college. This body reviews federal laws before they are submitted for approval. The FNC has the right to approve, amend, or reject these laws. The FNC also reviews the annual federal budget. Furthermore, it has the right to question ministers on their performance. Within the FNC, some social and economic issues are deliberated.

Unlike Kuwait, the FNC members are not directly elected. Moreover, these elected members are approved by each emirate before they take up their federal position. As a result, the FNC arguably is more reflective of the policy preferences of the executive and business elite as all members are approved by emirate-level governments. By contrast, Kuwait's National Assembly is more reflective of the interests of the average Kuwaiti citizen because, aside from the sixteen cabinet members, all Members of Parliament are directly responsible to their electorate. Another difference from Kuwait is that the structure of the FNC allows for a more streamlined implementation of energy policies from the executive, through the legislative to the bodies responsible for execution.

The UAE has managed to make a more significant turn to renewable energy transition because of a number of factors. First, it lacks the kind of populist opposition that Kuwait contends with. UAE's economic policy has been mostly top-down driven with the political decision-makers and major business families as the driving forces. Second, the UAE has historically cultivated market-based policies aimed at diversifying revenue sources beyond oil exports at a higher level compared to its neighbours. Market-based revenue diversification started before the UAE came together to form a federation state with the oil-poor Dubai being a trade hub since the early twentieth century when the leader of Dubai then built a port large enough to attract trade and investment from neighbouring ports and supplemented the port with favourable regulations such as low taxation and import fees. After independence, the Jabal Ali Free Zone was established and prompted numerous other free trade zones to be established in Dubai and also in other emirates, such as Al Sharjah Airport International Free Zone, Ras Al Khaimah Economic Zone, and Industrial City of Abu Dhabi, to name but a few.

Due to the lack of populist opposition and the presence of alternative sources of revenue, the executive leadership, which had been aware of the precarious nature of oil dependence since the 1980s, was therefore able to expand diversification to energy sources and invest in renewable energy. Additionally, UAE's reluctance to remain reliant on expensive imported natural gas at a time when the costs for solar photovoltaic systems have been falling made expansion into alternative sources more attractive (IRENA, 2015).

The UAE's inclination towards market-based policies since its early days has set it on a path that made the transition to cleaner energy sources smoother. Thus, Hertog's (2010) hypotheses regarding the profit-oriented performance of SOEs also applies to the case of renewable energy policy in the UAE. In other words, government bodies regulating clean energy are not shaped by social-based populist demands, nor are these bodies prone to pressure from interest groups, that is to say decision-making is autonomous.

11.7 Energy Policy in Mexico

Mexico is a traditional O&G producer and one of the first and most important countries in the world to nationalise oil resources with the expropriation of foreign companies in favour of the creation of the NOC Pemex in 1938 (Philip, 1992). The full nationalisation of the electricity sector came decades later, in 1960, when the Mexican president, Adolfo López Mateos, consolidated all activities in the wholly owned Federal Electricity Commission (CFE, in Spanish), a state-run company created in 1937.

Throughout the years, Pemex and CFE have grown together. As Pemex expanded production, it created a supply of fuel oil and natural gas that were sold, at subsidised prices, to CFE and used for electricity generation at thermal power stations. Selling fuel at subsidised prices discouraged further diversification of the country's energy matrix and was a bad deal for Pemex. Over the years, this practice drained Pemex's ability to invest in new O&G exploration (Meyer and Morales, 1990). However, this close link between Pemex and CFE was part of successive Mexican governments' plans to promote industrialisation through cheap energy prices and locked-in a carbon-heavy energy infrastructure in the country. According to data from Morales (1992, p. 215), in 1945, 40.6% of the electricity-generated capacity was met by thermal plants. By the end of the 1950s, 75% of the electricity produced in Mexico came from hydrocarbons.

This strong historical relationship shaped Mexico's energy matrix for years. Mexico still relies primarily on hydrocarbons in its energy mix. Petroleum and other liquids and natural gas make up 85%, of the mix, while renewables contribute 4%. The main source of electricity is hydrocarbons, with the share of natural gas at 56%, fuel-oil at 10%, and coal at 7% (EIA, 2020b). Renewables (mostly hydro) only make up 10% of the electrical energy sources (EIA, 2020b). This heavy reliance on O&G continued in spite of declining production since 2004, when production peaked at twice the current amount of 1.9 million barrels per day (mbpd) (EIA, 2020b).

In order to deal with an incoming energy crisis, the Mexican administration of Enrique Peña Nieto (2012–2018) approved a politically costly energy reform designed to attract private investments and reduce subsidies. The reform strengthened the role of the Ministry of Energy as a planner, decentralised regulation by creating regulatory agencies for the power and oil sector, and introduced governance reforms on the key state-owned companies, Pemex and CFE. Significantly, in 2015, an Energy Transition Law was passed which created incentives for alternative energies and had a target of 35% as the minimum share of clean energies in power generation by 2024.[1]

[1] See: www.diputados.gob.mx/LeyesBiblio/pdf/LTE.pdf.

While Pemex and CFE remained as fully state-owned companies, a number of auctions brought new players to the Mexican energy market, both for O&G exploration and production as well as electricity generation. Mexico is a country of large potential for renewable energy (Pérez-Denicia et al., 2017) and the first three auctions (which occurred in 2016 and 2017) attracted strong interest from investors and an estimated addition of 5.2 GW of capacity of solar and wind energy by 2030 (Fitch Solutions, 2021).

Peña Nieto was succeeded by Andres Manuel Lopez Obrador (known as AMLO) (2018–2024), a political opponent who is a staunch defender of Pemex and CFE and opposes the earlier energy reforms. He has closed the door for new energy auctions and redirected government efforts towards strengthening the role of Pemex and CFE (Villamil, 2020). A planning document from the Ministry of Energy makes it clear that the current administration has been focused on recuperating the energy generation capacity of CFE and adding more thermal power capacity (SENER, 2020, p. 7). Given the state company's legacy assets and expertise, that goes in the direction of reinforcing fossil fuel consumption and the close links between Pemex and CFE. Furthermore, a new energy bill approved in 2021 gives priority in the dispatch order to CFE-owned plants and creates other obstacles for wind and solar projects, seriously hurting renewable players (Fitch Solution, 2021).

Overall, Mexico's tradition of resource nationalism, historical fossil fuel abundance, and tight state control of state-owned companies create substantive barriers to energy diversification. The move *against* renewables benefits the incumbent players of Pemex and CFE (by tilting the rules in their favour) and the nationalistic rhetoric used by President Lopez Obrador enjoys wide popular support, further enhancing the political risks of investing in alternative sources in Mexico.

11.8 Energy Policy in Brazil

Brazil has a strong NOC, Petrobras, which was created in 1953 with monopoly rights. Although since the 1990s market reforms introduced competition to the domestic oil sector, Petrobras is still the dominant player, both upstream and downstream and its technicians have occupied key policy-making positions in the Ministry of Energy and the regulatory agency (Trojbicz and Loureiro, 2018). Brazil has had a steep growth trajectory in the oil sector: production volume went from less than 1 million barrels per day (bpd) in the 1990s to close to 3 million bpd in 2019 (BP, 2020). Standard accounts of the political economy of energy transition would point out that a major fossil fuel player with such entrenched power would be an obstacle to the development of renewable energy sources. Yet, Brazil has one of the most decarbonised electricity systems in the world for a large country and where the traditional power clash between fossil fuel and alternative energy players is not seen.

To understand why such a clash is not observed, it is necessary to delve into the history of Brazil's energy sector. While neighbouring countries such as Venezuela had access to easy-to-extract and abundant onshore oil resources, by the 1950s Brazil was meeting its oil demand only with imports. In the context of the aftermath of the Second World War, this situation was seen as an economic and security vulnerability. 'For sure such a large country would have its own oil reserves', was a common belief at the time. Following a nationalistic campaign that preached that 'the oil is ours', Petrobras was created to find and develop resources that the international oil majors were supposedly uninterested or purposefully hiding from Brazilians. Therefore, unlike most NOCs founded after large resources had already been discovered, Petrobras was born in a context of scarcity and was mostly run on a professional basis (Smith, 1976; Contreras, 1993; Freire, 2013).[2] This had an important effect in stimulating the early diversification of energy sources in Brazil towards renewables – particularly biofuels (sugarcane ethanol) for transportation and hydroelectricity in the power sector. Besides, an NOC under scarce oil resource conditions has limited ability to serve as a tool for social welfare provision.

As a reaction to the OPEC oil shock in the 1970s, the Brazilian government sponsored the Proálcool programme, an ambitious initiative to replace imported fuel with locally produced ethanol (Coelho and Goldemberg, 2013). Brazil already had experience with that during the Second World War when a blend of gasoline and ethanol was used to deal with import limitations. The Proálcool programme provided subsidies to the private ethanol distilleries and incentives for the conversion of gasoline-powered cars to run on 100% ethanol. In the 2000s, auto-manufacturers based in Brazil developed a flex fuel technology that allows consumers to use any mixture of gasoline and ethanol. Importantly, Petrobras was not a key player in Brazil's ethanol programme (Smith 1976; Philip, 1992; Nardon and Aten, 2008; Leite et al. 2009).

In the power sector, the lack of indigenous coal and natural gas reserves were an additional factor that drove Brazilian policy-makers to other energy sources. In particular, hydroelectricity received large public investments and even a nuclear programme was launched in the 1970s, led by state-owned companies like Eletrobras and subsidiaries (Leite, 2014). By the end of the 1990s, about 80% of the electricity generation came from hydro.

Fossil fuel scarcity gradually turned to abundance starting in the mid-1990s, when Petrobras was achieving records in offshore oil exploration (Priest, 2016). Despite encouraging findings, the country was still importing over 50% of its oil needs before the turn of the century. Without the fiscal resources to directly boost

[2] Although the Carwarsh corruption scandal showed the politicization of investment decisions and key appointments during the administrations of Luiz Inácio Lula da Silva and Dilma Rousseff (Lima-de-Oliveira 2020).

public investments in oil and electricity, and elected with a platform that included market-opening and privatisations, the government of Fernando Henrique Cardoso (1995–2002) took the decision to open up the energy sector to private investments. A constitutional amendment (n° 9/1995) ended Petrobras' monopoly and, in the power sector, the monopoly of electricity generation of the utility company Eletrobras was dismantled.

In 2001, the country's overreliance on hydroelectricity and the lack of substantive new investments in the generation park led to an energy crisis when a drought led to the imposition of nationwide energy rationing. The diversification of energy sources became imperative for system stability, including new gas-fired power plants. However, these new generators had a much higher cost than hydro plants and primarily operated as suppliers of peak power, operating in standby mode when hydro generation was able to supply the base load demand.

Following this energy crisis, the government launched the Programme of Incentives for Alternative Electricity Sources (PROINFA, in Portuguese) in 2002, which promoted wind, biomass, and small hydroelectric sources. Its initial target was 3,300 MW of renewable energy by 2007. Despite government changes, the programme was picked up and strengthened by subsequent administrations and largely led by a stable bureaucracy of strong technical skills, operating within different government agencies (the Ministry of Energy, Energy Research Enterprise, and National Electricity Agency) (Hochstetler, 2021).

To a large extent, energy politics in Brazil run on two separate tracks, where the growth of the oil production led by Petrobras and other oil companies does not clash with the development of renewables. Key arenas of political activity have been on energy access (universalisation), price (including of oil derivatives like gasoline and diesel), site location of new projects (such as new hydroelectric dams), the ownership of oil resources and industrial policy (local content in O&G projects). Petrobras was never a predominant actor in electricity generation and even in transportation the country had a history of experimenting with alternative energy, ethanol, and since 2005, biodiesel.

11.9 Discussion

While earlier studies on energy transition tended to focus on cost and technological factors in explaining the (mostly slow) rate of transition out of fossil fuels, the substantive cost declines in access to clean energy sources in the last ten years, together with their global availability, have opened new areas of inquiry. Domestic politics is increasingly seen as a critical area to understand the variation found among countries in enabling a faster rate of adoption of cleaner sources of energy (e.g. Hochstetler, 2021). In this vein, the chapter contributes to this expanding literature on the impact of political and institutional factors in shaping energy sources. It does so by uncovering the path-dependent influence of resource nationalism, an important feature found in oil-rich states, which can constrain and delay the transition out of it by placing expectations on how central the oil industry is to a country's economy and the expected benefits from the national control of it.

As the four cases of Kuwait, the UAE, Mexico, and Brazil have illustrated, domestic political factors have led to the pursuit of various types of resource nationalism. Under the first category, there are social-based policies such as those followed by Kuwait and Mexico, aimed at boosting welfare, creating jobs in the public sector, providing subsidies, and so on. These policies created path dependencies and strengthened incumbent interest groups who oppose policies that would limit the benefits they had been receiving. Therefore, the transition to renewable energy sources, with the associated loss of subsidies and cheap energy sources, has been more difficult in comparison with the second type of resource nationalism, market-based nationalism. In this second case, as exemplified by the UAE and Brazil, governments have been able to respond to market demands in a more agile manner as previous policies had not created reliant interest groups who would oppose a market-driven approach. Consequently, switching gradually to renewables has been relatively easier.

By process tracing the evolution of energy choices and the key actors involved in four countries, we show how past decisions have empowered segments of the society which can now hinder or facilitate the energy transition. One common characteristic found in Brazil and the UAE is to tie the growth of the clean energy sector to broader societal aims, such as technology achievements and energy security (as in the development of ethanol and nuclear capacity). This has created a supporting coalition with members from academia and the private sector for energy diversification. Innovation systems promoting energy diversification have indeed been making headway in Brazil and the UAE.

Freeman (1987, p. 1) defines an innovation system as 'the network of institutions in the public and private sectors whose activities and interactions initiate, import, modify, and diffuse new technologies'. In the case of the UAE and Brazil, this has taken the form of state investment in research and innovation, overall favourable state legislation, and private investment in clean energy projects. Examples include the Mubadala Investment Company in the UAE and the Proálcool programme in Brazil. Brazil's O&G regulatory framework also earmarks revenue from the sector to investments in energy R&D, which oil companies can use to partner with universities doing projects in biofuels and other renewables (Lima-de-Oliveira, 2019). The focus on innovation systems also shows that switching from a social-based to a market-based form of resource nationalism is possible and does not have to be a zero-sum game. Broadening the segment of society that benefits from the transition to a market-based resource nationalism could take the form of a reduction in hydrocarbon subsidies coupled with market-based incentives that would compensate would-be losers. For example, specialised state institutions could provide incentives for private investors, foreign and domestic, while also providing technical retraining programmes that service the demands of the new renewable energy sector. These interactions can help challenge the status quo in oil-exporting and oil-producing countries by providing incentives that favour market-based over social-based type of resource nationalism in the long run.

11.10 Conclusion

To summarise, this chapter investigates the causes behind the varying patterns of renewable energy transition among oil-rich countries. To discover this, we examine how four oil-rich countries, two from MENA and two from Latin America, adopted different policies addressing the urgent need to transition to renewable energy. The empirical data suggest that the two countries that pursued social-based policies, namely Mexico and Kuwait, have transitioned more slowly to the adoption of renewable energy. By comparison, the two countries that implemented market-based policies, namely Brazil and the UAE, have made more progress in the transition to renewable energy.

This chapter offers several contributions. It adds to the literature on energy transition by examining four oil-exporting countries from the developing world, two groups that have rarely been studied in the literature. Additionally, it uses a qualitative process tracing method, which is not often used in studies on energy transition. Finally, the study expands the literature on political determinants of energy transition, which thus far has not been sufficiently examined in studies on renewable energy.

The topic of political determinants of renewable energy transition can certainly benefit from continued research. One of the proposed areas of future research is a quantitative or mixed-methods approach using cross-section time-series data to map trends complementing our qualitative comparative approach. Moreover, additional case studies from other developing parts of the world such as Africa and other parts of Asia would further enhance our understanding of the determinants of energy transition – an area few scholars and informed policy-makers would argue is not of urgency.

References

Alam, M. M., and Murad, M. W. (2020). The impacts of economic growth, trade openness, and technological progress on renewable energy use in organization for economic co-operation and development countries. *Renewable Energy* 145, pp. 382–390. Doi .org/10.1016/j.renene.2019.06.054.

Andreasson, S. (2015). Varieties of resource nationalism in sub-Saharan Africa's energy and minerals markets. *Extractive Industries and Society* 2 (2), pp. 310–319. Doi.org/10.1016/j.exis.2015.01.004.

Arent, D., Arndt, C., Miller, M., Tarp, F., and Zinaman, O. (2017). Introduction and synthesis, in Arent, D. J. (ed.), *The Political Economy of Clean Energy Transitions*. 1st ed. Oxford: Oxford University Press, pp. 14–23.

Bamati, N., and Raoofi, A. (2020). Development level and the impact of the technological factor on renewable energy production. *Renewable Energy* 151, pp. 946–955. Doi.org/10.1016/j.renene.2019.11.098.

Bennett, A., and Checkel, J. T. (eds.) (2015). *Process Tracing*. Cambridge: Cambridge University Press.

BP (2020). *Statistical Review of World Energy*. London: BP.

Bremmer, I., and Johnston, R. (2009). The rise and fall of resource nationalism. *Survival* 51 (2), pp. 149–158. Doi.org/10.1080/00396330902860884.

Butler, N. (2019, September 10). Kuwait's action on green energy fails to match best intentions. *Financial Times*. Available online: www.ft.com/content/bdcee818-c35f-11e9-ae6e-a26d1d0455f4.

Cadoret, I., and Padovano, F. (2016). The political drivers of renewable energies policies. *Energy Economics* 56, pp. 261–269. Doi.org/10.1016/j.eneco.2016.03.003.

Carbon Tracker (2021). The sky's the limit – solar and wind energy potential is 100 times as much as global energy demand. Available online: https://carbontracker.org/reports/the-skys-the-limit-solar-wind/.

Coelho, S. T., and Goldemberg, J. (2013). Global energy policy: A view from Brazil, in Goldthau, A. (ed.), *The Handbook of Global Energy Policy*. Malden, MA: Willey-Blackwell, pp. 457–474.

Contreras, E. (1993). *Os Desbravadores: A Petrobrás e a Construção do Brasil industrial*. Rio de Janeiro: Relume Damará/ANPOCS.

Energy Information Administration (EIA) (2016). *Country Analysis Brief: Kuwait*, p. 14. U.S. Energy Information Administration. Available online: www.eia.gov/international/content/analysis/countries_long/Kuwait/kuwait.pdf.

Energy Information Administration (EIA) (2020a). *Country Analysis Executive Summary: United Arab Emirates*, p. 8. U.S. Energy Information Administration. Available online: www.eia.gov/international/content/analysis/countries_long/United_Arab_Emirates/uae_2020.pdf.

Energy Information Administration (EIA) (2020b). *Country Analysis Executive Summary: Mexico*, p. 10. U.S. Energy Information Administration. Available online: www.eia.gov/international/content/analysis/countries_long/Mexico/mexico.pdf.

Etheridge, J. (2009, 9 March). Power struggle hits Kuwaiti oil sector. *Financial Times*. Available online: www.ft.com/content/55b6a2f6-0cbe-11de-a555-0000779fd2ac.

Fitch Solutions (2021). *Mexico: Renewables Report: Includes 10-Year Forecasts to 2030 (Q3 2021)*. Available online: www.fitchsolutions.com.

Freeman, C. (1987). *Technology Policy and Economic Performance: Lessons from Japan*. London: Pinter.

Freire, W. (2013). Petrobras: das origens até os anos 1990, in Giambiagi, F., and Paulo Velloso Lucas, L. (ed.), *Petróleo: Reforma e Contrareforma do Setor Petrolífero Brasileiro*. Rio de Janeiro: Elsevier, pp. 3–36.

Gatzert, N., & Kosub, T. (2017). Determinants of policy risks of renewable energy investments. *International Journal of Energy Sector Management* 11 (1), pp. 28–45.

Hertog, S. (2010). Defying the resource curse: explaining successful state-owned enterprises in rentier states. *World Politics* 62 (2), pp. 261–301. Doi.org/10.1017/S0043887110000055.

Hochstetler, K. (2021). *Political Economies of Energy Transition: Wind and Solar Power in Brazil and South Africa*. Cambridge: Cambridge University Press.

Hussein, H. (2020, 27 December). Khalifa bin Zayed issues a law to establish the Supreme Council for Financial and Economic Affairs. Emirates News Agency. Available online: https://wam.ae/en/details/1395302898123.

International Energy Agency (IEA) (2018). *World Energy Investment 2018*. Paris: IEA/OECD.

International Energy Agency (IEA) (2020). The Oil and Gas Industry in Energy Transitions. Available online: https://iea.blob.core.windows.net/assets/4315f4ed-5cb2-4264-b0ee-2054fd34c118/The_Oil_and_Gas_Industry_in_Energy_Transitions.pdf.

International Energy Agency (IEA) (2021). *Energy Subsidies: Tracking the Impact of Fossil-Fuel Subsidies*. Available online: www.iea.org/topics/energy-subsidies.

International Renewable Energy Agency (IRENA) (2015). *Renewable Energy Prospects: United Arab Emirates*. Available online: www.irena.org/publications/2015/Apr/Renewable-Energy-Prospects-United-Arab-Emirates.

Kammermann, L., and Dermont, C. (2018). How beliefs of the political elite and citizens on climate change influence support for Swiss energy transition policy. *Energy Research & Social Science* 43, pp. 48–60. Doi.org/10.1016/j.erss.2018.05.010.

Kuwait National Petroleum Company (2021). *Clean Fuels Project*. Available online: www.knpc.com/en/strategic-projects/clean-fuel-project-cfp.

Leite, A. D. (2014). *A Energia do Brasil (3ª edição)*. Rio de Janeiro: Lexikon.

Leite, R. C. D. C., Leal, M. R. L. V., Cortez, L. A. B., Griffin, W. M., and Scandiffio, M. I. G. (2009). Can Brazil replace 5% of the 2025 gasoline world demand with ethanol? *Energy* 34 (5), pp. 655–661. Doi.org/10.1016/j.energy.2008.11.001.

Lima-de-Oliveira, R. (2019). Resource-led industrial development in the oil and gas global value chain: The case of Brazil, in Elisabeth, B. R., and Reynolds, B. (eds.), *Innovation in Brazil: Advancing Development in the 21st Century*. London: Routledge, pp. 283–302.

Lima-de-Oliveira, R. (2020). Corruption and local content development: assessing the impact of the Petrobras' Scandal on recent policy changes in Brazil. *Extractive Industries and Society* 7, pp. 274–282. Doi.org/10.1016/j.exis.2019.08.004.

MacDonald, F. (2020, September 10). Kuwait Parliament approves state budget with $46 billion deficit. Bloomberg. Available online: www.bloombergquint.com/markets/kuwait-parliament-approves-state-budget-with-46-billion-deficit.

Meyer, L., and Morales, I. (1990). *Petróleo y nación (1900–1987): La política petrolera en México*. México (DF): Fondo de Cultura Econónica.

Morales, I. (1992). The consolidation and expansion of Pemex, in Brown, J. C. and Knight, A. (eds.), *The Mexican Petroleum industry in the Twentieth Century*. Austin, TX: University of Texas Press, pp. 208–232.

Murshed, M., and Alam, M. S. (2021). Estimating the macroeconomic determinants of total, renewable, and non-renewable energy demands in Bangladesh: the role of technological innovations. *Environmental Science and Pollution Research* 28, pp. 30176–30196. Doi.org/10.1007/s11356-021-12516-6.

Nardon, L., and Aten, K. (2008). Beyond a better mousetrap: A cultural analysis of the adoption of ethanol in Brazil. *Journal of World Business* 43 (3), pp. 261–273.

Pérez-Denicia, E., Fernández-Luqueño, F., Vilariño-Ayala, D., Montaño-Zetina, L. M., and Maldonado-López, L. A. (2017). Renewable energy sources for electricity generation in Mexico: A review. *Renewable and Sustainable Energy Reviews* 78, pp. 597–613.

Philip, G. (1992). The expropriation in comparative perspective, in Brown, J. C. and Knight, A. (eds.), *The Mexican Petroleum industry in the Twentieth Century*. Austin, TX: University of Texas Press, pp. 173–189.

Priest, T. (2016). Petrobras in the history of offshore oil, in Schneider, B. R. (ed.), *New Order and Progress: Development and Democracy in Brazil*. New York: Oxford University Press, pp. 53–77.

Saadi, D. (2020, 28 December). Abu Dhabi merges Supreme Petroleum Council with new economic body. S&P Global. Available online: www.spglobal.com/platts/en/market-insights/latest-news/oil/122820-abu-dhabi-merges-supreme-petroleum-council-with-new-economic-body.

Saba, Y. (2020, 16 September). Kuwait cuts $3 billion from 2020–21 budget, lawmaker says. Reuters. Available online: www.reuters.com/article/kuwait-budget-int-idUSKBN25Z1GZ.

SENER (2020). *Programa de Desarrollo del Sistema Eléctrico Nacional: 2020–2034*. Mexico City: SENER.

Sequeira, T. N., and Santos, M. S. (2018). Renewable energy and politics: A systematic review and new evidence. *Journal of Cleaner Production* 192, pp. 553–568. Doi.org/10.1016/j.jclepro.2018.04.190.

Shehabi, M. (2020). *Kuwait Energy Outlook 2020: Current Policies and Necessity of Reform*. Oxford: Oxford Institute for Energy Studies. Available online: www.oxfordenergy.org/publications/kuwait-energy-outlook-2020-current-policies-and-necessity-of-reform/.

Smith, P. (1976). *Oil and Politics in Modern Brazil*. Toronto: Macmillan.

Stevens, P. (2008). National oil companies and international oil companies in the Middle East: Under the shadow of government and the resource nationalism cycle. *Journal of World Energy Law & Business* 1 (1), pp. 5–30. Doi.org/10.1093/jwelb/jwn004.

Trojbicz, B., and Loureiro, M. R. (2018). Brazilian oil sector reforms: the role of technical know-how and corporate ethos in Petrobras' dominance. *Energy Policy* 118, pp. 588–595. Doi.org/10.1016/j.enpol.2018.03.060.

UAE Government Portal (2021, 1 May). *UAE Energy Strategy 2050*. Available online: https://u.ae/en/about-the-uae/strategies-initiatives-and-awards/federal-governments-strategies-and-plans/uae-energy-strategy-2050.

UAE Ministry of Energy and Infrastructure (2017, 10 January). Vice President Unveils UAE Energy Strategy for Next Three Decades. Available online: www.moei.gov.ae/en/media-centre/news/10/1/2017/محمد-بن-راشد-يعلن-استراتيجية-دولة-الإمارات-للطاقة-للعقود-الثلاثة-المقبلة.aspx#page=1.

Villamil, J. (2020). Why Mexico is pushing to slow down clean energy. *Washington Post*. Available online: www.washingtonpost.com/business/energy/why-mexico-is-pushing-to-slow-down-clean-energy/2020/07/16/fbfcd0f4-c779-11ea-a825-8722004e4150_story.html.

Wilson, J. D. (2015). Understanding resource nationalism: Economic dynamics and political institutions. *Contemporary Politics* 21 (4), pp. 399–416. Doi.org/10.1080/13569775.2015.1013293.

World Bank (2021). *World Development Indicators Data Bank*. World Bank Data Bank. Available online: https://databank.worldbank.org/source/world-development-indicators#.

12

Toward Smart Buildings and Communities in the Gulf States

Analysis of Human and Social Dimensions in the Transition to Carbon-Neutral Cities Using Artificial Intelligence

AMMAR ABULIBDEH, ESMAT ZAIDAN, AND MOHSEN JAFARI*

12.1 Introduction

The global push towards achieving net zero and carbon-neutral buildings has gained significant momentum in recent years (Ye et al., 2017). As sustainability becomes a top priority, initiatives aimed at reducing energy consumption and increasing efficiency have taken center stage. The built environment plays a significant role in contributing to carbon footprints in urban communities worldwide, primarily due to the high energy consumption required for heating, cooling, and other building services (World Energy Outlook, 2019). However, by implementing demand-side management strategies and improving energy efficiency, it is possible to significantly reduce the energy usage and subsequently decrease the carbon footprint of buildings (Christensen & Olhoff, 2019). One effective approach is the adoption of advanced and smart human-in-the-loop control technologies, specifically designed to optimize building air conditioning, air quality, and overall comfort based on human needs and occupancy schedules.

These advanced technologies leverage near real-time data on occupancy behavior, including individual set points, occupancy numbers, and schedules. By integrating artificial intelligence (AI) and machine learning (ML) techniques, these technologies can predict and adjust energy demand and load in a highly efficient manner (Abulibdeh et al., 2022; Alabi et al., 2022) Furthermore, load flexibility can be utilized to shift peak energy consumption periods, thereby maximizing the utilization of renewable energy sources (World Energy Outlook, 2019). In essence, smart building technologies are crucial for achieving carbon neutrality in the built environment. However, it is important to recognize that the effectiveness and cost-effectiveness of these solutions depend on the seamless interaction

* This publication was made possible by an NPRP award (NPRP13S-0206-200272) from the Qatar National Research Fund (a member of Qatar Foundation). The statements made herein are solely the responsibility of the authors.

between humans and the control systems and AI algorithms. Human behavior and preferences play a pivotal role in optimizing energy usage and ensuring occupant comfort. Therefore, a holistic approach that combines human input with machine intelligence is essential to achieve the desired outcomes in terms of carbon neutrality and sustainable building practices (Liu et al., 2022).

By understanding and leveraging the symbiotic relationship between humans and smart technologies, we can unlock the full potential of the built environment in transitioning towards carbon neutrality. This requires a collaborative effort between technology developers, building occupants, and policymakers to create an ecosystem that promotes effective interaction, energy conservation, and sustainable practices (Abulibdeh et al., 2024). While, smart building technologies are crucial for achieving carbon neutrality in the built environment, it is imperative to acknowledge the significant role of human–machine interaction. By integrating human needs and behaviors with advanced control systems and AI algorithms, we can optimize energy usage, reduce carbon footprints, and create sustainable and comfortable living spaces for urban communities (Charfeddine et al., 2023). However, in the midst of technological advancements and energy-efficient solutions, an often overlooked aspect is the crucial role of occupant–building interactions in realizing carbon-neutral goals. The chapter delves into this understudied area, exploring the connections between occupant behavior, building performance, and carbon neutrality.

While considerable attention has been given to the development of innovative technologies and sustainable practices in building design and operation, the human dimension remains a critical yet relatively unexplored aspect (Chen et al., 2022; Cureau et al., 2022). Understanding how occupants use and interact with buildings is essential for achieving carbon neutrality. Their behaviors, preferences, and comfort significantly impact energy consumption patterns, making it imperative to comprehensively address occupant–building interactions.

The Gulf Cooperation Council (GCC) countries' national innovation systems play a critical role in facilitating a holistic transition to carbon neutrality. These systems encompass various institutions, policies, and mechanisms that foster innovation and technological advancements in sustainable practices. By integrating innovation into the transition process, GCC countries can effectively address the challenges associated with achieving carbon neutrality and create a sustainable future (Ammar Abulibdeh et al., 2019; Zaidan et al., 2019). One key insight is that GCC national innovation systems need to prioritize research and development (R&D) in clean energy technologies and solutions (Shahwan & Zaman, 2023). This includes investing in renewable energy sources such as solar and wind, as well as developing energy storage and grid integration technologies. By supporting R&D efforts, GCC countries can accelerate the deployment and adoption of sustainable energy solutions, contributing to their carbon neutrality goals.

Additionally, the innovation systems should focus on creating a conducive environment for entrepreneurship and startups in the clean energy sector. This involves providing funding mechanisms, incubation programs, and regulatory frameworks that promote innovation and the commercialization of sustainable technologies (Zaidan, Abulibdeh, et al., 2022). By nurturing a thriving ecosystem for clean energy startups, the GCC can tap into the entrepreneurial spirit and drive innovation towards carbon neutrality. Collaboration and knowledge exchange are also crucial aspects of GCC national innovation systems (Mutambik et al., 2023). Establishing partnerships with international institutions, research organizations, and industry leaders can facilitate the transfer of knowledge, expertise, and best practices in sustainable development. This collaboration can enhance the GCC's capacity to develop and implement innovative solutions that address regional challenges while aligning with global sustainability goals. Furthermore, fostering a culture of innovation and sustainability within the GCC societies is essential. This involves promoting awareness, education, and capacity-building programs that empower individuals and communities to embrace sustainable practices. By encouraging behavioral changes and promoting a mindset of innovation and sustainability, the GCC can create a supportive social environment that complements the efforts of the national innovation systems.

By filling the existing research gap, this chapter provides valuable insights into the multifaceted nature of occupant–building interactions and their relationship to carbon neutrality. It aims to shed light on the intricate dynamics between technical, behavioral, socioeconomic, and demographic factors that influence occupant behavior and, subsequently, building performance. By unraveling these connections, we can develop a more holistic approach towards achieving carbon neutrality in buildings. The empirical analysis conducted in Doha, Qatar, serves as the foundation of this research, incorporating the perspectives of 2,600 respondents. This chapter investigates the factors influencing human–building interactions (HBIs), including indoor environmental quality, occupant well-being, work performance, building operations, and perceived thermal comfort. By examining the interplay between these factors, a comprehensive conceptual framework is developed to comprehend and model occupant behavior and its implications for carbon neutrality.

In line with the broader theme of the book, this chapter emphasizes the vital connection between occupant–building interactions and carbon neutrality. It underlines the significance of considering the human factors involved in building design, operation, and occupant well-being, alongside technological advancements. By empowering occupants and optimizing their comfort and satisfaction, we can drive sustainable practices, reduce energy consumption, and ultimately contribute to the overarching goal of carbon neutrality. Through a holistic and interdisciplinary approach that integrates occupant behaviour, preferences, and comfort, we can unlock the full potential of buildings as key contributors to carbon neutrality. By bridging the gap between technological advancements and human factors, this chapter sets the stage for further research and the development of targeted strategies to optimize occupant well-being, energy efficiency, and sustainability. By recognizing and harnessing the power of occupant–building interactions, we can pave the way towards a greener, more carbon-neutral future in the built environment.

12.2 Human–Building Interactions

Typically, people spend 65% of their day at home. However, when different demographic factors (e.g. type of job, age) are taken into account, this percentage significantly increases (Elessawy & Zaidan, 2014; Pais-Magalhães et al., 2022). The performance of buildings is closely linked to the health and well-being of their occupants. In recent years, there has been growing recognition of the influence of indoor environmental conditions on well-being, leading to an increased demand for healthier living spaces and improved living standards (Ghofrani, Zaidan, & Jafari, 2021; Jafari et al., 2022). Consequently, researchers have undertaken studies to assess the factors that affect occupant comfort and health with respect to buildings. The emerging field of building occupant behavior draws on insights from both building science and psychology to investigate this issue (Zaidan, Ghofrani, et al., 2022). Researchers such as Humphreys & Nicol (1998) introduced the concept of homeostasis as a principle of human adaptability in the energy research sector. According to Humphrey, people react to changes in the indoor environmental conditions of a space in a way that restores their comfort condition if discomfort arises.

Research has demonstrated that occupants who perceive a higher level of control over their indoor environment report higher levels of satisfaction compared to those with a lower perceived level of control, with a difference of up to 85% (O'Brien & Gunay, 2014; Von Grabe, 2016). The perception of having control over the indoor environment has been shown to result in greater comfort (Xu et al., 2014). However, occupants may perceive persuasion and prohibition of certain actions as constraints, which can lead to increased desire for restricted activities and a repulsion towards persuasive messages (D'Oca & Hong, 2014). Additionally, behavioural selection can be perceived as stressful, particularly as the number of options increases. Occupants commonly express dissatisfaction with their choices, leading to demotivation (González et al., 2008). Behavioural and personality psychology can help explain the choices made regarding control options (D'Oca & Hong, 2015). The functioning of heating, ventilation, and air conditioning (HVAC) and control systems in buildings is subject to change due to the dynamic and nonmechanistic aspects of human needs, requirements, comfort preferences, and behaviors. Simulation studies have indicated the positive impact of proactive attitudes towards building control aimed at energy saving. Proactive workers who engage in control actions, such as unplugging equipment and turning off HVAC systems and lights, consume 50% less energy than those who are not involved in control actions (Lin & Hong, 2013). Furthermore, a field study by Masoso & Grobler (2010) revealed the "dark side" of building energy use by analyzing energy-intensive consumption patterns, such as leaving lights and screens on after leaving the space and working long hours, among occupants of monitored office buildings.

In recent years, there has been a growing interest in an interdisciplinary research field aimed at reducing energy consumption in the building sector and increasing energy efficiency by combining knowledge from various fields such as building physics, data science, social psychology, and sociology. This approach involves the use of social science, artificial intelligence, and human–building interaction-related data to identify energy consumption behavioral patterns in both residential (D'Oca et al., 2014) and commercial sectors. In particular, it has been argued that interventions targeting employee behavior in the commercial sector require an interdisciplinary approach since such behavior affects the economic, environmental, and energy performances of an organization.

In order to gain a comprehensive understanding of a building's energy consumption, it is crucial to have a deep knowledge of human–building interactions. This chapter provides a thorough explanation of HBIs in both residential and non-residential buildings, which can be used to estimate the impact of HBIs on energy consumption. The study analyzes human behavior in relation to the indoor environment, including interactions with building facilities such as air conditioning, ventilation, and lighting, and how these interactions directly and indirectly affect energy consumption. The term "HBI" refers to the experiences of building occupants in relation to the building's energy network and HVAC systems, such as thermostats and lighting, as they attempt to meet their own comfort requirements. In modern buildings, the importance of HBIs has been increasing due to growing recognition of individual differences in thermal control and the demand for highly personalized comfort (Davoodi et al., 2018). HBIs are also crucial to occupant response control systems in order to improve occupants' comfort and performance (Boerstra et al., 2015).

HBIs are critical for assessing not only the comfort and health of building occupants but also the building's energy consumption. Therefore, it is recommended to establish a comprehensive HBI framework to regulate the built environment. Given the increasing importance of HBIs in modern buildings, new instruments have been developed (Deme Belafi et al., 2019) and simulations of HBIs have been carried out (Mijorski & Cammelli, 2016). Occupational activities have a significant impact on the role and efficiency of buildings concerning HBI. Occupants in shared environments generally experience less comfort (Karjalainen, 2012) and rely more on emotional treatment (Foster & Oreszczyn, 2001) than on environmental changes, mainly due to poor management of energy-building tools (Angizeh et al., 2021 Nazemi et al., 2021).

In addition to influencing living standards, indoor climate also has a significant impact on occupant health. Indoor air quality (IAQ) is affected by various factors including building location, architecture, HVAC operation, pollutants, building materials, and occupants. Effective indoor control methods cannot only improve occupant comfort but also reduce CO_2 emissions, independent of the building's architectural design (Vázquez-Canteli et al., 2019). The type of ventilation system used in buildings, for instance, can also affect indoor temperature and air quality (Ye et al., 2017). Furthermore, the indoor thermal effects on specific building control elements such as windows and fans have been discussed in previous studies.

The primary hindrance to achieving significant energy sustainability in buildings is the lack of knowledge regarding the critical factors that affect the HBI and its relation to energy consumption. The difference between the anticipated and actual energy usage in buildings is frequently substantial but has been commonly attributed to human behavior rather than building design. This chapter identifies four major factors that not only affect energy consumption in buildings but also the HBI, which include the environmental factors (comprising both indoor environmental quality (IEQ) and the impact of the outdoor environment), building-related factors (including the energy systems), occupants' related factors, and overall comfort of occupants. While most studies have mainly concentrated on the first three factors, the present chapter emphasizes the importance of considering all four of these factors.

12.3 Relation of Different Variables Affecting Human–Building Interaction

This section delineates the outcomes of investigations that aimed to discern the diverse constituents influencing the HBI, including IEQ, the outdoor milieu, occupant traits, building features, and occupant contentment, which are the primary parameters. Although the mentioned factors are examined in this section individually, they demonstrate strong associations. Many scholars have observed that augmented noise levels result in inferior thermal gratification as opposed to standard conditions. Nonetheless, it is worth mentioning that numerous analyses have uncovered no adverse effects on thermal comfort resulting from the noise level (Schust M et al., 1991).

12.3.1 Impact of Occupant Characteristics

It is unquestionable that human factors have a significant impact on both HBI and energy consumption. According to various studies across multiple domains, technological advancements alone are insufficient to ensure the attainment of net zero energy consumption buildings or to enhance the effectiveness of HBI and building comfort. Frequently, human factors are crucial, and despite their increased importance, they are often overlooked in building design and planning. Many research studies have investigated the influence of occupant characteristics on the HBI framework. As depicted in Figure 12.1, different building variables have an effect on occupant comfort. Designers and construction managers should consider both the building attributes and the occupants' characteristics while prioritizing the comfort factors. Among the numerous factors that affect the occupants' comfort level in their building interactions, the environment component appears to be one of the most crucial.

Gender differences are a significant factor in determining differences in comfort levels. For instance, as reported by (Karjalainen, 2007), men tend to use thermostats more often than women and have a greater awareness of HVAC systems, leading to better regulation and consequently improved thermal comfort. Women tend to be more sensitive to temperature than men and may wear more clothing

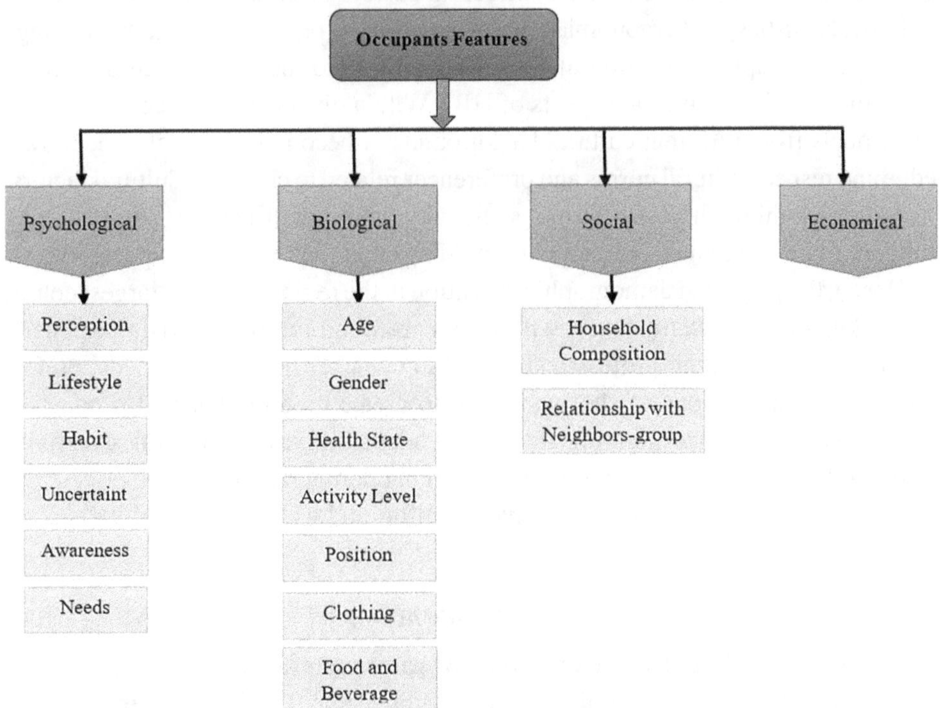

Figure 12.1 Effective human factors in HBI.

to compensate for colder environments (Xue et al., 2015). These differences in behavior and response to environmental changes may be attributed to various factors, such as biological and psychological variations and differing behavioral adaptations between genders (Karjalainen, 2012; Mehnert et al., 2002). In addition, the age of occupants is another crucial factor affecting their satisfaction with indoor conditions (Lee et al., 2011; Zalejska-Jonsson & Wilhelmsson, 2013). Younger occupants tend to be less satisfied with urban indoor environments and have a lower approval rate than their older counterparts. However, Hwang & Chen (2010) suggests that older individuals are highly susceptible to temperature fluctuations and have limited thermal comfort options compared to younger occupants.

The increased working-age population presents both opportunities and challenges in HBI. On the one hand, the diverse workforce will have varying comfort preferences and requirements, necessitating flexible and adaptable building environments. Different age groups, genders, and cultural backgrounds will have unique comfort expectations, and buildings will need to accommodate these diverse needs to ensure occupant satisfaction. Additionally, the changing demographic landscape will influence the demand for different types of buildings and spaces. As the working-age population grows, there may be an increased demand for office spaces, co-working spaces, and other work-related environments. These spaces will need to be designed with occupant comfort in mind, considering factors such as temperature control, lighting, acoustics, and ergonomic features to promote productivity and well-being.

The demographic transition also brings attention to the importance of considering the social and cultural aspects of HBI. With a diverse workforce comprising individuals from different cultural backgrounds, it becomes essential to acknowledge and respect cultural norms and preferences related to comfort. Cultural factors, including clothing choices, thermal sensitivity, and indoor activity patterns, may influence how occupants interact with buildings and their comfort expectations.

Hence, the projected demographic transition in the region, with the largest cohort of working-age population ever, will have a profound impact on HBI. Designers, architects, and building professionals need to consider the diverse needs, preferences, and expectations of the workforce to create comfortable and productive environments. By incorporating flexibility, adaptability, and cultural sensitivity into building design and operation, the changing demographics can be effectively addressed, leading to enhanced occupant comfort and well-being.

12.3.2 Environment Impact

The impact of environmental factors on HBI parameters and their association with various aspects of human comfort is highly noticeable. For instance, the outdoor environment has an effect on the occupants' thermal needs and indoor temperature

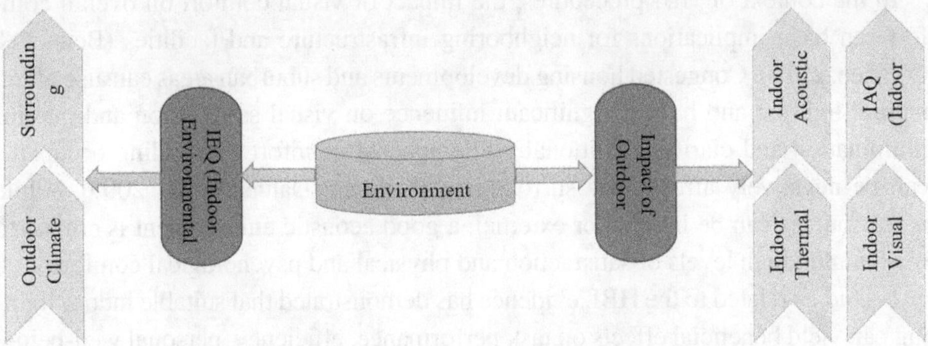

Figure 12.2 Effective environmental factors in HBI.

adjustment levels (Chan et al., 2008). High humidity and temperature have been found to negatively affect the indoor air quality and occupants' satisfaction, while colder and drier air has been deemed more comfortable and suitable (Lan et al., 2011). The assessment of the influence of the environment on HBI involves the examination of two primary categories, namely the indoor environmental quality (IEQ) and its associated subfactors, as well as the effects of the outdoor environment as shown in Figure 12.2.

The interactions between the visual and acoustical environments have only been studied in a limited number of cases. Some studies suggest that low levels of noise and ambient light can enhance performance (Liebl et al., 2012). However, the impact of these factors on self-reported comfort remains unclear (Knez & Hygge, 2002), while others suggest a link between noise and light levels and indoor comfort (Huang et al., 2012). The acceptability of air quality can be significantly affected by introducing high levels of noise in a polluted environment with high temperatures. Furthermore, according to Dahlan (2013), thermal conditions can also affect satisfaction with acoustics, as discomfort due to temperature can negatively impact acoustic satisfaction.

In previous research, it has been observed that higher levels of lighting can result in increased air acceptance (Jiang & Yang, 2011). Furthermore, there is evidence to suggest that user comfort can have a significant impact on IAQ (Kempton et al., 2022; Rolando et al., 2022). Psychological factors, such as the level of tolerance of the occupants, can also play a crucial role in this regard. For example, in dwellings where the occupants have adapted to their environment and noise pollution, tests have indicated a decrease in irritation among high-tolerance individuals (Ye et al., 2017). Additionally, (Choi & Yeom, 2019) studied the impact of mixed environmental conditions on occupant stress, finding that accounting for variations in brain activity could be useful in measuring resident discomfort. Their study involved two stages, with a paper survey followed by an electroencephalogram (EEG) examination.

In the context of HBI procedures, the impact of visual comfort on overall comfort can have implications for neighboring infrastructure and facilities (Bennet & O'Brien, 2016). Congested housing developments and suburban areas can also affect natural lighting and have a significant influence on visual satisfaction and interior illumination and clarity. Additionally, the acoustic comfort of building occupants can be negatively affected by surrounding facilities (Dahlan et al., 2009). While noise sources can be internal or external, a good acoustic environment is crucial to maintaining high levels of satisfaction and physical and psychological comfort.

In studies related to the HBI, evidence has demonstrated that suitable indoor lighting can yield beneficial effects on task performance, efficiency, personal well-being, and security (Newsham et al., 2002). Additionally, it has the potential to enhance the aesthetic attractiveness of the environment and induce positive psychological effects on occupants (Newsham et al., 2004). Furthermore, the examination of occupants' physiological and psychological responses plays a crucial role in evaluating the dynamic interplay between humans and artificial lighting systems within buildings.

The comprehensive examination of the HBI encompasses various aspects related to the openings within a building, such as windows and doors. The comfort experienced by occupants is influenced by several factors, including external environmental conditions, the efficiency of glazing and shading systems, and other comfort-related characteristics that necessitate attention to enhance the effectiveness and utilization of these openings (Zomorodian & Tahsildoost, 2017). Dwellings equipped with balconies offer greater satisfaction with regard to thermal and acoustic conditions compared to those lacking such features (Bennet & O'Brien, 2016). The size, dimensions, and placement of openings, as well as their operational aspects, significantly impact occupants' comfort by modulating optical, auditory, thermal conditions, and IAQ satisfaction (Lyons et al., 2000). The utilization of roof overhangs for shading purposes contributes to reduced solar exposure and overheating, thereby enhancing the comfort level for inhabitants. It is crucial to carefully consider and optimize these aspects to provide improved HBI conditions for occupants (Dahlan et al., 2009). Moreover, the vertical location of a residence within a building has a notable influence on the satisfaction levels of its occupants. Research suggests that individuals residing on higher floors generally experience higher satisfaction and exhibit greater preference for their surrounding environment compared to those living on lower floors (Jamaludin et al., 2013; Wong et al., 2002).

12.4 A Comprehensive Relations Pattern of HBI Factors

To design energy-efficient and comfortable buildings, it is crucial to comprehend the intricate interactions among multiple elements within the HBI, encompassing architecture, construction, and building service engineering. A comprehensive understanding of these interrelationships is indispensable for achieving satisfactory levels of occupant comfort in residential buildings, as it directly influences energy conservation and sustainable energy consumption. Adopting a user-centric approach to HBI is therefore imperative for a holistic design approach. Satisfaction with HBI can also yield enhanced productivity and effective recreational experiences. Consequently, there has been a recent surge in studies examining the factors influencing HBI in residential buildings, although many of these studies tend to focus on singular aspects such as building type or environmental conditions. Consequently, translating the findings into a multifactorial study can pose challenges due to the need for simultaneous consideration of diverse influential factors.

The evaluation of behavioral energy savings is frequently limited to the examination of the interplay between occupant behavior and building control systems and tools. However, this approach overlooks other critical factors such as occupant comfort levels and indoor/outdoor environmental conditions, which can significantly affect the efficacy of energy-saving strategies. To ensure an optimal interaction between occupants and building control systems, it is imperative to develop a comprehensive understanding of all major elements involved. The proposed framework, which highlights the influential factors shaping the HBI, can contribute to the formulation of energy-saving policies and decision-making frameworks. Addressing the identified gap in previous research, the authors put forth a conceptual model that elucidates the relationships among four key factors influencing HBI, encompassing both environmental and non-environmental aspects, with the aim of conducting a comprehensive assessment of occupants' comfort levels. This proposed framework sheds light on the reasons why energy savings achieved in practice often fall short of their predicted potential, as corroborated by recent studies (Ehrhardt-Martinez, 2013).

The inadequate exploration of the intricate interactions between diverse environmental and non-environmental factors, including occupant attributes and building characteristics, and their consequential effects on long-term occupant comfort within the context of HBI assessments indicates a dearth of comprehensive analysis. The available range of environmental conditions, building features, and occupant attributes that must be considered to ensure occupant comfort in various building types is also limited. To tackle this issue, the objective of this chapter is to identify the key factors influencing HBI and to present their interrelationships within a conceptual framework as shown in Figure 12.3.

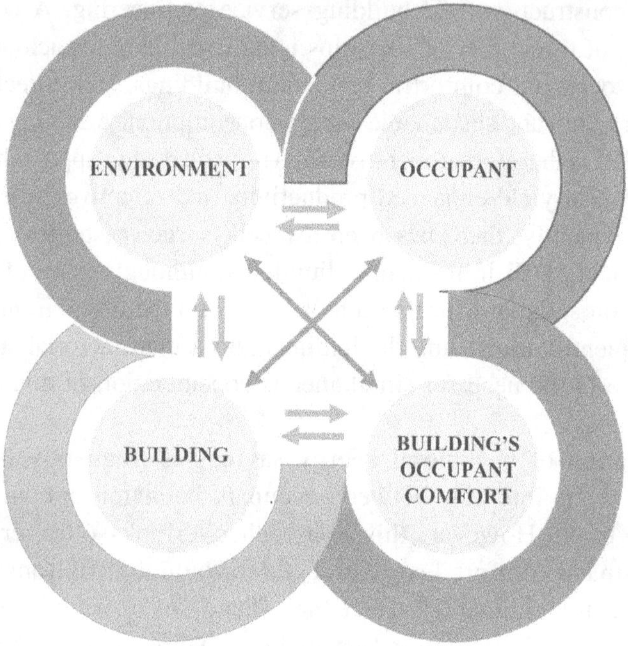

Figure 12.3 Human–building interactions.

12.5 Concept Mapping for Planning Human–Building Interaction

Concept mapping (CM) is a technical approach employed by teams to construct a conceptual model that aids in independent assessment and organization (Trochim & McLinden, 2017). In this chapter, a concept mapping methodology is proposed, as depicted in Figure 12.4, which comprises several steps: (1) preparation, involving the selection of major parameters in the HBI and effective factors categorized into four main categories; (2) collection of energy-related behavior data; (3) monitoring and modeling of occupants behavior; (4) occupants behavior simulation; (5) modeling the HBI by considering the simultaneous impact of technical and human factors, encompassing both physical and nonphysical aspects; and (6) utilization and analysis of the results.

The introduced concept mapping approach promotes optimal energy consumption among occupants by fostering a comprehensive understanding of their interactions with building systems, as well as the internal and external environment of their buildings, while ensuring overall comfort. Furthermore, the proposed framework visually represents all major concepts and their interrelationships, enhancing the evaluation of HBI through a Feedback Loop. This loop offers an opportunity to assess the impact of adopting the framework on the initial

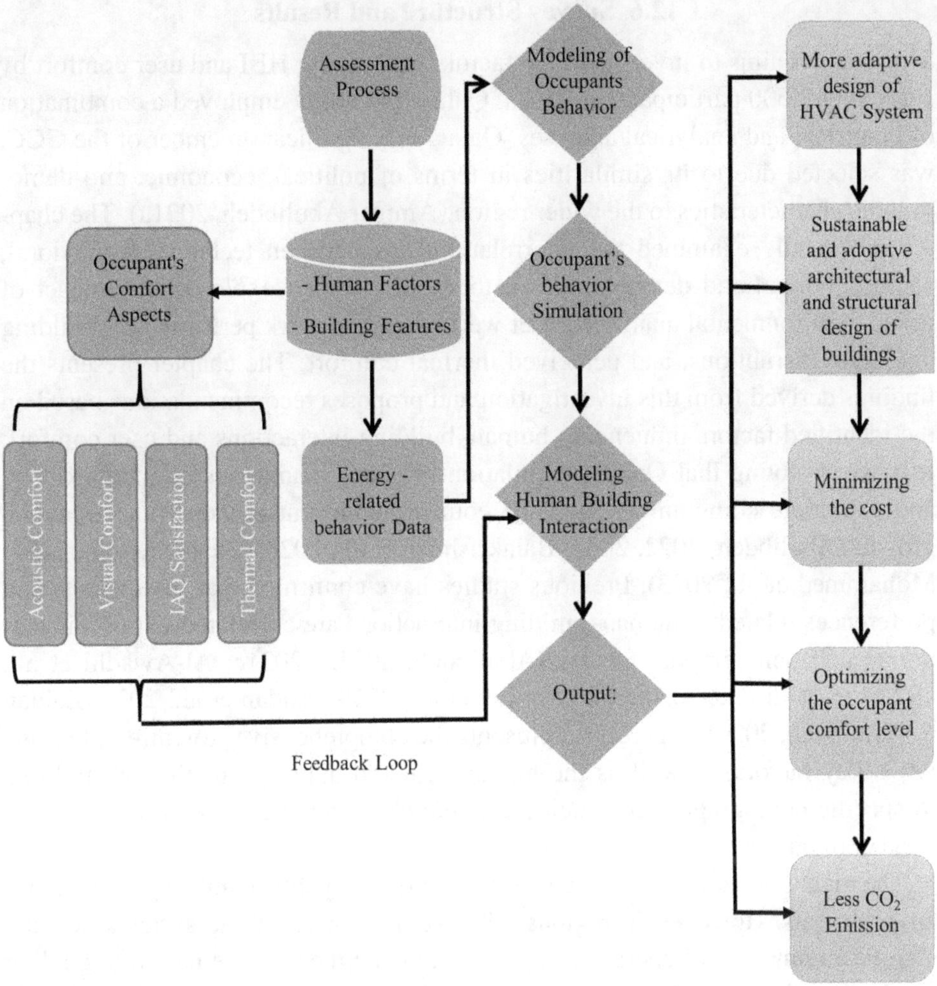

Figure 12.4 Concept mapping for planning human–building interactions.

influencing factors in HBI analysis. For instance, following the implementation of the HBI framework, the Feedback Loop enables the evaluation and comparison of the application and performance of an improved and upgraded HVAC system (as an output approach) under desirable comfort levels, considering various factors such as occupant behavior and building features. This iterative process facilitates the optimization of the occupants' interactions with the building and their environments to achieve optimal comfort. Although CM has been utilized in diverse engineering contexts, to the best of our knowledge, limited work has been conducted using this methodology for the generation of procedures related to the modeling and analysis of HBI.

12.6 Survey Structure and Results

This chapter aims to investigate the factors influencing HBI and user comfort by surveying 2,600 participants in Doha, Qatar. The study employed a combination of empirical and analytical analyses. Qatar, as a significant member of the GCC, was selected due to its similarities in terms of political, economic, and demographic characteristics to the wider region (Ammar Abulibdeh, 2021a). The chapter specifically examined the interrelationships between technical, behavioral, socioeconomic, and demographic factors and HBIs. It explored the impact of indoor environmental quality on user well-being and work performance, building operation disruptions, and perceived thermal comfort. The chapter presents the findings derived from this investigation and proposes recommendations based on the identified factors influencing human–building interactions and user comfort. It is worth noting that Qatar's population primarily comprises migrant workers and expatriate communities, and the country is currently undergoing dynamic growth (Abulibdeh, 2022, 2023; Balakrishnan et al., 2023; Mansour et al., 2022; Mohammed et al., 2023). Previous studies have confirmed that the impacts and preferences related to human–building interactions are correlated with socioeconomic and demographic factors (Abulibdeh, 2021b, 2021c; Al-Awadhi et al., 2022; Al-Saidi & Zaidan, 2020; Sintov et al., 2019; Zaidan et al., 2021; Zaidan & Abulibdeh, 2020). Figure 12.5 presents the comprehensive structure of the survey's key factors, as well as the human-centered applications that are tailored to specific demographic and socioeconomic characteristics of both migrant and local communities within the society.

The main goal of HVAC systems is to ensure occupants' comfort within indoor environments. However, in regions with warm climates, these systems demand significant amounts of energy for operation. Given the variable nature of cooling needs, there is a considerable potential for elevated electricity consumption. This is primarily due to the fact that users' preferences play a substantial role in defining what is considered a comfortable indoor environment. While energy conservation is of utmost importance, it is equally vital to examine its impact on occupant comfort, as it is closely intertwined with their well-being.

In Figure 12.6, the importance of indoor thermal comfort for overall well-being is influenced by factors such as ethnicity, income, and gender. Generally, females tend to prefer a warmer indoor environment to achieve a higher level of comfort at home compared to males (Figure 12.6a). The gender-based categorization demonstrates that women assign greater significance to indoor comfort than men. Categorization by household income level reveals the correlation between income and the importance of comfort and perceived comfort (Figure 12.6b). Additionally, different ethnic groups exhibit varying levels of comfort, with

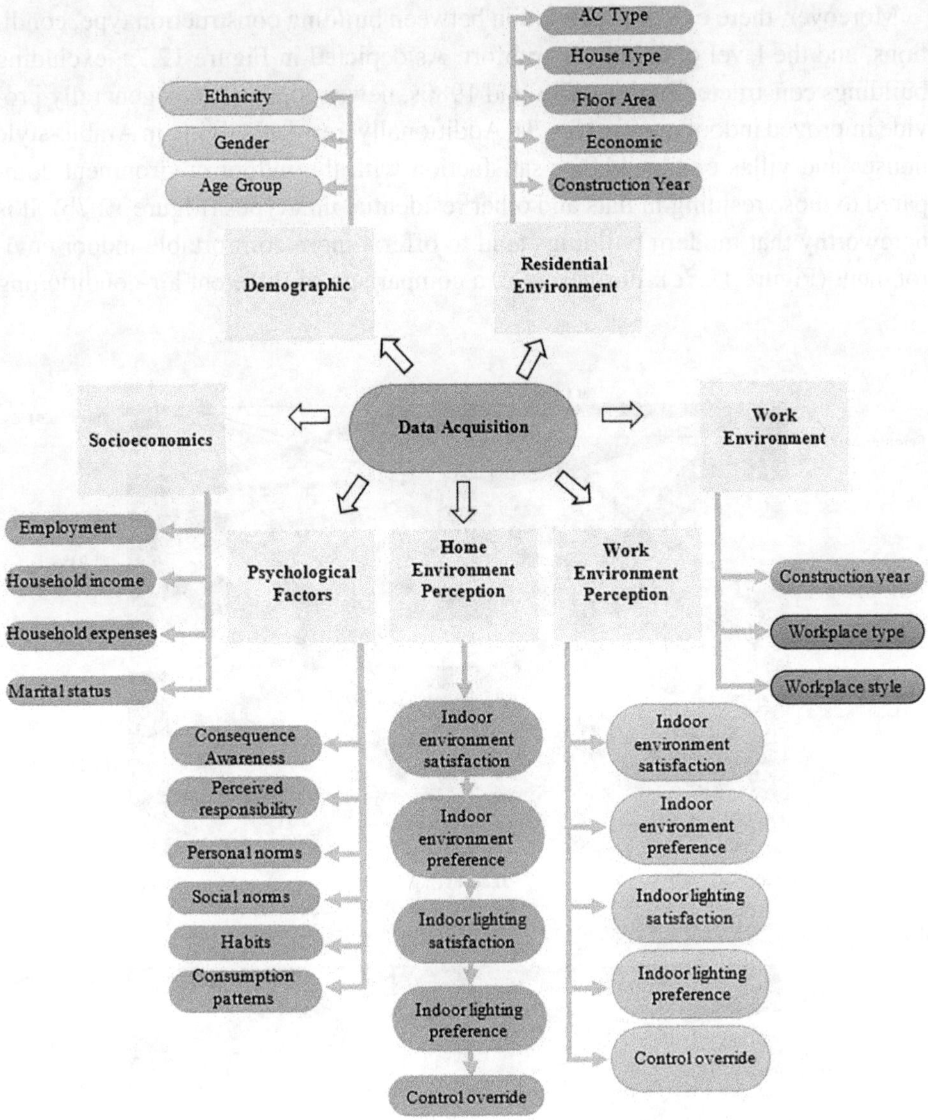

Figure 12.5 The survey framework composed of the data acquisition of human dimensions and building properties.

Arabs, Qataris, and Europeans valuing indoor comfort more than Indians, Asians, and North Americans (Figure 12.6c). This finding suggests the potential to develop electricity pricing plans incorporating financial incentive models that aim to enhance the overall well-being of entire communities. Moreover, penalty factors can be quantified for deviations from comfort and building control regulations, operations, and designs.

Moreover, there exists a correlation between building construction type, conditions, and the level of occupant comfort. As depicted in Figure 12.7a, excluding buildings constructed in the 1970s and 1980s, newer constructions generally provide improved indoor comfort levels. Additionally, residents living in Arabic-style houses and villas exhibit higher satisfaction with the indoor environment compared to those residing in flats and other residential unit types (Figure 12.7b). It is noteworthy that modern buildings tend to offer a more comfortable indoor environment (Figure 12.7c). Furthermore, a comparison of different air-conditioning

(a)

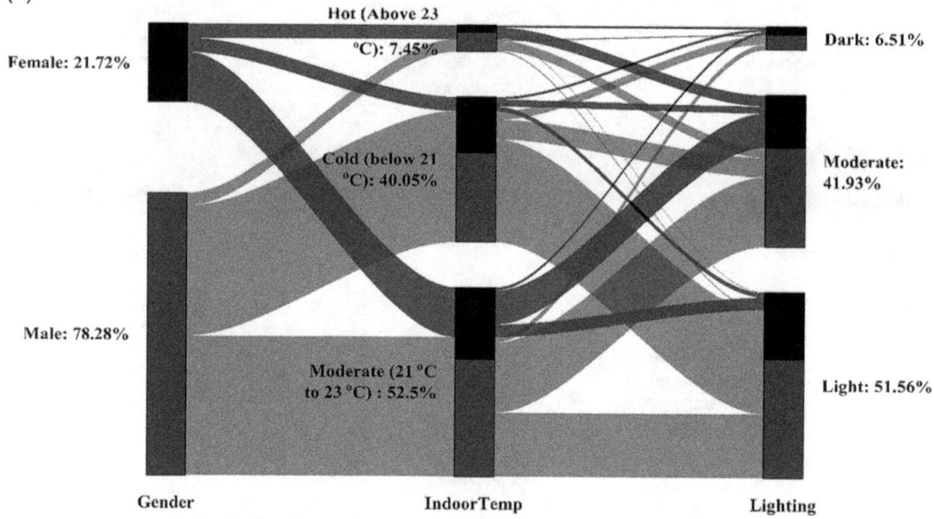

(b)

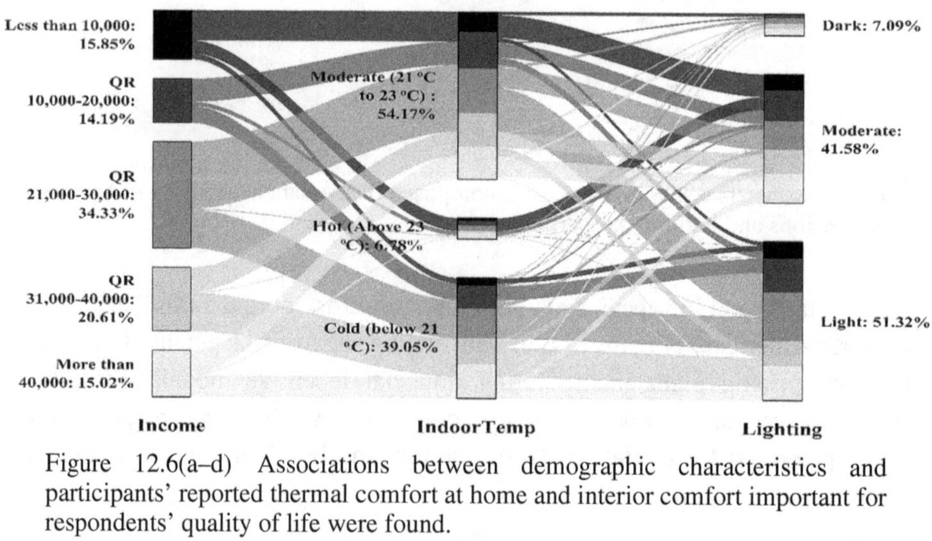

Figure 12.6(a–d) Associations between demographic characteristics and participants' reported thermal comfort at home and interior comfort important for respondents' quality of life were found.

(c)

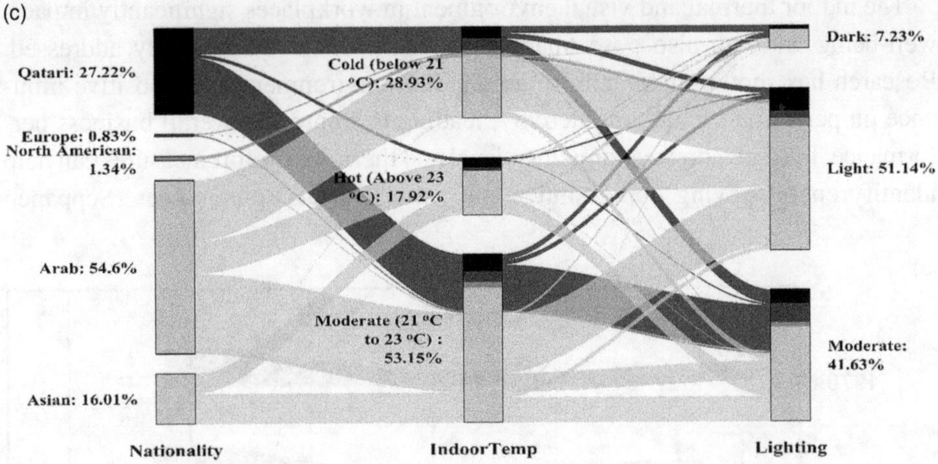

(d)

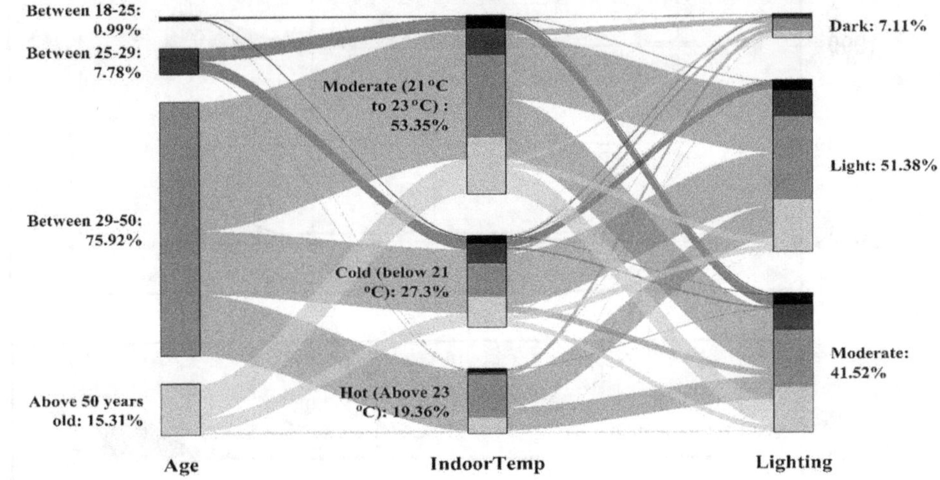

Figure 12.6(a–d) (cont.)

systems reveals that wall-mounted units and central ducted systems contribute to higher indoor comfort levels than ceiling fans and window air conditioners (Figure 12.7d). In summary, a comprehensive investigation of the aforementioned factors, along with human factors, is crucial in exploring human–building interactions within residential systems. For instance, offering energy efficiency incentives and retrofitting programs can be considered to improve the overall well-being of society while simultaneously enhancing energy efficiency indicators by ensuring minimal comfort levels (and consequently minimizing energy inefficiencies).

The indoor thermal and visual environment in workplaces significantly impacts well-being and can also pose financial challenges if not adequately addressed. Research has shown that a comfortable indoor environment has a positive influence on performance and productivity, leading to improved overall business performance. Furthermore, customizing visual and thermal comfort measures can help identify energy-saving opportunities and cater to users' preferences (Seppänen

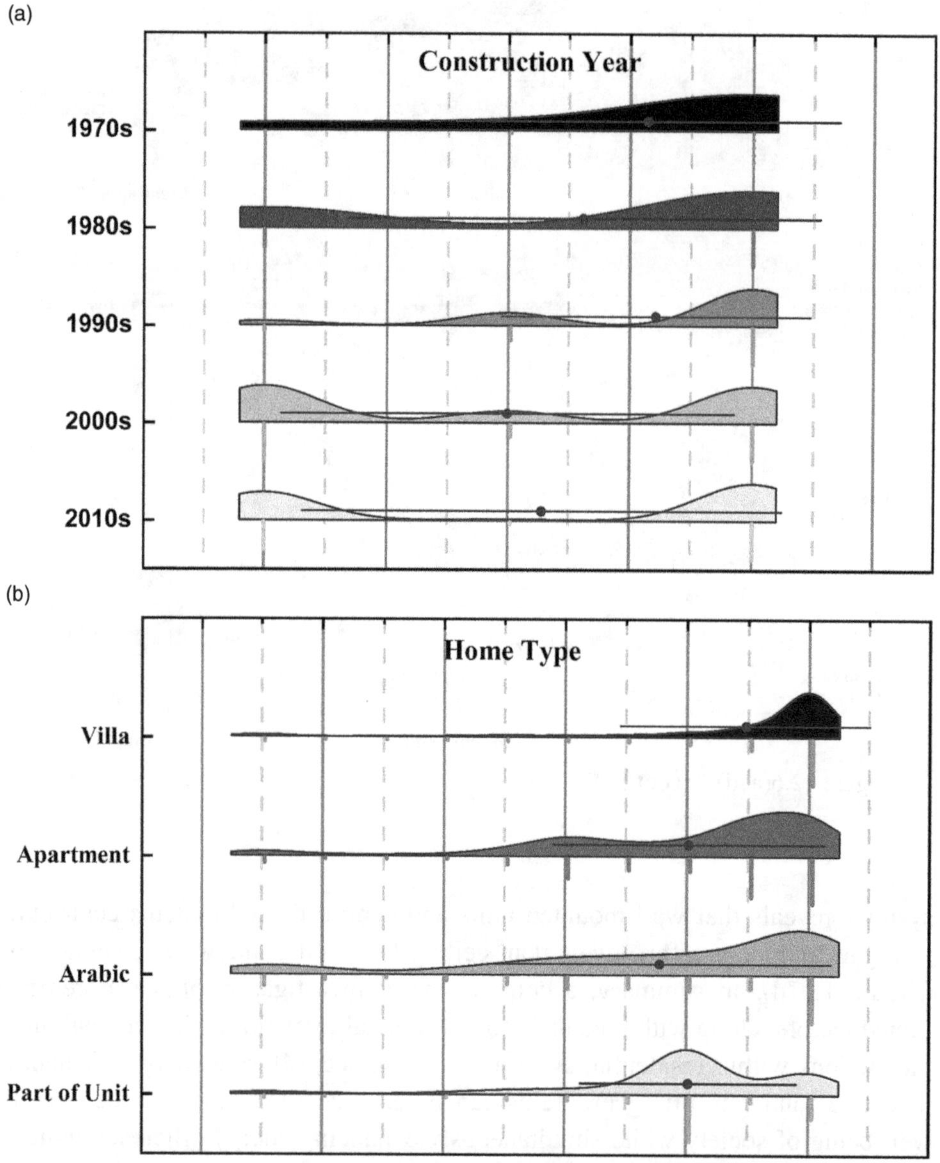

Figure 12.7(a–d) Correlation between dwelling characteristics and perceived thermal comfort at home. Analysis of thermal comfort in workplaces.

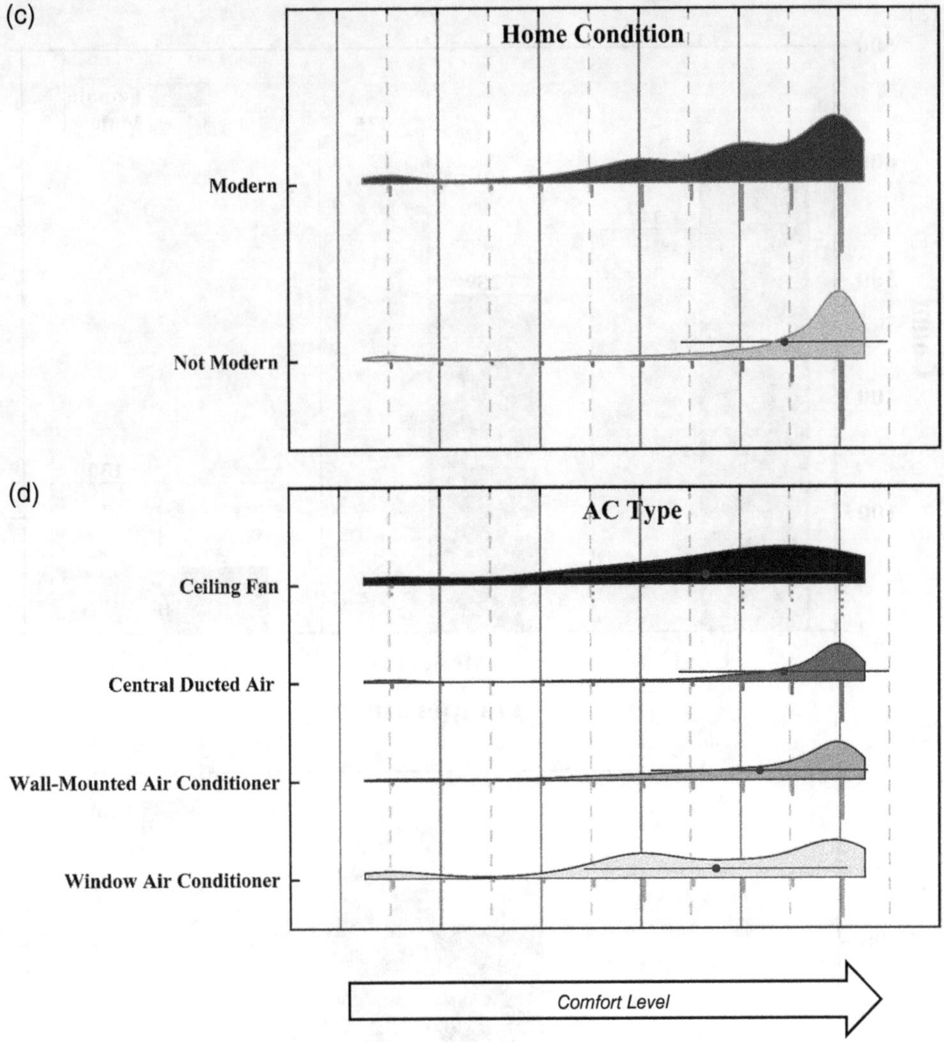

Figure 12.7(a–d) (cont.)

et al., 2006). Figure 12.8 illustrates the considerable influence of gender and ethnic groups on perceived comfort in the indoor environment. Women tend to find colder temperatures (below 22°C) more comfortable, while men prefer moderate indoor temperatures (22°C to 24°C). Similarly, Asian ethnic groups express a preference for warmer indoor environments, while North Americans and Arabs lean towards colder temperatures. Additionally, preferences regarding lighting systems were explored, revealing that Asians generally prefer a brighter working space. Figure 12.9 presents patterns of human–building interactions, indicating that Asians tend to adjust thermostat settings at work, in contrast to female respondents. These

(a)

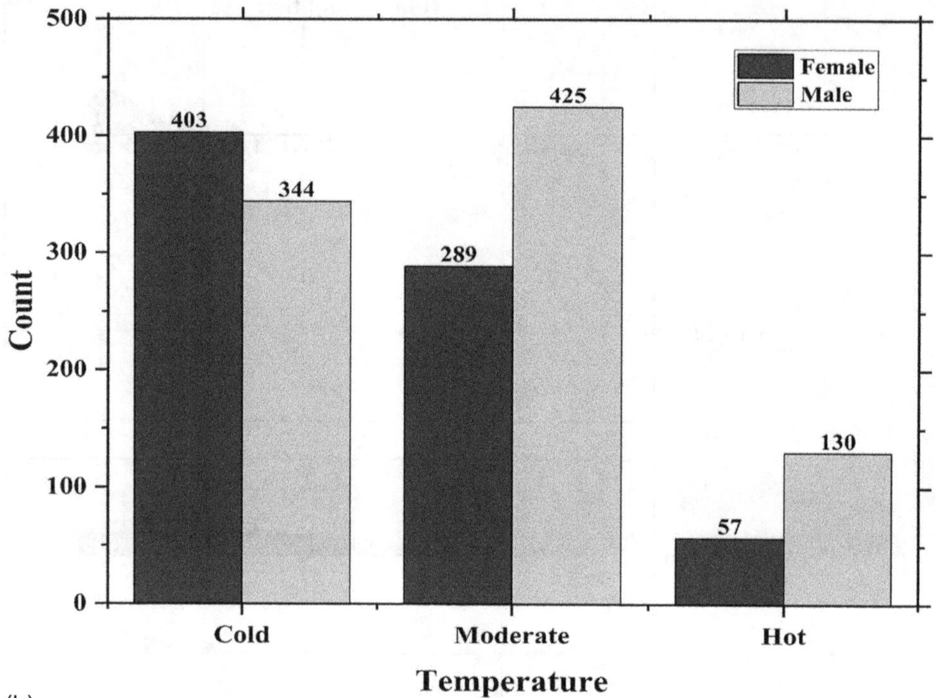

(b)

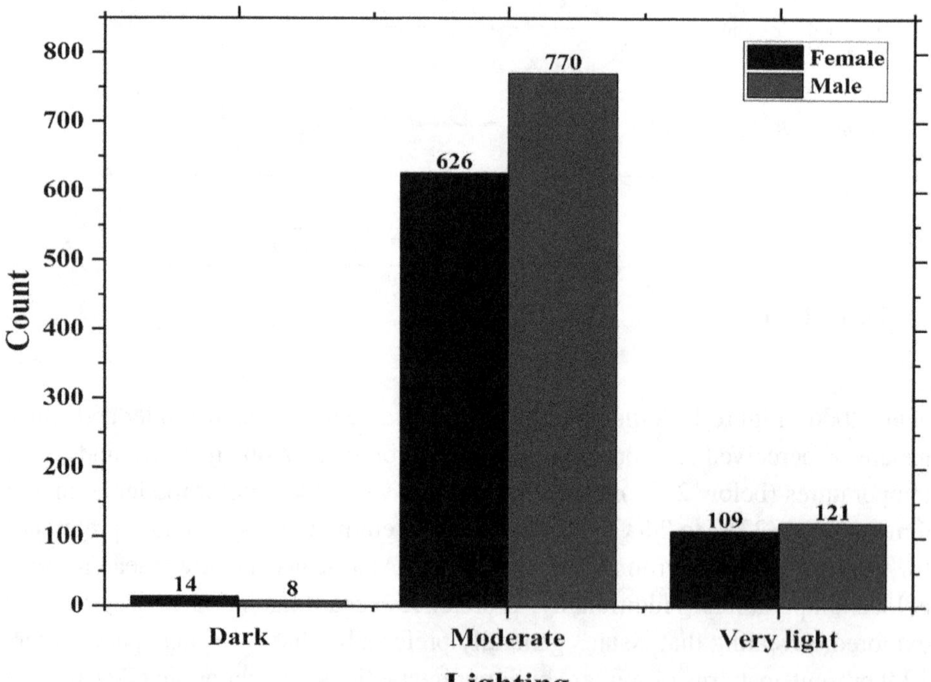

Figure 12.8(a–d) Intercorrelations between demographic characteristics and workplace interior environment user preferences.

(c)

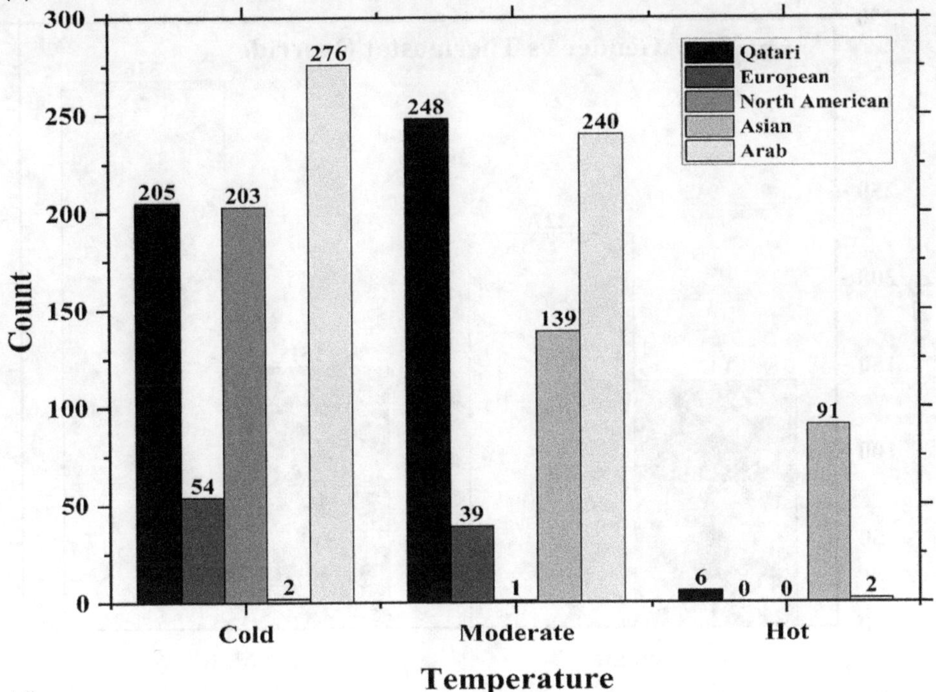

(d)

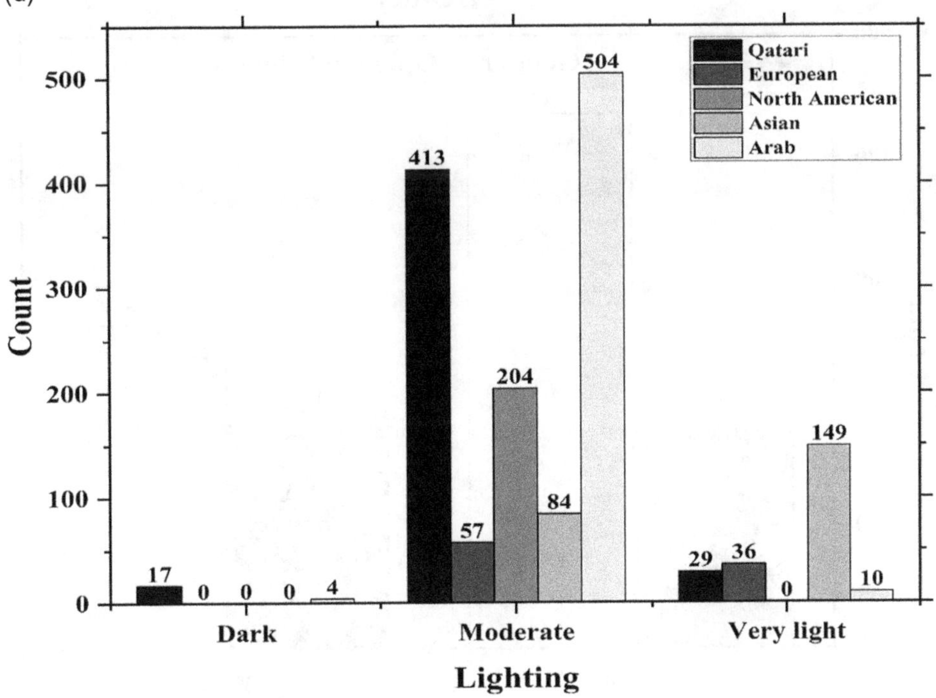

Figure 12.8(a–d) (cont.)

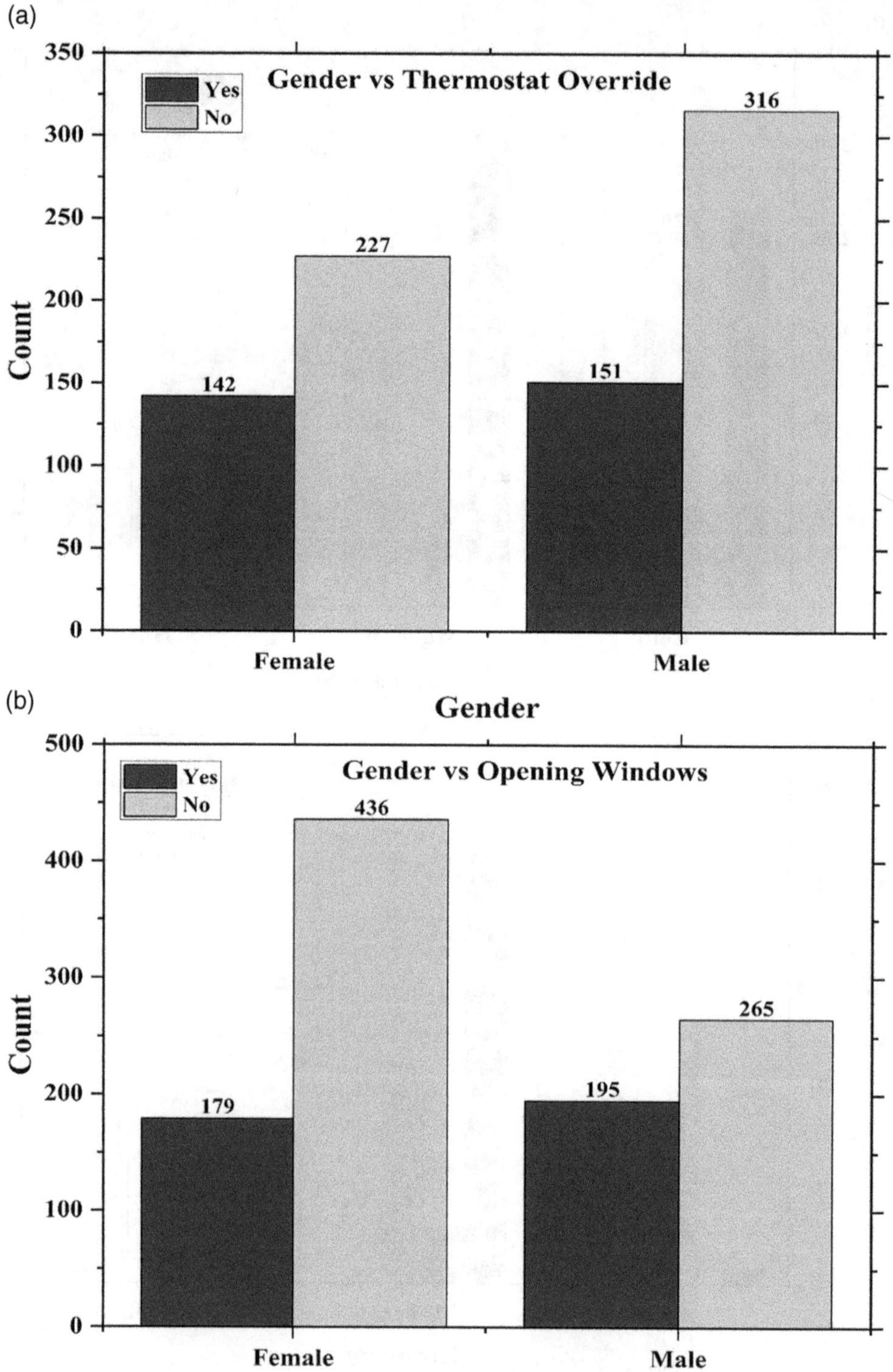

Figure 12.9(a–d) Intercorrelations between demographic characteristics and building–user interactions.

(c)

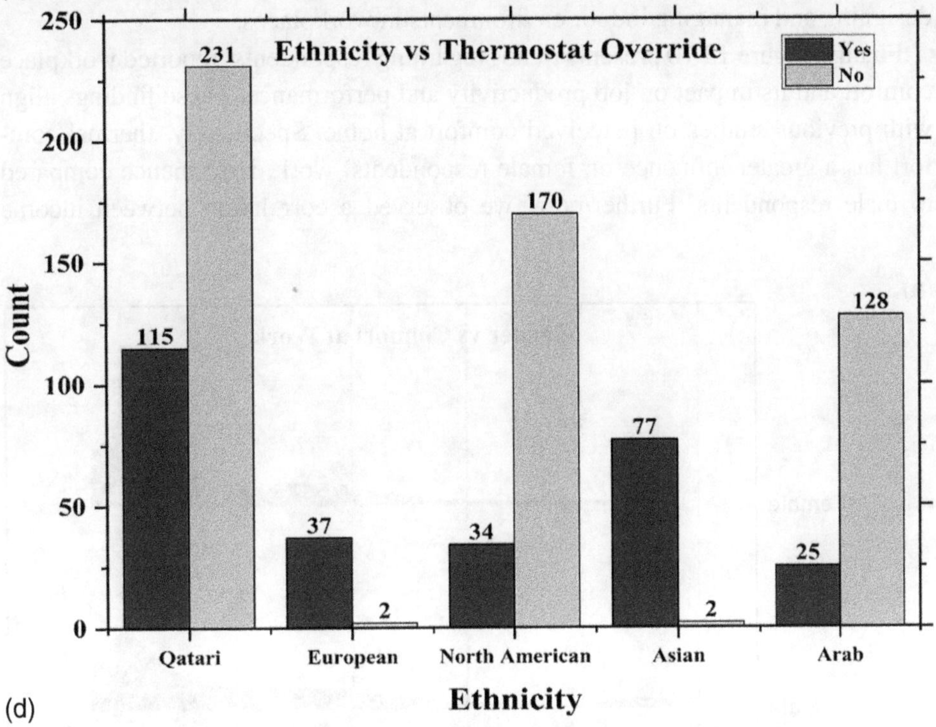

(d)

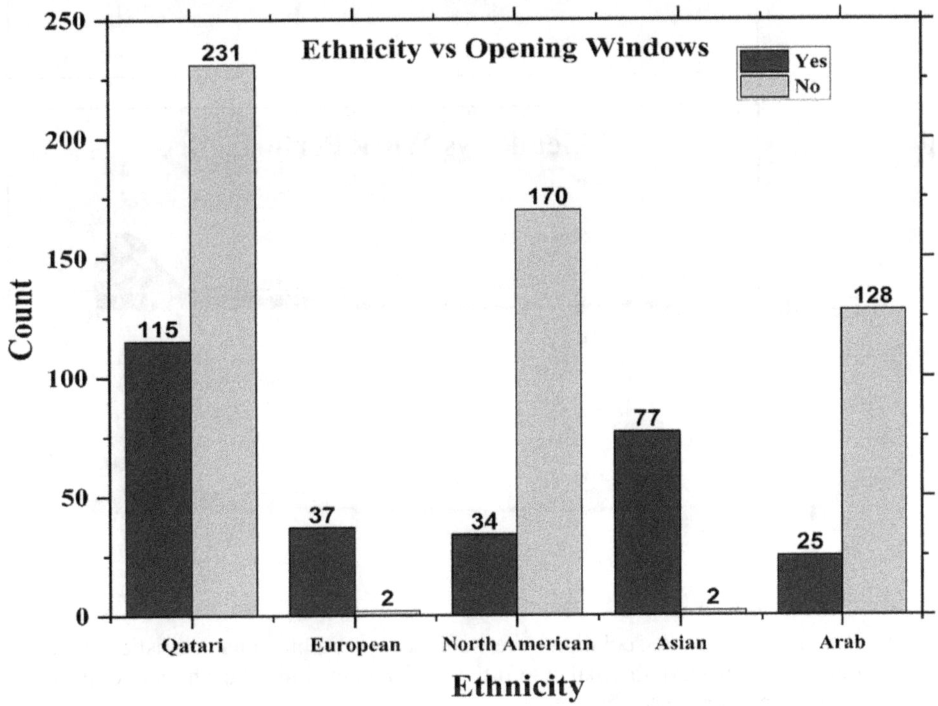

Figure 12.9(a–d) (cont.)

findings emphasize the need to consider cultural and gender-related factors when designing and managing indoor environments in workplaces.

Finally, Figure 12.10 presents trends regarding respondents' reported workplace comfort and its impact on job productivity and performance. These findings align with previous studies on perceived comfort at home. Specifically, thermal comfort has a greater influence on female respondents' work performance compared to male respondents. Furthermore, we observed a correlation between income

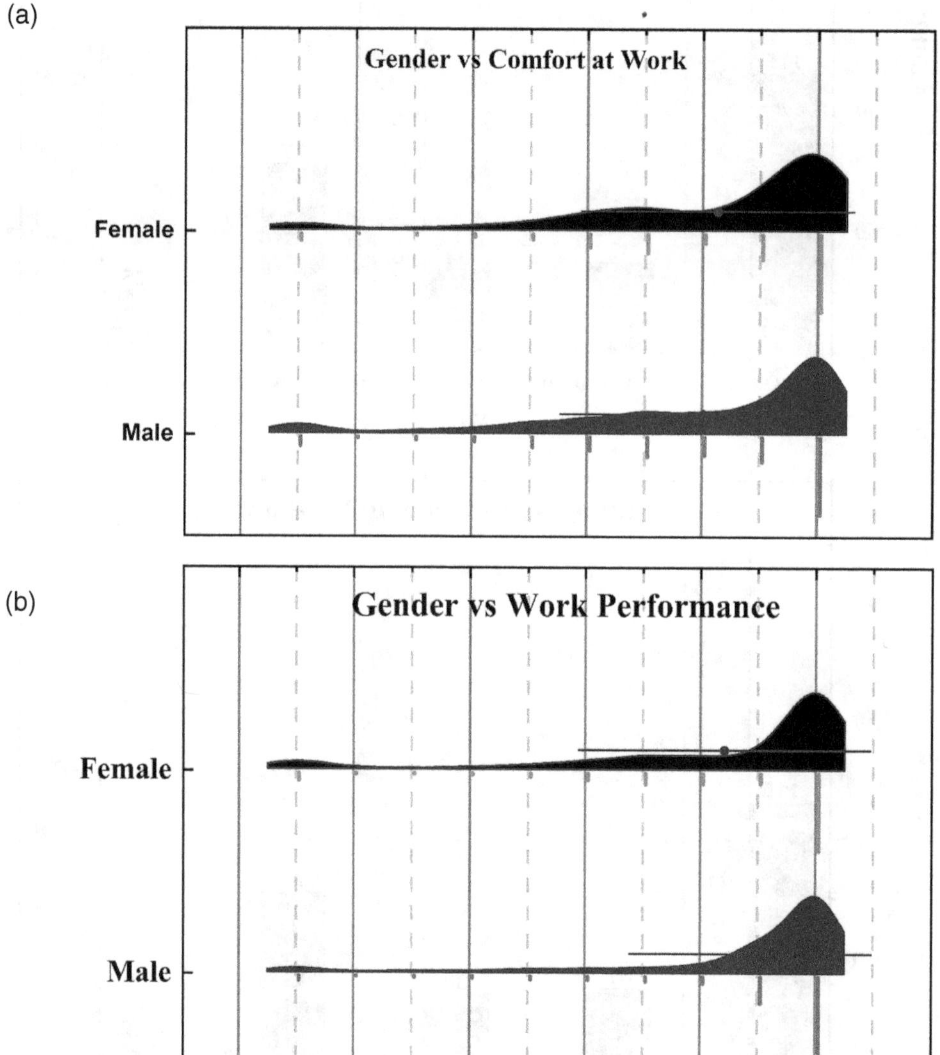

Figure 12.10(a–f) Associations between demographic characteristics and participants' subjective thermal comfort at work and the impact of indoor comfort on respondent work performance.

(c)

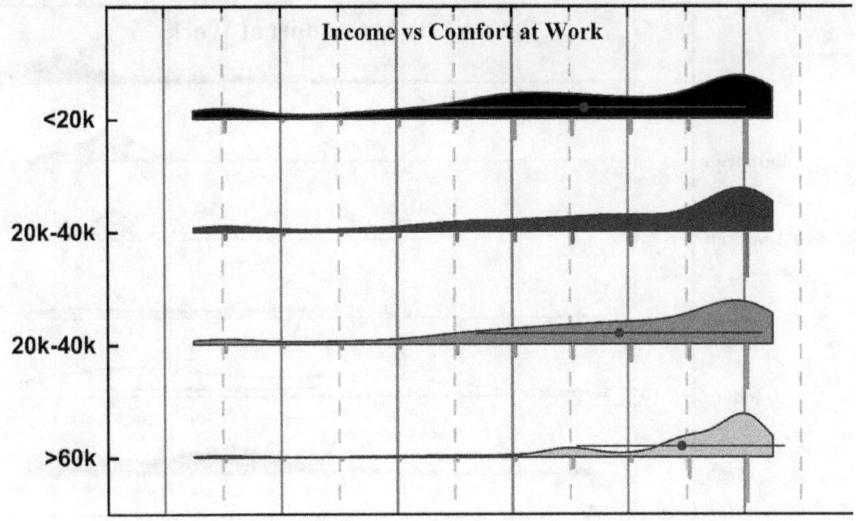

(d)

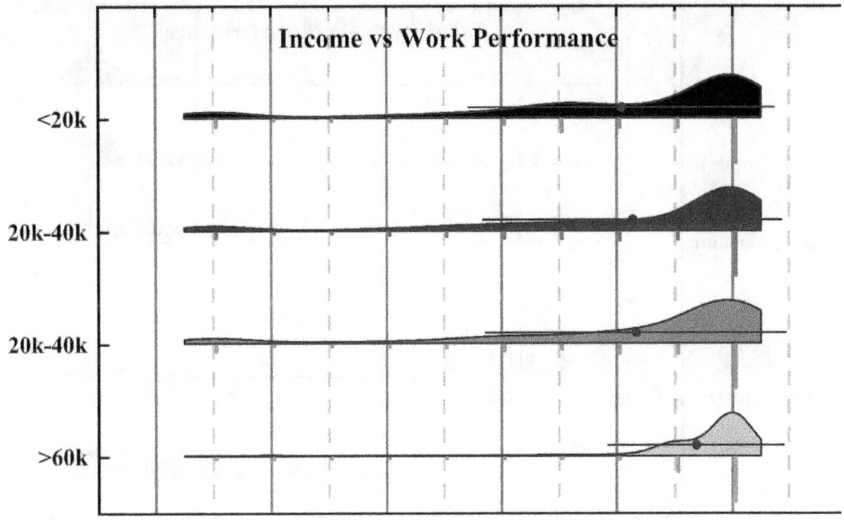

Figure 12.10(a–f) (cont.)

and its influence on productivity and perceived workplace comfort. For instance, thermal comfort is less crucial for Asian and Indian productivity, even though they reported experiencing less comfort at work. In Figure 12.11, we explore the correlations between human–building interactions and indoor environment preferences with perceived comfort levels at work. The results indicate that respondents who prefer a hotter indoor environment are more likely to experience discomfort. Additionally, respondents who frequently open windows and override the thermostat tend to have higher levels of thermal discomfort. These findings highlight the

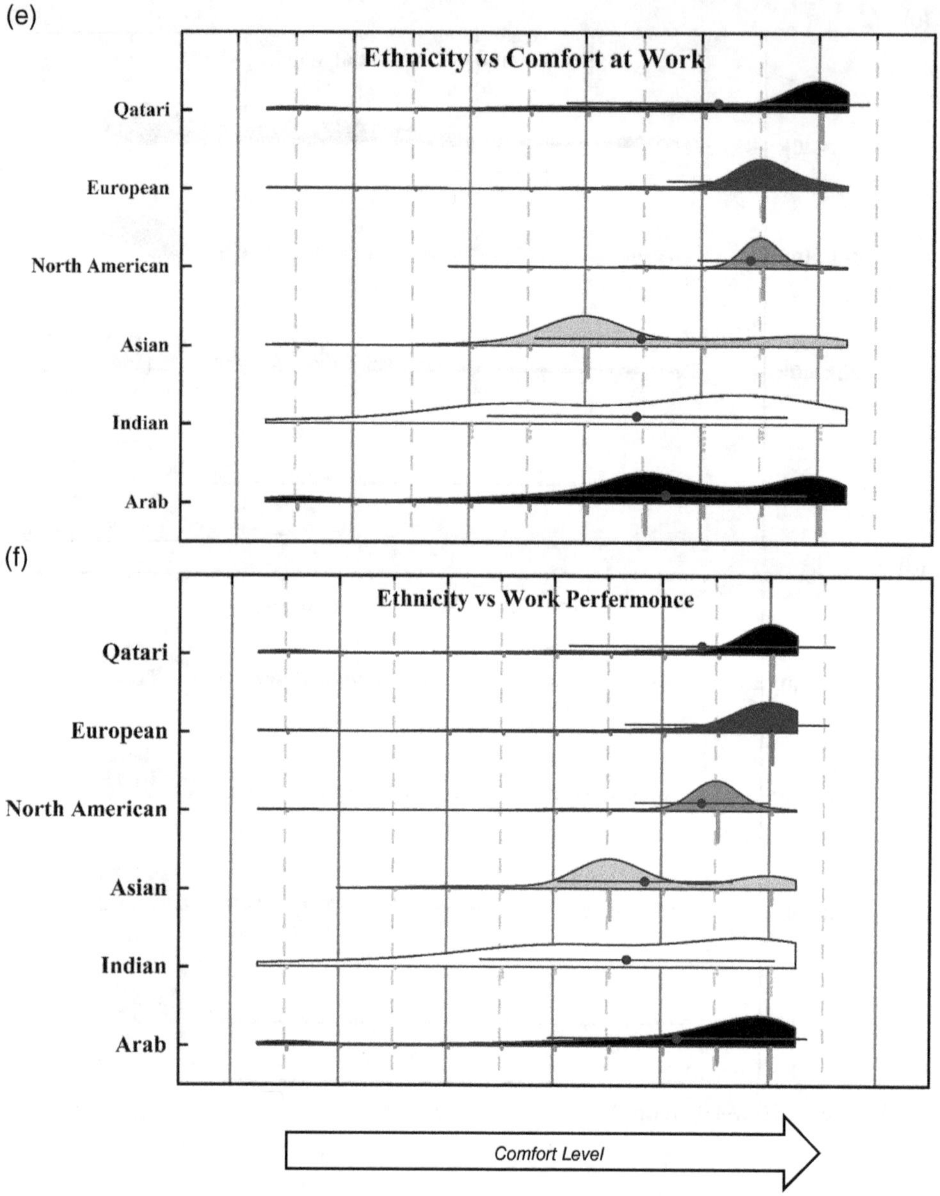

Figure 12.10(a–f) (cont.)

significance of thermal comfort in mitigating negative human disruptions. Figure 12.12 illustrates the impact of building construction and features on perceived comfort levels. Notably, individuals working in personal offices reported a higher level of comfort compared to those in open office settings. This emphasizes the importance of considering the design and features of the workspace when aiming to enhance perceived comfort levels at work.

In summary, the survey results revealed several significant findings. Gender differences were observed, with men demonstrating a better understanding of HVAC systems and more effective regulation of thermal comfort compared to women.

(a)

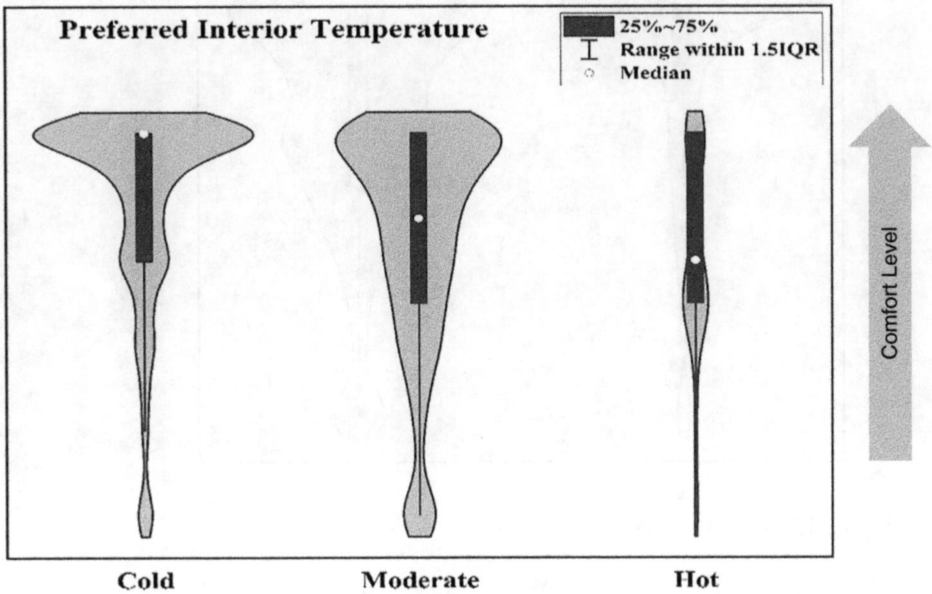

(b)

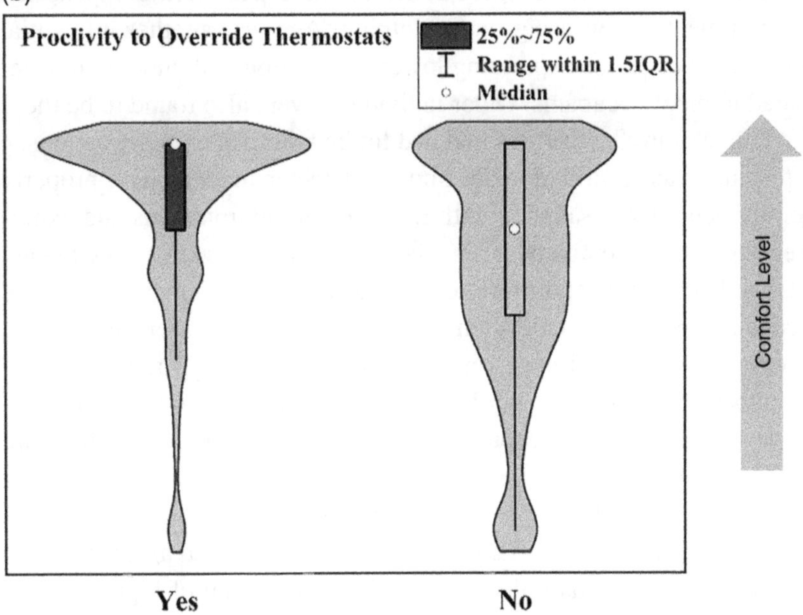

Figure 12.11(a–c) Relationship between respondents' perceived comfort and (a) preferred interior temperature, (b) proclivity to override thermostats, and (c) proclivity to open windows.

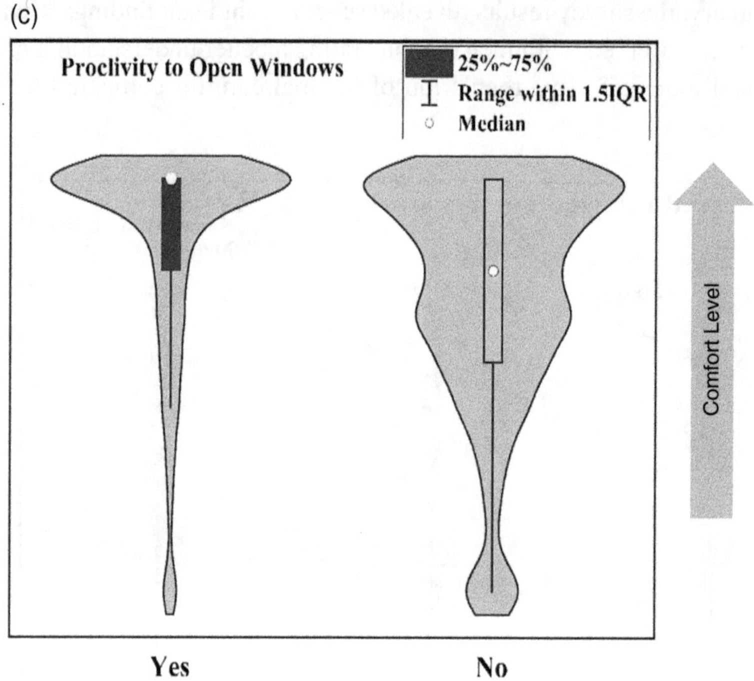

Figure 12.11(a–c) (cont.)

Women were found to be more sensitive to temperature and often compensated for colder environments by wearing more clothing. Age was another influential factor, with younger occupants expressing lower satisfaction with indoor environments compared to older occupants. Older individuals were also found to be more susceptible to temperature fluctuations and had limited thermal comfort options.

Ownership status was identified as an important factor in HBI, with property owners generally being more satisfied with their indoor environments and exhibiting a greater degree of receptiveness. Psychological factors, such as occupants' living conditions, knowledge, and lifestyle, were also found to play a crucial role in HBI. Occupants' psychological strain was shown to affect their acceptance and reactivity to acoustic conditions. Environmental factors were found to have a significant impact on HBI. The outdoor environment, including temperature and humidity levels, influenced occupants' thermal needs and indoor temperature adjustments. The visual and acoustical environments were also found to affect comfort levels, with low levels of noise and ambient light enhancing performance and comfort. Indoor lighting levels were associated with improved air acceptance, and air quality acceptability was influenced by the introduction of high levels of noise in polluted environments.

(a)

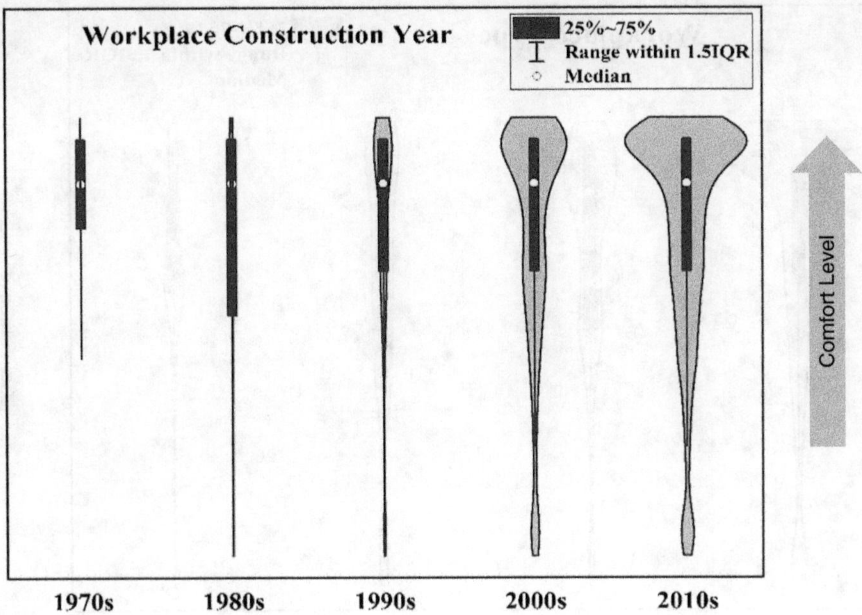

(b)

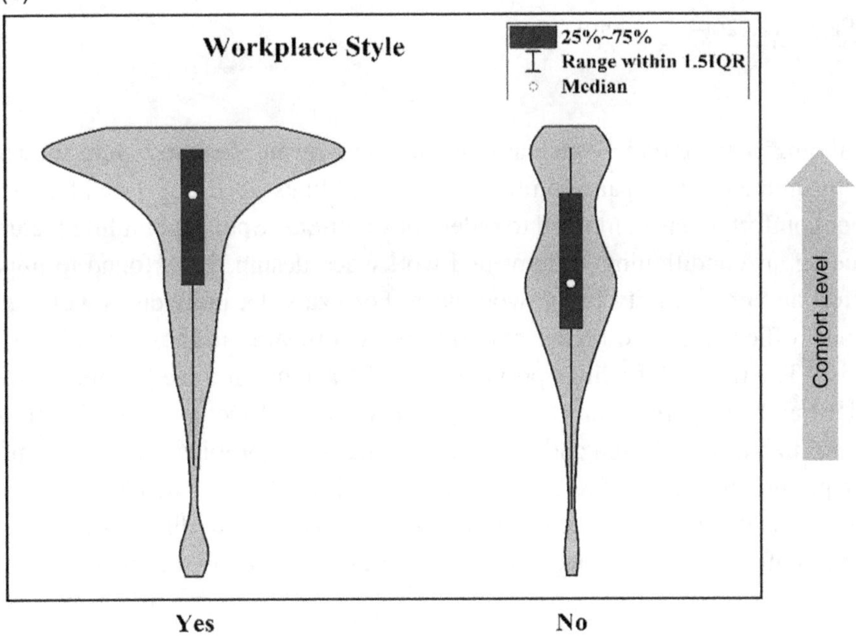

Figure 12.12(a–c) Relationship between the respondents' perceived comfort and (a) workplace construction year, (b) workplace style, and (c) workplace type.

(c)

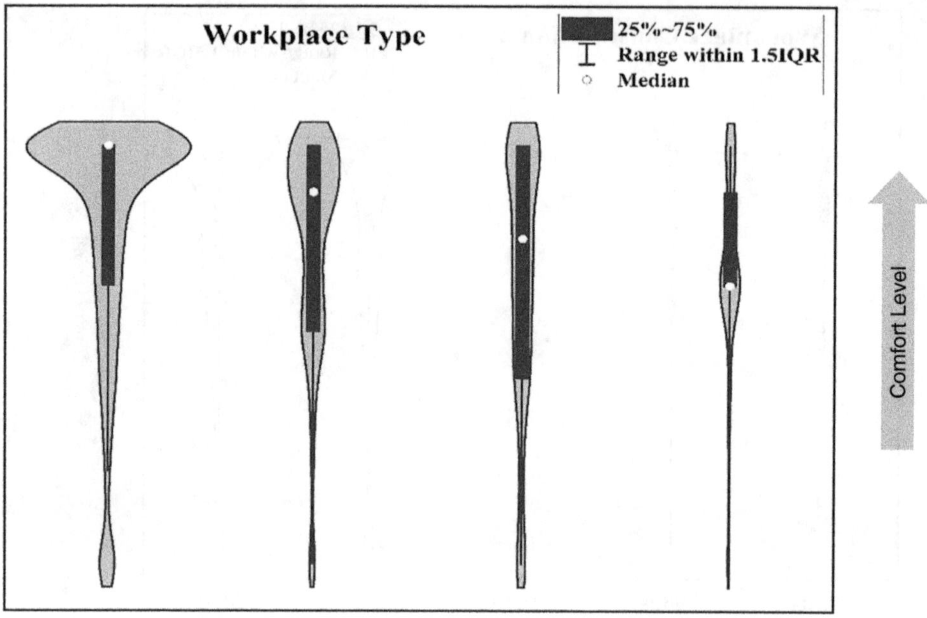

Personal office **Shared office** **Open office** **Cubicle office**

Figure 12.12(a–c) (cont.)

Building characteristics, such as construction type and features, were shown to directly influence occupant comfort. Newer buildings generally provided better indoor comfort levels compared to older constructions. Specific building features, including air-conditioning systems and workspace design, were found to impact comfort and productivity in the workplace. For example, individuals working in personal offices reported higher comfort levels compared to those in open office settings. The research findings provide valuable insights into the factors influencing HBI and occupant comfort in the specific context of Doha, Qatar. The results can inform building design and operation strategies to optimize occupant comfort while promoting energy efficiency. Designers and construction managers can consider occupant characteristics, environmental factors, and building features to prioritize comfort factors and create more comfortable and energy-efficient buildings.

12.7 Conclusion

The initiative to achieve net zero and carbon-neutral buildings is gaining momentum worldwide. However, a significant gap exists in understanding the role of occupant–building interactions in achieving sustainable outcomes. While studies often focus on technological advancements, they tend to overlook how people use and interact with these technologies. This chapter addresses this gap by emphasizing the importance of occupant–building interactions as a key element in the transition to net zero and carbon-neutral buildings. This chapter has shed light on the crucial role of human–building interaction and occupant behavior in the transition towards carbon-neutral buildings and communities. While technological advancements are important, achieving carbon neutrality goes beyond just implementing energy-efficient systems and technologies. It requires a comprehensive understanding of the human and social dimensions involved in building design, operation, and occupant comfort.

By examining the factors influencing HBI and occupant comfort, this chapter has emphasized the need to prioritize occupant behavior, environmental factors, and building characteristics in achieving sustainable outcomes. The survey conducted in Doha, Qatar, has provided valuable insights into the specific influences on HBI, such as gender differences, age, ownership status, psychological factors, and building features. These findings highlight the importance of considering the diversity of occupants and their specific needs and preferences in designing carbon-neutral buildings. Furthermore, the conceptual framework and concept mapping approach presented in this chapter offer a systematic and holistic approach to understanding the complex interactions within HBI. By considering the interplay between environmental factors, building attributes, and occupant characteristics, it becomes possible to optimize occupant comfort and energy efficiency in buildings. This approach supports the development of targeted strategies and interventions that can enhance the efficiency of energy policies and sustainability performance indicators.

In the context of carbon neutrality, the findings of this chapter have important implications for the Gulf States and other regions aiming to achieve sustainable development. The integration of innovation and technological advancements, supported by national innovation systems, is crucial in driving the transition to carbon-neutral buildings and communities. By investing in clean energy technologies, fostering entrepreneurship and startups in the clean energy sector, and promoting collaboration and knowledge exchange, the Gulf States can accelerate the adoption of sustainable energy solutions and address regional challenges while aligning with global sustainability goals.

Ultimately, the transition to carbon-neutral buildings and communities requires a multidimensional approach that considers not only technological advancements but also the human and social dimensions of sustainability. By prioritizing occupant behavior, environmental factors, and building characteristics, and by leveraging concepts such as concept mapping, it is possible to design and operate buildings that achieve carbon neutrality while providing optimal occupant comfort and well-being. This chapter serves as a foundation for further research and the development of targeted strategies to facilitate the transition towards a sustainable and carbon-neutral future.

References

Abulibdeh, A. (2021a). Analysis of urban heat island characteristics and mitigation strategies for eight arid and semi-arid gulf region cities. *Environmental Earth Sciences* 80, Article 259. Doi.org/10.1007/s12665-021-09540-7.

Abulibdeh, A. (2021b). Modeling electricity consumption patterns during the COVID-19 pandemic across six socioeconomic sectors in the State of Qatar. *Energy Strategy Reviews* 38, p. 100733. Doi.org/10.1016/J.ESR.2021.100733.

Abulibdeh, A. (2021c). Spatiotemporal analysis of water-electricity consumption in the context of the COVID-19 pandemic across six socioeconomic sectors in Doha City, Qatar. *Applied Energy* 304, p. 117864. Doi.org/10.1016/J.APENERGY.2021.117864.

Abulibdeh, A. (2022). Time series analysis of environmental quality in the state of Qatar. *Energy Policy* 168, p. 113089. Doi.org/10.1016/J.ENPOL.2022.113089.

Abulibdeh, A. (2023). Analysis of mode choice affects from the introduction of Doha Metro using machine learning and statistical analysis. *Transportation Research Interdisciplinary Perspectives* 20, p. 100852. Doi.org/10.1016/J.TRIP.2023.100852.

Abulibdeh, A., Zaidan, E., and Al-Saidi, M. (2019). Development drivers of the water–energy–food nexus in the Gulf Cooperation Council region. *Development in Practice* 29 (5), pp. 582–593. Doi.org/10.1080/09614524.2019.1602109.

Abulibdeh, Ammar, Zaidan, E., and Jabbar, R. (2022). The impact of COVID-19 pandemic on electricity consumption and electricity demand forecasting accuracy: Empirical evidence from the state of Qatar. *Energy Strategy Reviews* 44, p. 100980. Doi.org/10.1016/J.ESR.2022.100980.

Abulibdeh, A., Jawarneh, R. N., Al-Awadhi, T., Abdullah, M. M., Abulibdeh, R., and El Kenawy, A. M. (2024). Assessment of carbon footprint in Qatar's electricity sector: A comparative analysis across various building typologies. *Renewable and Sustainable Energy Reviews* 189, Part A, p. 114022. Doi.org/10.1016/J.RSER.2023.114022.

Al-Awadhi, T., Abulibdeh, A., Al-Masri, A. N., Bin Touq, A., Al-Barawni, M., and El Kenawy, A. M. (2022). Spatial and temporal changes in electricity demand regulatory during pandemic periods: the case of COVID-19 in Doha, Qatar. *Energy Strategy Reviews* 41, p. 100826. Doi.org/10.1016/J.ESR.2022.100826.

Al-Saidi, M., and Zaidan, E. (2020). Gulf futuristic cities beyond the headlines: Understanding the planned cities megatrend. *Energy Reports* 6, pp. 114–121. Doi.org/10.1016/J.EGYR.2020.10.061.

Alabi, T. M., Aghimien, E. I., Agbajor, F. D., Yang, Z., Lu, L., Adeoye, A. R., and Gopaluni, B. (2022). A review on the integrated optimization techniques and machine learning approaches for modeling, prediction, and decision making on integrated energy systems. *Renewable Energy* 194, pp. 822–849. Doi.org/10.1016/J.RENENE.2022.05.123.

Andargie, M. S., Touchie, M., and O'Brien, W. (2019). A review of factors affecting occupant comfort in multi-unit residential buildings. *Building and Environment* 160, p. 106182. Doi.org/10.1016/j.buildenv.2019.106182.

Angizeh, F., Ghofrani, A., Zaidan, E., and Jafari, M. A. (2021). Resilience-oriented behind-the-meter energy storage system evaluation for mission-critical facilities. *IEEE Access*. Doi.org/10.1109/ACCESS.2021.3085410.

Balakrishnan, P., Abulibdeh, A., Abul, K., and Kabir, T. (2023). Assessment of the impact of anthropogenic evolution and natural processes on Shoreline Dynamics Using Multi-Temporal Satellite Images and Statistical Analysis. *Water 2023* 15 (8), p. 1440. Doi .org/10.3390/W15081440.

Bennet, I. E., and O'Brien, W. (2016). Field study of thermal comfort and occupant satisfaction in Canadian condominiums. *Architectural Science Review* 60 (1), pp. 27–39. Doi.org/10.1080/00038628.2016.1205179.

Bodin Danielsson, C., Chungkham, H. S., Wulff, C., and Westerlund, H. (2014). Office design's impact on sick leave rates. *Ergonomics* 57 (2), pp. 139–147. Doi.org/10.1080/00140139.2013.871064/SUPPL_FILE/TERG_A_871064_SM0001.JPG.

Boerstra, A. C., Kulve, M. te, Toftum, J., Loomans, M. G. L. C., Olesen, B. W., and Hensen, J. L. M. (2015). Comfort and performance impact of personal control over thermal environment in summer: Results from a laboratory study. *Building and Environment* 87, pp. 315–326. Doi.org/10.1016/J.BUILDENV.2014.12.022.

Chan, E. H. W., Lam, K. S., and Wong, W. S. (2008). Evaluation on indoor environment quality of dense urban residential buildings. *Journal of Facilities Management* 6 (4), pp. 245–265. Doi.org/10.1108/14725960810908127/FULL/PDF.

Charfeddine, L., Zaidan, E., Alban, A. Q., Bennasr, H., and Abulibdeh, A. (2023). Modeling and forecasting electricity consumption amid the COVID-19 pandemic: Machine learning vs. nonlinear econometric time series models. *Sustainable Cities and Society* 98, p. 104860. Doi.org/10.1016/J.SCS.2023.104860.

Chen, S., Liu, J., Zhang, Q., Teng, F., and McLellan, B. C. (2022). A critical review on deployment planning and risk analysis of carbon capture, utilization, and storage (CCUS) toward carbon neutrality. *Renewable and Sustainable Energy Reviews* 167, p. 112537. Doi.org/10.1016/J.RSER.2022.112537.

Choi, J. H., and Yeom, D. (2019). Development of the data-driven thermal satisfaction prediction model as a function of human physiological responses in a built environment. *Building and Environment* 150, pp. 206–218. Doi.org/10.1016/J .BUILDENV.2019.01.007.

Christensen, J. M., and Olhoff, A. (eds.) (2019). Lessons from a Decade of Emissions Gap Assessments. Nairobi: United Nations, Environment Programme. Available online: www.un.org/Depts/.

Cureau, R. J., Pigliautile, I., Pisello, A. L., Bavaresco, M., Berger, C., Chinazzo, G., Deme Belafi, Z., Ghahramani, A., Heydarian, A., Kastner, D., Kong, M., Licina, D., Luna-Navarro, A., Mahdavi, A., Nocente, A., Schweiker, M., Vellei, M., and Wang, A. (2022). Bridging the gap from test rooms to field-tests for human indoor comfort studies: A critical review of the sustainability potential of living laboratories. *Energy Research & Social Science* 92, p. 102778. Doi.org/10.1016/J.ERSS.2022.102778.

D'Oca, S., and Hong, T. (2014). A data-mining approach to discover patterns of window opening and closing behavior in offices. *Building and Environment* 82, pp. 726–739. Doi.org/10.1016/J.BUILDENV.2014.10.021.

D'Oca, S., and Hong, T. (2015). Occupancy schedules learning process through a data mining framework. *Energy and Buildings* 88, pp. 395–408. Doi.org/10.1016/J .ENBUILD.2014.11.065.

D'Oca, S., Corgnati, S. P., and Buso, T. (2014). Smart meters and energy savings in Italy: Determining the effectiveness of persuasive communication in dwellings. *Energy Research & Social Science* 3 (C), pp. 131–142. Doi.org/10.1016/J.ERSS.2014.07.015.

Dahlan, N. D. (2013). Perceptive-cognitive aspects investigation in relation to indoor environment satisfaction collected from naturally ventilated multi-storey student accommodations in Malaysia. *Indoor and Built Environment* 24 (1), pp. 116–127. Doi.org/10.11 77/1420326X13506449.

Dahlan, N. D., Jones, P. J., Alexander, D. K., Salleh, E., and Alias, J. (2009). Evidence base prioritisation of indoor comfort perceptions in Malaysian typical multi-storey hostels. *Building and Environment* 44 (10), pp. 2158–2165. Doi.org/10.1016/J.BUILDENV.2009.03.010.

Davoodi, F., Hassanzadeh, H., Zolfaghari, S. A., Havenith, G., and Maerefat, M. (2018). A new individualized thermoregulatory bio-heat model for evaluating the effects of personal characteristics on human body thermal response. *Building and Environment* 136, pp. 62–76. Doi.org/10.1016/J.BUILDENV.2018.03.026.

Deme Belafi, Z., Hong, T., and Reith, A. (2019). A library of building occupant behaviour models represented in a standardised schema. *Energy Efficiency* 12 (3), pp. 637–651. Doi.org/10.1007/S12053-018-9658-0/TABLES/2.

Ehrhardt-Martinez, K. (2013). Behavior wedge profiles for cities: a new tool for identifying opportunities and targeting behavioral programs. Behavior, Energy and Climate Change Conference, Berkeley, University of California. Available online: https://escholarship.org/uc/item/9gh2g6x2.

Elessawy, F., and Zaidan, E. (2014). Living in the move: Impact of guest workers on population characteristics of the United Arab Emirates (UAE). *Arab World Geographer* 17 (1), pp. 2–23. Doi.org/10.5555/ARWG.17.1.04502312V8G83U76.

Foster, M., and Oreszczyn, T. (2001). Occupant control of passive systems: The use of Venetian blinds. *Building and Environment* 36(2), 149–155. Doi.org/10.1016/S0360-1323(99)00074-8.

Ghofrani, A., Zaidan, E., and Abulibdeh, A. (2021). Simulation and impact analysis of behavioral and socioeconomic dimensions of energy consumption. *Energy* 240, p. 122502. Doi.org/10.1016/J.ENERGY.2021.122502.

Ghofrani, A., Zaidan, E., and Jafari, M. (2021). Reshaping energy policy based on social and human dimensions: an analysis of human–building interactions among societies in transition in GCC countries. *Humanities and Social Sciences Communications* 8 (1), pp. 1–26. Doi.org/10.1057/s41599-021-00904-9.

González, M. C., Hidalgo, C. A., and Barabási, A. L. (2008). Understanding individual human mobility patterns. *Nature* 453 (7196), pp. 779–782. Doi.org/10.1038/nature06958.

Huang, L., Zhu, Y., Ouyang, Q., and Cao, B. (2012). A study on the effects of thermal, luminous, and acoustic environments on indoor environmental comfort in offices. *Building and Environment* 49 (1), pp. 304–309. Doi.org/10.1016/J.BUILDENV.2011.07.022.

Humphreys, M., and Nicol, F. (1998). Understanding the adaptive approach to thermal comfort. *ASHRAE Transactions* 104, pp. 991–1004.

Hwang, R. L., and Chen, C. P. (2010). Field study on behaviors and adaptation of elderly people and their thermal comfort requirements in residential environments. *Indoor Air* 20 (3), pp. 235–245. Doi.org/10.1111/J.1600-0668.2010.00649.X.

Jafari, M. A., Ghofrani, A., Zaidan, E., and Abulibdeh, A. (2022). Improving building energy footprint and asset performance using digital twin technology. *Smart Infrastructure and Construction* 174 (2), pp. 57–65. Doi.org/10.1680/JSMIC.21.00001.

Jamaludin, A. A., Keumala, N., Ariffin, A. R. M., and Hussein, H. (2013). Satisfaction and perception of residents towards bioclimatic design strategies: residential college buildings. *Indoor and Built Environment* 23 (7), pp. 933–945. Doi.org/10.1177/1420326X13481614.

Jiang, J. T., and Yang, C. Z. (2011). Investigation of the subjective evaluation of indoor illumination level on perceived air quality. 7th International Symposium on Heating, Ventilating and Air Conditioning, *Proceedings of ISHVAC 2011*, 2, pp. 453–458.

Karjalainen, S. (2007). Gender differences in thermal comfort and use of thermostats in everyday thermal environments. *Building and Environment* 42 (4), pp. 1594–1603. Doi.org/10.1016/j.buildenv.2006.01.009.

Karjalainen, S. (2009). Thermal comfort and use of thermostats in Finnish homes and offices. *Building and Environment* 44 (6), pp. 1237–1245. Doi.org/10.1016/J.BUILDENV.2008.09.002.

Karjalainen, S. (2012). Thermal comfort and gender: A literature review. *Indoor Air* 22 (2), pp. 96–109. Doi.org/10.1111/J.1600-0668.2011.00747.X.

Kempton, L., Daly, D., Kokogiannakis, G., and Dewsbury, M. (2022). A rapid review of the impact of increasing airtightness on indoor air quality. *Journal of Building Engineering* 57, p. 104798. Doi.org/10.1016/J.JOBE.2022.104798.

Knez, I., and Hygge, S. (2002). Irrelevant speech and indoor lighting: Effects on cognitive performance and self-reported affect. *Applied Cognitive Psychology* 16 (6), pp. 709–718. Doi.org/10.1002/ACP.829.

Lan, L., Wargocki, P., Wyon, D. P., and Lian, Z. (2011). Effects of thermal discomfort in an office on perceived air quality, SBS symptoms, physiological responses, and human performance. *Indoor Air* 21 (5), pp. 376–390. Doi.org/10.1111/J.1600-0668.2011.00714.X.

Lee, T. K., Cho, S. H., and Kim, J. T. (2011). Residents' adjusting behaviour to enhance indoor environmental comfort in apartments. *Indoor and Built Environment* 21 (1), pp. 28–40. Doi.org/10.1177/1420326X11420120.

Liebl, A., Haller, J., Jödicke, B., Baumgartner, H., Schlittmeier, S., and Hellbrück, J. (2012). Combined effects of acoustic and visual distraction on cognitive performance and well-being. *Applied Ergonomics* 43(2), pp. 424–434. Doi.org/10.1016/J.APERGO.2011.06.017.

Lin, H. W., and Hong, T. (2013). On variations of space-heating energy use in office buildings. *Applied Energy* 111, pp. 515–528. Doi.org/10.1016/j.apenergy.2013.05.040.

Liu, Z., Sun, Y., Xing, C., Liu, J., He, Y., Zhou, Y., and Zhang, G. (2022). Artificial intelligence powered large-scale renewable integrations in multi-energy systems for carbon neutrality transition: challenges and future perspectives. *Energy and AI* 10, p. 100195. Doi.org/10.1016/j.egyai.2022.100195.

Lyons, P. R., Arasteh, D., and Huizenga, C. (2000). Window performance for human thermal comfort. *Transactions-American Society of Heating Refrigerating and Air Conditioning Engineers* 106(1), pp. 594–604.

Mansour, S., Alahmadi, M., and Abulibdeh, A. (2022). Spatial assessment of audience accessibility to historical monuments and museums in Qatar during the 2022 FIFA World Cup. *Transport Policy* 127 (August 2021), pp. 116–129. Doi.org/10.1016/j.tranpol.2022.08.022.

Masoso, O. T., and Grobler, L. J. (2010). The dark side of occupants' behaviour on building energy use. *Energy and Buildings* 42 (2), pp. 173–177. Doi.org/10.1016/j.enbuild.2009.08.009.

Mehnert, P., Bröde, P., and Griefahn, B. (2002). Gender-related difference in sweat loss and its impact on exposure limits to heat stress. *International Journal of Industrial Ergonomics* 29 (6), pp. 343–351. Doi.org/10.1016/S0169-8141(02)00073-2.

Mijorski, S., and Cammelli, S. (2016). Stack effect in high-rise buildings: A review. *International Journal of High-Rise Buildings* 5 (4), pp. 327–338. Doi.org/10.21022/IJHRB.2016.5.4.327.

Mohammed, S., Alkhereibi, A. H., Abulibdeh, A., Jawarneh, R. N., and Balakrishnan, P. (2023). GIS-based spatiotemporal analysis for road traffic crashes; in support of sustainable transportation Planning. *Transportation Research Interdisciplinary Perspectives* 20, p. 100836. Doi.org/10.1016/J.TRIP.2023.100836.

Mutambik, I., Lee, J., Almuqrin, A., and Zhang, J. Z. (2023). Transitioning to smart cities in Gulf Cooperation Council countries: the role of leadership and organisational culture. *Sustainability* 15 (13), p. 10490. Doi.org/10.3390/SU151310490.

Nazemi, S. D., Zaidan, E., and Jafari, M. A. (2021). The impact of occupancy-driven models on cooling systems in commercial buildings. *Energies* 14 (6), p. 1722. Doi .org/10.3390/EN14061722.

Newsham, G. R., Arsenault, C., and Veitch, J. A. (2002). Preferred surface illuminances and the benefits of individual lighting control: a pilot study. National Research Council Canada. NRCC-45354, pp. 1–13.

Newsham, G., Veitch, J., Arsenault, C., and Duval, C. (2004). Effect of dimming control on office worker satisfaction and performance. *Proceedings of the IESNA Annual Conference*. New York, NY, pp. 19–41.

O'Brien, W., and Gunay, H. B. (2014). The contextual factors contributing to occupants' adaptive comfort behaviors in offices – a review and proposed modeling framework. *Building and Environment* 77, pp. 77–87. Doi.org/10.1016/J.BUILDENV.2014.03.024.

Pais-Magalhães, V., Moutinho, V., and Robaina, M. (2022). Is an ageing population impacting energy use in the European Union? Drivers, lifestyles, and consumption patterns of elderly households. *Energy Research & Social Science* 85, p. 102443. Doi .org/10.1016/J.ERSS.2021.102443.

Rijal, H. B., Tuohy, P., Humphreys, M. A., Fergus Nicol, J., Samuel, A., Raja, I. A., and Clarke, J. (2008). Development of adaptive algorithms for the operation of windows, fans, and doors to predict thermal comfort and energy use in Pakistani buildings. *American Society of Heating Refrigerating and Air Conditioning Engineers (ASHRAE) Transactions* 114 (2), pp. 555–573.

Rolando, D., Pallard, W. M., and Molinari, M. (2022). Long-term evaluation of comfort, indoor air quality and energy performance in buildings: the case of the KTH live-in lab testbeds. *Energies* 15 (14), p. 4955. Doi.org/10.3390/EN15144955.

Schust, M., Gaebelein, H., Meister, A., and Rothe, R. (1991). The effect of combined noise and heat exposure upon thermal regulation, hearing and subjective state. *Archives of Complex Environmental Studies* 3 (2), pp. 25–30.

Schweiker, M., Huebner, G. M., Kingma, B. R. M., Kramer, R., and Pallubinsky, H. (2018). Drivers of diversity in human thermal perception – a review for holistic comfort models. *Temperature* 5 (4), pp. 308–342. Doi.org/10.1080/23328940.2018 .1534490.

Seppänen, O., Fisk, W., and Lei, Q. (2006). *Effect of Temperature on Task Performance in Office Environment*. Berkeley, CA: Lawrence Berkeley National Laboratory, 11.

Shahwan, R., and Zaman, T. (2023). Role of universities as knowledge creators in a national innovation system: An open innovation paradigm. in El Ebrashi, R., Hattab, H., Hassan, R. S., and Bouchra, N. H. (eds.), *Industry Clusters and Innovation in the Arab World*. Leeds: Emerald Publishing Limited, pp. 259–280. Doi .org/10.1108/978-1-80262-871-520231012.

Sintov, N. D., White, L. V., and Walpole, H. (2019). Thermostat wars? The roles of gender and thermal comfort negotiations in household energy use behavior. *PLoS ONE* 14 (11), pp. 8–10. Doi.org/10.1371/journal.pone.0224198.

Trochim, W. M., and McLinden, D. (2017). Introduction to a special issue on concept mapping. *Evaluation and Program Planning* 60, pp. 166–175. Doi.org/10.1016/j .evalprogplan.2016.10.006.

Vázquez-Canteli, J. R., Ulyanin, S., Kämpf, J., and Nagy, Z. (2019). Fusing TensorFlow with building energy simulation for intelligent energy management in smart cities. *Sustainable Cities and Society* 45, pp. 243–257. Doi.org/10.1016/J.SCS.2018.11.021.

Von Grabe, J. (2016). The systematic identification and organization of the context of energy-relevant human interaction with buildings – a pilot study in Germany. *Energy Research & Social Science* 12, pp. 75–95. Doi.org/10.1016/J.ERSS.2015.12.001.

Wong, N. H., Feriadi, H., Lim, P. Y., Tham, K. W., Sekhar, C., and Cheong, K. W. (2002). Thermal comfort evaluation of naturally ventilated public housing in Singapore. *Building and Environment* 37(12), pp. 1267–1277. Doi.org/10.1016/S0360-1323(01)00103-2.

Xu, X., Taylor, J. E., and Pisello, A. L. (2014). Network synergy effect: establishing a synergy between building network and peer network energy conservation effects. *Energy and Buildings* 68 (Part A), pp. 312–320. Doi.org/10.1016/J.ENBUILD.2013.09.017.

Xue, P., Mak, C. M., Cheung, H. D., and Chao, J. (2015). Post-occupancy evaluation of sunshades and balconies' effects on luminous comfort through a questionnaire survey. *Building Services Engineering Research & Technology* 37 (1), pp. 51–65. Doi.org/10.1177/0143624415596472.

Ye, W., Zhang, X., Gao, J., Cao, G., Zhou, X., and Su, X. (2017). Indoor air pollutants, ventilation rate determinants and potential control strategies in Chinese dwellings: a literature review. *Science of The Total Environment* 586, pp. 696–729. Doi.org/10.1016/J.SCITOTENV.2017.02.047.

Zaidan, E., and Abulibdeh, A. (2020). Master planning and the evolving urban model in the Gulf cities: principles, policies, and practices for the transition to sustainable urbanism. *Planning Practice & Research* 36 (2), pp. 193–215. Doi.org/10.1080/02697459.2020.1829278.

Zaidan, E., Al-Saidi, M., and Hammad, S. H. (2019). Sustainable development in the Arab world–is the Gulf Cooperation Council (GCC) region fit for the challenge? *Development in Practice* 29 (5), pp. 670–681. Doi.org/10.1080/09614524.2019.1628922.

Zaidan, E., Ghofrani, A., and Dokaj, E. (2021). Analysis of human–building interactions in office environments: to what extent energy saving boundaries can be displaced? *Frontiers in Energy Research* 9, p. 450. Doi.org/10.3389/FENRG.2021.715478.

Zaidan, E., Ghofrani, A., Abulibdeh, A., and Jafari, M. (2022). Accelerating the change to smart societies – a strategic knowledge-based framework for smart energy transition of urban communities. *Frontiers in Energy Research* 10, p. 158. Doi.org/10.3389/FENRG.2022.852092.

Zaidan, E., Abulibdeh, A., Alban, A., and Jabbar, R. (2022). Motivation, preference, socioeconomic, and building features: new paradigm of analyzing electricity consumption in residential buildings. *Building and Environment* 219, p. 109177. Doi.org/10.1016/J.BUILDENV.2022.109177.

Zalejska-Jonsson, A., and Wilhelmsson, M. (2013). Impact of perceived indoor environment quality on overall satisfaction in Swedish dwellings. *Building and Environment* 63, pp. 134–144. Doi.org/10.1016/J.BUILDENV.2013.02.005.

Zomorodian, Z. S., and Tahsildoost, M. (2017). Assessment of window performance in classrooms by long term spatial comfort metrics. *Energy and Buildings* 134, pp. 80–93. Doi.org/10.1016/J.ENBUILD.2016.10.018.

13

EU–GCC Cooperation Opportunities on Behavioural Energy Efficiency

KONSTANTINOS KOASIDIS, NIKOLAOS VOURGIDIS, VANGELIS MARINAKIS, FILIPPOS SEREPAS, AND HARIS DOUKAS*

13.1 Introduction

Efforts to battle climate change have intensified in recent years. However, the world is not yet on track to achieve the goals set by the Paris Agreement of 2015. Climate policies, if fully implemented, will likely put the world on track to 2.3–2.9°C (Sognnaes et al., 2021). On top of that, net zero pledges and the nationally determined contributions (NDCs) appear to be able to put the 2°C target within grasp (Hausfather & Moore, 2022; Meinshausen et al., 2022; Höhne et al., 2021; Sognnaes et al., 2021), highlighting a gap from Paris-compliant targets (Baptista et al., 2022). This indicates that current policies up to 2030 need to be implemented fast while ensuring that the road to achieving the net zero pledges is pursued with a raised ambition to close this gap.

Heading towards and in the aftermath of the 2021 United Nations Climate Change Conference (COP26), many countries renewed their pledges and presented their plans to raise ambition, committing themselves to lower carbon emissions. The countries of the European Union (EU) and the Gulf Cooperation Council (GCC) were among the regions that presented their updated plans. These two regions are of vital importance in the battle against climate change considering historically the former's major economic and emissions impact and the latter's fossil fuel production (Doukas et al., 2012). The EU published its roadmap based on the European Green Deal (EGD), committing to carbon neutrality by 2050, while the GCC states

* Part of the study presented is based on research carried out within the framework of the projects 'ATOM—Innovative Personalised Apps to Motivate and Support Behavioural Energy Efficiency', 'EU–GCC Clean Energy Technology Network', and 'PARIS REINFORCE—Delivering on the Paris Agreement: A Demand-Driven, Integrated Assessment Modelling Approach'. ATOM has received funding from the Hellenic Foundation for Research and Innovation (HFRI) and the General Secretariat for Research and Innovation (GSRI), under grant agreement No. HFRI-FM17-2566. 'EU–GCC Clean Energy Technology Network' has received funding from the European Commission – FPI service contract No. PI/2015/370817 (www.eugcc-cleanergy.net). PARIS REINFORCE has received funding from the European Union's Horizon 2020 Research and Innovation Programme, under grant agreement No 820846.

published their updated NDCs, most of them also committing to net zero futures (Gebeily, 2021).

However, the road to these pledges may be challenging. Such a path is expected to require going beyond supply-side measures, such as increasing the share of renewable energy sources (RES) in the mix, to also incorporating demand-side transformations like energy efficiency (Creutzig et al., 2018; Creutzig et al., 2022). Both the EGD and the updated NDCs of the GCC head in this direction, including relevant energy efficiency initiatives. However, although the importance of accompanying such initiatives with behavioural changes to battle climate change is widely recognised (Whitmarsh et al., 2021), only a handful of provisions for behavioural change measures is present in the current plans. This leaves a large potential for mitigation unexploited, especially in the residential sector, which is a key energy consumer in the GCC countries with high per capita consumption (Ahmed & Asif, 2021).

In this context, the chapter aims to identify opportunities for cooperation on behavioural energy efficiency between the EU and the GCC, by enhancing the ability of the two regions to trigger end-users' behavioural changes and help them achieve their climate pledges and energy efficiency targets. In particular, we analyse the updated pledges of the GCC in comparison with the EU to showcase the current role of energy efficiency in the recent plans. This analysis includes the current energy system context to identify areas with high demand reduction potential. By facilitating a knowledge transfer between the two regions that exploits strengths and weaknesses in each case, we finally present a framework that will help both regions reach the behavioural energy efficiency potential and achieve challenging climate targets. This framework builds on existing innovative personalised applications to motivate and support behavioural energy efficiency (Koasidis & Psarras, 2021) and is based on smart infrastructure in buildings. Within the framework, we suggest exploiting technologies such as energy disaggregation and machine learning techniques, as well as devices for smart planning, and we propose the implementation of a novel digital energy currency mechanism to motivate consumers to reduce their consumption.

13.2 Updated Pledges and the Representation of Energy Efficiency

Moving towards COP26 the EU pledged to reduce greenhouse gas (GHG) emissions by 55% by 2030 with the ratification of the EGD and the accompanying 'Fit for 55' package, increasing ambition compared to the previous target setting a goal of 40% emissions reduction (Jäger-Waldau et al., 2020). The EGD is an action plan to make the EU's economy sustainable by enhancing the effective use of resources through the transition to a clean and circular economy, restoring biodiversity, and cutting pollution.

Among the main elements of the EGD which are focused on climate action, clean energy and eliminating pollution, the building sector and the role of efficiency emerged as key priorities in the battle against climate change (Lapierre & McDougall, 2021), considering the significant potential for mitigation not only based on how energy is produced, but also on how it is consumed. In particular, buildings account for approximately 40% of the EU's energy consumption and 36% of energy-related GHG emissions (Gupta & Chakraborty, 2021). For this reason, the EU Green Deal requires cleaner construction and building sectors by inter alia leveraging technology to increase energy efficiency as well as promote the uptake of sustainable behaviours from dwellings' occupants, by introducing a target to reduce GHG emissions in the building sector by 60% by 2030.

Achieving this updated target requires building on lessons from years of efforts in the EU to exploit the energy efficiency potential (Knoop & Lechtenböhmer, 2017), as well as the identified key challenges hindering progress on this front, i.e. on a policy (Forouli et al., 2019) or on a behavioural level (Doukas et al., 2019). Apart from underpinning the EU's own future steps, such lessons can also inform other parties currently starting to pursue energy efficiency improvements. The GCC states are also starting to take initiatives to increase the role of energy efficiency, on top of ongoing efforts to reduce fossil fuel dependence in their economies. Being among the world's most significant fossil fuel producers has led to significantly high per capita energy consumption and emissions, a potential that needs to be exploited to assist the energy transition of the region. Like the EU, GCC member states are currently adjusting their national strategies in the form of updating their NDCs. With most GCC states incorporating measures to enhance the role of energy efficiency (and renewable energy) in their new plans (Figure 13.1), opportunities for constructive cooperation between the EU and GCC countries emerge. In the next sections we delve into the updated NDCs of the GCC states with a focus on identifying the pledged role of energy efficiency.

13.2.1 Bahrain

In October 2021, Bahrain's cabinet declared that the kingdom aims to reach net zero emissions by 2060, in response to CO_2 emissions from energy use quickly rising (Alnaser et al., 2022). In its NDC update, and following the country's National Renewable Energy Action Plan (NREAP), a target was set to achieve the penetration of 5% renewable energy at peak capacity by 2025 and 10% by 2035, focusing mostly on solar photovoltaics (PVs) and wind energy (Alnaser & Alnaser, 2019). The NDC also emphasised energy efficiency by building on the National Energy Efficiency Action Plan (NEEAP), launched in 2017. The NEEAP outlines a comprehensive set of 22 activities, spanning all sectors, to assist Bahrain meet

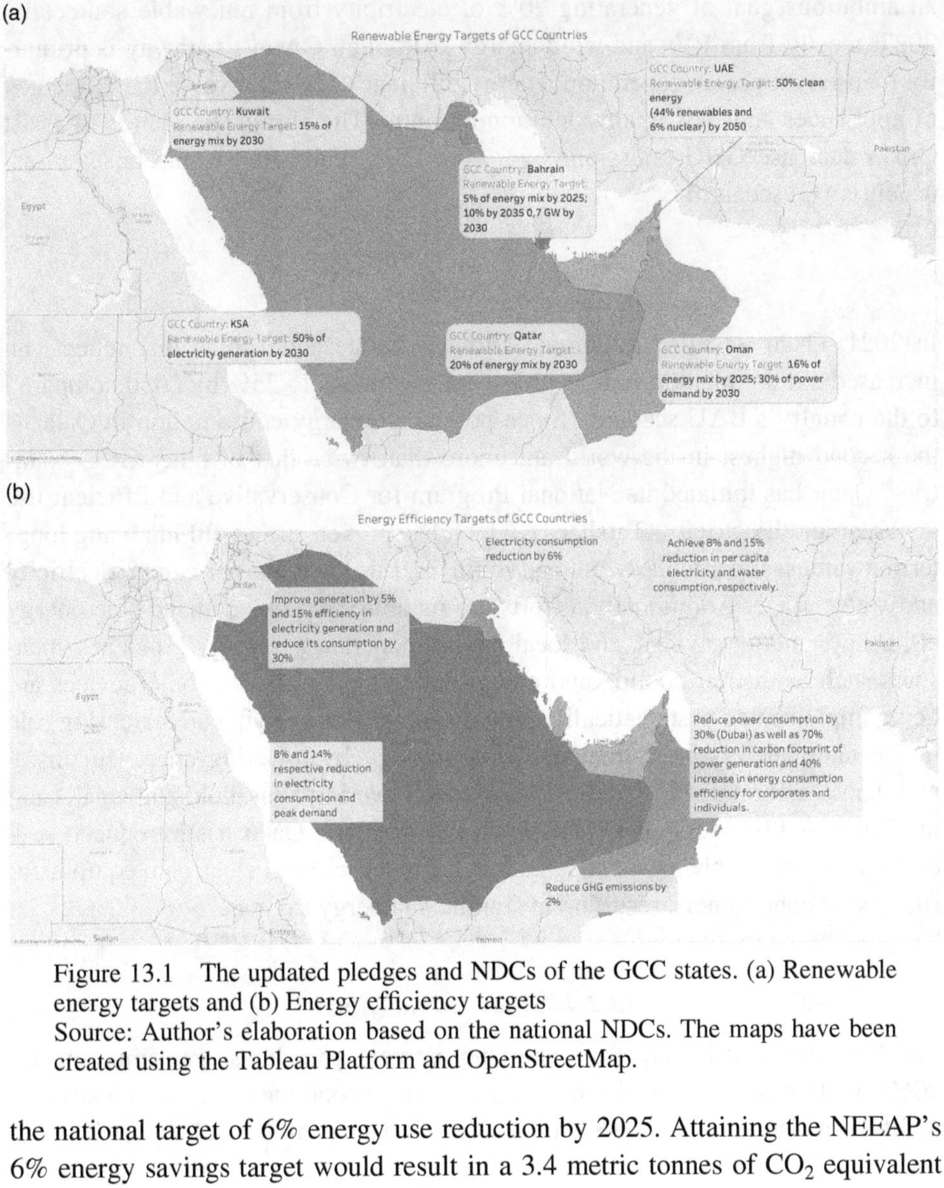

Figure 13.1 The updated pledges and NDCs of the GCC states. (a) Renewable energy targets and (b) Energy efficiency targets
Source: Author's elaboration based on the national NDCs. The maps have been created using the Tableau Platform and OpenStreetMap.

the national target of 6% energy use reduction by 2025. Attaining the NEEAP's 6% energy savings target would result in a 3.4 metric tonnes of CO_2 equivalent ($MtCO_2eq$) reduction in GHG emissions.

13.2.2 Oman

The Second NDC of Oman is centred on the country's Vision 2040 and the National Energy Strategy, aiming to foster a gradual transition to a low-carbon economy. The 2030 carbon reduction plan's pillars focus on expanding renewable energy and strengthening energy efficiency efforts. The strategy has set an ambitious goal of generating 20% of electricity from renewable sources by 2027, mostly from PVs and wind energy. Although Oman's pathway is primarily focused on power generation, energy efficiency efforts involve the efficiency of appliances and mostly air-conditioning units. The aim of the plan is to assist Oman decrease GHG emissions by 7% in 2030, compared to the business-as-usual (BAU) scenario.

13.2.3 Qatar

In 2021, Qatar unveiled a national climate change action plan that reflects an increased commitment to reduce its overall emissions to 25% by 2030 compared to the country's BAU scenario. Since per capita energy consumption in Qatar is the second highest in the world and more than twice that of other GCC countries, Qatar has initiated its National Program for Conservative and Efficient use of Water and Electricity (Tarsheed), which has proven successful in raising long-term awareness, particularly among youth, and in lowering per capita electricity and water usage. Additionally, efforts are made to improve demand-side energy efficiency, energy savings, and local energy generation. Energy efficiency measures such as district cooling and energy labelling for all electronic devices are being implemented systematically. As a result, they are playing an increasing role in the national economic diversification strategy by lowering energy intensity and the need for energy subsidies, while also lowering household and small- and medium-sized business GHG emissions. Furthermore, Qatar has introduced several specification enhancement standards for electrical and electronic equipment, such as air conditioners, resulting in significant energy savings.

13.2.4 Saudi Arabia (KSA)

The KSA declared its target of achieving net zero greenhouse gas emissions by 2060, while launching a series of comprehensive economic reforms with sustainability as a central principle (KSA 2021). The country aims to achieve 50% penetration of RES in mix by 2030. Regarding the core pillar of energy efficiency, the country states that strategies, policies, measures, and initiatives should actively promote and support co-benefits of mitigation across the economy. The Saudi Energy Efficiency Center manages an energy efficiency programme establishing strict efficiency criteria aimed at three major sectors that account for 90% of the country's energy consumption: industry, construction, and land transportation. The goal of the NDC is to expand such initiatives in the building sector to increase the efficiency of home appliances and air conditioning units. Additionally, the National Energy Services Company was founded to promote energy efficiency in government buildings and the involvement of the private sector in energy efficiency services, intending to retrofit the whole inventory of public and governmental assets and facilities.

13.2.5 United Arab Emirates (UAE)

In 2021, the UAE committed to becoming the first Gulf petrostate to fully decarbonise its economy, achieve net zero GHG emissions, and pursue a clean energy target in the mix of 50% by 2050, through the National Climate Change Plan 2017–2050, the National Energy Strategy 2050, and Green Agenda 2030. The UAE is also taking steps to reduce energy consumption through regulatory measures, pricing signals, technology deployment, and energy-saving programmes to reduce energy consumption by 40% by 2050. More specifically, green building laws and rating systems for new buildings have been adopted, and a federal-level initiative for retrofitting government buildings has been implemented to target existing buildings. Similarly, Abu Dhabi's Building Retrofit initiative focuses on upgrading government buildings and will be expanded to include non-government buildings in the future, while Dubai has set a goal of retrofitting 30,000 structures by 2030. Tariff reforms for residential, commercial, and industrial electricity use are implemented periodically across the Emirates to promote cost-effective pricing and energy saving. Emphasis is placed on enhancing the efficiency of cooling appliances with district cooling being applied in high-density regions and the implementation of an Energy Efficiency Standardization and Labelling Program.

13.2.6 Kuwait

Kuwait amended its first NDC, committing to cut GHG emissions by 7.4% by 2035 compared to a BAU scenario. As Kuwait's per capita consumption is among the top ten highest in the world, Kuwait's Vision 2035 intends to decrease energy consumption by 30%, and boost RES penetration in the mix to 15% by 2030 (Abdullah et al., 2019). Kuwait's strategy for decarbonisation is centred on enhancing energy efficiency, raising awareness, providing incentives for clean energy, and lowering subsidies (Kuwait, 2021).

13.3 The Energy Generation and Consumption System of the GCC

The updated pledges hold a lot of promise, with Gulf states actively participating in the global decarbonisation agenda, as clearly indicated by their new and more ambitious targets. By taking a more active role in combating climate change and accelerating the energy transition through the rapid deployment of

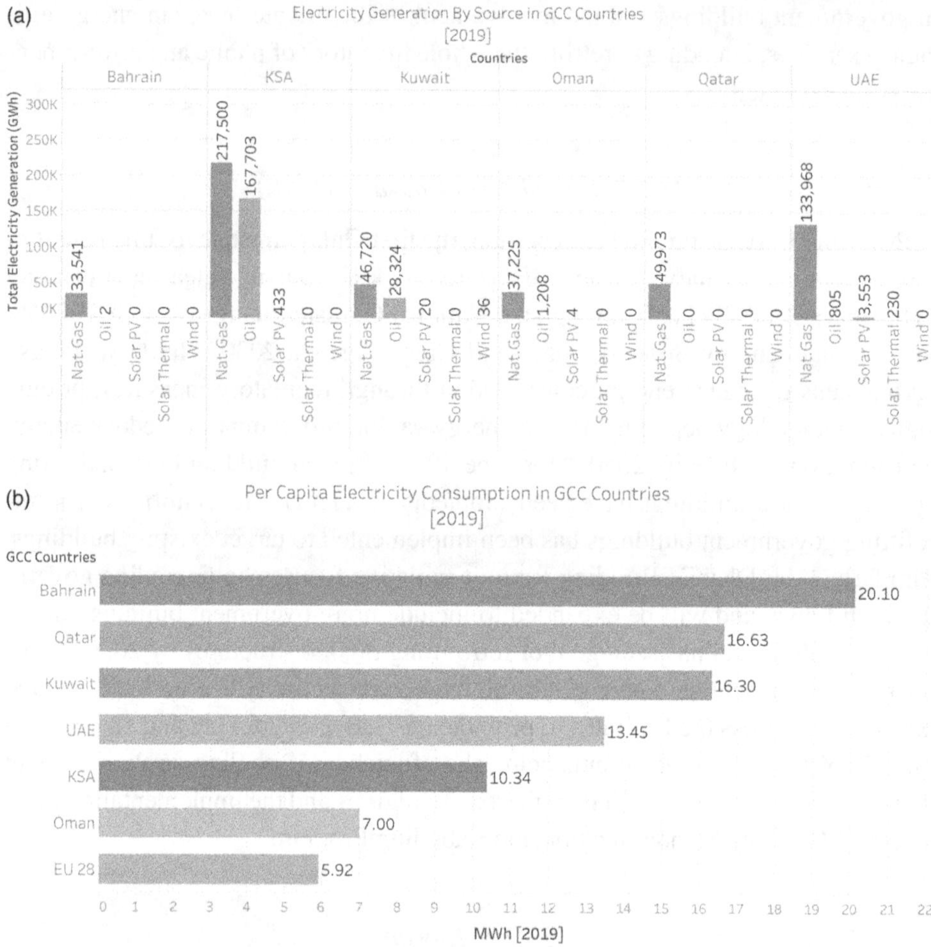

Figure 13.2 The electricity generation (a) and consumption (b) system in the GCC. Source: Own elaboration based on data from the International Energy Agency (IEA, 2019)*.
* This is a work derived by Koasidis et al. from IEA material and Koasidis et al. are solely liable and responsible for this derived work. The derived work is not endorsed by the IEA in any manner.

renewables, the Gulf States envisage achieving a stable low-carbon shift and reducing fossil fuel reliance (Figure 13.2a). However, the large role of fossil fuels, mostly natural gas and occasionally oil, and the small role in the current energy and electricity generation system forced the updated NDCs to primarily focus on targets and policies for RES deployment. Although provisions for energy efficiency exist in the plans, the level of detail on the demand side is much lower than on the supply side. Considering the high per capita electricity consumption in the GCC states (Figure 13.2b), energy efficiency should be regarded as a critical enabler of the desired decarbonisation of the fossil fuel-dominant GCC power sectors.

In particular, as a result of the region's abundance of oil and gas resources, the GCC states ranked among the world's highest per capita electricity consumers. Electricity demand is growing constantly and is predicted to double by 2025, reaching 1,094 Terawatt-hour (TWh) (Al-Badi & AlMubarak, 2019), as a result of the region's high population growth due to labour migration, a high birth rate, rising living standards, and most notably the rapid economic expansion increasing the electrical power required to sustain the growth in large-scale infrastructure construction, heavy industry, and petrochemicals (Al-Badi & AlMubarak, 2019).

As shown in Figure 13.2b, Bahrain's electricity usage per capita was the highest in the GCC region (20.1 Megawatt-hours per capita (MWh/capita)) in 2019 (increasing by 11% since 2010), and about 300% higher than the European average (5.92 MWh/capita). Between 2010 and 2019, electricity consumption in Qatar increased by 17%, becoming the region's second-highest electricity consumer on a per capita basis (16.63 MWh/per capita in 2019). Oman achieved the region's lowest consumption, of 7 MWh/per capita, which is still 18% higher than the European average. Kuwait's electricity consumption per capita has decreased slightly by 3.6% over the last decade but remains the region's third highest. In contrast, the UAE and the KSA experienced the fastest energy consumption per capita growth over the last decade, increasing by 29.5 and 30.4%, respectively. The disparity in per capita consumption between the GCC countries and the EU-28 is due to the developing nature of the GCC economies, which rely heavily on electricity consumption for economic growth (AlKhars et al., 2020). Still, this indicates that there is a large potential for energy efficiency in the region's pathway to decarbonisation, without hampering overall economic progress.

From a sectoral perspective, residential buildings accounted for the majority of electricity consumption, representing 43% of electricity demand and 18% of the total final energy intake (Almasri & Alshitawi, 2022). In Oman, Qatar, the KSA, and the UAE, the residential sector accounts for the majority of electricity consumption at 44.56%, 44.65%, 43.71 %, and 33.26%, respectively, whereas, in Bahrain and Kuwait, the industrial sector is the largest electricity consumer. In the region as a whole, the residential sector accounted for most of the region's total final electricity consumption, at 38.91% (Table 13.1), highlighting the importance of exploring the potential for mitigation in buildings.

The importance of the residential sector is further highlighted if the increasing trend in terms of energy and electricity consumption is considered. In particular, the total electricity consumption per capita in buildings in Bahrain, Kuwait, Oman, Qatar, the KSA, and the UAE in 2015 was 20,190, 14,951, 6588, 17,460, 9926, and 12,916 kWh, respectively (Krarti, 2019). The average building energy

Table 13.1 *Share of electricity consumption by sector in EU 28 and GCC countries in 2019.*

Sectors	Final electricity consumption (%) EU 28	Final electricity consumption (%) GCC countries
Residential	29.82	38.91
Industry	37.8	20.07
Commercial and public services	30.18	34.26
Non-specified	0.11	5.62
Agriculture / Forestry	2.09	1.13

Source: Own elaboration based on data from IEA (2019)*.
* This is a work derived by Koasidis et al. from IEA material and Koasidis et al. are solely liable and responsible for this derived work. The derived work is not endorsed by the IEA in any manner.

consumption per capita in the region significantly increased over the past two decades (Bumajdad et al, 2020), while the energy use intensity (EUI) of residential and commercial buildings in the GCC region has increased by 31% and 50%, respectively, between 2000 and 2015. This trend is most likely due to the widespread use of energy-intensive equipment in the building sector, including air conditioning systems that maintain indoor thermal comfort, due to high temperature conditions.

Considering the importance of energy cooling needs, many studies investigated the electricity shares for AC systems, as well as equipment, lighting, heating water (HW), and other devices from each GCC member's total electricity intake. For example, according to Krarti and Dubey (2018a), the electricity consumption share of ACs in Bahrain is 73%. In Kuwait, Azar et al. (2021) estimated the share to be between 39% and 49%, while Park et al. (2019) estimated it to be 60%. In Oman, Al-Saadi and Al-Jabri (2020) discovered that the share of AC for various locations in the country ranged from 57% to 71%. In the UAE, the electricity consumed for ACs was around 63% (Al Amoodi & Azar, 2018; Alremeithi et al., 2020; Radhi, 2011), while multiple studies in the KSA found the share varying between 30% and 80% (Almasri & Alshitawi, 2022). Despite intraregional fluctuations in the share of AC consumption, the overall high share of cooling needs across the GCC countries underlines the importance of this consumption area, as well as the large potential for energy efficiency.

The share of lighting fluctuated between 10% and 15% (Alardhi et al., 2020; Alaidroos & Krarti, 2015; Krarti et al. 2020), while the share of heating water and other appliances ranged between 4% and 25% (Alaidroos & Krarti, 2015; Alardhi et al., 2020; Almasri et al., 2021; Krarti, Dubey et al., 2017; Al Amoodi & Azar, 2018). Usually, the highest consumption shares were associated with multi-story buildings (Almasri and Alshitawi, 2022).

13.4 Reinforcing Energy Efficiency with Behavioral Changes

Based on the previous analysis, the residential sector in the GCC, not unlike the EU, presents a significant opportunity to combat climate change, as a result of the huge mitigation potential from energy efficiency in buildings. Recent pledges in the GCC attempted to incorporate relevant initiatives (see Section 13.2). However, the road to achieving the pledges might be more challenging than envisaged. For example, the energy efficiency targets in the EU have historically been among the most difficult to achieve, due to inter alia the large investments required (Claeys et al., 2019). To reinforce these efforts, supplementing energy efficiency initiatives with behavioural changes and a more sustainable lifestyle has been proposed (Nikas et al., 2020). As outlined in the recent 'net zero by 2050' scenario (Cozzi et al., 2020; IEA, 2021), decarbonisation of the energy system, apart from supply-side measures, will require a combination of end-use efficiency gains, electrification, but also the incorporation of behavioural changes.

In this respect, individuals and household occupants can optimise their energy use through modest, low-cost, and quickly adopted adjustments in daily routines that reduce residential energy costs, cut carbon emissions, and alleviate pressure on the power grid while, over time, yielding energy and monetary savings (Cornago, 2021). In the EU, the energy savings potential from behavioural factors is estimated at around 20% (Lopes et al., 2015). However, without proper engagement and the necessary motives, end-users are not expected to behave in a more energy-conscious way (Doukas et al., 2019). For this reason, providing monetary incentives to trigger such behavioural actions has been suggested (Marinakis et al., 2020a; Koasidis et al., 2022). In the next sections, we explore specific behavioural measures usually pursued as well as the tendency of the GCC communities towards accepting such interventions. We then proceed with suggesting a framework for achieving this potential in the GCC, drawing from EU lessons, based on providing tips to end-users through machine learning algorithms and smart devices and then incentivising energy savings through digital energy currencies.

13.4.1 Behavioural Interventions

The European Commission, in collaboration with the International Energy Agency (IEA), issued small-scale and individual-based recommendations to raise European citizens' awareness of the benefits of energy savings and assist them in reducing their energy consumption and fuel costs. Recommendations targeted specific energy-intensive household activities and appliances, such as heating and cooling, which account for 75% of all residential energy consumption in the EU (European Commission, 2020).

For heating and cooling, these included lowering the heating temperature to 19°C or 20°C and setting the cooling temperature to 26°C without compromising thermal comfort, which could save approximately 7% of the energy used for heating and 10% for cooling, depending on the region. This is of particular importance, since exploiting the behavioural energy efficiency potential in the EU, especially in northern countries, requires primarily focusing on reducing energy needs for heating, while in the GCC the largest potential is found in the energy needs for cooling. Across the GCC region, a 10% reduction in cooling needs translates to around 25 TWh of electricity saved in the residential sector.

Additionally, lowering the boiler's temperature to a maximum of 60°C, avoiding using the dishwasher, and attempting to turn off electric devices that consume electricity even when in standby mode are some of the small steps that a household can take to reduce electricity consumption (IEA, 2022). Residential energy demand could be reduced further through sustainable consumer choices, by upgrading to more energy-efficient appliances, such as refrigerators and dishwashers with an EU Energy Label or similar initiatives in the GCC like the Energy Efficiency Rating Labels for Air Conditioners, as well as replacing incandescent or halogen light bulbs with energy-efficient LED bulbs or installing smart metering systems that could save 5–15% of energy use (European Commission, 2020; Sovacool et al., 2017). Drawing from EU lessons as well as the literature (e.g. Lopes et al., 2019), Table 13.2 presents

Table 13.2 *List of potential behavioural energy efficiency interventions.*

	Convenient behavioural measures and low-cost, energy-saving tips
1	Use of thermostats in heating/cooling systems and frequent maintenance
2	Ventilation of heating radiators, cleaning/replacing system filters
3	Set water heater temperature at 50°C, insulate water heater pipes
4	Use of timers, dimmers and photocells for lighting automation/control
5	Selection of energy class A electrical appliances and energy efficient lamps
6	Shift the demand load by using energy-intensive household equipment (e.g. washing machine, dishwasher) during the off-peak period
7	Power saving mode in electronic devices coupled with standby killers
8	Correct appliance placement (e.g. refrigerator) to avoid heat losses
9	Exploit smaller and low consumption appliances (e.g. kettle, hobs)
10	Proper tree/plant planting/placement for optimum shading and wind protection

an indicative list of behavioural measures and tips to enable households to reduce their energy consumption in a convenient and low-cost way.

On the other hand, the recent increase in per capita electricity consumption in the GCC exceeded the growth in per capita GDP, indicating that the former was driven by underlying behaviours (The Ideation Center, 2018). In many GCC countries, washing machines and dishwashers are operated with partial loads, while many consumers leave lights, air conditioning units, and electronic appliances on when not in use. In 2017, it was reported that more than 70% of homes lacked adequate insulation, leading to the operation of approximately 25 million, not necessarily efficient, AC units.

Numerous studies in Oman (Krarti & Dubey, 2017), the UAE (Krarti & Dubey, 2018b), Qatar (Krarti et al., 2017), and Bahrain (Dubey & Krarti, 2017) found that installing an energy-efficient air conditioning system has the most significant impact on lowering annual energy consumption and peak demand. In the UAE, the second most impactful measure is decreasing the cooling temperature settings, whereas in Bahrain, the second most impactful measure was reducing air leakage from the building shell. In Oman, setting the cooling temperature to 26°C instead of 24°C was effective in reducing energy consumption, whereas in Qatar, adding wall insulation and employing high-efficiency lighting was instrumental in achieving the same result.

According to a survey (Abdmouleh et al., 2018) investigating residential consumers' knowledge about efficiency measures and awareness about best practices in Qatari homes and performed in the community of a university (hinting at a sample skewed towards the younger generation, but also including non-academic administrative staff), the most common measures to conserve electricity at home were turning off unused electrical appliances and using energy-efficient light bulbs. However, purchasing energy-efficient appliances (other than light bulbs) was the least common conservation measure. Moreover, although the study revealed a low level of familiarity with smart metres (29.87%), there was a high level of eagerness to install them (76.43%), particularly with in-home displays, as respondents viewed this setting as an incentive to assume a more active role in managing their electricity consumption. This eagerness to reduce energy consumption is primarily due to the feedback information provided by smart metres, with the level of commitment increasing through mobile applications and simple graphical illustrations of electricity consumption data, electricity costs, and appliance electricity usage.

13.4.2 A Framework to Motivate and Support Behavioural Changes in the GCC

From the discussion above, some key lessons can be drawn. First, large-scale and costly energy efficiency retrofits or the replacement of appliances face implementational difficulties. As such, like the EU, achieving the pledges on the energy efficiency front will be challenging. Second, early attempts towards behavioural energy efficiency indicate that enhancing conventional energy efficiency efforts with behavioural changes can have a positive impact in the GCC. The high level of eagerness to engage with smart metres indicates that GCC citizens are keen to enhance their energy literacy, and with the proper tips and incentives become more energy conscious. Here we present a framework to motivate and support behavioural changes in the GCC based on three levels: (1) machine-learning-based energy disaggregation algorithms to provide appliance-level behavioural tips, (2) a raspberry-based smart device for cooling load planning, and (3) a digital energy currency to incentivise energy savings.

13.4.2.1 Energy Disaggregation Algorithms

Providing tailored tips and advice to end-users is key to unlocking the behavioural energy efficiency potential in a household. However, the provision of such tips on an appliance level requires the existence of multiple smart metres and sensors within a single dwelling, which is both challenging and expensive. Although the transition to smart metres has already started in the GCC (Saleh et al., 2019), it is unlikely that their diffusion will quickly reach such penetration levels. For this, the employment of energy disaggregation algorithms has been proposed. Such algorithms receive only the signal from the total aggregated consumption and attempt to forecast the consumption of individual appliances (Shin et al., 2019), thus requiring only one smart metre per household. To achieve this, optimisation and machine-learning-based algorithms are used, like inter alia Factorial Hidden Markov Models, Combinatorial Optimisation, Long Short-Term Memory Neural Networks and Decision Trees (Zou et al., 2021), and trained based on historical data on the consumption profiles of the appliances present in a household. This could be done through measuring the appliances on the household itself for a certain amount of time (e.g. a week), to compile a training dataset for the algorithms and then start the forecasting process. However, for households that lack the energy literacy to perform such tasks, already available datasets can be used (e.g. Kolter & Johnson, 2011; Barker et al., 2012).

Figure 13.3 presents an example of an energy disaggregation implementation on an electric water heater in a Greek household, showcasing both the accuracy (Figure 13.3a) and the potential for energy efficiency using energy disaggregation and behavioural tips in real conditions (Figure 13.3b). After identifying the timestamp of when the water heater is on (green and red area), it is obvious that the water heater should have been turned off much earlier than it was, since for around half the time the heater operated, it was not used to produce useful energy. With energy disaggregation showing high accuracy potential in other appliances as well (Rahimpour et al., 2017), including AC units, an important area in the GCC context, there is huge potential in appliance-level tips. Utility companies

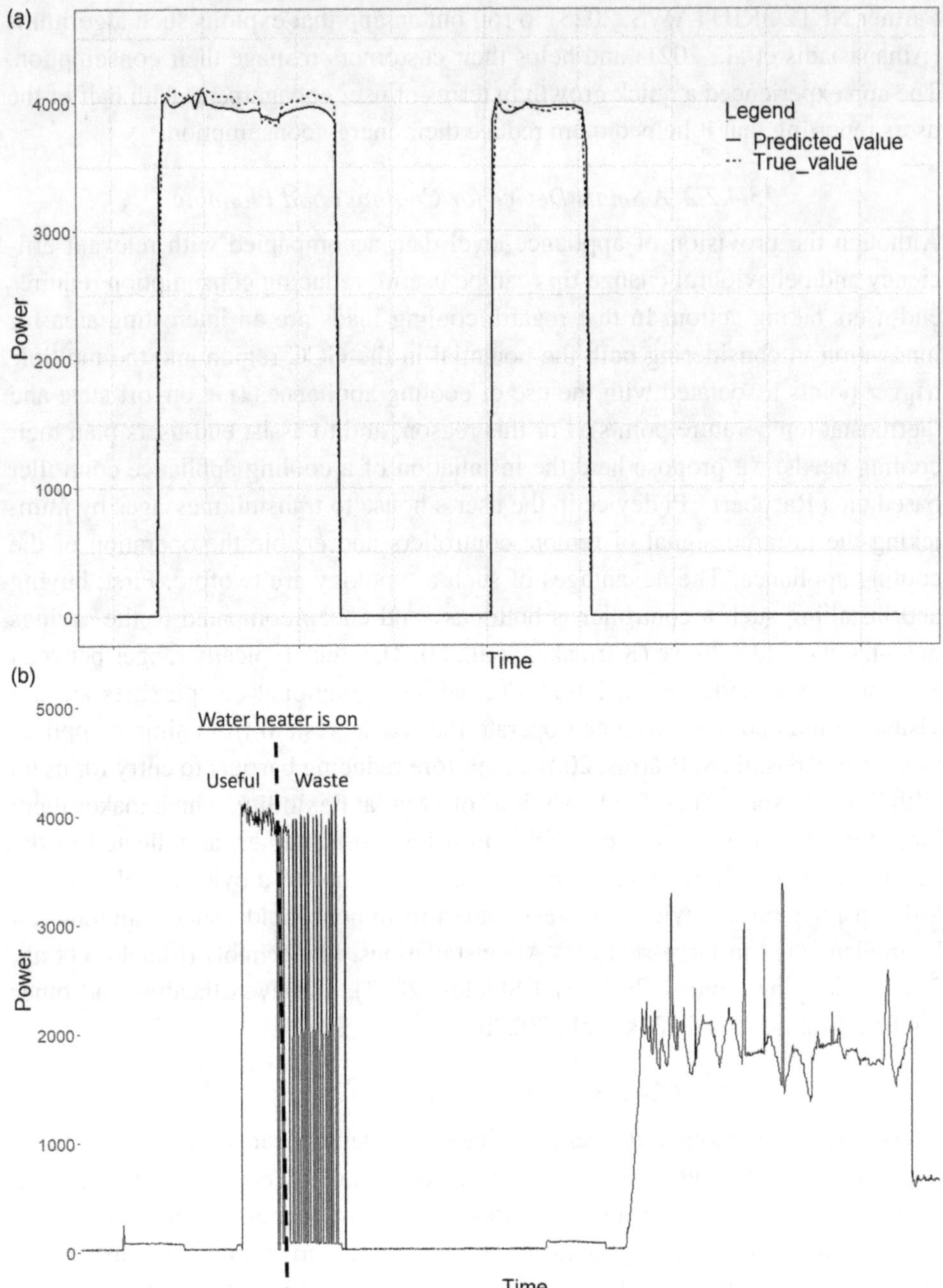

Figure 13.3 Energy disaggregation on an electric water heater: (a) accuracy and (b) behavioural tip.

and energy/electricity providers could rely on such technologies to offer relevant services to their customers and empower them to reduce their consumption. For example, in 2022, the Belgian energy provider Luminous collaborated with AWS

Partner NET2GRID (AWS, 2023) to roll out an app that exploits such algorithms (Athanasiadis et al., 2021) and helps their customers manage their consumption. The app experienced a quick growth in terms of user engagement, with half of the users reporting that it helped them reduce their energy consumption.

13.4.2.2 A Smart Device for Cooling Load Planning

Although the provision of appliance-level data accompanied with relevant efficiency and behavioural change tips can be useful, reducing consumption requires end-users taking action. In that regard, cooling loads are an interesting area for innovation in considering both the potential in the GCC region and the multiple trigger points associated with the use of cooling appliances (i.e. on–off state and thermostat temperature points). For this reason, and to assist end-users plan their cooling needs, we propose here the installation of a cooling appliance controller based on a Raspberry Pi device in the user's house to transmit messages by mimicking the infrared signal of remote controllers and enable the operation of the cooling appliance. The advantages of such a typology are twofold. First, buying and installing such a controller is both easy and cheap compared to the savings potential it could achieve (Karmakar et al., 2018), which typically ranges between 8% and 17% (Pandey et al. 2021). Second, computational complexities are not visible to the end-user, who can operate the whole system from simple applications (e.g. Koasidis & Psarras, 2021), therefore reducing barriers to entry for users with limited experiences. Such solutions offer great flexibility, which makes them ideal for implementing in households in a low-cost manner, as reflected in the rapid expansion of the 'smart home' concept in Europe (Vujović & Maksimović, 2015) using similar devices. However, apart from households, such solutions can be implemented in large-scale HVAC installations, like schools (Mataloto et al., 2019), shopping centres (Industrial Shields, 2023), and even theatres and other public buildings (Marinakis et al., 2020b).

13.4.2.3 A Digital Energy Currency

Unlocking the behavioural energy efficiency potential can be beneficial for a household since it reduces energy needs and consequently contributes to reducing energy bills. However, because this financial benefit appears in small quantities over time it is not always visible to end-users, who end up dropping the sustainable changes adopted after a while and return to previous norms and habits. Therefore, it is argued that triggering long-lasting behavioural changes requires both the implementation of a set of advanced information and communication technologies (Marinakis, 2020a; Hernández-Moral et al., 2021), as well as incentives (Bastida et al., 2019). For this reason, the energy disaggregation algorithms and the cooling load planning application can be combined with a digital energy currency, aiming

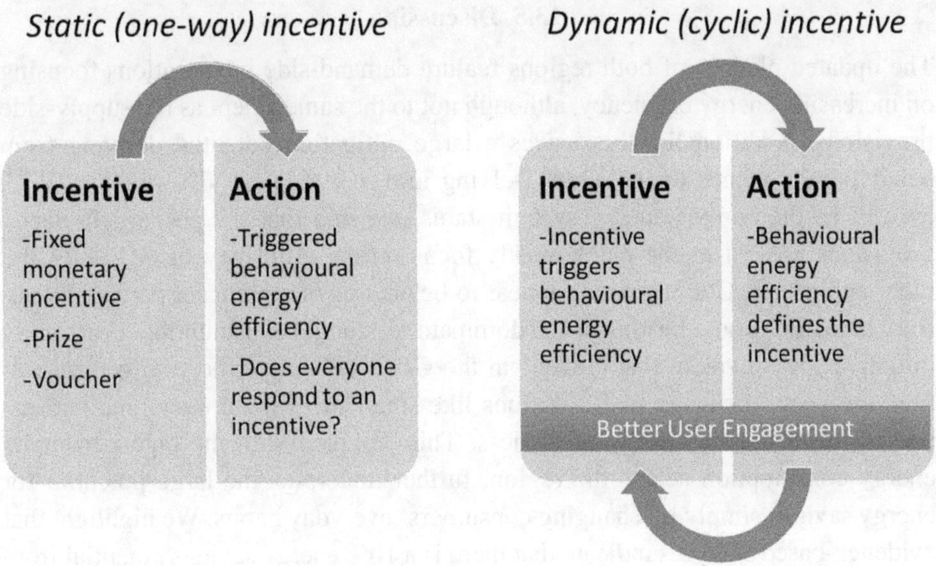

Figure 13.4 The ATOM digital energy currency novelty.

to monetise behavioural changes by providing a financial incentive to households that contribute towards saving energy. One such currency, the ATOMcoin, was presented by Marinakis et al. (2020b) and Koasidis et al. (2022), which provides an incentive to households that change their behaviour towards energy efficiency, providing a coin for 1kWh of saved energy, implemented in the context of a state, a municipality, utility, or even an energy community. The price of the currency was defined based on a dynamic pricing mechanism, ensuring that if more people adopt sustainable habits and reduce their consumption the higher the rate (Figure 13.4). This is contrary to a static incentive (e.g. coupons) since the ability of such a mechanism to trigger the expected changes depends on the background of the participants (Alberts et al., 2016; Azarova et al., 2020).

Based on simulations in Bahrain (Marinakis et al., 2020a) and the EU (Koasidis et al., 2022) it was found that such a mechanism could provide an additional financial incentive of around USD200 per household depending on the ability to contribute towards reducing energy consumption. This benefit far outweighs the installation cost of the equipment, if the household implements the behavioural changes discussed (see Section 13.4.1). In fact, it was showcased that this financial incentive would be more than adequate for certain categories of end-users (e.g. non-high-income households) (Ito et al., 2015). This, combined with the tendency of citizens in both regions to increase their engagement, indicates that the implementation of such a digital energy currency scheme could be desirable and assist towards unlocking the behavioural energy efficiency potential.

13.5 Discussion

The updated pledges of both regions feature demand-side interventions focusing on increasing energy efficiency, although not to the same extent as the supply-side provisions. Additionally, this leaves a large mitigation potential deriving from behavioural changes unexploited. Delving into the updated NDCs of the GCC, as well as the current energy system status, we find that the energy efficiency provisions present in the plans mostly focus on the efficiency of AC units and other appliances. Cooling needs appear to be an area of significant potential, contrary to the EU where heating needs dominate residential consumption. From early initiatives, it is evident that citizens in the GCC, especially the younger generation, are keen to engage with solutions like smart metres and overcome barriers present from limited energy awareness. This, coupled with the high per capita energy consumption across the region, further underpins the large potential for energy savings simply by changing consumers' everyday habits. We highlight that evidence-based analyses indicate that there is a 10% energy savings potential from efficiently adjusting the thermostat of an AC unit to conserve energy without sacrificing thermal comfort. For the GCC, this could translate to around 25ThW energy savings, a potential that could increase if we consider the high per capita energy consumption.

To achieve this potential and even unlock the full range of energy savings from behavioural changes, which could reach up to 20%, we suggest the employment of a behavioural energy efficiency framework consisting of autonomous technical solutions, that could also be employed in an integrated manner. This framework is based on energy disaggregation algorithms to provide consumption data on an appliance level without the need for extensive equipment, coupled with a Raspberry Pi device for smart cooling load planning, with user actions being informed by energy savings tips from a detailed list of behavioural changes. Such solutions have been systematically employed in Europe with significant success and could present great opportunities for the GCC region. To supplement this smart infrastructure, a digital energy currency could be implemented to provide financial incentives to consumers who contribute towards reducing their energy consumption. We highlight that considering the high savings potential, the financial benefit would significantly outweigh the small investment cost required. Overall, these common opportunities should be framed in consideration of the different political contexts and norms of the two regions, and notably regarding the highly subsidised energy within the context of the GCC's social contract. The interventions proposed in this chapter could help reduce the amount of energy consumed and, therefore, directly contribute to the reduction of subsidies required, reducing – rather than shifting – the financial burden for both the states and the citizens. Additionally, the reward mechanism could act as a supplementary scheme, providing financial support to citizens, while at the same time encouraging and supporting them to save energy and adopt more sustainable habits.

13.6 Conclusion

Meeting the Paris Agreement targets entails introducing divergent policies to battle climate change and raise ambition, as current trajectories are not aligned with a 1.5°C pathway. As a result of COP26, EU and GCC states, regions that constitute major economies and significant emitters, introduced updated plans and pledges towards carbon neutrality. In this chapter, we attempt to capture EU–GCC cooperation opportunities to unlock the energy savings potential from behavioural factors and share lessons from areas of strength and weakness in both regions, to assist them towards realising demand-side provisions of their updated pledges. We first delve into the updated pledges of the EU and the GCC to understand the current role of energy efficiency. Then we analyse the current power generation and electricity consumption context to identify areas with large efficiency potential from behavioural changes, highlighting parallels between energy needs for heating in the EU and cooling in the GCC. Finally, we suggest a set of measures focusing on behavioural changes to supplement current energy efficiency strategies and present a framework for exploiting existing opportunities for behavioural energy efficiency, drawing from proven technical solutions in the EU context that could be exploited in the GCC. The presented framework could assist in overcoming the barriers to achieving the energy efficiency targets established by the updated pledges, like high investment costs, by focusing on small low-cost actions and adapting everyday life habits, which could significantly lower demand and thus make it easier for supply-side transformations to be met as well.

References

Ahmed, W., and Asif, M. (2021). A critical review of energy retrofitting trends in residential buildings with particular focus on the GCC countries. *Renewable and Sustainable Energy Reviews* 144, p. 111000. Doi: 10.1016/j.rser.2021.111000.

Alam, M. M., and Murad, M. W. (2020). The impacts of economic growth, trade openness, and technological progress on renewable energy use in organization for economic co-operation and development countries. *Renewable Energy* 145, pp. 382–390. Doi .org/10.1016/j.renene.2019.06.054.

Al Amoodi, A., and Azar, E. (2018). Impact of human actions on building energy performance: a case study in the United Arab Emirates (UAE). *Sustainability* 10 (5), p. 1404. Doi: 10.3390/su10051404.

Al-Badi, A., and Al-Mubarak, I. (2019). Growing energy demand in the GCC countries. *Arab Journal of Basic and Applied Sciences*, 26 (1), pp. 488–496. Doi: 10.1080/25765299.2019.1687396.

AlKhars, M., Miah, F., Qudrat-Ullah, H., and Kayal, A. (2020). A systematic review of the relationship between energy consumption and economic growth in GCC countries. *Sustainability*, 12 (9), p. 3845. Doi: 10.3390/su12093845.

Almasri, R. A., and Alshitawi, M. S. (2022). Electricity consumption indicators and energy efficiency in residential buildings in GCC countries: extensive review. *Energy and Buildings* 255, p. 111664. Doi: 10.1016/j.enbuild.2021.111664.

Alnaser, N. W., Albuflasa, H. M., and Alnaser, W. E. (2022). The transition in solar and wind energy use in Gulf Cooperation Council Countries (GCCC). *Renewable Energy and Environmental Sustainability* 7 (4). Doi: 10.1051/rees/2021034.

Alnaser, N. W., and Alnaser, W. E. (2019). Analyzing the impact of Bapco 5 MW Solar PV grid-connected project on Bahrain's outlook for energy-mix production. *International Journal of Modern Nonlinear Theory and Application* 8 (3), pp. 72–91. Doi: 10.4236/ijmnta.2019.83006.

AlRemeithi, A., Kamal, H., and Alraeesi, M. (2020). Building simulation, solar potential and consumption analysis of residential dwellings, in Dubai. Thesis. Available online: https://scholarworks.rit.edu/theses/10471.

Andreasson, S. (2015). Varieties of resource nationalism in sub-Saharan Africa's energy and minerals markets. *Extractive Industries and Society* 2 (2), pp. 310–319. Doi .org/10.1016/j.exis.2015.01.004.

Arent, D., Arndt, C., Miller, M., Tarp, F., and Zinaman, O. (2017). Introduction and synthesis, in Arent, D. J. (ed.), *The Political Economy of Clean Energy Transitions (First)*. Oxford: Oxford University Press, pp. 14–23.

Athanasiadis, C. L., Doukas, D. I., Papadopoulos, T. A., and Barzegkar-Ntovom, G. A. (2021). Real-time non-intrusive load monitoring: a machine-learning approach for home appliance identification, in *2021 IEEE Madrid PowerTech*, pp. 1–6. Doi: 10.1109/PowerTech46648.2021.9494962.

AWS (2023). *Luminus and AWS Partner NET2GRID Offer Energy Insights That Help Users Reduce Their Energy Consumption*. Available online: https://aws.amazon.com/partners/success/luminus-net2grid/?advocacy_source=everyonesocial&trk=global_employee_advocacy&sc_channel=sm&es_id=9e5c22bec7.

Azar, E., Alaifan, B., Lin, M., Trepci, E., and El Asmar, M. (2021). Drivers of energy consumption in Kuwaiti buildings: insights from a hybrid statistical and building performance simulation approach. *Energy Policy* 150, p. 112154. Doi: 10.1016/j.enpol.2021.112154.

Bamati, N., and Raoofi, A. (2020). Development level and the impact of the technological factor on renewable energy production. *Renewable Energy* 151, pp. 946–955. Doi .org/10.1016/j.renene.2019.11.098.

Barker, S., Mishra, A., Irwin, D., Cecchet, E., Shenoy, P., and Albrecht, J. (2012). Smart*: an open data set and tools for enabling research in sustainable homes. *Proc. SustKDD* 111 (112), p. 108.

Bennett, A., and Checkel, J. T. (eds.) (2015). *Process Tracing*. Cambridge: Cambridge University Press.

Bremmer, I., and Johnston, R. (2009). The rise and fall of resource nationalism. *Survival* 51 (2), pp. 149–158. Doi: 10.1080/00396330902860884.

BP (2020). *Statistical Review of World Energy*. London: BP.

Bumajdad, A., Bouhamra, W., Alsayegh, O. A., Kamal, H. A., and Alhajraf, S. F. (eds.) (2020). *Gulf Conference on Sustainable Built Environment*. Cham: Springer International Publishing. Doi: 10.1007/978-3-030-39734-0.

Butler, N. (2019). Kuwait's action on green energy fails to match best intentions. *Financial Times*. Available online: www.ft.com/content/bdcee818-c35f-11e9-ae6e-a26d1d0455f4.

Cadoret, I., and Padovano, F. (2016). The political drivers of renewable energies policies. *Energy Economics* 56, pp. 261–269. Doi.org/10.1016/j.eneco.2016.03.003.

Carbon Tracker (2021). The sky's the limit – solar and wind energy potential is 100 times as much as global energy demand. Available online: https://carbontracker.org/reports/the-skys-the-limit-solar-wind/.

Coelho, S. T., and Goldemberg, J. (2013). Global energy policy: a view from Brazil, in Goldthau, A. (ed.), *The Handbook of Global Energy Policy*. Malden, MA: Willey-Blackwell, pp. 457–474.

Contreras, E. (1993). *Os Desbravadores: A Petrobrás e a Construção do Brasil industrial*. Rio de Janeiro: Relume Damará/ANPOCS.

Cornago, E. (2021). The potential of behavioural interventions for optimising energy use at home. Available online: www.iea.org/articles/the-potential-of-behavioural-interventions-for-optimising-energy-use-at-home.

Cozzi, L., Gould, T., Bouckart, S., Crow, D., Kim, T. Y., McGlade, C., Olejarnik, P., Wanner, B., and Wetzel, D. (2020). *World Energy Outlook 2020*. Available online: www.oecd-ilibrary.org/energy/world-energy-outlook-2020_557a761b-en.

Creutzig, F., Niamir, L., Bai, X., … Ürge-Vorsatz, D. (2022). Demand-side solutions to climate change mitigation consistent with high levels of well-being. *Nature Climate Change* 12 (1), pp. 36–46. Doi: 10.1038/s41558-021-01219-y.

Creutzig, F., Roy, J., Lamb, W. F., … Weber, E. U. (2018). Towards demand-side solutions for mitigating climate change. *Nature Climate Change* 8 (4), pp. 260–263. Doi: 10.1038/s41558-018-0121-1.

Doukas, H., Makarouni, I., Karakosta, C., Marinakis, V., and Psarras, J. (2012). EU–GCC clean energy cooperation: from concepts to action, in Tortora, M. (ed.), *Sustainable Systems and Energy Management at the Regional Level: Comparative Approaches*. Hershey, PA: Information Science Reference, pp. 288–308. Doi: 10.4018/978-1-61350-344-7.ch015.

Doukas, H., Marinakis, V., Tsapelas, J., and Sgouridis, S. (2019). Intelligent energy management within the smart cities: an EU–GCC cooperation opportunity, in Samad, W. A. and Azar, E. (eds.), *Smart Cities in the Gulf: Current State, Opportunities, and Challenges*. Singapore: Springer Nature, pp. 123–147. Doi: 10.1007/978-981-13-2011-8_8.

Energy Information Administration (EIA) (2016). *Country Analysis Brief: Kuwait*. U.S. Energy Information Administration, p. 14. Available online: www.eia.gov/international/content/analysis/countries_long/Kuwait/kuwait.pdf.

Energy Information Administration (EIA) (2020a). *Country Analysis Executive Summary: Mexico*. U.S. Energy Information Administration, p. 10. Available online: www.eia.gov/international/content/analysis/countries_long/Mexico/mexico.pdf.

Energy Information Administration (EIA) (2020b). *Country Analysis Executive Summary: United Arab Emirates*. U.S. Energy Information Administration, p. 8. Available online: www.eia.gov/international/content/analysis/countries_long/United_Arab_Emirates/uae_2020.pdf.

Etheridge, J. (2009). Power struggle hits Kuwaiti oil sector. *Financial Times*. Available online: www.ft.com/content/55b6a2f6-0cbe-11de-a555-0000779fd2ac.

European Commission (2021). *Tips for Your Home*. Available online: https://ec.europa.eu/clima/citizens/climate-tips/tips-your-home_en#wash-smart.

Fitch Solutions (2021). *Mexico: Renewables Report: Includes 10-Year Forecasts to 2030 (Q3 2021)*. Available online: www.fitchsolutions.com.

Forouli, A., Gkonis, N., Nikas, A., Siskos, E., Doukas, H., and Tourkolias, C. (2019). Energy efficiency promotion in Greece in light of risk: evaluating policies as portfolio assets. *Energy* 170, pp. 818–831. Doi: 10.1016/j.energy.2018.12.180.

Freeman, C. (1987). *Technology Policy and Economic Performance: Lessons from Japan*. London: Pinter.

Freire, W. (2013). Petrobras: das origens até os anos 1990, in Giambiagi, F. and Paulo Velloso Lucas, L. (eds.), *Petróleo: Reforma e Contrareforma do Setor Petrolífero Brasileiro*. Rio de Janeiro: Elsevier.

Gebeily, M. (2021). Analysis: Gulf energy giants pledge net zero – but plan to stick with oil. Reuters, 28 October. Available online: www.reuters.com/business/cop/gulf-energy-giants-pledge-net-zero-plan-stick-with-oil-2021-10-28/.

Gatzert, N., and Kosub, T. (2017). Determinants of policy risks of renewable energy investments. *International Journal of Energy Sector Management* 11 (1), pp. 28–45.

Hausfather, Z., and Moore, F. C. (2022). Net-zero commitments could limit warming to below 2°C. *Nature* 604(7905), pp. 247–248. Doi: 10.1038/d41586-022-00874-1.

Hertog, S. (2010). Defying the resource curse: explaining successful state-owned enterprises in rentier states. *World Politics* 62 (2), pp. 261–301. Doi.org/10.1017/S0043887110000055.

Hochstetler, K. (2021). *Political Economies of Energy Transition: Wind and Solar Power in Brazil and South Africa*. Cambridge: Cambridge University Press.

Hussein, H. (2020). Khalifa bin Zayed issues a law to establish the Supreme Council for Financial and Economic Affairs. *Emirates News Agency*. Available online: https://wam.ae/en/details/1395302898123.

Höhne, N., Gidden, M. J., den Elzen, M., … Rogelj, J. (2021). Wave of net zero emission targets opens window to meeting the Paris Agreement. *Nature Climate Change* 11 (10), pp. 820–822. Doi: 10.1038/s41558-021-01142-2.

Industrial Shields (2023). Better monitoring and control of HVAC for Shopping Malls. Available online: www.industrialshields.com/success-story-hvac-equipment-with-raspberry-pi-gprs-plc.

International Energy Agency (IEA) (2018). *World Energy Investment 2018*. Paris: IEA/OECD.

International Energy Agency (IEA) (2019). *Data and Statistics*. Available online: www.iea.org/data-and-statistics.

International Energy Agency (IEA) (2020). The Oil and Gas Industry in Energy Transitions. Available online: https://iea.blob.core.windows.net/assets/4315f4ed-5cb2-4264-b0ee-2054fd34c118/The_Oil_and_Gas_Industry_in_Energy_Transitions.pdf.

International Energy Agency (IEA) (2021). *Energy Subsidies: Tracking the Impact of Fossil-Fuel Subsidies*. Available online: www.iea.org/topics/energy-subsidies.

International Renewable Energy Agency (IRENA) (2015). *Renewable Energy Prospects: United Arab Emirates*. Available online: www.irena.org/publications/2015/Apr/Renewable-Energy-Prospects-United-Arab-Emirates.

Jäger-Waldau, A., Kougias, I., Taylor, N., and Thiel, C. (2020). How photovoltaics can contribute to GHG emission reductions of 55% in the EU by 2030. *Renewable and Sustainable Energy Reviews* 126, p. 109836. Doi: 10.1016/j.rser.2020.109836.

Kammermann, L., and Dermont, C. (2018). How beliefs of the political elite and citizens on climate change influence support for Swiss energy transition policy. *Energy Research & Social Science* 43, pp. 48–60. Doi.org/10.1016/j.erss.2018.05.010.

Karmakar, G., Arote, U., Agarwal, A., and Ramamritham, K. (2018). Adaptive hybrid approaches to thermal modeling of building, in *Proceedings of the Ninth International Conference on Future Energy Systems*. New York: Association for Computing Machinery, pp. 477–479. Doi: 10.1145/3208903.3212068.

Knoop, K., and Lechtenböhmer, S. (2017). The potential for energy efficiency in the EU member states – a comparison of studies. *Renewable and Sustainable Energy Reviews* 68, pp. 1097–1105. Doi: 10.1016/j.rser.2016.05.090.

Koasidis, K., and Psarras, J. (2021). Innovative personalised applications to motivate and support behavioural energy efficiency, in *2021 12th International Conference on Information, Intelligence, Systems & Applications (IISA)*, pp. 1–6. Doi: 10.1109/IISA52424.2021.9555498.

Koasidis, K., Marinakis, V., Nikas, A., Chira, K., Flamos, A., and Doukas, H. (2022). Monetising behavioural change as a policy measure to support energy management in the residential sector: a case study in Greece. *Energy Policy* 161, p. 112759. Doi: 10.1016/j.enpol.2021.112759.

Kolter, J. Z., and Johnson, M. J. (2011). REDD: a public data set for energy disaggregation research, presented at the Workshop on data mining applications in sustainability (SIGKDD), San Diego, CA. Available online: www.semanticscholar.org/paper/REDD-%3A-A-Public-Data-Set-for-Energy-Disaggregation-Kolter/db3ea129add716192f11d41e605c0020ee2488d7.

Krarti, M. (2019). Evaluation of energy efficiency potential for the building sector in the Arab region. *Energies* 12 (22), p. 4279. Doi: 10.3390/en12224279.

Kuwait National Petroleum Company (2021). *Clean Fuels Project*. Available online: www.knpc.com/en/strategic-projects/clean-fuel-project-cfp.

Leite, A. D. (2014). *A Energia do Brasil (3ª edição)*. Rio de Janeiro: Lexikon.

Leite, R. C. D. C., Leal, M. R. L. V., Cortez, L. A. B., Griffin, W. M., and Scandiffio, M. I. G. (2009). Can Brazil replace 5% of the 2025 gasoline world demand with ethanol? *Energy* 34 (5), pp. 655–661. Doi.org/10.1016/j.energy.2008.11.001.

Lima-de-Oliveira, R. (2019). Resource-led industrial development in the oil and gas global value chain: the case of Brazil, in Elisabeth, B. R., and Reynolds, B. (eds.), *Innovation in Brazil: Advancing Development in the 21st Century*. London: Routledge, pp. 283–302.

Lima-de-Oliveira, R. (2020). Corruption and local content development: assessing the impact of the Petrobras' scandal on recent policy changes in Brazil. *Extractive Industries and Society* 7, pp. 274–282. Doi.org/10.1016/j.exis.2019.08.004.

MacDonald, F. (2020, 10 September). Kuwait Parliament approves state budget with $46 billion deficit. Bloomberg. Available online: www.bloombergquint.com/markets/kuwait-parliament-approves-state-budget-with-46-billion-deficit.

Marinakis, V., Doukas, H., Koasidis, K., and Albuflasa, H. (2020a). From intelligent energy management to value economy through a digital energy currency: Bahrain city case study. *Sensors* 20 (5), p. 1456. Doi: 10.3390/s20051456.

Marinakis, V., Doukas, H., Tsapelas, J., … Sgouridis, S. (2020b). From big data to smart energy services: an application for intelligent energy management. *Future Generation Computer Systems* 110, pp. 572–586. Doi: 10.1016/j.future.2018.04.062.

Meinshausen, M., Lewis, J., McGlade, C., … Hackmann, B. (2022). Realization of Paris Agreement pledges may limit warming just below 2°C. *Nature* 604 (7905), pp. 304–309. Doi: 10.1038/s41586-022-04553-z.

Meyer, L., and Morales, I. (1990). *Petróleo y nación (1900–1987): La política petrolera en México*. México, DF: Fondo de Cultura Económica.

Morales, I. (1992). The consolidation and expansion of Pemex, in Brown, J. C., and Knight, A. (eds.), *The Mexican Petroleum industry in the Twentieth Century*. Austin, TX: University of Texas Press., pp. 208–232.

Murshed, M., and Alam, M. S. (2021). Estimating the macroeconomic determinants of total, renewable, and non-renewable energy demands in Bangladesh: the role of technological innovations. *Environmental Science and Pollution Research* 28, pp. 30176–30196. Doi.org/10.1007/s11356-021-12516-6.

Nardon, L., and Aten, K. (2008). Beyond a better mousetrap: a cultural analysis of the adoption of ethanol in Brazil. *Journal of World Business* 43 (3), pp. 261–273.

Park, J., Kim, T., and Lee, C. (2019). Development of thermal comfort-based controller and potential reduction of the cooling energy consumption of a residential building in Kuwait. *Energies* 12 (17), p. 3348. Doi: 10.3390/en12173348.

Pérez-Denicia, E., Fernández-Luqueño, F., Vilariño-Ayala, D., Montaño-Zetina, L. M., and Maldonado-López, L. A. (2017). Renewable energy sources for electricity generation in Mexico: a review. *Renewable and Sustainable Energy Reviews* 78, pp. 597–613.

Philip, G. (1992). The expropriation in comparative perspective, in Brown, J. C. and Knight, A. (eds.), *The Mexican Petroleum Industry in the Twentieth Century*. Austin, TX: University of Texas Press, pp. 173–188.

Priest, T. (2016). Petrobras in the history of offshore oil, in Schneider, B. R. (ed.), *New Order and Progress: Development and Democracy in Brazil*. New York: Oxford University Press, pp. 53–77.

Radhi, H. (2011). Viability of autoclaved aerated concrete walls for the residential sector in the United Arab Emirates. *Energy and Buildings* 43 (9), pp. 2086–2092. Doi: 10.1016/j.enbuild.2011.04.018.

Rahimpour, A., Qi, H., Fugate, D., and Kuruganti, T. (2017). Non-intrusive energy disaggregation using non-negative matrix factorization with sum-to-k constraint. *IEEE Transactions on Power Systems* 32 (6), pp. 4430–4441. Doi: 10.1109/TPWRS.2017.2660246.

Saadi, D. (2020). Abu Dhabi merges Supreme Petroleum Council with new economic body. S&P Global. Available online: www.spglobal.com/platts/en/market-insights/latest-news/oil/122820-abu-dhabi-merges-supreme-petroleum-council-with-new-economic-body.

Saba, Y. (2020, 16 September). Kuwait cuts $3 billion from 2020–21 budget, lawmaker says. Reuters. Available online: www.reuters.com/sarticle/kuwait-budget-int-idUSKBN25Z1GZ.

Saleh, M., Khdour, T., and Qasaymeh, M. (2019). Analysis of AMI, smart metering deployment and big data management challenges, in *Proceedings of the 3rd International Conference on Big Data and Internet of Things*. New York: Association for Computing Machinery, pp. 3–7. Doi: 10.1145/3361758.3361759.

SENER (2020). *Programa de Desarrollo del Sistema Eléctrico Nacional: 2020–2034*. Mexico City: SENER.

Sequeira, T. N., and Santos, M. S. (2018). Renewable energy and politics: a systematic review and new evidence. *Journal of Cleaner Production* 192, pp. 553–568. Doi.org/10.1016/j.jclepro.2018.04.190.

Shehabi, M. (2020). *Kuwait Energy Outlook 2020: Current Policies and Necessity of Reform*. Oxford: Oxford Institute for Energy Studies. Available online: www.oxfordenergy.org/publications/kuwait-energy-outlook-2020-current-policies-and-necessity-of-reform/.

Shin, C., Rho, S., Lee, H., and Rhee, W. (2019). Data requirements for applying machine learning to energy disaggregation. *Energies* 12 (9), p. 1696. Doi: 10.3390/en12091696.

Sognnaes, I., Gambhir, A., van de Ven, D.-J., … Peters, G. P. (2021). A multi-model analysis of long-term emissions and warming implications of current mitigation efforts. *Nature Climate Change* 11 (12), pp. 1055–1062. Doi: 10.1038/s41558-021-01206-3.

Smith, P. (1976). *Oil and Politics in Modern Brazil*. Toronto: Macmillan.

Sovacool, B. K., Kivimaa, P., Hielscher, S., and Jenkins, K. (2017). Vulnerability and resistance in the United Kingdom's smart meter transition. *Energy Policy* 109, pp. 767–781. Doi: 10.1016/j.enpol.2017.07.037.

Stevens, P. (2008). National oil companies and international oil companies in the Middle East: under the shadow of government and the resource nationalism cycle. *Journal of World Energy Law & Business* 1 (1), pp. 5–30. Doi.org/10.1093/jwelb/jwn004.

Trojbicz, B., and Loureiro, M. R. (2018). Brazilian oil sector reforms: the role of technical know-how and corporate ethos in Petrobras' dominance. *Energy Policy* 118, pp. 588–595. Doi.org/10.1016/j.enpol.2018.03.060.

UAE Government Portal (2021). *UAE Energy Strategy 2050*. Available online: https://u.ae/en/about-the-uae/strategies-initiatives-and-awards/federal-governments-strategies-and-plans/uae-energy-strategy-2050.

UAE Ministry of Energy and Infrastructure (2017, 10 January). *Vice President Unveils UAE Energy Strategy for Next Three Decades*. Available online: www.moei.gov.ae/en/media-centre/news/10/1/2017/محمد-بن-راشد-يعلن-استراتيجية-دولة-الإمارات-للطاقة-للعقود-الثلاثة-المقبلة.aspx#page=1.

Villamil, J. (2020). Why Mexico is pushing to slow down clean energy. *Washington Post*. Available online: www.washingtonpost.com/business/energy/why-mexico-is-pushing-to-slow-down-clean-energy/2020/07/16/fbfcd0f4-c779-11ea-a825-8722004e4150_story.html.

Whitmarsh, L., Poortinga, W., and Capstick, S. (2021). Behaviour change to address climate change. *Current Opinion in Psychology* 42, pp. 76–81. Doi: 10.1016/j.copsyc.2021.04.002.

Wilson, J. D. (2015). Understanding resource nationalism: economic dynamics and political institutions. *Contemporary Politics* 21 (4), pp. 399–416. Doi.org/10.1080/13569775.2015.1013293.

World Bank (2021). *World Development Indicators Data Bank*. World Bank Data Bank. Available online: https://databank.worldbank.org/source/world-development-indicators#.

Zou, M., Zhu, S., Gu, J., Korunovic, L. M., and Djokic, S. Z. (2021). Heating and lighting load disaggregation using frequency components and convolutional bidirectional Long short-term memory method. *Energies* 14 (16), p. 4831. Doi: 10.3390/en14164831.

Part VI

Conclusion

14

Outlook of Net Zero GCC States

WAEL A. SAMAD, AHMED BADRAN, AND ELIE AZAR

14.1 Overview and Contributions

The Gulf region is home to some of the world's largest oil reserves and is a major contributor to global carbon emissions, both directly and indirectly. As the world grapples with the challenges of climate change, the Gulf countries have been forced to take a closer look at their carbon footprint and their role in the global effort to reduce emissions. Carbon neutrality is the concept of achieving net zero carbon emissions by balancing carbon emissions with carbon removal or offsetting. It has become a popular buzzword in recent years, with many countries and even companies making pledges to become carbon neutral in the coming years.

The Gulf countries have joined global efforts, announcing several ambitious pledges to achieve carbon neutrality by 2050 or earlier, with varying degrees of commitment between the countries. However, several challenges exist and need to be tackled for a successful transition, including but not limited to geographical, socioeconomic, institutional, and political challenges. Therefore, research efforts are needed to critically evaluate the stated challenges, assess promising opportunities, and inform strategies that enable a carbon neutrality transition in the different sectors of the Gulf Cooperation Council (GCC) economies.

This edited volume provided the first systematic assessment and understanding of the current trends, challenges, and opportunities for the GCC region to achieve carbon neutrality. Through a compilation and synthesis of scholarly essays and case studies, it offered unique insights into the policy frameworks, technological innovations, and behavioural changes needed to transition from oil-based to cleaner, knowledge-based economies. More specifically, the volume features twelve chapters organised along four themes focused on particular aspects of the transition: (1) *Circular Carbon Economy and Pathway Frameworks*; (2) *Infrastructure*; (3) *Policy and Data Transparency*; and (4) *Behavioural Aspects and Human Factors.*

The following section provides a key takeaway from each of the four themes, before concluding the book with some final thoughts.

14.2 Takeaways

14.2.1 Takeaway #1: The Role of Cities and the GCC in Carbon Neutrality

Delving into the theme of 'Circular Carbon Economy and Pathway Frameworks' in Part II, a multifaceted exploration unravels the intricacies of the GCC's path to carbon neutrality. 'Circular Cities: One of the Pathways to Carbon Neutrality' (Chapter 2) dives into the potential of transitioning from a linear to a circular economy model, especially within urban environments. The discourse brings into light the extensive resources cities offer, coupled with the intrinsic power they possess in spearheading the carbon neutrality campaign. While a pragmatic step-by-step methodology to foster circularity in urban contexts emerges as the cornerstone, the chapter also underscores the potential for cities to innovate and adapt these strategies over time.

Shifting focus to the broader region, 'The GCC and the Circular Carbon Economy: Progress and Potential' (Chapter 3) offers a comprehensive assessment of the GCC's strides in the circular carbon economy. Through a comparative lens, GCC's performance is benchmarked against both its regional and global peers. The findings spotlight the vast potential lying in underutilised technologies such as renewables and nuclear energy. Also, the narrative underscores the critical importance of sustainable finance and investments, suggesting that for the GCC to truly ascend in the global green transition, a concerted effort in these domains is indispensable.

Zeroing in on the Saudi context, 'Net Zero Saudi Arabia: How Green Can the Oil Kingdom Get?, (Chapter 4) paints a nuanced picture of the nation's ambitious decarbonisation goal. Against the backdrop of its deep-rooted oil legacy, Saudi Arabia's pledge for a net zero 2060 presents both challenges and advantages. A holistic perspective reveals Saudi's robust resource landscape, which, combined with its human talent and geopolitical ambitions, may just offer the right recipe for its ambitious 2060 target.

Together, these explorations furnish a holistic view of the trials and triumphs that mark the GCC's journey within the circular carbon domain, sketching a portrait of a region fervently pursuing its carbon-neutral aspirations.

14.2.2 Takeaway #2: Infrastructure's Pivotal Role in GCC's Carbon Ambitions

Within the theme of 'Infrastructure' in Part III, various facets of the GCC's approach to carbon neutrality are explored. 'Energy Efficiency and Carbon Neutrality Potentials for the Building Sector in the GCC Region' (Chapter 5) investigates the energy demands of the GCC's building sector. The analysis underscores historical energy efficiency trends, with a significant emphasis on the role of air conditioning in energy consumption. It reveals an immense potential for enhancing energy performance in the region's buildings. Key interventions, such as implementing Minimum Energy Performance Standards and comprehensive energy efficiency codes, emerge as pivotal. A spotlight on retrofitting existing structures suggests that ambitious energy efficiency initiatives could save up to 600 TWh by 2030.

Transitioning to Dubai's efforts in public transport, 'Electrifying Public Transport Networks in Dubai: Environmental Benefits, Urban Improvements, and Social Challenges' (Chapter 6) offers a comparative perspective with European experiences in public transport electrification. The discussion contrasts the potential of hydrogen-fuelled technology with electrification, emphasising the critical roles of user engagement, cultural adaptability, and strategic urban planning. Drawing from European lessons, it becomes clear that Dubai's unique cultural and geographical context demands custom solutions, with electrification appearing as a more promising route than hydrogen technology for urban mobility.

Examining to the potential of green hydrogen, 'Net Zero Emissions in the GCC Region: Challenges and Opportunities for Green Hydrogen Applications' (Chapter 7) illuminates how this energy source can be instrumental in the GCC's aspiration for net-zero emissions. With the region's distinct advantages, such as abundant oil reserves and renewable energy sources, green hydrogen stands out as a transformative solution. However, realising its full potential requires a systematic roadmap, encompassing policies for technology readiness and market expansion. With strategic planning, the GCC countries can not only achieve their environmental goals but also position themselves as global pioneers in the burgeoning hydrogen economy.

Collectively, these insights provide a comprehensive perspective on the challenges and opportunities inherent in the GCC's infrastructure landscape, portraying a region fervently navigating its ambitious path towards carbon neutrality.

14.2.3 Takeaway #3: Policy, Data Transparency, and Forward-Thinking in GCC's Climate Strategy

Under the overarching theme of 'Policy and Data Transparency' in Part IV, a series of analyses provide an intricate examination of the GCC region's response to climate change. 'GCC Carbon Neutrality and Net Zero Policy Tracker: Framing, Methodology, and Findings' (Chapter 8) underscores the global decarbonisation policy gap, highlighting the urgent need for GCC countries to adopt tangible carbon neutrality policies. By introducing policy tracking as a tool to bolster accountability, this analysis evaluates the GCC's adherence to the Paris Agreement's commitments. While the United Arab Emirates (UAE) stands out with its proactive renewable energy investments, countries like the Kingdom of Saudi Arabia remain caught up in a gap between public relations claims and substantive action. This disparity raises concerns about the region's genuine commitment to the objectives of the Paris Agreement and their own Nationally Determined Contributions.

Transitioning to data governance, 'Data Policies and Governance for Greenhouse Gases Reports and Initiatives' (Chapter 9) emphasises the central role of open environmental data. Through the lens of the Kingdom of Bahrain's endeavour to present its greenhouse gas inventory, the significance of robust data governance in safeguarding transparency and accountability becomes evident. The success of such inventory projects hinges on the strength of data governance, with challenges like data availability and quality surmountable through a structured governance system, stakeholder trust, and precise data integration.

Exploring the complexities of long-term climate planning, 'Key Issues for Long-Term Climate Policy Design in GCC Countries with a Focus on Qatar' (Chapter 10) explores the complexities of devising an effective global climate policy tailored for the GCC. Assessing the macroeconomic implications of the Paris Agreement's emissions abatement targets and spotlighting Qatar, strategies for drastic greenhouse gas emissions reduction emerge. The imperative of technologies such as Carbon Capture and Storage and Direct Air Capture is highlighted, essential for achieving zero net emissions both globally and locally. As the landscape of global oil and gas demand shifts, propelled by innovations like electric mobility, the GCC nations must anticipate these changes, pioneering cleaner fossil fuel programmes and advancing innovative energy policies synergised with cutting-edge technologies like the Internet of Things.

In summation, these insights offer a comprehensive view of the intertwined domains of climate policy, data transparency, and futuristic planning in the GCC, reiterating the pressing need to strategise, adapt, and innovate.

14.2.4 Takeaway #4: Human Behavior and Societal Implications in Energy Transition

The theme of 'Behavioural Aspects and Human Factors' in Part V analyses the dynamics nexus of human behaviour, societal interactions, and the overarching challenges of energy transition in the Gulf States. By intertwining sociopolitical, technological, and economic viewpoints, it offers a holistic exploration of energy transitions in oil-rich nations.

'Energy Transition in Oil-Rich Countries: The Role of Resource Nationalism' (Chapter 11) examines the profound impact of a country's resource nationalism on its adaptability to a post-hydrocarbon economy. By juxtaposing the renewable energy adoption rates of nations like Kuwait and Mexico, which lean towards social-based policies, with those of the UAE and Brazil, which prefer market-based strategies, it becomes evident that national policies hold significant sway over energy transition speeds. The segment also highlights the necessity for broader research, emphasising the political determinants of these transitions to enrich existing academic discourses.

Transitioning to the interplay between individuals and their built environments, 'Toward Smart Buildings and Communities in the Gulf States: Analysis of Human and Social Dimensions in the Transition to Carbon-Neutral Cities Using Artificial Intelligence' (Chapter 12) employs a detailed survey from Doha, Qatar, to emphasise the pivotal role of understanding and optimising the bond between occupants and buildings in designing sustainable infrastructure. The introduction of the innovative Human Building Interaction framework provides groundbreaking insights. This framework presents a harmonious blend of energy efficiency and occupant comfort, advocating for their centrality in the design of sustainable, carbon-neutral edifices.

Concluding this theme, 'EU–GCC Cooperation Opportunities on Behavioural Energy Efficiency' (Chapter 13) acts as a conduit for knowledge exchange between the European Union and the GCC. This segment underscores the untapped potential of behavioural shifts in reaching energy efficiency aspirations. It suggests the harmonious marriage of incentive-based mechanisms with advanced machine learning. Such an amalgamation promises to furnish personalised energy-saving recommendations for consumers, amplifying their efficacy. In a world now reflecting on the outcomes of COP26 and the pressing need to steer back to the 1.5°C pathway, this segment showcases the avenues for the EU and GCC to collaboratively traverse the energy domain, learning and drawing from their shared and individual strengths.

Collectively, this theme not only illuminates the intricate tapestry of energy transition but firmly places the human element, spanning macropolicies to individual behaviours, at the heart of the discourse on achieving ambitious energy and sustainability milestones.

14.3 Final Thoughts

Achieving carbon neutrality requires more than just investments in renewable energy. It requires a fundamental shift in the way we live and work, from our consumption patterns to our transportation systems. It also requires a commitment to innovation and the development of new technologies that can help us reduce emissions in a cost-effective manner. This includes, in addition to investing in renewable energy, promoting energy efficiency, developing low-carbon transportation systems, and engaging the public in the conversation about climate change. It also requires a commitment to international cooperation and collaboration; the Gulf countries are part of a global community that must work together to address the challenges of climate change. This includes sharing knowledge and best practices, collaborating on research and development, and supporting international efforts to reduce emissions and promote sustainable development. Finally, achieving carbon neutrality requires a long-term vision and commitment. It will not happen overnight and it will require sustained effort and investment over many years. On the positive side, the rewards of carbon neutrality are significant, both in terms of mitigating the impacts of climate change and promoting sustainable development and economic growth. Research efforts originating from and focused on the local GCC context are increasingly needed to guide the anticipated transformation of GCC economies from oil-based to low-carbon and resilient knowledge-based economies, while accommodating the unique needs and context of the region. The current edited volume is a contribution towards steps taken in that direction, supporting the good-intentioned pledges of GCC countries toward carbon neutrality and providing pathways to face the harsh reality of the complex challenges ahead.

Index

abatement, 61, 168, 202, 210, 212, 218, 312
Abu Dhabi, 15, 70, 88, 91, 128, 171–172, 233–235, 287
AC. *See* air conditioning
academia, 20, 240
acclimatisation, 128
accountability, 172, 178, 180, 194–195, 198, 311–312
acidification, 121
activism, 233–234
adaptability, 248, 252, 311–312
adaptation, 157, 176, 182, 184, 192
affordability, 123
Africa, 24, 32, 34–35, 38, 49, 65, 77, 164–165, 170, 228, 241
agriculture, 180–181, 290
AI. *See* artificial intelligence
air conditioners, 94–95, 113, 261, 286
air conditioning, 88, 91–92, 94, 106, 245, 248–249, 260, 274, 286, 290, 293–294, 298, 311
aluminium, 75
ammonia, 48, 58, 70, 72, 74–75, 78, 137–138, 143, 216
aquifers, 58, 74, 206
architecture, 129, 176, 193, 250, 255
aridity, 146
artificial intelligence, 6, 197, 245–246, 313
Asia, 77, 145, 164, 203, 229, 241
atmosphere, 30, 118, 124, 136, 138, 201–202
automation, 292
autonomy, 125, 154, 230, 233
Aviation, 167, 214
awareness, 4, 19, 127, 182, 184–185, 198, 226, 247, 251, 286–287, 291, 293, 298

Bahrain, 3, 6, 12, 33, 36, 38, 42, 44, 46, 85, 88, 91, 93, 95–96, 102–104, 159, 161, 164, 167, 177, 179–180, 182–185, 187–189, 191, 193, 197, 284, 289–290, 293, 297, 312
batteries, 69, 76, 119–121, 124–125, 127, 215
biodiesel, 14, 239
biodiversity, 153, 155, 158, 283
bioenergy, 202
biofuels, 70, 76, 238, 240
biogas, 46, 69, 140
biology, 137
biomass, 70, 139, 202, 206–207, 239

carbon capture, 72, 143, 202, 205–206, 312
cement, 71–72
circular cities, 5, 13, 16, 18, 310
circular economy, 12–16, 19, 21, 26, 30, 124, 171, 283, 310
circularity, 12–21, 24–27, 30, 32, 44, 310
citizen, 113, 191, 235
combustion, 58, 60–62, 64, 67, 69, 73, 76, 119, 122, 124, 142, 144, 187
comfort, 6, 58, 88, 91–92, 106, 128, 245–256, 258, 260, 262, 268, 271–275, 290, 292, 298, 313
Conference of the Parties, 77, 167–170, 172, 176
construction, 37, 60, 92, 96, 105, 119–120, 126, 129, 145, 161–162, 169, 184, 251, 255, 260, 270, 273–274, 284, 286, 289
contaminants, 138
contractors, 99
cooling, 88, 90, 92, 98, 106, 109, 138, 158, 167, 203–204, 214, 216–218, 245, 258, 286–287, 290, 292–294, 296, 298–299
COP. *See* Conference of the Parties
coronavirus, 61, 135, 153–154, 160–165, 231
COVID-19. *See* coronavirus
crowdsourcing, 163
currency, 79, 163, 283, 294, 296–298
cybersecurity, 191

data transparency, 178, 312
datasets, 33, 35, 43, 162, 294
daylighting, 92
debt, 39
decarbonisation, 117–119, 122–123, 125–126, 129–130, 148, 287, 289, 291
demand-side management, 69, 245
democracy, 154
density, 122, 125, 129–130, 287
desalination, 58

designers, 90
diesel, 70, 76, 127, 167, 171, 239
diplomacy, 155
disability, 165
discomfort, 106, 128, 248, 253, 269
discrimination, 164
diversification, 42–43, 62, 78, 85, 113, 117, 166, 170, 204–205, 229, 235–240, 286
Doha, 247, 258, 274–275, 313
drought, 239
Dubai, 5, 12, 14–16, 46, 59, 70, 91–92, 127–128, 171–172, 234–235, 287, 311

ecology, 92
ecosystem, 20, 27, 246–247
education, 160, 164–165, 233, 247
electric vehicle, 69–70, 205
electrification, 33, 37, 46, 49, 69–70, 78, 119–121, 123, 125, 130, 167, 215, 291, 311
electrolysis, 48, 75, 136, 138–140, 143, 145–146, 216
employment, 26, 105, 163–164, 233, 294, 298
entrepreneurship, 247, 275
equipment, 46, 90, 92, 94, 98, 109, 113, 138, 146, 249, 286, 290, 292, 297–298
equity, 25
ethanol, 137, 238–240
ethnicity, 258
ethylene, 71–72
EVs. *See* electric vehicle
expatriate, 258
expertise, 21, 24–25, 74, 79, 182, 190, 237, 247

facility, 37, 48, 72, 141, 169–170, 234
factory, 171
feedstock, 60, 65, 72, 75, 135, 137–139, 143, 145–146
fermentation, 140
fertiliser, 69, 72, 137
fission, 137
fleet, 46, 70–71
forestry, 176, 181, 186, 290
freezers, 93

gasification, 140
gasoline, 65, 70, 76, 167, 171, 232, 238–239
gender, 128, 251, 271
generators, 110, 239
geology, 71, 74–75, 77, 79
geothermal, 46, 119
glazing, 113, 254

halogen, 292
happiness, 161
hazards, 161
health, 118, 160, 163–165, 248–250
healthcare, 3, 165, 233
heating, 90, 92, 106, 109, 143, 245, 248, 290, 292, 298, 299
highways, 129
hotels, 172
humidity, 253, 272
HVAC, 248–251, 257–258, 271, 296
hydroelectricity, 238–239
hydrogen, 6, 32–33, 37, 39–40, 45–46, 48–49, 58, 60, 69–72, 74–75, 78, 118–119, 123–126, 130, 134–148, 166, 170, 215–219, 311

IAQ. *See* indoor air quality
ideology, 161, 228
IEQ. *See* indoor environmental quality
inclusion, 111
inclusivity, 179
indigenous, 47, 238
indoor air quality, 250, 253–254
indoor environmental quality, 250, 253
industrialisation, 229, 236
infiltration, 98
infrastructure, 4–5, 13–14, 26, 33, 38, 49, 71, 78–79, 121–122, 129, 141, 144, 169, 171, 193–194, 197, 204, 236, 254, 283, 289, 298, 311, 313
insulation, 96, 98, 113, 293
integration, 127, 146, 187, 191–193, 196, 198, 246, 275, 312
integrity, 154, 191, 196–198
intermittency, 69, 215

Jeddah, 111–112
justice, 155, 211

KSA. *See* Saudi Arabia
Kuwait, 3, 14, 34, 37, 39, 42–44, 46, 77, 85, 88, 91, 93, 95–96, 102–105, 159, 161, 164, 167, 226, 229–235, 240–241, 287, 289–290, 313

legislation, 15, 155, 240
lifecycle, 25, 111, 192–194, 197–199
lifestyle, 203, 272, 291
liquefaction, 147
literacy, 294
lithium, 121, 215
LNG. *See* natural gas

machine learning, 245, 283, 291, 294, 313
MENA, 127, 165, 171, 230, 241
metallurgy, 137
metals, 71
meteorology, 93
methane, 43, 127, 138–140, 170
methanol, 37, 58, 70, 72, 74, 137–138, 143
metro, 169
microclimate, 92
mobility, 92, 123, 127, 171, 205, 215, 219, 311–312
modernism, 129
monopoly, 76–77, 237, 239
monoxide, 137
motor, 167
municipality, 171, 297

nationalisation, 229, 236
nationalism, 6, 226–230, 237, 240, 312
natural gas, 42, 47, 49, 58–59, 64, 67–69, 71–72, 74–75, 77, 85–86, 119, 123–124, 126–127, 137, 139, 142–145, 147, 158, 166, 169–171, 203–204, 206, 216–217, 231, 234–236, 238, 288
negotiations, 16, 155, 176, 186, 201–204, 211, 219
neighbourhood, 21, 92, 128
Neom, 37, 141
NGOs. *See* non-governmental organisations
nitrogen, 75
noise, 250, 253–254, 272
non-governmental organisations, 18, 156–157
norms, 154, 161, 252, 296, 298
nuclear, 47, 59, 69, 85, 201, 231

oil, 3–6, 32–35, 37–38, 40–47, 49, 57–65, 67–69, 71, 73–79, 85–86, 113, 120–121, 127, 134–135, 137–138, 144, 148, 158, 166, 168, 170–171, 196, 201, 204–205, 217, 219, 225–233, 235–241, 288–289, 309–312, 314
Oman, 3, 14, 34, 37, 39–40, 43, 45–46, 49, 74, 77, 85, 88, 91, 93, 95–96, 102–104, 141, 159, 161, 164, 168, 171, 173, 205, 285, 289–290, 293
osmosis, 138, 172
outdoor, 88, 92, 250, 252, 255, 272
overcrowding, 122
overhangs, 254
overheating, 254
oxygen, 74, 124, 139

pandemic. *See* coronoavirus
parliament, 232, 234–235
participation, 18, 27, 183, 191
pedestrian, 128
petrochemical, 58, 60, 71, 137, 231
photocells, 292
photovoltaic, 68, 110–111, 140, 146, 167–169, 171–172, 215, 235
policymaking, 76
pollution, 92, 121, 125, 129, 134, 137, 145, 155, 158, 171, 253, 283–284
precipitation, 203
privacy, 100, 128, 191–192, 198
profitability, 63, 233
prosperity, 142, 145
psychology, 248–249
PV. *See* photovoltaic

Qatar, 3, 6, 14, 30, 34, 37, 39, 43–46, 49, 63, 77, 85, 88, 90–91, 93, 95–96, 102–105, 142, 159, 161, 164, 166, 169, 171, 173, 201, 203–205, 212, 215, 217–218, 247, 258, 274–275, 286, 289, 293, 312–313
quality assurance, 178–179, 181, 187, 190–191, 196

radiation, 68, 74
radiators, 292
railway, 171
rainfall, 146
recycling, 14, 18, 24
refineries, 58, 232
refrigerators, 88, 94–95, 292
resilience, 25–26, 145, 157, 205
restoration, 12, 122
retrofit, 98–105, 114, 137, 167, 287

safety, 123, 128, 138, 163, 202, 205, 207
Saudi Arabia, 3, 5, 12, 14, 34, 37, 39–46, 49, 57–60, 62–63, 65, 67–79, 85–88, 91, 93–96, 100, 102–109, 110, 128, 140–141, 146, 158–161, 164, 166, 170, 173, 205, 286, 289–290, 310, 312
sequestration, 60, 65, 73–74, 202, 208
settlement, 79
sociology, 249
sodium, 121
sovereignty, 211
stakeholder engagement, 19, 191
standardisation, 190
startups, 247, 275
symbiosis, 13, 20, 24, 26

tariffs, 79
taxation, 20, 235
teleworking, 164
tourism, 169

UAE. *See* United Arab Emirates
unemployment, 160, 163–165
United Arab Emirates, 3–4, 12, 14–16, 34, 37, 39–41, 43–46, 49, 59, 63, 69, 74, 77, 85, 88, 91, 93–96, 102–105, 117–118, 125–127, 130, 140–141, 159–161, 164, 166, 171–173, 204–205, 225–226, 230, 233–235, 240–241, 287, 289–290, 293, 312–313
uranium, 68, 138

VAT. *See* taxation
ventilation, 92, 248–250

wealth, 27, 113, 204–205, 234
weather, 143
well-being, 158

For EU product safety concerns, contact us at Calle de José Abascal, 56–1°,
28003 Madrid, Spain or eugpsr@cambridge.org.

www.ingramcontent.com/pod-product-compliance
Lightning Source LLC
LaVergne TN
LVHW062207200926
848484LV00006B/1341

* 9 7 8 1 0 0 9 4 7 1 5 5 8 *